LET'S MAKE A PLAN

By Eilidh Craster

Let's Make a Plan

Spiderwize
Mews Cottage
The Causeway, Kennoway
Kingdom of Fife
KY8 5JU
Scotland UK

www.spiderwize.com

ISBN: 978-1-907294-49-5

To Mark, Heath and Vicki,
with gratitude for your help,
encouragement, support.

Table of Contents

A NORMAL LIFE

A t first, when good friends, Marchal and John, suggested I write this book, I had very mixed emotions. They had commented on what an 'exciting' life I'd led in Zimbabwe, and assured me that people from 'outside' would be interested in what I had to tell. I didn't quite share their confidence, but decided to give it a go anyway. The one aspect that I did promise myself that I would not touch on was that of politics. There were several reasons for this. Political views, especially in a volatile environment such as Africa, tend to be emotive and are usually misconstrued, or considered racially biased, even if this is not the intention. Another reason for steering clear of the subject is for a very basic reason, that of survival. Depending which regime is in power in my country at the time, life could be made most unpleasant if 'they' didn't like or approve of what I'd written. It's not a cop out; it's survival instinct. Unlike people in the Western world, who have complete freedom of speech, we have to tend to be a bit more circumspect when speaking.

A whole book could be dedicated to the 'land invasions' of the farms beginning in 2000, but it won't be by me. Books have been written about the Unilateral Declaration of Independence in 1965; numerous books written about the 'war' years of the 1970s; and books have been, and will be, written about the years of 'Black' Independence, the early hey-days, and the later extremely difficult years. Even saying that I'm shying away from the political side of events in Zimbabwe, it is still impossible to ignore them completely. It is as a result of these weird and wonderful happenings in our land, that many of the incidents in this book have arisen; and as a result, have moulded and shaped my life, the lives of my family and the lives of all those with whom I have come into contact in this beautiful land. I'll leave the political rhetoric to someone else who will be far more qualified to write on the subject than I will ever be.

There has always been an impression that there is something exciting, exotic, daring, debonair, and so very not boring, about living in Africa. I wouldn't know about that. I was born and brought up in Africa and it all just seemed normal to me. Life in Africa if nothing else, is certainly interesting and entertaining. My parents arrived in the then Federation of Rhodesian and Nyasaland in 1952 shortly after their marriage in Scotland. They were to spend fifty years of their lives here, and they too, had an interesting, albeit sometimes difficult, life here, but they somehow always managed, in good old "Rhodie" (Rhodesian) and now Zimbo (Zimbabwean) parlance, to 'make a plan'.

According to my birth certificate, I was born in Salisbury, Southern Rhodesia, according to my passport I was born in Harare, Zimbabwe, a bit confusing at times. Harare was named after Chief Neharwa as part of his kingdom included Harare and its surrounds. In 1965 the then government of Ian Smith, of the Rhodesian Front, declared Unilateral Independence from Britain so that we well and truly became Rhodesia. In March 1978 Bishop Abel Muzorewa of the ANC (African National Council) formed an interim government with the Rhodesian Front and we became known as Zimbabwe-Rhodesia. In December 1979 we had a cease-fire with the liberation fighters, terrorists, freedom fighters or whatever depending which side you were on, and the country was handed back to the British. February 1980 saw elections in which Bishop Muzurewa gained three seats and Robert Gabriel Mugabe of the ZANU (PF) party (Zimbabwe African National Union [Patriotic Front]) had a resounding success. Prince Charles attended and Bob Marley performed at the Independence Day ceremonies on 18th April 1980 whereby Mr. Mugabe took the reins and Zimbabwe was created and an exodus of whites began. The word Zimbabwe means the 'house of stone' and comes from 'dzimba dza mabwe'.

The most part of my earliest childhood was spent in Southern Rhodesia. U.D.I (Unilateral Declaration of Independence) was declared from Britain on 11th November 1965, by Ian Smith and the Rhodesian Front and we became known as Rhodesia. Britain and the West applied economic sanctions and although you couldn't go into a shop and buy all the imported brands, as a nation we were very self-reliant and innovative, with the ability to produce basically anything that was needed, and if we couldn't produce it, we made a plan. Being a land-locked country was difficult; and as our nearest port was in Beira, Mozambique about 560 kilometres (350 miles) away, we had many periods when obtaining fuel was a problem. We were rationed to the amount of fuel we could get. It was worked out on a system of the distance you had to travel to and from work every day and coupons were allocated accordingly. Lift-clubs (or car-pools) were formed and we somehow managed.

The majority of children went to government schools in the area in which they lived, in most cases this was in either walking or cycling distance from home. Those pupils who lived too far away from school usually became boarders.

The family holidays that we took were mainly to Mozambique or South Africa if we were not holidaying locally. Occasionally, we would make the trek to the United Kingdom, flying BOAC with airhostesses who looked like models and gave children the most wonderful activities to do during the journey. I made this journey when I was three years old and then again when I was eleven. The flight left Salisbury (now Harare) and we stayed overnight in a hotel in Wadi Halfa in Sudan; the airport was a huge, dark, cavernous lounge with ceiling fans. There was goats' milk that I thought was disgusting as I wasn't used to it — but it was possible to get the most delicious bottled chocolate milk that was such a treat for us sanction-ridden, deprived Rhodesian children!

Even as a child there were dark shadows looming over us in Africa, and although I had no inkling of their depth of despair, I do know that they disturbed me. Even now, I can vividly remember going with my parents as a young child one day to a suburb known as Cranborne, and taking clothes, food, blankets and other essentials for the people who had fled the atrocities in the Congo. At that young age I had no idea of where the Congo was. Nor did I know the meaning of the word 'refugee'; but I can remember being upset at seeing all the 'mummies and daddies' walking around in the middle of the day in their pyjamas – only to be told many years later, that these tragic people literally left the Congo in the clothes that they were wearing at the time. Forty-something years later, I can still clearly picture the distressing scene.

Many, many years later in 1976, my husband Mike, and I were on our honeymoon in Durban, South Africa. We had spent a few hours wandering around the docks and looking at ships when we came to a huge open piece of ground that was fenced off. Inside it were hundreds, if not thousands, of abandoned cars. This time it was as a result of a war much closer to home, that of Mozambique, and these were the cars of the Portuguese nationals and other Mozambicans who had fled for their lives by driving to Durban, abandoning their cars and getting on ships to take them to safety to places such as Portugal and the island of Madeira. The civil war in Mozambique had raged on for about ten years and in 1974 the fighting between the Frelimo rebels and the colonial Portuguese was almost at an end, with the outcome being that most of the Portuguese had to flee for their lives. Mozambique has not had a very happy recent history, not long after one civil war had ended another began, this time between the Renamo rebels and the new Frelimo government. Politics in Africa seems to come in waves and is constantly changing with innocent civilians being stuck in the middle. Again, this picture of the car graveyard is indelibly stuck in my memory. I have often wondered when 'our' turn is coming.

EARLY YEARS

We were proud to be Rhodesians. We thought we were invincible. We worked hard, we played hard and we fought hard. It was an almost idyllic childhood for me. My parents both worked, but I would never consider myself a latchkey kid. During the school term, the week was taken up with the usual academic and school activities, and for me, the weekends were taken up with the Girl Guides and church. When I was a child not many people had home swimming pools, so the 'in' place to be was the local municipal swimming baths where we all went to meet our friends and socialise.

When I was at Alfred Beit junior school in Mabelreign on the days we had swimming lessons, the class had to walk in a 'crocodile' formation to the Mabelreign municipal swimming pool. We loved going there as it meant that we were out of class on an 'outing'. The walk must have taken about twenty minutes and there were usually two classes at a time. When I look back, it must have been quite a responsibility for the teachers involved. My class usually went with big Mrs. Bennett and little Mrs. Bennett, both of whom were strict disciplinarians and we thought they were scary. I'll never forget an occasion when one child got into trouble in the deep end of the swimming pool, and big Mrs. Bennett pulled her dress off over her head and dived into the pool in her petticoat. We were shocked. Firstly, big Mrs. Bennett was a 'mean' diver and we were all most impressed, we never actually thought that either of our teachers could swim, and secondly, we were mortified to see a half-naked teacher in flimsy underwear.

My father used to work for the Railways and as a result we would get free rail travel. It was such a treat to go on holiday to South Africa by train that was part of the holiday in itself. It would be such a festive time at the Railway station on Railway Avenue, which was situated at the bottom end of town, in an area that we called the Cow's Guts. All our friends would come to see us off. It was a great social occasion. The restaurant and bars did a roaring trade. I always found it most humiliating how the Railways found it necessary to put my age against my name on the passenger manifest and on the card outside our compartment! The last time my family did such a journey was when I was thirteen and a half. I was mortified! Why couldn't the Railways at least have put my age down as fourteen, I was so very nearly there! We had a compartment for the three of us, bunk beds with starched white sheets that were made up with hospital corners by the stewards while we were having our dinner in the dining car. Early morning tea and coffee brought to our compartment before we made our way to the dining car for breakfast; that was the life. The Customs and Immigration officers came to the compartments to complete their formalities, which meant that when we reached our destination we could disembark and be on our way.

THE ANORAK

I loved receiving parcels from Britain especially from my grandparents. It was exciting to receive the parcel slip in the post, then to rush up to the post office to collect the parcel. One year my grandmother sent me a present from Scotland and I thought I had died and gone to heaven, I was now the proud owner of a blue, quilted anorak. It was more of a luxury than a necessity in our climate, that didn't bother me; the only thing that did matter was that none of my friends possessed such a luxury. I went by train on a Girl Guide camp to Beira, Mozambique one August – September school holidays. I took my anorak with me on the camp and anyone who has been to Beira, especially in August, will know that an anorak is probably the last thing that was needed in that climate, but I was so proud of it. We stayed in a children's camping facility in the middle of the Estoril campsite. You can imagine the fun the fifty or so of us guides had; I'm not sure how much our guiders in charge would agree. It must have been hard work for them and such a responsibility. Beira was paradise. A beautiful, safe beach, gentle seas in the morning, but with rough waves in the afternoons. The old wreck in the shallow water was a landmark and a great meeting place, but it was 'out of bounds' to us guides in case one of us injured ourselves on the rusting metal.

I have never been a fussy eater, but one of the things that I have never been able to eat is Maltabella, a popular brown porridge. Our senior guider insisted that for breakfast every morning we had Maltabella before our eggs and bacon. We had to show our empty porridge bowl before we were dished up with the rest of breakfast. No matter how hard I tried, I could just not get the Maltabella down, I was gagging on it. To solve my problem I made a plan. I used to wear my anorak to breakfast every morning, it was like being in a portable sauna and then I would surreptitiously spoon the

Maltabella into the hood of my anorak, take my empty bowl up to the kitchen and enjoy my eggs. It was then necessary to get out of the dining hall as quickly as possible to dig a hole in the sand and bury the porridge, as by now, the soggy, brown mess was beginning to seep through the material. I was never able to remove the brown stain from the hood, and it remained as a constant reminder.

YOUNG LIVES

Another unfortunate part of the history of our country was our war, which was known as the terrorist war or the war of liberation, depending which side you were on. Thousands of innocent lives were needlessly lost and much heartache endured. The Africans use the word "Chimurenga" which means the War of Liberation. The first Chimurenga took place in the late 1800s when the white settlers were attacked. This then was the reason that the Africans called this our war, the Second Chimurenga that started in the 1960s with an attack by the Zimbabwe African National Liberation Army (ZANLA) against the government forces in a place called Sinoia, now known as Chinhoyi. The 'war' was just another fact of life for us. Fathers, sons, brothers, boyfriends, all were called-up to the various forces to fight for their country. So many lives were affected in the long-term by the war. For boys who were leaving school it was sometimes almost impossible to get an exemption from military service to go to university or follow other career paths. Many careers were shaped by military call-up; so many boys in the late 70s had their lives disrupted by the call-ups. People who decided to leave were described as taking the 'chicken run' as it became disparagingly known. They left the country to try and lead a more meaningful, normal life, usually in South Africa, Australia or Britain.

Life went on, war or no war. On Friday nights, all roads lead to Glamis Stadium in the then Salisbury Show grounds for the weekly stock car races. The place was always packed to capacity, as apart from the entertainment of the cars, it was the place to see and to be seen! In the 70s, as teenagers or young adults, we had a fantastic social life; stock cars on Friday nights, followed at the weekend by motor racing at the Marlborough race track, with the supposedly haunted building on top of the hill in the middle of the

9

track.   The Mabelreign and Metro drive-in cinemas were also great favourites. New Year was celebrated in First Street, which was a seething mass of humanity and usually ended up on the Kopje, overlooking the city of Salisbury (Harare), where we watched the sunrise. A chief named Mbari lived on the Salisbury kopje prior to the white occupation of Mashonaland. Salisbury was renamed Harare in 1980, and this is a corruption of 'Harawa' which came from the name of Chief Neharawa. When he died, his remains were interred in the Salisbury kopje.

It was the 'in' thing to go overseas to Britain and Europe to work and see the world. It was such a culture shock for us 'Rhodies' who came from a fairly sheltered environment. We were always a season or two behind in the fashion scene and I felt out of place on my arrival in Britain when I was twenty-one, in my hot-pants and mini skirts when the British and European hemlines had gone way down south to below the knee to mid calf or longer. I thought I was another Twiggy or Mary Quant on my return to Rhodesia a year later with all my new, fashionable clothes. I will never forget standing outside the OK Bazaars on the corner of First Street and Baker Avenue waiting for the traffic lights to change just shortly after my arrival home; I was wearing a blue denim ankle length skirt and platform shoes and I thought I was fashion personified. I soon changed my mind and just couldn't wait to get home; the stares and weird looks I was getting from the Rhodies who still wore mini skirts were unbelievable.

My sister-in-law, Yvonne, married in 1975, she and her husband lived on a dairy farm in the Beatrice farming area to the south of the capital. The farmhouse was built during the Second World War by Italian prisoners of war who were billeted in the area. The prisoners had been given the plans of the house and had gone ahead to build it, not realizing that the plans were drawn up in imperial measurements and they had built it with metric measurements. The place was huge. For years there was no running water or electricity in the house, and one particularly wet rainy season we went out to the farm for a party. I sat with my friend Charmaine sharing an umbrella in the lounge as the water was pouring in through the holes in the roof. Charmaine and I decided that we needed to go to the loo, so we went off together with a candle and the brolly. We had to step down into the central passage, which bisected the house from front to back, to find ourselves ankle deep in a raging torrent flowing through the house. This was nerve wracking as our imaginations ran riot, but, when Nature calls, it calls.

The bathroom was unusual to say the least. It was a huge, vast room with the toilet on a raised dais, fortunately there were walls built around the loo to give some privacy, but it was a surreal experience answering the call of nature in these surroundings. In one corner of the room, under the window, was an old white enamel bath. The archaic plumbing in the house provided only cold water. In order to overcome this slight problem, Yvonne and her husband made a plan. There was a wood-burning, Rhodesian boiler immediately outside the bathroom window. The fire was kept alive twenty-four-seven, to enable an adequate supply of boiling hot water for bathing purposes. Taking a bath was a two-man process whereby a person outside the bathroom window collected buckets of boiling water from the boiler, and then emptied them into the bath by way of the window. Primitive, but effective.

Yvonne's ex-husband, the farmer, certainly made good use of their house and if nothing else, he was a practical man. When his maize crop had matured and he wanted a safe place to keep the cobs to prevent them from being stolen, what better place than one of the empty rooms in the house? It was simple, reverse the tractor to the window and deposit the cobs through the open window. Getting to the house itself was an adventure. There was a river to cross, which in the dry season was no trouble at all, but in the rainy season, it was a completely different scene. One time we were following Yvonne and her husband in their truck and we came to the engorged river that was flowing rapidly. Mike was concerned about crossing the black, swirling water. The truck continued on its way straight into the churning black water, we had no choice but to follow exactly in the same place. Wonder of wonders we got through, but I must admit that we were both feeling tense until we'd reached the safety of the land on the other side of the river.

We had some fantastic times on the farm. Mike went springhare shooting at night with Yvonne's husband, racing straight through fences when they were in full pursuit. I was intrigued watching Yvonne and her mother-in-law who lived with them, cooking the most delectable meals on their woodstove; I have never sampled roast meat or vegetables that tasted so delicious! Unfortunately Yvonne's marriage ended and so did our trips to the farm, but we will always have fond memories of our escapades.

MARRIED LIFE

Mike and I became engaged in 1975 and were married in October 1976. Wedding planning can be a nightmare at the best of times, but trying to organize a wedding in a country that's had economic sanctions for ten years was quite a feat in logistics. Material for the wedding dress had to be imported from South Africa, as was the dried fruit to make the wedding cake. There was the problem of getting foreign currency (forex) to pay for goods and then there was the question of how we were going to get the commodities delivered to us in Rhodesia. Our long-suffering friends and relations in South Africa were so helpful and somehow, we always managed, 'we made a plan'. October is known as the 'suicide' month in Zimbabwe as it is one of the hottest and driest months, but this wasn't the case on 9th October 1976. The heavens opened and we had torrential rain, I was so tired of people telling me it's 'lucky' if it rains on your wedding day – they weren't the ones trying to keep the hem of their long, white dress clean and dry, and they weren't the ones whose high-heels were sinking in the mud in the neighbour's garden while we were having photographs taken.

Our wedding ceremony took place in the Greencroft Presbyterian Church followed by the reception in the Great Indaba Room at the Monomatapa Hotel in Salisbury. We left the following day for our honeymoon in South Africa. The on-going terrorist war meant that there were strict travel restrictions to adhere to and it was forbidden to travel at night by car in case we were ambushed. We drove to the Lion and Elephant motel at Bubi River and spent the night there; next morning at the crack of dawn, we joined other southward bound travellers in the convoy that were known as 'Pookies' that would take us to the Beit Bridge border post. The Pookies were mine-detecting vehicles that moved at quite a speed and must have been nerve-wracking for slower drivers or those with older, more unreliable cars. We were not permitted to overtake while in the convoy, and the security vehicle (which was almost prehistoric-looking) would race up and down the convoy with the men armed to the teeth.

Just to add a bit of spice to life we had car problems that morning and were experiencing difficulties starting. We were worried we wouldn't be able to join the convoy in time, in which case, we would have to take our chances on our own with any would-be 'terrs' (terrorists) along the route we had to follow as we wouldn't have the back up of the convoy. The only alternative would be to wait until the following morning, which would mean incurring the added expense of staying another night at the hotel, and being newly-weds, finances were limited. With much gnashing of teeth and a lot of luck, Mike managed to get our car into line in the convoy just in the nick of time.

South Africa was a haven for shopping for us sanction-ridden 'Rhodies'. It was a dream come true to actually be able to walk into a shop and buy HP Sauce, Appletiser, Nescafe, Marmite, Mars Bars, white chocolate, Smarties, tinned fish, dried fruit, the list was endless. We all bought Pineware toasters, electric frying pans, pressure cookers and all the other electrical appliances that were unavailable to us back home. I used to love browsing in the bookstores seeing all the books that were just not obtainable at home. I still have this 'U.D.I mentality' of hoarding precious books 'just in case' I'll need them in the future. I could spend hours in the department stores just looking at everything. Whenever friends asked what I'd like to look at in particular, it was impossible to explain that all I wanted to do was 'look', to be able to read labels, to see things that I didn't even know existed. We had had sanctions for so much of my formative life and to give credit where credit is due, Rhodesia managed incredibly well in supplying everything that we needed, but we were brought up with the mindset that locally produced items were homemade and therefore, inferior.

Once we got to South Africa, our first night was spent at the Ranch Motel, near Petersburg, then to Jo'burg to our adopted extended family, the Hemmings, for a night. It wasn't until we arrived at the Beach Hotel, Marine Parade, Durban, that our real holiday started. Lazing on the beach by day, going for long walks around the Marine Parade by night; being able to eat seafood washed down with South African wines, was just heaven to us. In my lifetime we have always been restricted for foreign currency in our beautiful country. This made our holiday spending different from other holidaymakers, we had different priorities; purchasing items that were unobtainable at home.

The honeymoon over, it was back home and the start to proper married life. My late father-in-law, Yvo, had a property in an area called Maryvale, just past Christon Bank in Mazowe, which is about twenty-five kilometres north of the city of Salisbury (Harare). Mazowe, known to the earlier local inhabitants as 'Maswe', was used by the first Portuguese explorers who travelled down the Mazoe River for over 300 years. An indication of the Portuguese presence was found near Jumbo mine (which is located in the area) where fragments of Delft pottery were found, including Nankin china. Mike and I decided that this is where we wanted to live and build our house. We bought the adjoining piece of land, which turned out to be a stroke of luck in that all the water we use is found on this plot of land, and the original plot that Mike's Dad bought is as dry as a bone. Considering this hilly part of Maryvale lies in a rain shadow, and that we have never been particularly flush with water, if you'll excuse the pun, the purchase of the second plot was necessary. We built the house north facing and it is situated on the top of a hill with a wonderful view of the Mazoe dam.

Readers will note the difference in the spelling of Mazoe and Mazowe. There are huge citrus estates in the Mazowe farming area and they produce among other things, the famous Mazoe orange cordial drink, prized by locals. Before Zimbabwe's Independence in April, 1980, the farming area in which we live was spelt "Mazoe", after Independence, the ruling government decided to change place names, road names, names of hospitals, and Mazowe was now spelt with a 'w', but the orange juice is still spelt the old way. Changing names of towns and streets is confusing. When I used to go to the Central Business District of Salisbury (Harare), if I wasn't sure where a certain street was, it was easy, all I had to remember was, 'Speak to Stanley Gordon about the Bakers Union'. Change 'speak' to 'Speke', and you have: Speke Avenue, Stanley Avenue, Gordon Avenue, Baker Avenue and Union Avenue. Somehow 'Speke to Jason Moyo and George Silundika about the Baker's Union' doesn't quite have the same ring to it.

WAR YEARS

In the early days of our marriage the Terrorist War was still in full swing and each house in rural and farming areas had 'agric-alert' radios. These radios were connected to the local police station in the area and were sometimes the only form of communication people had with each other and the security forces, as often the old party-line telephones were occupied or out of order in an emergency. We had Roll call every morning and evening. If for any reason we were not going to be at home, it was incumbent upon us to notify either a neighbour who would answer for us, or to inform the police post.

The radio was never switched off in case of an emergency. I will never forget hearing people calling in when they were under attack, sometimes we could even hear the shooting in the background. One case in particular was when a woman was in tears begging the reaction stick (a small group of armed forces patrolling an area) to get to their farm as quickly as possible as they were under attack and her husband had been shot, but it was too late, and he died in her arms. The sound of her sobs over the radio was heart wrenching. There were lighter moments as well. We had elderly neighbours who lived on the farm next to us, one night the wife called in to say that they had heard a shot really close to them, a few minutes later she sheepishly came back on the radio to say that it had all been a mistake and that it was just the top of a soda-water bottle exploding off!

The white population living in the rural areas all had weapons during the war and we carried these weapons with us everywhere. I have never liked guns as such, but they were a fact of life, and I actually surprised myself to find that I wasn't a bad shot, not quite in the league of Annie Oakley though, but nevertheless, pretty good. It was a 'given' that the men would know how to use a weapon as they all had either done military service or were in active military service in the form of call-ups, depending on their age. A lot of women had never handled a gun before, so it was crucial for us to attend shooting practice on either a Tuesday afternoon or a Saturday morning. As I worked during the week, I opted for the Saturday mornings. The training sessions were held in a field behind the Mazowe dam in the most beautiful bush setting.

There were usually fifteen or so women who attended and we were instructed by a police reservist who lived in the area and who thought he was God's gift to the world. He was the most infuriating, nauseating little man ever and we women called him the Sergeant Major. He tried to treat the training sessions as if we were in boot camp and he absolutely hated if any of the husbands decided to stay and watch. We used to stand in a line facing a row of targets and the array of weapons would have made any museum drool. I'm positive that some of the weapons arrived on the Ark with Noah they were so old, as I'm sure some of the women did too. There were a couple of women who were in their late eighties. We had to shoot at the target standing, kneeling and then lying down. After each practice shot the weapons were left on the ground and each woman moved to the weapon on her right, and the whole process was repeated. This was to enable us to be able to use any weapon in any given situation. As I was by the far the youngest in our sessions, it was always my role to go along the line and help the women who were unable to get back up on to their feet. The arthritic knees, creaking joints, huffs and puffs, panting, grunts and groans did not go down well with The Sergeant Major. It was awe-inspiring to watch the older women cope; they would have put many a younger woman to shame.

A firm of gunsmiths in Salisbury was making a semi-automatic weapon called the GM16, which was based on the Israeli Uzi weapon. There was a long waiting list to get one. Mike was away on call-up and the best man at our wedding Gordon, said he had a contact at the gunsmiths. Gordon told the contact that I was a woman on my own and lived in a rural area and that my husband was away on call-up. As a result of this, he was told that I would be able to jump the queue and get a GM16 immediately. Nothing has changed in this country, it's not what you know, it's who you know. I didn't have enough money on me to pay for the weapon and Gordon very kindly allowed me to borrow money out of the petty cash at work to pay for it.

Gordon and I went together to buy the gun and I was given a demonstration on how it all worked. I very proudly, but gingerly, took my new acquisition home. Whenever Mike was away on call-ups, I wouldn't sleep in the bedroom, as the outside wall was entirely made up of a glass sliding door onto a balcony. We had put strips of sellotape down the entire length of the glass every few inches apart to try and reduce the glass shattering too much if we were under attack, and the balcony railings were also clad with benox (bullet-proof) plates. I never felt safe sleeping in the room on my own, so I used to put up a camp bed in the passage between the bedroom and the bathroom and I slept in there with my faithful, but totally soppy, Doberman, called Rinke. I got the gun on a Monday night and wasn't due at the shooting training until the following Saturday, so I determined to be expert in handling my GM16 before having to face the Sergeant Major. I took the weapon apart, re-assembled it, timed myself doing it, then did it blindfolded and by the end of the week, I had it down pat. I would have been a credit to any military unit!

Saturday morning came and bursting with pride and confidence, I went off to training with my state-of-the-art weapon. There were many oohs and aahs when the other women admired my weapon, even the Sergeant Major showed a faint glimpse of being human and almost made a civil comment about the gun. So you can imagine how my bubble burst and how devastated I felt when I discovered that the GM16 would not fire. It transpired that it was a manufacturing fault with the weapon, and the guns had to be recalled. Thank goodness I wasn't attacked.

Farmers and people from areas that lay outside the main towns and cities, always travelled with a weapon. Mike and I usually travelled to and from work together and when we did, Mike would drive and I would ride 'shotgun' with whichever weapon we were taking with us, laying on my lap in easy reach. Most major roads leading into a town or city had a police station where a weapon could be left in safe custody. In our case, we drove to my parents-in-law's house where we deposited our weapon in their sturdy, upright Chubb safe. For motorists going out of the main towns and cities, there wasn't a curfew as such, but for insurance purposes, if you were ambushed or attacked in your vehicle after about five thirty or so in the afternoon, you weren't covered by your policy. You travelled at dusk or later, at your own risk. This made our social life a bit more complicated.

First priority was to inform the neighbours and / or the agric alert monitors that we would be away for a night and therefore would not be present for roll call. Following this we had to organise our staff with food rations for two days. During the war years many of the farm labourers and domestic workers had part of their wages paid in food. The rationale behind daily rationing of food was that it would provide only enough for personal use and could not be given to any terrs who might be hiding in the area. If we were going out at night it meant spending the night in town where we had no shortage of beds amongst friends and relations. But it was a lot of palaver to go to, just for a night at the movies or to go to dinner with friends. All through our early-married life, all I wanted to do was to be able to entertain at home at night! Our entertaining was restricted to the weekends during daylight hours and friends were on their way back home usually by four or five in the afternoon. Our house was so tiny that it was almost impossible to have anyone stay the night.

Mike and I were travelling home at dusk one evening as we were running late. We'd got just past the Marlborough police station on the outskirts of town and were nearing the bridge, when a stationary car facing towards us, on the other side of the bridge, suddenly put its headlights on full, temporarily blinding Mike. This was a deliberate attempt to blind any drivers going towards the bridge as there were two, huge, concrete blocks in the road blocking the vehicle's way. Fortunately we didn't disable the car as we crashed into the blocks. This attack was literally just a couple of kilometres away from a police station and armed personnel. Mike hadn't been driving fast, and he also had a gut feeling that something wasn't right; so although we did hit the concrete blocks, we didn't smash into them at speed. Just after impact, Mike managed a handbrake turn, headed the car back towards town, and we limped into the police station on square tyres, while gunshots rang out behind us. It was a wake-up call for us.

During the war years each area had a military reaction stick made up of volunteers who lived in the vicinity. They would attend to a call first and if it was out of their league, then the big guns would be called in. As our house was on top of a hill, it not only afforded a good view of the area, but there was also good radio communications. As a result, the reaction stick was at our house three or four times a week in the late afternoons and stayed for hours unless they were called away. They were a great bunch of men, but Mike and I were concerned that they would be more of a hindrance than a help, as they were quite elderly and we thought that if there was any 'action' the shock and excitement might be too much for them. When they first started coming, we provided beers, but we eventually had to ask them to provide their own, as it was getting a bit expensive, and being newly-weds, we were on a tight budget. They loved my homemade ginger biscuits and I always made sure that I had plenty in stock for them, what a combination, beer and ginger biscuits.

One evening when Mike was away on call-up and I was on my own, I decided that I was going to pamper myself and have a beauty treatment guaranteed to make me look absolutely gorgeous. I massaged coconut oil into my hair, which was then covered with a plastic bag and a towel. My face was covered in a green seaweed facemask that smelt foul and I daren't even twitch or it cracked and started peeling off. With my feet soaking in a basin of warm water and oil, and my nails manicured and the varnish still wet, I was furious when the telephone rang. We were on a party-line system, and our call was one short ring followed by one long ring. The party line was our only means of communication apart from the agric-alert. There was nothing for it but to take my feet out of the basin and go and answer the phone. It was a neighbour to say that there had been a terrorist attack close-by in our area and that the reaction stick was on their way up the hill to collect me so that I could spend the night in their house.

I was devastated. There wasn't even time to try and make myself look human, by the time I had put the phone down, the reaction stick had used strong bolt-cutters to cut the lock and chain on our security gates and came tearing up the driveway. I was mortified. This wasn't Dad's army; this was the real thing, a jeep full of young, dishy guys in uniform armed to the teeth, and me looking like some extra-terrestrial being that had been rejected from the mother ship. Needless to say after that absolutely humiliating experience I dolled myself up every night, not an eyelash out of place, perfectly manicured and coifed, and all for nothing. I never needed to be rescued again. In any event, the guys were probably still in a state of shock after seeing me, and had been sent home for a bit of R&R.

HELL'S BELLS

My late father-in-law, Yvo, was an upright, hard-working, God-fearing man whose motto was 'Work hard. Pray hard'. He was a mason, an active member of his church and also a Gideon, distributing bibles at school assemblies and to hotels. He lived a clean, ordered life and was a prominent member of many professional organizations. He tended to be puritanical at times and could also be a bit intimidating until you got to know him. My first 'run-in' with him was early in my marriage when a school friend of mine was getting married while Mike was away on army call-up, so my mother was roped in to be my partner. The wedding definitely had a surplus of women with the men of all ages away fighting the war. We left the wedding ceremony at a church in Marlborough, Harare and drove to the reception at the Jameson Hotel in Jameson Avenue (now Samora Machel Avenue). Mike and I had a Citroen GS Club car, as I was driving along, mum and I were busy gossiping about the guests, old school friends, clothes, the bride, her dress, I was vaguely aware that there was a noise coming from the car which was getting louder and louder the further we drove. Finally, even mum noticed the noise. When she asked what I thought the racket was, I shrugged it off saying that I thought we were getting the beginnings of a hole in the exhaust and it was nothing to worry about.

We had a lovely time at the reception. It was great catching up with friends I hadn't seen since we'd all left school. As mum knew a lot of my friends, we had plenty to talk about. Mum and I were enjoying ourselves and hadn't noticed the time, with a start we looked at our watches and thought it was high time we left the celebrations. About nine o'clock we were on our way home, I was spending the night at my parents, because it was unsafe for me to drive home at night. The car was getting noisier and noisier, it was also getting slower and slower. Even I had to admit that a hole in the exhaust couldn't cause those symptoms. Dad was waiting for us when we drove up the driveway to their house. He'd expected us back much earlier and was getting concerned. He heard the noise and walking round the car, came back to me with a strange expression on his face. "What have you been up to?"

"Oh we had a wonderful time and the food was great and everyone was there and ...."

"No. I don't mean the wedding. What have you done to the car?"

Mum and I looked at each other. "W-e-l-l," I hesitantly replied, "the car was getting noisy and slowing down."

Dad took my hand and walked me round to the back passenger tyre, well, to what should have been the back passenger tyre. It wasn't there. What should have been a tyre was ribbons of rubber worn almost down to the rim. Somewhere in the very deep recesses of my mind I vaguely remembered that Citroens could run on three wheels for a limited time in the event of a puncture. I should have pulled over and changed the tyre (and break a nail, I think not!) when I first heard the noise and not continue driving for approximately eighteen kilometres!

Dad said that he'd change the wheel for me and asked where Mike kept the tools. I said that I didn't think that Mike used tools and that he did it by hand. I know, I know – it wasn't my brightest moment. I'm just not the slightest bit interested in mechanics and all that goes with it! I've been blessed to be married to a very capable and practical man, so why make extra work for myself? Mike had given me lessons on changing tyres and it was obvious that I hadn't paid much attention. Mum and I went inside and dissected the wedding over some coffee. Then we remembered poor dad. I must point out here that my father was great at woodwork and home décor, but his mechanical knowledge is not a whole lot more advanced than mine. We went outside to see how dad was doing. His fingers were raw and the wheel wasn't any closer to coming off. I finally remembered that the car's owner's manual was in the cubbyhole and looked up the part about changing wheels. The book was in French, so this took a bit longer as the French I did in school didn't include mechanical vocabulary. Like most things, when you know how to do them, it's easy. Once I'd read the manual

I did remember about tyres and hydraulics so it wasn't long before dad was inside sharing coffee with us.

I was trying to get up the courage to tell my father-in-law, Yvo, about the tyre. He was a fair man, but didn't suffer fools easily. There was no excuse, if I'd been listening to Mike when he demonstrated changing tyres, I wouldn't be in this mess. My father-in-law never used profanity. When he was very, very, very, extremely very angry, he'd say "hell's bells!" I think Mike and his sister Yvonne, can count on their hands the number of "hell's bells" they've had in their entire lives. Within the space of a couple of days, I outdid the two of them together. I phoned Yvo. I explained what had happened. I accepted my "hell's bells" and put it down to experience. If nothing else, it meant that I was most definitely one of the family. Isn't it funny how things come in threes? A couple of days later the Citroen wouldn't start. Would I be blamed for this? I mean, I hadn't done anything wrong, just got into the car, put the key in the ignition and turned it, nothing happened. What could I possibly have done wrong. Living in a rural area, but most especially in a war situation, it is vital to have a car that runs. With much trepidation I phoned my father-in-law and gave him the details of the car. He said it sounded as if I had a flat battery and then proceeded to ask me if I'd left the lights on or some such thing! As if I'd do anything like that! I did go out to the garage to check that everything was in order and that I hadn't inadvertently left lights on before dad's arrival.

Yvo arrived with a pair of jumper cables that he attached to his battery and told me to take the other end of the cables and attach them to my presumably dead battery. People shouldn't take things for granted. I mean just because they have an engineering background (like Yvo), they shouldn't expect that everyone else is practically minded. They shouldn't take for granted that we all know that there are different coloured leads that go on the corresponding colour terminal on the battery! I didn't know. It's quite spectacular when you do get it wrong. Though I wouldn't advise it as a form of entertainment, it's fairly costly. Guess what? My second "hell's bells" in about as many days, followed. Yvo was shaking. It wasn't a particularly cold day so I don't suppose it was from that. He didn't suffer from verbal diarrhoea at the best of times, but you could cut the atmosphere with a knife on this day with the very pregnant silence. He then informed me that he was going to tow me into town to take the car for repairs. I hate being towed. It's not so bad with a tow-bar, but with a rope I find it distinctly nerve-wracking. He connected the rope to the two cars, told me to get into mine and make sure that the key was off and nothing was switched on.

"But dad …."

"Just do as you are told."

"But dad, …"

"Do it!"

Muttering under my breath I got into my car and did as I was told. This time I knew I was in the right, but the look on Yvo's face and the tone of his voice didn't encourage any contradiction. I was towed out of our driveway, which was an up hill road, then out onto the road that would lead to the main Mazowe road.   This entailed an extremely steep descent of about two kilometres and as we were nearing the main road I had beads of sweat on my brow and my hands were like saturated rags. The main road is always busy with passenger vehicles, public buses and commercial trucks transporting agricultural produce, therefore it is always circumspect to not only give way at the bottom of our road, but to come to a complete standstill. Yvo did so – and I went ramming up his backside at quite a speed!

"Hell's bells girl!"

Three! I'd beaten both Mike and Yvonne. It must have been some kind of record.

"Hell's bells girl," FOUR! "What on earth do you think you're doing?"

"What I was told to do." I wasn't prepared to take the blame for everything.

"What do you mean? Look at the damage to my boot!"

"You told me to switch every thing off," I'm not usually assertive, but after four "hell's bells" it was time to stand up for myself.

"So?"

"Well when everything's switched off in a Citroen and the engine's not running, there are no brakes." Remember, I'd read the manual just a few days prior! I could see the differing emotions passing through dad's eyes. He had forgotten. He of all people would know about hydraulics and brakes, after all, he had the very first Citroen DS ever brought into this country. If he could forget an important piece of information like this, he couldn't really get mad and blame me. Mike did point out to me later that I could have used the hand brake. Technicalities. I thought that a brake was a brake, so if one didn't work, the others wouldn't either. You learn something new every day. Soon all was forgiven. And I think I seriously impressed both Mike and Yvonne with my four "hell's bells"!

Yvo used to own, at one time, the largest engineering firm in Zimbabwe. His staff respected him and though many of them had completely different religious beliefs to his, they respected his. He lived by his beliefs and his word was his bond. He started every meeting with a prayer and didn't exactly enamour himself to outside members of the board when he stated that he was not in business to make a profit, but to fulfil a need in the community. The annual staff Christmas parties used to take place at the Ambassador Hotel in Union Avenue. Every year before the festivities began in earnest, Yvo would give his speech. We were sitting at a table with a crowd of younger employees who were raring to party. Yvo's speech always took the same format, a synopsis of the firm's past year, any important staff announcements such as a death, promotions and, always, the Second Coming of Christ. The waiter service at the hotel this particular year left much to be desired, it would have been hard to tell the difference between them being on a go-slow, or just going slow! While dad was exhorting us to make sure that we were ready for Christ's return, one wag at our table quipped, "I hope the waiter gets back here with my drink before Christ returns, I'm bleep thirsty!" The eruption of laughter from our table nearly earned us all a collective "hell's bells"!

THE HIDDEN VALLEY OF THE BIRDS

The Hidden Valley of The Birds is the headline of a newspaper article by Stella Day and Allan Gray that appeared in The Sunday Mail of April 6th 1975 on page eleven. It was an article about my father-in-law, Yvo and Mike and "the biggest privately owned bird sanctuary known to exist in Rhodesia" that they had just finished constructing. Mike and Yvo built the aviary over a period of time at the weekends and whenever they had any spare time – which wasn't often as they were both involved in the running of the family-owned engineering business in Harare. Stella Day went on to say, "The steep valley, about half a hectare in extent, has been completely enclosed and roofed with strong wire mesh stretched like a continuous spider web over the bush, rocks and tall trees."

Yvo and Mike collected differing species of birds to stock their sanctuary and these included guinea fowl, pheasants, peacocks, several varieties of game birds, wild ducks and geese. The presence of these birds attracted other wild birds and it could be quite noisy to be in the vicinity at times. Stella also mentioned, "As an engineering feat the building of this huge bird-cage posed some very complicated problems." That was an understatement. All the wire and equipment had to be transported from Harare and then be taken down to the site of the sanctuary by means of the treacherously steep road, which was actually not much more than a track that led down the hill. The fence was 12 metres high in places and the planning that went into the placing of the network of support wires was impressive. The choice of the site of the birdcage was daring. It was positioned over a steep-sided gully with a small river running through it, this water eventually ending up in our dam. River is a bit of a misnomer as the water only runs in the rainy season and is bone dry the rest of the year.

Mike's sister, Yvonne, bought a rabbit from a street vendor as she felt sorry for the plight of the poor animal imprisoned in a tiny box. The vendors prey on us softies, knowing that we can't bear to see an animal ill treated. Yvonne reckoned that if she didn't take this rabbit, then it would end up on someone's table as stew. The vendor assured her that the rabbit was a male. I know, I know. We've all been caught like this. It's easy to be gullible where cute, furry little animals are concerned. It wasn't long before the tsuro (rabbit) dropped her furry little bundles of joy – many of them. Yvonne had been prepared to look after one rabbit, but she was landed with far more than she bargained for. She asked if the Family Tsuro could be re-located to Mazowe, namely to the Valley of The Birds.

With hindsight we all have twenty-twenty vision, it was not a bright thing to do to put the rabbits in the birdcage. They multiplied and they multiplied. Apart from their ever-increasing numbers, they also attracted predators, namely pythons. Whilst the tsuros were multiplying and attracting undesirables, they were also burrowing AND burrowing, it was as if they were trying to find the shortcut to the land Down Under, in fact I'm sure one time I caught a glimpse of the Sydney Opera House. Finally it got out of hand. No wonder Australia was a tad anti rabbits a few years back, I know exactly how they felt. Mike had no choice but to say to our staff that it was open season on the rabbits. Talk about efficiency. Within a week we were rabbit free and our staff were replete and there were soon some Davey Crockett wannabes sporting an unusual assortment of head apparel.

We did experience incidents with theft of the birds, especially the more exotic ones. Even though we tried to keep the location of our home and therefore the sanctuary, a well-guarded secret, some people seemed to develop radar where the birds were concerned. One Sunday afternoon Mike and I thought we'd go for a walk down to the birdcage, only to find that there was a carload of aggressive picnickers there who threatened us and chased us away – on our own land. That was the only incidence of that type, but it was somewhat unnerving. It was sad, but the sanctuary died a natural death. Some birds were stolen, but most of them succumbed to predators such as snakes. Eventually Mike and Yvo decided that enough was enough and that they should just call it quits. The wire was dismantled and it was the end of an era. It was a great disappointment for Yvo. He had envisioned breeding the birds and expanding it into a business of providing live birds for sale and birds for the pot. It obviously just wasn't meant to be. Even if we hadn't made the fatal error of introducing tsuro and her progeny, we would still have had the problems of theft and the snakes.

Hidden Valley of the Birds

OLD MADALA

During the war years of the 60s and 70s, as previously mentioned, the security forces were concerned about the terrorists obtaining supplies of food and thereby being able to stay in an area and cause havoc. As a result, we had to inform the police via the agric-alert radio as to the number of staff we employed and the number of dependants staying on our property. We provided the mealie-meal, milled maize kernels, which was the staple diet for the majority of people in the country, and rationed it out daily to our staff to prevent it from falling into the wrong hands. This was a time-consuming, but necessary chore. As we had quite a large piece of land our staff was fortunate in that they could supplement their diets by growing fruit and vegetables near to their houses.

The plot of land on our western border was vacant. It had belonged to an elderly man, who had bought the land in the area and subsequently sub-divided it into plots for resale. In time, he would most probably have recouped his money, but not many people were prepared to buy land in rural areas during a terrorist war. He died shortly before we got married, his widow had to leave the area and take a job as a school matron at a boarding school. Their house stood empty for years and was stripped of virtually everything that was removable: window and door frames, pipes, circuit breakers and other electrical fittings, bathroom fittings, whatever could be removed was removed. The poor house was just a shell of its former self. This stripping of the house was not only done by locals living in the area, but opportunists from Salisbury (Harare) drove all the way out to Mazowe to do a little cheap, self-service D.I.Y shopping. It's amazing how people got to hear about the house in the first place. We reported the matter to the police on several occasions but there wasn't much they could do about it. There was a war going on which took priority over everything.

During this period, an old 'madala', the Shona word for an old person, decided that he was going to squat on the vacant land. He built himself a grass hut and lived there for quite some time. Technically he was not meant to be there, apart from the fact that he was squatting, the security forces did not permit anyone to stay in an area if they did not have a legitimate reason for so being. Somehow the madala managed to slip through the net, nobody ever bothered him and he never bothered anyone else. None of our staff knew his name or anything about him. One Sunday night in winter, we were informed by a member of our staff that the old madala had died in his sleep.

We weren't quite sure what to do about him, but 'we made a plan'. We were loath to bury him on our land, as we didn't know what the legal implications would be. At the time, we had a Citroen DS20 station wagon, a fantastic old car that we made good use of over the years. We used it to transport furniture, fifty-kilogram sacks of fertilizer, building materials and anything else that we needed. We drove to the madala's hut and put his body into the back of the car with the backseat down. Whatever he died of must have been nasty, because the poor old man stank so badly that we had to have all the car windows wide open to stop ourselves gagging and in the middle of winter, this was no joke. Winters, even in Africa, *can* get cold. The nearest police station to us was Mazowe, about twelve kilometres away so we took the body there. The policeman on duty said that they were not equipped to deal with dead bodies and that we had to take the madala into Salisbury (Harare) a journey of approximately thirty-seven kilometres.

Our makeshift hearse was accordingly turned around and we went back in the direction we had just come. The nearest police station in Harare was at Marlborough on the outskirts of the city, so we headed there, me with my head stuck out the window – I have a weak stomach! Marlborough police weren't interested in our deceased madala as he had died in the district of Mazowe and therefore it was nothing to do with them, and they suggested that we go to the morgue at Harare hospital. The stench from madala was getting riper all the time. Another long trek through central Harare to the morgue just to be told that they could not accept the body, as they had to have a death certificate from Mazowe police! By now Mike was beginning to have a sense of humour failure and I wasn't impressed with life, as apart from the fact we were driving all over the place with a dead body in the back of our car, I was missing my favourite soapy, 'Dallas' and the Ewing family.   Again, more precious fuel and the trek back to Mazowe police station. Another refusal to accept the body. Mike and I had tried to do everything that we could to treat the madala with respect, but this was the final straw. So, with the constable watching us, the two of us removed him from the back of the car which was no easy task as he was quite a tall man, all the while I was swallowing rapidly to prevent myself from vomiting and we left him lying in the car park and drove off. We never heard another word about him. Hopefully he is resting in peace and perhaps having a quiet smile.

SHING AND THE OTHER CATS

When we had gone to collect madala's body from his hut, I noticed the most beautiful little Siamese kitten. It looked far too young to be away from its mother and I have no idea where the madala had found it. I named the kitten Shing. The poor little mite had at sometime fallen into the fire as parts of his fur were quite badly singed and he also had lumps of sadza (mealie meal porridge) matted in his coat. He was a lovely colour, but a bit deformed with a very rounded potbelly and short, stumpy, bandy legs. He always insisted in accompanying me to the bathroom when I was having a bath and seemed to make a habit of falling into the water. I would have to wrap him in a towel to dry him, then finish the job with a hairdryer. The cats' food has always been put up on one of the kitchen counters to prevent the dogs from helping themselves; poor stumpy Shing couldn't manage the jump up so had to be helped in order to enable him to eat and when he was finished, had to be helped down again. The odd time when he did try to get down by himself, he more tumbled than jumped. The other cats were tolerant towards him, but the dogs treated him as a joke. Unfortunately one year when we were on holiday in South Africa, the dogs chased, caught and killed Shing. I suppose those stubby little legs just weren't up to the job of helping him to escape. He has joined the rest of the occupants in our animal graveyard near our reservoir at the back of the house.

Maxi

Maxi was given to us as a young kitten. He was jet black, glossy, handsome and a male chauvinist. He would tolerate me, but was most definitely Mike's cat. We had the pleasure of Maxi's company for twenty-one years and he was certainly one of the family. Mike had gone to bed before me one night. He was lying on his back with the blankets up under

31

his chin and looking peaceful. I came into the room just in time to see Maxi passionately rubbing himself against one side of Mike's face, then the other. I knew what was coming, but my warped sense of humour wouldn't let me interfere. Maxi turned round, tail ramrod straight in the air, posterior facing towards my snoozing, unsuspecting husband, and commenced to mark his territory! Poor Mike. It took a while for it to hit him what the warm, fuzzy feeling that he was experiencing was all about. It doesn't pay to have a perverted sense of humour. It backfired on me as guess who had to change the bed linen while Mike had a shower.

Maxi loved Mike so much he was always leaving him little feline billet-doux in unusual places. Take the time that Mike was hurrying out in the morning taking children to school en route to a board meeting. He was in his suit and was just putting on his shoes. He slipped his one foot into a shoe, it momentarily felt nice and warm, then the wetness pervaded. Yes, Maxi just wanted Mike to remember him throughout the day. We built our house over a period of many years depending on the state of our finances. Maxi claimed the position of 'clerk of works' and took it upon himself to supervise every aspect of the building. My father helped Mike with a lot of the work on the house and often complained that he would just have a timber balanced ready to nail, when, out of no-where, Maxi would jump on it, scaring everyone half to death and nearly causing the timber to come crashing down.

Maxi had the dogs under control and the other cats knew who was boss. Humans loved him and he always made such a good impression on visitors. He was a very civilized cat. By the time Maxi had reached his human age of majority, he was no longer the sleek, arrogant being that we had all come to know and love. There were a few teeth missing and his fur was still black but a tad tatty. As most of us do, he'd mellowed with age and was more charitable towards the rest of our animal and human family. He died in his sleep one night and we found him dead on the kitchen floor in the morning. It definitely was the end of an era when Maxi too went to join our other beloved pets in our animal cemetery.

Snowy

It was like the Beatles' song, 'Ebony and Ivory'; we went from jet-black Maxi, to snow white, Snowy. My parents were given an adorable kitten by a gardener who was walking past their property. The gardener had found the kitten on the road and was concerned that it would be run over by a car. He had asked other gardeners roundabout if they knew where the kitten belonged, but to no avail. My parents did not want a kitten; their days as pet owners were over. They had recently had to put their beloved little dog down and had decided, no more pets! Dad phoned me to see if we wouldn't take the stray, he had fallen in love with it and said it had such a wonderful nature, but I had to steel myself and say 'no'. Left to my own devices, I would have been at their house like a shot to collect the kitten. Mike and I had come to a near parting of the ways because I kept bringing home stray animals. At one stage we had seven cats and seven dogs, I think that's when Mike decided that it would be a good idea to have a human family of our own, and perhaps I'd slow down on the animals. He all but barred me from going to the SPCA, so when Dad phoned about the kitten, I had to say, 'Get thee behind me Satan', thanks, but no thanks. Begrudgingly, my parents took the kitten to the SPCA.

Snowy

A few days after the kitten incident, Mark (our eldest son) came home from junior school with a tabby kitten that he'd been given by one of the teachers. He named her Purdy. What a beautiful cat she turned into and was faithful to Mark. She was also spunky and gave the other cats a run for their money and was clearly the Alpha female. Purdy liked to explore and she would often spend a night or two away from home, but she always came back. One school holidays we had gone to Kariba for a few days and on our return, there was no Purdy. At first we weren't unduly concerned, after all, she'd done this before. When days turned into weeks, weeks into months, we had to face up to the fact that she wasn't coming back. The Zimbabwean bush can be a hostile place for domestic cats, not only would she have to contend with snakes, wild cats, baboons and so on, there was also the added danger of the snares that the local people set up to catch small game and birds. I felt desperately sorry for Mark. He truly loved Purdy.

I am constantly grateful for being an only child – my parents had it easy. Shortly after Mark had got Purdy I had the whining from Heath (our younger son), it's not fair, Mark's got a kitten and I haven't, why can't I have one? I could see Heath's point of view. I had a brilliant idea, they don't happen very often to me, so when they do, I have to act on them immediately! I made a plan. I contacted the SPCA to see if the white kitten was still available. It was, but had to stay at the kennels for the regulation ten days. I booked the kitten and kept it a secret from the boys. I did have to tell my big boy, Mike, and although he wasn't ecstatic, he was far more amenable than I had thought he'd be! The day arrived, 6th October 1994. I collected the boys from school and said that we were going out to the SPCA to deliver some books and old toys for their charity shop. Mark and Heath helped me carry the boxes in to the office, and then I wish you could have seen Heath's face when I mentioned to the woman behind the counter that we had come to collect 'our' kitten. I wish you could have seen my face when we went to the enclosure to collect 'our' kitten and I saw it for the first time. He was a bag of bones held together with stringy white fur.

No one in their right minds would have chosen him. The SPCA attendant took me aside and said that they were concerned about the kitten and didn't think it would survive, as it would just not eat. Honestly, you would think that an organisation like the SPCA would know how to feed a kitten properly. They tried to treat him like a feline instead of the junk-food addict that he was. Within a few weeks we had Snowy looking lovely. It was truly a 'before' and 'after' picture. Forget about cats' mince; try olives, chocolate, cashew nuts, Nik-Naks, popcorn (preferably salted), gem squash, potato crisps – and all the junk food you can think of! That cat had radar where junk food was concerned. If ever you couldn't find him, all you had to do was rustle a packet of sweets or chips and he'd be there like a shot! I would love to know who Snowy's original owner was and what their diet consisted of! Heath wanted to call the kitten, Hercules, but Mike, when he first saw the kitten, in his usual diplomatic way, said, "this kitten isn't going to make it, it'll be dead in a few days." We then had one distraught child and a scrawny, half-dead kitten. I soothed Heath and we dissuaded him from calling the kitten Hercules, and finally Heath came up with 'Snowy'. Hercules would never have suited. He turned out to be the most affectionate, soppy, lovable, floppy cat imaginable – definitely not a Hercules.

Snowy and I had one thing in common, we both loved the sun. The difference being that I wear a sun block with a very high UV factor and don't get the tips of my ears burnt to blisters like he was constantly doing. I tried putting sun block on his ears and as fast as I'd apply it, he'd lick it off. I don't know what it did for his digestion, but it certainly wasn't helping his ears and he was developing nasty sores on them. I took Snowy to the vet and explained our predicament. The only suggestion the vet had was that we tattoo Snowy's ears, which may prevent the UV rays damaging the pigmentation. The boys thought that this was a really cool idea, having a cat with tattooed ears. I think they had visions of wild designs and garish colours all over his ears.

We've had so many pets over the years that have had ops of one kind or another, so we know what to expect of an animal when it is recovering from an anaesthetic. Snowy has proved to be different from the norm in every way. He wasn't at all groggy when we collected him in the afternoon, but kept trying to stand, which didn't work, and as he fell, he'd bang his head which in turn, caused pain to his swollen, blue-black ears. He refused anything to eat or drink, and was in such a bad way, that I decided to sleep on the settee in the lounge to be near him. I didn't get a wink of sleep and the next morning I was like a zombie.

I phoned the vet in quite a state and was advised that as Snowy hadn't eaten, his blood sugar levels were low and I had to get them up quickly. The vet said that they had had to give Snowy almost double the dose of anaesthetic than normal in order to get both ears done. The vet suggested a couple of drops of golden syrup might do the trick. Easier said than done. Have you ever tried to give runny, sticky syrup to a demented animal that won't keep still, and I couldn't even hold his head to steady him, as he really seemed to be in pain from his ears. I managed a couple of drops. They slipped down his throat. It worked like magic. Within a matter of minutes, he'd calmed down and was soon eating well. For weeks after the op, poor Snowy had balance problems; he'd aim for one chair and land up on another. He'd either go too far left or right, or be completely off kilter altogether. With time, he eventually came right. His ears were sore and he hated anyone touching them, and this was the case until the end of his days.

Snowy always looked so regal when he was lying down with his front paws crossed over each other, completely relaxed. Shortly after his op, he was lying on my dressing table and I went to talk to him – to find him lying in his usual sphinx pose – but with the tips of his ears lying on the dressing table next to him. Never having experienced anything like this before, I wasn't sure what to do. I put Snowy in the cat basket and his ear tips in an envelope and went back to the vet. I took one of the tips out of the envelope and said to the vet, "We seem to have a slight problem here." A look of horror crossed the vet's face. He said, "I'm sorry, there's not much I can do, I can't re-attach the tip to the ear." From the vet I went to school to pick up the boys.

Mark was out first and I told him about the ear and showed it to him in the envelope. He thought it was 'cool'. On Heath's arrival, before I could even get a word in edgeways, Mark had taken the ear out of the envelope and said, "Hey, look! It's Snowy's ear!" Poor Heath. I thought he was about to faint. After it had been explained to him that there was still a cat that went with the ear, he visibly relaxed and Snowy got lots of T.L.C on the way home. When people met Snowy for the first time they thought he was some exotic breed with the blue-black oblong formations he had on the top of his head. Unfortunately, the tattooing wasn't that successful and his right ear was a continual mess from cancerous blisters, and, as I'm sure you'll have guessed, Snowy loved to spend his time sunbathing.

In August 2005 Snowy went walk-about and we couldn't find him. That's one of the downsides of living in the bush, we can keep the dogs within our property by means of a security fence, but cats can't be kept in. We looked everywhere for Snowy. We passed the worried, desperate stage to the hopeless and resigned to the fact that we were never going to see him again stage. We thought it was going to be a re-run of the Purdy scenario. He had been away for the odd day or two before, but this was now five days. He could have been snared, killed by a snake or a wild cat, anything could have happened to him, and we just didn't know where else to look. We had an elderly gardener working for us called Loya, it gave me a kick to say, "I'll have to ask my lawyer," I mean, not many people have a lawyer mowing their lawn for them, do they? One Monday lunchtime Loya had been walking through the bush and heard a strange noise, on investigation, found Snowy in a snare. Fate works in mysterious ways. This was not the path that Loya normally took, he was in a hurry so was taking a shortcut; he was also a bit deaf, so it was amazing that he even heard Snowy's pitiful meow.

When I opened the door in answer to Loya's knock and saw the pathetic white bundle in his arms, I thought the cat was dead. August is hot and dry, and the snare had been in the open under the blazing sun, I didn't think Snowy stood a chance of surviving. Miracles *do* happen. I rushed him to the vet and it was touch and go for a while. The vet said that we were fortunate that the wire snare had been around his stomach and lower back as if it had been around his neck he would almost certainly be dead, and if it had been around a limb, it would more than likely have to be amputated. There were concerns about damage to internal organs, but another of his nine lives was used up, and he survived. It wasn't all plain sailing though. He had a fetish about water, although we left saucers of water throughout the house we'd find him trying to drink out of the toilet bowl and I was terrified that he'd fall in and drown. He also refused to eat. Heath and I would take turns holding him whilst the other tried forcing morsels of food down his throat. The stench from his mouth made us want to gag, it was awful. Back to the vet. Snowy was kept in for a few more days as it was discovered that he had an infection, hence his not wanting to eat and the stench from his stomach as all the gastric juices worked on one another, as they had no food to work on.

Back home, eating and drinking normally. Then Heath discovered a chunk of flesh hanging off his hind paw. Back to the vet to have a partial amputation of the paw. It was thought that he had damaged his paw trying to scrape away the wire from his stomach when he'd been snared. It took several months and many costly visits to the vet to get Snowy on the road to recovery.

Mike and I used to regularly walk around the fence surrounding our property, dismantling wire snares. When the boys were younger, they used to go 'snare-hunting' as well. These snares are usually put out to catch small animals such as rabbits and ground birds, and it is a cruel, painful way to die. As fast as we'd dismantle the snares, they'd be back. Of course no one ever owns up. According to our staff it's always 'the neighbours', and according to the neighbours, it's our staff. With the dire economic situation in present-day Zimbabwe it is very hard to castigate someone for merely trying to stay alive. It's a no-win situation.

Poor Snowy still suffered with his ears. He loved to lie in the sun. The effect of this was that his right ear in particular, developed huge black blisters, most likely cancerous, these in turn irritated him; he'd scratch and draw blood. And did he draw blood! The ear was raw and every time he shook his head, we had blood splatters on walls, furniture, everywhere. Between the vet and ourselves, we'd tried all sorts of remedies, but to no avail; the only course of action was the drastic one – that of removing his ear altogether! This was duly done at the end of November 2007, and once again poor Snowy had a traumatic recovery time. We were convinced that his nine lives must surely be up, but one thing's for sure, he never learnt his lesson, he still spent his days lazing under the blistering African sun.

At the beginning of 2008 we thought he was dying. He refused to eat and we had to keep him alive by syringing raw egg mixed with milk into his mouth. This went on for weeks and I eventually suggested that we do the humane thing. Mike loved that cat – as did we all – and he refused to give up. Snowy did perk up for a while but was a shadow of his former self. Towards the end of the year he was pitiful, he was like a lost soul. He couldn't settle and always wanted to be near one of us. This went on for a few weeks and I finally made the 'decision'; by now it seemed as if the cancer was spreading throughout his head and he was again having trouble eating on his own. On Thursday 30th October 2008 we took Snowy to the government Veterinary training institute in Mazowe. True to form, Snowy didn't make things easy and he fought to cling on to life. He was so dehydrated that the vet struggled to find any veins on his legs and this led to Snowy getting agitated thus necessitating an injection to sedate him. Even this wasn't going well and finally there was nothing for it but to inject him directly into his heart. This all took forty-five minutes of gut-wrenching emotion, followed by 'negotiations' with the vet re payment. Zimbabwe was going through a crazy financial free-fall with our own currency deemed worthless but no one really knowing what to charge. Mike and the vet made a plan and the negotiations were amicably settled with the vet suggesting that we pay either ten US dollars or one hundred South African rands, we chose the former. The next step was a sombre journey home to bury Snowy in our animal graveyard.

Ditch

In January 1996, we spent a week on holiday in Nyanga, staying at the Village Inn in the Nyanga village. Nyanga is in the eastern districts of Zimbabwe near the Mozambican border. There's not a whole lot to Nyanga village. There's a main street with widely spaced shops, a few pavements, but more often than not, these are bare earth and clumps of grass. The shops are basic. There is a general store cum hardware, called Cha-Cha Store. I used to love browsing around in there. There was a clothes shop cum furniture shop, a dingy café, Bata shoe shop, Athlete's world, CABS building society and a Standard Chartered bank. At one time there was a quaint gift shop, but as with many business concerns in Zimbabwe, as we started our landslide fall towards and during, the new millennium, this too died.

We were doing a bit of window-shopping walking along the 'natural' pavement, which was cluttered with grass, mud and other debris. Mike was in the lead and was just passing the one and only public call box, which stood incongruously on its own on a patch of barren earth sprinkled with a few tufts of grass. As he was about to put his right foot down Mark let out a piercing yell, "Lookout Dad!" and there, just where his foot would have landed, was a tiny, black and white bundle of fur. It was a scrawny, vermin infested, kitten. Mark and Heath went to try and pick it up, but not only was this kitten street-wise; it was plain wild and took off like a banshee.

We often saw it around the shopping centre when we were in the vicinity, but this was one wily kitten with an amazing survival instinct diving into the storm water drains that abound in the area. Nyanga is mountainous and as such these drains are massive to cope with the huge volumes of water in the rainy season. It would have been easy for either of the boys to follow the kitten into the drain, but I would not entertain the idea as I had visions of gaboon vipers (highly venomous snakes which are native to this part of the country) lurking in the drains.

Ditch

The Village Inn was a family establishment. There were no frills and no fuss, but it was clean and basic yet comfortable and reasonable, if a bit staid. Mark likes to talk. He had started chatting to the receptionist on duty during our stay, a woman called Julie. It transpired that Julie was a cat lover, as was evidenced by the number of extremely well fed, sleek felines frequenting the hotel. In the course of their conversations, Mark had told Julie about the little kitten that we had seen, and she told him that if he was ever able to catch it, to bring it to her and she would look after it. That was definitely easier said than done as this kitten had other ideas. We seemed to spend an awful lot of time in the village, which is not one of life's most scintillating places, purely so Mark and Heath could try and catch the kitten.

The last day of our holiday was 13th January 1996. I had an ear infection and took myself off early in the morning before breakfast to the local doctor in the village, Dr. Dambanemwiya, known as Dr. Damba due to ease of articulation. He has been in the area forever and over the years we have used his services for our family, the last time being years back when Heath had a mild bout of malaria. I was chatting to another woman and her daughter while we were both waiting for the surgery to open and just then the kitten darted past us and dived into the drain. I told the women about how my sons had been trying to catch the kitten for a week, when the daughter took herself off, bent down, looked inside the drain, called the kitten *and* it came to her! To this day I don't know what her secret was. I was now in possession of a wild, tick infested kitten, but I still had an appointment with a doctor to go through before I could get the struggling wee beastie back to Julie. Dr. Damba's wife, who is his assistant and the pharmacist, 'made a plan' and came to my rescue by providing me with a small cardboard carton. I shudder to think what the other patients in the waiting room thought of me as we all sat stoically awaiting the arrival of Dr. Damba and I had a moving box on my lap, which was making the most hideous noises.

My turn came to see the doctor I was not prepared to leave the kitten and the box in the waiting room after finally having caught it. I only had a few minutes to wait for Dr. Damba. When he entered the consulting room, he looked a bit bemused. He looked at me, looked at the box, listened to the box, looked back at me, hesitated and said, "I'm not sure if you realise, but I'm a doctor for humans, I'm not a vet." We both had a bit of a laugh when I explained the circumstances. It was with great relief that he attended to my ears, I think he had the feeling that his expertise was going to be tested to its limit.

Back at the hotel, my euphoria on obtaining the kitten soon dissipated. Both the boys were excited to see me with the kitten, and Mark ran off to the reception to inform Julie, only to find out that she was off work for four days, and her replacement, in no uncertain terms, definitely did *not* like cats! We explained things to the duty receptionist and she said that she would keep the kitten for Julie, but the boys and I just knew that the moment our car drove out the gates, she'd open the box and let the kitten go. We were under no illusions about her feelings towards cats. We left the kitten in an office with a feast of roast beef and a saucer of milk while we had our breakfast. There were serious discussions at our table. Mike was adamant that we were not taking the cat home. We were adamant that we weren't leaving the cat with this receptionist. Mark came up with a brilliant solution. He'd been learning about democracy at school and decided that we should decide the fate of the cat in a democratic manner. We had a vote. Mike was outvoted three to one. We were now the proud owners of a mutinous black and white kitten, and a somewhat mutinous husband and father. There was obvious relief on the receptionist's face when we reclaimed the newest member of our family.

I sat in the bedroom with the kitten trying to get as many ticks off it as possible as his poor body was alive with them. Mike and the boys were out in the gardens surreptitiously digging up some of the flowerbeds so that we could provide a sandbox of sorts in order to transport the kitten back home. I'm not sure if the kitten grasped the fact that we were trying to help him, or if it was just so replete after its recent feast, but he didn't seem quite so wild. We were finally ready to make our way home with our latest acquisition. The feast must have just been too much for the kitten, we'd hardly got going and the most awful pong pervaded the car. It was so bad it brought tears to our eyes and our teeth started buckling. We had to stop at the side of the road under a tree and change the soil in the sandbox. Not the easiest thing to do without a spade – or even a spoon!

For a considerable part of the journey home, we discussed various names for the kitten. There was the usual, Sooty (as he was black), Socks (as he had little white socks), Nyanga (as we quite often name our animals after the places they came from), or my contribution, Damba. Nothing clicked. Then Mike said, "What about Ditch? We found him in a ditch." That seemed to be the perfect name. It was short, catchy, and different, just like the kitten. We still hadn't been able to find out whether Ditch was male or female, he wasn't that tame yet! One of the boys piped up, "If we find out that the kitten's a girl, will we change the 'D' to a 'B' in his name?" I told him emphatically that it would most definitely NOT change to a 'B'. Luckily Ditch is male, so we never had to go there.

Ditch decided that he belonged to me. I have an old, favourite, long red dressing gown I've had for years and I hope I have it for years to come. I love it, it's comfortable and every cat we've ever had has loved it as well. I was convinced that I was suffering from Yuppie 'flu or some debilitating disease after Ditch came to live with us. I used to get up first in the morning and went through to the kitchen to make tea and coffee. I'm not a morning person. I don't 'do' mornings well. It seemed more and more difficult to go down the passage in the mornings, until I found out the cause. Ditch was getting a free ride down the passage to the kitchen on the tails of my gown. He'd cling on with his front paws to the hem of my dressing gown and got pulled along the passage on his stomach!

LUCKY

I have never been particularly keen on horses, the only one that I was ever able to conquer was the one in Woolworths, which took a twenty-cent coin and my feet could touch the ground. For some strange reason, after we were married I decided that I rather fancied owning a donkey. I didn't consider them quite as frightening as horses; we live and learn. I answered an advert in the newspaper for a donkey for sale. That evening after work, Mike and I went to look at it. What a magnificent creature. He was the crème de la crème of donkeys with a haughty manner and his name was Lucky. Lucky had been brought up in a stable with real horses and genuinely believed he was no mere donkey.

We weren't sure how we were going to transport Lucky from his stable in Harare to our house in Mazowe, a distance of about thirty-five kilometres. We discussed the matter with two members of our staff, Peter and Raphael. The men were adamant that they would be able to walk him back taking shortcuts through fields and neighbouring farms, so they made a plan. This was all before we got to know Lucky, and Peter and Raphael found out the hard way! The two men were utterly exhausted when they finally arrived home and Lucky had a mean glint in his eye challenging all and sundry to try and take him on. Peter and Raphael told of having to chase Lucky out of fields, of it taking the two of them to hold onto the reins and of almost being dragged along.

Lucky had free rein of our garden and the dogs learned very early on never to get too close to the hind legs. We used to have a stable door that led straight in to our lounge and Lucky would stand for hours with his head resting over the closed bottom half of the door staring in and watching us. I suppose it was quite a change for him to be on the outside looking in instead of the other way round. One Sunday we had visitors for lunch and as our

44

house then only consisted of two rooms, neither being a dining room, guests had to eat off their laps in the lounge. Our elderly guest, Rose, was sitting with her back to the stable door and wasn't aware that Lucky had been observing us for ages, gazing at us with those big innocent eyes and fluttering luscious eyelashes. He suddenly gave a huge heehaw, which reverberated around the room in stereo almost giving poor old Rose a heart attack. We were picking up food from every-which way as Rose's lunch plate was airborne.

On another occasion we were having an afternoon tea on the lawn with both sets of parents and Mike's aunt and uncle. I had my beady eye on Lucky who was hovering around in the background, I knew from the glint in his eyes and the way that he kept looking over at us, that he was up to no good. I kept asking Mike to put Lucky away in his stable while we had our tea, but Mike thought I was just being neurotic. I really, really wish people, especially my family, would just listen to me, I get *feelings* about these kind of things and once again was proved right. With no warning, Lucky galloped up, well maybe it was more of a fast walk, viciously kicked out left and right, and helped himself to the apple pie. Fortunately no one was injured, but Mike's elderly, and somewhat rotund uncle, saw his life flash before his eyes as he was firmly wedged in his chair and was utterly helpless as Lucky's menacing hooves whipped through the air.

Our house had polished wooden parquet floors. The one and only time that Lucky managed to get into the house was an experience that I never want to repeat. A large, heavy, angry donkey and highly polished floors is a recipe for disaster. Finally after much shoving and pushing, huffing and puffing we managed to get Lucky back onto his feet and out the door. It was providential that the passage in which Lucky found himself was fairly narrow so that it restricted his kicking ability, apart from the fact that he was too heavy to balance on three legs on a polished surface. It took four of us to manhandle him, and it was hard work.

Lucky was a past master of escape, we should have renamed him Houdini. He went out on the town one night and decided to pay a visit to our neighbours. It was after midnight and everyone was asleep, so you can imagine the panic he caused by sticking his head through a bedroom window and announcing to the world at the top of his lungs that he was there. Not the brightest of things to do during the war years in an area where people usually keep a weapon handy. He so very nearly went to meet his maker and retire to the big stable in the sky. He often would go down to the boundary of our land and hee-haw over the valley to a hill in Christon Bank from where he was answered by Peggy's dulcet hee-hawing. Peggy was a tatty, elderly donkey and certainly not in the same league as Lucky. Her owner and I made contact and it came to pass that Peggy and her brother, Percy, came to live with us. A short while later, we were then given another really tatty, ugly, but oh so lovable old male called Hager, and another female, Daisy. When Lucky saw her, it was love at first sight. You could see the stars in his eyes, and over the years, the loving couple produced four foals. Our garden comprised of four acres surrounded by a security fence and gates, the remaining one hundred acres were demarcated with a four-strand barbwire fence. Now that our equestrian family was increasing so rapidly, it was decided that we would keep them outside the security fence, but within the bounds of the rest of our land, so every night they trekked back to the stable area and were locked in for the night.

It was a win-win situation with the donkeys. We derived great enjoyment from them and they in turn kept the grass short which greatly reduced the danger of the annual bush fires. Our cook's son asked if he could try riding one of the donkeys and with a grin from ear to ear, had great delight a few weeks later, in informing me that he had 'tamed' Percy. The enthusiastic jockey asked if I'd like a ride. I didn't want to be a whimp and disappoint the youngster, but I was nervous, very nervous. I had never been aware just what cunning creatures donkeys were. The youngster 'parked' the donkey next to the water trough so that I could stand on top of it and mount the donkey. I'm no expert with a saddle, but bareback was worse than impossible. I just seemed to slide to the left, then to the right, then to the left. My legs felt like they were the pendulums of a clock.

Percy was more subtle than Lucky, he didn't kick or rear up, he just walked slowly – going as close as he possibly could to every tree or shrub he could find to try and scrape me off. If this method didn't unseat me, it certainly left me with physical reminders of the day; my legs were covered in long, raw, bloody scratches. Then to compound the situation, Percy loved going up steep slopes, then turning round and going back down again. The young jockey took his responsibility seriously by walking next to the donkey and I had one hand clutching for dear life to Percy's mane, and the fingers of my other hand firmly entwined in the coils of the boy's hair! It's a miracle that he had any hair left by the time I got off I was so terrified. That was my first and last attempt at riding our donkeys.

We had a constant battle with some local neighbours who kept stealing our fencing standards. This facilitated the donkeys being able to get out of our property and get on to the neighbours' land and eat their crops. It would appear that donkeys, as with humans, hold true to the 'grass is greener' adage. The neighbours would complain to us about the donkeys and we in turn, would complain about the theft of the standards. We tried reasoning with them that it was impossible for us to contain the donkeys if the fences were constantly being sabotaged, but it fell on deaf ears. The situation came to a head when all of our donkeys died within three days of each other. I was devastated. We had a post mortem done on Lucky and it showed that he had been poisoned. We thought about taking the matter to the police, but decided against it. We would never have been able to prove anything conclusively, nothing would have been done to our neighbours other than perhaps a warning; it would have caused animosity in a small community and all we would have gained by it, would be a dent in our bank account. Our animal cemetery was filling up fast.

FELIX

Late one night, we heard strange noises outside and went to investigate. We're used to the nocturnal 'bush' noises, we know the screech of the bush-babies, the hoot of the owl and other birds; but this sound was different. It plainly was the sound of an animal in distress. There was a young serval cat lying in the grass inside our security fence and it had been injured. The markings were beautiful. It was so traumatized that it allowed us to carry it back to the house where we proceeded to clean the wounds and do what first aid we could. I decided, with hindsight rather foolishly, that I wanted to try and keep him as a pet, and duly named him Felix. While he was convalescing I kept him in a storeroom in the garage. It was during the war years and we had to ration out the food to our staff, so Mike had erected a nissen hut inside our garage for extra storage.

The garage was a huge, cavernous affair easily accommodating three cars and at a push, with lots of manoeuvering we could squeeze a fourth one in. The nissen hut kept the fifty-kilogram bags of mealie meal under lock and key and I kept my deepfreeze there. As all true Zimbabweans will understand, you never throw anything away and the contents of the hut would testify to that. Empty glass jars, old coffee tins, empty plastic juice bottles – all very necessary items to be used for either jam making or as planters in the garden or as containers for muti (medicine or pesticides) for the vegetable garden or the livestock.

It was into this cluttered and dark hut that Felix was placed in a corner on some old sacks. He had to be taken outside at regular intervals to relieve himself and we had to make sure that the dogs and cats had been locked up so that they wouldn't upset him any more. I know that he was in shock and possibly quite a bit of pain, but it was amazing how he would permit me to handle him. His wounds were healing, albeit slowly. He did not have a pleasant odour and that was putting it mildly, it would be truer to say that he stank! Our domestic family of animals was less than impressed with his presence. Whenever I had been handling Felix, the dogs and cats would sniff me and were very wary and took their time to come to be with me. He was about the size of a small dog so it wasn't too difficult to carry him but I knew that we were on borrowed time and as soon as he was up and about the situation would be quite different. I was also fully aware that I had to be extremely careful when handling him to ensure he didn't scratch or bite me. I had been told what signs to look for in case he had rabies and occasionally wondered if this was part of the reason for his docility; but as he never showed any signs of aggression other than a weak hiss, I think he was just in too much pain to worry about what was happening to him.

Mike's cousin, Richard, was curator of mammology at the museum in Bulawayo, and before this, he'd been in National Parks. Richard had kept many weird and wonderful animals over the years including an aardvark, so if anyone could advise us, it would be him. We contacted him enquiring how best to care for Felix. His opinion wasn't what I wanted to hear. He reckoned that the best thing we could do for Felix was to give him away to a game-park or wildlife shelter. I knew in my heart that it was the right thing to do, but it wasn't going to be easy. Richard said that it was necessary for servals to incorporate live birds and feathers into their diets to aid digestion, and as we were keeping ducks and chickens at the time we could see problems looming in the future when Felix was fully healed. I couldn't stand the thought of him being in a cage, so the painful, but necessary decision was made to take him to the National Parks department, which in turn, re-located him. I was grateful for the privilege of being able to actually handle such a magnificent animal, and although I know we made the right decision, it was still very painful parting with Felix.

WHITEY

My mother worked with a woman who had a pet leghorn cockerel, named Whitey. The family had had Whitey since he was a day-old chick and he had been hand-reared, but was now getting a bit aggressive and the children were scared of him. Mother volunteered on our behalf to re-home Whitey, and I was *not* impressed. We had told the family that they could come and visit whenever they wanted; I should have known there was something amiss when the kids gave huge whoops of delight as I drove out of their garden, and we never did hear from them again. Very sensible people. I am not the greatest fan of birds at the best of times, but I could foresee all kinds of problems with our dogs. Needless to say, my fears were groundless and Whitey ruled the roost. He was big, white, had a mean streak, a vicious beak, and terrorized me, the dogs, my father and later our sons, and like most tyrants, seemed to live forever.

Whenever we came home Whitey would be the first at the security gates to greet us, even before the dogs. As much as its nice to know that we'd been missed, it wasn't very nice to have to make a dash from the car to the house with the vicious bundle of feathers nipping at your ankles all the way. He had the complete run of the house and if we were packing to go away on holiday, he seemed to sense what the suitcases were for and he wasn't a happy chappy. He would fly onto the bed and scratch around in the cases pulling clothes out as fast as we were putting them in. Keeping up with the Jones' was out of the question for us when we had pets like Whitey and Lucky. If we had guests when the meal was over, Whitey would fly onto the table and go round all the wine glasses finishing off the dregs. He never broke any of the glasses; in fact he was quite agile. Depending on how much wine he'd consumed he'd sometimes tipsily stagger around. Some strangers arrived at our house when we'd just finished a very merry lunch with friends. The foreigners were lost and asking for directions; we weren't able to help so suggested that they come in and use our phone for directions. Our phone is in the dining room and the look on the woman's face was indescribable as she was having her phone conversation while at the same time watching our slightly inebriated cockerel helping himself to the remains of the wine.

Whitey adored my chocolate mousse that was laced with brandy. Another of his favourites was pecking the marrow out of the dogs' bones while they stood by helplessly waiting for him to have his fill. Whitey and my late father-in-law loved and respected each other, and whenever Yvo came out to visit, the two of them were inseparable. One Saturday afternoon we couldn't find Whitey and hunted high and low for him, Mike was worried that the dogs had put a contract on him, and I was secretly hoping that they had. Eventually we found Yvo and Whitey curled up on the settee in the lounge sharing a *chicken* sandwich. I hope Whitey never realised exactly what it was that he was eating.

The presence of Whitey meant I could never go out of the house without a big stick, as he had loved inflicting vicious, painful pecks on my ankles. Every time our sons wanted to go outside and play, we would have to round up Whitey and put him in the chicken run as the boys were terrified of him, and rightly so. Whitey knew my parents' car and he and my father hated the sight of each other. It was mutual hatred. If Dad forgot to roll his window up, Whitey would fly up and attack Dad through the open window, eventually drawing blood. The cockerel with an attitude finally met his match when we acquired two vervet monkeys, Tsoko and Susie. One day, there was an ear-splitting screech and we rushed outside to find a totally naked cockerel streaking down the driveway being pursued by two laughing monkeys, at least I could have sworn that they were laughing. Tsoko and Susie had plucked out all his feathers. We couldn't stop ourselves laughing, he was such a pathetic sight without all his finery and when we finally caught him, he was very subdued, and for once, I actually felt sorry for the poor mite, needless to say, it didn't last for long.

I used to have a miniature Doberman called Zoe who was like a baby to me. She sat on my lap, slept in our bed under the blankets and I loved her. She always used to run to the gate to meet us when we came home from work, along with Whitey. Mike and I had a routine when we arrived at our gates in case we were ambushed as the war was at its height. Mike would get out of the car and unlock the security gates, while I would slide over to the driver's side of the car so that if we were attacked, I could put my foot down and race the length of the driveway towards the house, the agric alert radio and hopefully, security. One afternoon we were later than usual as we'd had car problems and had to borrow a VW Combi to get home. This vehicle was much bigger than I was used to and I had problems with the gears and driving through the gates. All the time this was going on, Whitey and Zoe were excitedly running around waiting for us, and unbeknown to me, Whitey chased my precious little dog under the car and I drove over her. To say I was heartbroken was an understatement. We rushed her back into Harare to the vet, but nothing could be done. I can't even begin to explain how guilty I felt. If only we had been in our own car, if only we hadn't been later than usual, if only Whitey hadn't chased her, if only I'd been more alert, if only!

Whitey always helped himself to the dogs' food first and they had to wait for him to finish. The dogs had tolerated this for years, but finally, our big, male Doberman, Roddy, cracked. It was too much for him, he couldn't take the humiliation any longer so he killed Whitey, but surprisingly didn't try to eat him. I'd like to think there was a bit of respect there. Whitey was buried in our animal cemetery behind the water reservoir in the back garden. It was the end of an era. Mike and his father sorely missed the old bird, but the boys and I, and no doubt the dogs, all heaved a sigh of relief.

SNAKES ALIVE!

S nakes are not amongst my favourite beasties. Let's face it, a snake is a snake. There are snakes, and then there are snakes. Living on top of a rocky hill in a rural area meant that we had our fair share of these reptiles over the years and they always provided us with amusing dinner conversation. It was when we had the vervet monkeys, Tsoko and Susie that we became aware of just how many snakes were around. The monkeys were forever excitedly chattering a warning that there was a snake in the vicinity, and if they hadn't pointed it out to us, we wouldn't have been any the wiser. If I'm gardening or walking in the bush, I'm always on the lookout for snakes. Both Mike and I have had several close encounters nearly standing on snakes mainly puff adders, but happily no human has ever had a lethal encounter with a snake on our property yet, which goes a long way in dispelling the myth of dangerous snakes.

We were fighting a particularly fierce bush-fire, which was an annual occurrence in our area. Mike and the staff had been battling the fire for hours but it was getting the better of them. In desperation, Mike jumped into our dam to flee the raging flames. He wasn't the only one with the same idea, and when he and the puff adder met in the water, the traumatised reptile took a stab at Mike. Fortunately it was a rather half-hearted attempt, but it was enough to make Mike feel quite nauseous and woozy for a few hours.

We used to keep chickens and there was a magnificent resident python that looked upon our chicken run as his 'One stop shop'. We really were fighting a losing battle with this imposing reptile. The python would arrive and take his pick of the birds, then would gorge himself, and have problems trying to get back out through the diamond mesh fence with his huge, swollen, bird-filled body. Mike would disengage the snake from the fence once he'd digested the meal, and then into a sack in the boot of our car he'd go to be driven quite a distance away and released in a field. Days, weeks even, would go by, then we would hear a commotion in the chicken run, rush outside, just to find that the snake was back! Then suddenly, he disappeared from our lives.

Another python came into our lives, fortunately very much smaller than our first visitor, I say fortunately, as when it was found, it was in our house curled up having a little siesta under Mark's baby-cot! I don't know who got more of a fright – the snake, or me and take it from me, python's don't move too well on polished wooden parquet floors! When I think of what could have happened if the snake had decided to climb into the cot and keep cozy with a nice warm baby, I get goose bumps.

We were having lunch with some friends at home and were at the table when our domestic worker, Taundi (pronounced Town), came into the dining room through the front door instead of using the door to the kitchen. This was most unusual behaviour for Taundi, so I went into the kitchen to see if everything was all right. Taundi was in quite a flap and said that there was a cobra in the kitchen. I decided to close the door leading to the dining room as an added precaution and then proceeded to search the kitchen, but to no avail. I went back to lunch and tried to behave as if nothing had happened, but Taundi used the front door on two more occasions, and on each, Mike went into the kitchen to look for the elusive reptile, again, it was nowhere to be seen. We were beginning to wonder if there really was a snake.

Finally our guests left and I went into the kitchen just in time to see a large cobra weaving in and out of the wire vegetable baskets! My scream brought Mike running on the double. We were trying to decide how to deal with the situation when the snake slithered into the back of the washing machine. Mike, ever the pragmatist, decided that the best course of action would be to put the machine on 'fast spin' and that hopefully would solve our problem. When the spin cycle came to an end, as the machine was a front-loader, Mike had to take the top off it and we were hoping to extract what was left of the cobra. So you can imagine our consternation, when on lifting the top of the washing machine, one *extremely* angry cobra emerged. Mike grabbed a broom and started trying to direct the snake towards the back door, while at the same time telling me to get the door open, stand outside it and see where the snake went. Get real! I'm too young to die. There was absolutely no way that I was going to try and get in between a snake that's just had a fast spin and the door. I left that technicality to Mike, who dealt with the situation admirably. I can't tell you the details, as I wasn't there, I was as far away as I could possibly get.

We get our fair share of Mozambique Spitting Cobras. I had by now replaced my Miniature-Pincher, Zoe, with another miniature called Minky. Minky was far more adventurous than Zoe, she might have been tiny in stature, but she more than made up for it in spirit. We were all at home on the 11th February 1992 when there was a terrible noise and we rushed out of the house in time to see Minky tackling a spitting cobra. She lost her left eye as a result of the altercation, despite our efforts to wash the venom out with milk before rushing her to the vet.

Heath our youngest son, used to be our resident snake-spotter. When he was much younger, he was in our bedroom one morning when a beautiful light green snake decided to climb up the creeper from the patio below, up on to the balcony which runs along the whole length of the bedrooms. Heath couldn't even find the words to tell me about the snake, but I saw it a fraction of a second after him, and it looked very much like it was coming in my bedroom. As it was summer, all the bedrooms had the sliding doors open onto the balcony to let the cool air waft through the house. Looking back, I reckon Heath and I would have been serious Olympic contenders. Talk about teamwork. Without a word to each other, I managed to close the sliding door in my room just as the snake arrived at it, Heath did the same in Mark's room which was next to ours, I did the same in Heath's room which was next to Mark's, and Heath did the same in the dining room which was next to his! Most summer evenings see us sleeping with our sliding doors open and we have never had a problem with snakes coming into the house.

The patio is directly below the balcony and we have palm trees growing in it. It was Heath again, who called me to his room to watch a snake (another green one! I know that that's not a very technical description, but I wasn't getting any closer to get more details) that was climbing up the palm tree towards the numerous Weaver birds' nests that had eggs and in some cases, chicks in them. The palm tree is tall, and the snake was doing well. It was almost at the top, when it lost its grip, or whatever it is that snakes use, and fell to the patio – thus allowing the Weavers to live another day. If snakes have feelings, I'd say this one was looking pretty sheepish.

WEE BEASTIES

I seem to be a magnet for scorpions. When I think of all the children we've had here over the years, playing in the garden, lifting rocks in the bush, sleeping in tents – and then *Moi*, who would never, never ever, put my hand in a drawer without looking inside first, I never ever put on a shoe without first giving it a good shake, I never walk around the house barefoot .... and that's right, you've guessed it, I was, and am, the one who gets zapped every time. Mark and Heath have never been stung by a scorpion and Mike has only once felt the wrong end of the tail. I've been stung thirteen times! And as far as I'm concerned, that's thirteen times too many. The very first time I had an altercation with a scorpion was when we were newly married and the nasty wee animal took exception to my foot.

I was a 'townie'. I had always lived in civilisation. I had never seen a real scorpion before. So you can imagine my panic when I was stung. I was alone at home. There was no one to help me. So there was nothing for it, but for me to sit down and wait to die. Twenty minutes or so passed. An hour passed. I thought that perhaps I'd have time for a cup of coffee before I died. When it was coming up for two hours I decided that maybe I wasn't meant to be meeting my maker at this particular time and maybe I could squeeze in a quick snack. My foot was excruciatingly painful. I couldn't wear a shoe for a couple of days, so at least the upside of that was that I had a couple of sickie days off work. The next time I crossed paths with a scorpion was when it connected with my back somehow. Again, not the most pleasant experience. I could only hope that it hadn't been a pleasant experience for the scorpion either. I was learning. I knew that our scorpions could inflict serious pain, but weren't killers.

Mike used to frequently travel to South Africa on business, and in December 1991, we decided that on the last day of term, once I had collected the boys from school, the three of us would fly down to Johannesburg and join Mike for a bit of a holiday. It had been a bit hectic for me getting the boys and myself ready for South Africa and getting them off to school in the morning. My first port of call en route to our departure was at Pooh Corner Nursery School to collect Heath. It was a disaster. Father Christmas had been in the morning and handed out presents, and somehow the labels on Heath and Russell's presents were mixed up. Russell was grinning from ear to ear. Father Christmas had really come through for him this time and he was more than pleased with the outcome of the morning visit and was overjoyed with the gift that he was given. Heath was beside himself. Although Russell was a good friend this was stretching friendship just a bit too far, it wasn't fair that Russell had been given the present that Heath had asked for! And that, unbeknown to him, his mummy had trudged into town to virtually every toyshop to buy it for him! There was no comparison between the little box of wax crayons that Heath was given in error and the Lego tractor that Russell had acquired. I was so busy trying to console Heath and tell him that maybe he didn't get the Lego set now because Father Christmas was going to give him one on Christmas Day (and hoping like crazy that I'd still be able to buy the identical set!) that I put my handbag on the roof of the car as I was strapping my tearful child in.

As I was driving to collect Mark from school, there was a car behind me hooting. At first I didn't pay much attention, I was trying to soothe my desolate son, but as it went on, I wondered what it was all about and decided to stop. Talk about my guardian angel. The woman in the car behind me had picked up my handbag. Not only do I always carry the kitchen sink in my bag, but also on this day, I had my passport, air tickets and travellers cheques! I can't even begin to imagine what would have happened if this wonderful Good Samaritan hadn't been there. I made it to St. John's Preparatory School and collected Mark without any further mishap. The last port of call was at my parents' flat in Mount Pleasant as they were going to take the boys and me to the airport, and I would leave the car and all our keys at their place. Only someone who has lived in Africa can fully appreciate just what I mean when I say *all* the keys. Mike and I each have a bunch of keys that would give Fort Knox a run for its money. There's the front door, back door, side door, veranda door and any other doors; then there's every cupboard that we possess, pantry, deepfreezes, drawers, garages, workshops – I reckon that I have about twenty keys on my bunch and Mike has a *whole* lot more than I have!

At the flat I bent down to get the house keys out of my suitcase – and I felt instant pain! I jumped up with a cry. My parents were most concerned and wanted to know what the problem was. When I said that a scorpion had just zapped me, I got 'that' look – you know the one, yes dear, we believe you dear, but we think you're out of your little mind, dear! I whipped off my trousers and the offending scorpion escaped and ran across the carpet. I never knew that my father could move so fast! The scorpion was swiftly dealt with. I was vindicated. It felt good, to be taken seriously I mean, but it didn't take the pain away.

I did not want to go on this trip! I had a miserable, weepy younger child, I had a hyper excited older child, I had nearly lost all my worldly possessions (well, you know what I mean, I carry most of them with me in my handbag) and to top it all, my thigh was throbbing. I don't remember much of getting to the airport, boarding the plane or the journey. Mike met us at the airport and he was full of all the things he'd done and places he'd been – and not the least bit sympathetic to my plight, as yet, he hadn't sampled the delights of the wrong end of a scorpion. You know the adage that trouble comes in pairs, well it's true. We arrived at our accommodation in Johannesburg and as I was unpacking, lo and behold, scorpion number two who'd just had the experience of a lifetime in the hold of the Air Zimbabwe plane, came scuttling out of the suitcase to make its escape. At least this time I wasn't in the firing line, it was, - with the sole of my shoe. One deceased scorpion.

On another occasion I was in bed and almost asleep when I felt something moving in my hair. I brushed it with my hand and for my effort I got stung on the side of my face and on my hand! Two stings for the price of one. At least this way, the one sting was so painful that it helped to keep my mind off the other one. I shot up and switched on the light and made sure that Mike was awake to share my pain. When he saw the tiny (and it was really tiny) scorpion on my hand, he was rather scathing and said something that went along the lines of, "You're not really making all that fuss over something that small!" Every dog has its day. Not too long after this incident, Mike was taking a shower when a scorpion decided to investigate the leg of his trousers, and Mike had his first (and to date, one and only) experience of being at the wrong end of a scorpion's tail. The Oscar performance would have done him credit. You'd have thought he was being measured up for his coffin en route to the Pearly Gates. The next time I made contact with a scorpion, he was so solicitous, so caring, and so helpful that I hate to admit it, but I milked it for all it was worth. My performance would have won me a double Oscar!

In the rainy season we are plagued with rose beetles. They are little brown non-descript beetles, some evenings after we've had rain there are literally thousands of these insects and if we didn't have gauze on the windows, we'd be totally overrun. Sometimes the balcony is a couple of inches deep in rose beetles and it resembles peanut brittle, and we all are extremely careful about either leaving lights on in rooms (which attract the beetles) and / or leaving outside doors or windows open. This particular evening Mike was asleep when he awoke with a start and commenced shaking his head and rubbing his ear – a rose beetle had decided to go on safari and had gone into the depths of Mike's ear. Mike was in agony. I actually think I'd prefer to be stung by a scorpion than have a rose beetle in my ear. Come to think of it, it must have been a terrifying experience for the beetle as well.

These insects have serrated legs that feel as if mini knives are at work in the ear. Mike was going demented. He was banging his head against the wall trying to make the beetle fall out and blood was pouring out of his ear. I managed to get Mike to stay still for long enough to get a few drops of oil into his ear and then we held a lighted torch to his ear to attract the beetle. It worked. Mike reckons that he's never experienced anything that painful and wouldn't wish it on his worst enemy. He was not amused when I said that I'd hold the torch to his other ear and that the beetle could follow the light out.

Beetles

The bush around us is plagued with ticks. It's amazing to see the ticks on a blade of grass just waiting to snag a helpless victim. One of the reasons that we've always tried to keep shorthaired dogs is to try and win the war against the ticks and it's fairly easy to keep them under control by means of regular dipping. With cats, it's not as easy; they don't exactly take to the idea of being dipped. It's not unusual to find a tick in the sheets when we go to bed courtesy of the cats. My mother is the only member of our family who's ever had the misfortune to have tick-bite fever, and my mother is the only member of our family who never walked in the bush. Makes you wonder doesn't it?

If you know any Zimbabweans, you'll notice that they like their clothes ironed. It's not that we like to be sartorially elegant, it's that by having well ironed clothes we hopefully will avoid the unpleasantness of putzi flies. I hate flies at the best of times, but these ones are high on my list of undesirables! They lay eggs on un-ironed clothes, especially on the likes of elastic waistbands of shorts or damp swimming towels. They manage to get from the damp material to burrow under the skin. The eggs become maggots, which look like boils on the surface of the skin, and if left to their own devices, emerge as full-blown flies. When Heath was a toddler, he had a putzi right on his forehead on his hairline, a gentle squeeze and hey presto, out popped a maggot the size of my finger nail! It's not the most pleasant experience for a mother to take a maggot out of her child's head. It was revolting. As a young child my arm was full of maggots and my mother took me to the doctor to have them removed; I have a fairly high pain-threshold, but I wouldn't like to go through that again. Recently Mike had six putzis in his back and his first inkling that something was amiss was when he said that he felt he had something moving under his skin. I tried squeezing them out, but Mike wasn't having any of it, so we covered the 'boils' with Vaseline and tried to suffocate the eggs that way. I was on a bit of a guilt trip. I'd been getting a bit lax about having shirts ironed and when I took them out of the washing machine, I'd just put the shirts on a hanger and let them drip-dry – with dire consequences for my husband's back. I have learnt my lesson and now if I'm going to cut down on the chore of ironing, I make sure that the laundry is not hung outside to dry.

With the changing seasons, we get changing insect life. In every nook and cranny we find stink bugs, we have the rose beetles, flies, fruit flies, cockroaches, wasps, hornets, bees, big ants, small ants, white ants, red ants, black ants, flying ants, worms of varying shapes and colours, things with forked tails that sting, things with forked mouths that bite and things that I'm positive have never even made it into an entomology book. The rainy season brings hordes of unmentionables including the tshongololo, or the black millipede. In a good rainy season, the roads and gardens are full of these black, plump, sort-of, worm-like insects. They're most entertaining for children; they don't bite or sting, and when lifted up, they curl tightly into a ball. However as far as I'm concerned, by far the most gruesome of these other beasties belong to the arachnid family. I am well aware that spiders do have their place on this planet, but I object to them having their place in my house. I'm not objecting to the flat wall-spiders or the daddy longlegs. They both belong to the good guys and help us fight the war against dreaded mozzies. It's the big, hairy, orange, speedy, ugly ones that really freak me out!

Mark, in his younger days, used to suffer quite badly from leg cramps in the middle of the night. When he called for me in the night, I'd go to him, and walk up and down the passage with him as the cool parquet floor seemed to alleviate the cramps. We were walking up and down the passage one night and as Mark was half asleep, he didn't notice the *huge*, orange monster straight out of some sci-fi movie that was at the end of the passage. This spider must have been the size of my hand and it had an evil, malevolent gleam in its beady eyes. I decided the best course of action was to turn round and walk in the opposite direction. OK I was being a wimp. When we turned to go back up the passage, we were faced with a whole herd of spiders! Mark woke up instantly. The desperate race down the passage to safety was the best remedy we could have thought of. The idea of the wild herd of gruesome spiders waiting for him to emerge from his bed, miraculously cured Mark's cramps. We were tempted to patent our miraculous, if a bit unorthodox cure.

Not long after this incident, also in the rainy season, I was opening the door to the pantry one night, and what I saw made me give out the most piercing scream. Men ran from every direction to my aid. Mike from the T.V. lounge, and Mark and Heath from their respective bedrooms. There, in all its splendour, 'sitting' on the doorframe of the pantry was one of the largest baboon spiders I have ever had the misfortune to encounter. Baboon spiders are so-called as their feet resemble monkey's padded fingers, and they are Zimbabwe's answer to tarantulas. The spider was almost the size of my hand – not that I actually laid it on my hand to measure it, mind you, but it looked pretty close.

Both Mark and Heath had bug-barns that were wooden and mesh structures really designed for the keeping of locusts and other little bugs, not – as we learnt to our dismay, for keeping larger beetles with sharp pincers! Mark had tried keeping a huge beetle similar to a dung beetle in his bug barn and it made short work of the mesh. Mike managed to get the baboon spider into Mark's bug-barn and we were all fascinated by the creature. I am most definitely not a fan of spiders but this one had us entranced. Its legs were so silky with fine hairs that you almost felt like stroking it – I did say almost! If it was frightened or angry, it reared up on its hind legs and the underneath of its body was covered in beautiful reddish, silky hairs.

Mark had been given one of the 'Bundu Series' of books on spiders for Christmas; he read that they made wonderful pets and that they could live for something like up to twenty years. He wanted a baboon spider as a pet. For once in my life I put my foot down in no uncertain manner. I had done my bit looking after cats, dogs, rats, mice and fish, to help out the boys. But I was NOT going to be a surrogate mummy for something that belonged in a horror movie. Mark was upset. I was adamant. Mike took the bug-barn up to the ground near the reservoir and released the spider. The Bundu Book mentioned that baboon spiders usually move around in pairs – just what I needed to hear. A few days later, lo and behold, on the step at the kitchen door, was a baboon spider. We're not sure if this was the original one come back to visit, or whether it was its mate. Mike again made the journey up to the reservoir, and thankfully, they seem to have decided to give our house a miss for the time being. But they have not gone.

Just the other day, (many years after Mark's abortive attempt at getting a spider for a pet) Mike took me to the security fence near the reservoir and showed me a hole in the ground. To the uninitiated it's just a hole in the ground, but in actual fact, it's the entrance of the baboon spider's residence. The entrance is approximately three inches in diameter and goes down a long way. According to our gardener, Weighton, these spiders are clever. They know when it's going to rain and just before the heavens open, they get to work covering the entrance of their burrows with a mass of spider-webs that keep the hole below, nice and dry. Weighton reckons that if we ever want to know when, or if, it's going to rain, we should just keep a check on the activities of the baboon spider.

According to my Scottish parents, they were told when they came to this part of the world in 1952, that the scourge of Africa was white ants and Scots. They were to be found everywhere. I must say, I know which ones I'd rather have around. Just in case you're not sure which I'm referring to, lets just say that white ants (or termites) have proved to be extremely costly to us. One of the reasons we keep a few free-range chickens, guinea fowl, pigeons and other birds, is not only because Mike is a great bird-fancier (both of the human and feathered variety), but also, to help to keep the white ant population in check. The times that we have had problems with these insects, are the times when for one reason or another, our bird population has been in decline or non-existent. In the 1980s we were the proud owners of a 'new' kitchen. That is a story in itself. Mike has built our house and made a wonderful job of it, and he would have been more than capable, in fact, as it turned out, *much* more capable, than the twit we got to re-model the kitchen. But, and it was a huge 'but', Mike was so busy on the work front at the time, that I could envision me being on my Zimmer frame and still not having a kitchen.

Eventually I was the proud new owner of a modern kitchen. I don't know how I ever managed with the old one. We'd been away for a few days and on our return we encountered a disaster in one of the kitchen units. From the outside there was no sign of anything being amiss, but when I opened the door it was unbelievable. The white ants had decided to invade the cupboard. They had completely destroyed the back of the unit and one of the shelves, they were demolished beyond repair. The chaos that the white ants caused in the cupboard had to be seen to be believed. It wasn't much fun clearing it all out but it had to be done. I am constantly grateful that Mike is so versatile and was able to replace the back and the shelf and had it looking as good as new in no time at all. That was our introduction to these insects in our house. The next visitation was a lot more costly and could have been dangerous if we hadn't discovered it in time.

As a part of our entrance hall we have a wooden walkway that leads to a window facing our magnificent view and that also forms the roof for the flight of stairs that lead to our main lounge, which is underground. I know this sounds a bit confusing, but our house is built on the side of hill so part of it is 'upstairs' which is essentially ground level and what could be the ground level, is essentially underground. The walkway was built out of strips of pine and then covered with fitted carpeting. Mike was going downstairs, in essence, underground, and happened to look up and was shattered to see that the white ants had moved in. There was a huge hole in a couple of the pine strips where the ants had been busy. If a heavy person had walked on the offending bits of wood, it could have had disastrous repercussions, as they'd only have had the carpeting to bear their weight.

I thought we'd have to rip up the carpeting, and gouge out the ruined wood; all I could see were dollar signs. Oh ye of little faith. I keep under-estimating Mike. With careful planning, he was able to remove the damaged wood and patch it up with new strips of wood. After a couple of coats of varnish, it was almost impossible to see where the repair had been affected. He was even able to cope with the carpet only having to lift a section to enable the repair of the wood to be carried out, and then successfully replaced the carpet. Another disaster averted. For the time being, that is. We have a house in Borrowdale, Harare which is closed up for days when we're not there, so one of the first things I do on arrival is to go round opening curtains and windows. A lot of the curtaining and furniture in the house is courtesy of my parents when they left the country to return to their native Britain. The curtains on the lounge window are a bronze-gold colour shantung material that my parents had in their house when I was still living at home before I married. Considering that at the moment I've been married almost thirty-one years that says a lot for the firm of Benatars in Harare, which made the curtains.

I went to pull the curtain and as my hand touched the material, it disintegrated into thousands of pieces. It was bizarre. The fabric had the texture of ash with small lumps – which turned out to be white ants. They had had a field day with the curtains. They had completely destroyed them. The ants had come through the floor and made straight for the curtains and not any of the furniture. For this I was thankful. Taking pride of place in the lounge is a magnificent sideboard that had belonged to my parents. They had had it made specially. It's made out of mukwa and comprises of three sideboards together to make one long one. The doors at the front are all carved with African scenes and wild animals. It is a piece of art, its only drawback being its length. It definitely isn't the most practical piece of furniture about, but it is greatly admired. I shudder to think of the damage that the white ants could have inflicted if they'd decided that they preferred the furniture instead of the curtains!

Not all the wee beasties were of the animal variety. There is the dreaded 'buffalo bean'. They are Zimbabwe's secret weapon! They are indigenous. They grow in the bush. They are beautiful, at the same time, insignificant looking. They are little brownish-mink coloured pods with minute, lethal, silky hairs that grow on a creeper. They are a piece of Africa that you don't want to have the pleasure of encountering. We were planning to sink a new borehole and wanted to make sure of the best site. We had a Portuguese friend who managed a farm near us and was renowned for his water divining. His name was Mandinga, but Mark and Heath had trouble pronouncing this, so they used to call him Mr. Farmer. We had invited Maria and Mandinga for dinner one Saturday, and they came in the afternoon to allow time for Mike and Mandinga to check the area for a suitable borehole site.

The two men went off trekking through the bush.   Mike said it was fascinating to watch Mandinga with his forked stick; at first, Mike was sceptical and thought that Mandinga might be faking it – the stick was wildly jumping up and down. So Mandinga made Mike put his hands on top of his, which were holding the stick.   Mike said it was a bizarre feeling. The stick was definitely moving of its own accord.   And it was definitely telling them that there was water there – but not very much of it! Which we later proved when we sunk the borehole! Mandinga discovered what we already knew; there wasn't a whole lot of water on our place, although he did manage to find one reasonable hole for us. The bush around our borehole sites is thick and there is a steep hill to climb back to the house. It was getting dusk and the two men were heading back to the house when they both regrettably had an encounter with buffalo beans. At first the silky hairs from the beans are just irritating, then they really start getting to work and they can bring a grown man to tears.   We had a friend, now in Australia, who, during the terrorist war had the disastrous misfortune to come into contact with these unpleasant beans, and it resulted in him having to be medivaced out of the area.

Mike and Mandinga made it back to the house, but by that time, they were both scratching like crazy. Both went and had showers to remove the offending hairs, but as Mandinga was a much heavier build than Mike, we weren't able to offer him any clothes. He put on as little of his clothing as was decently possible and took himself off home where he had another shower and changed into fresh clothes. Mike's not sure that what he went through that afternoon is worth the paltry amount of water we receive from the borehole. Mike took me to see the buffalo beans so that I would be aware of them in my meanders through the bush. They look so attractive and innocent and their appearance and texture just makes you want to stroke them – it's just the kind of thing that I would have done if I didn't know about their villainous reputation.

Maria and Mandinga have made a new life for themselves in Madeira running a restaurant. They have been there for a few years and are doing very well. We enjoyed their company and their hospitality when they lived in Zimbabwe. Before they left they taught us the many delights of Portuguese cuisine.

One of the reasons we've always preferred shorthaired dogs is because of the bush in winter, it's just a mass of burrs, seeds and sticky thingies that attach themselves to anything that they possibly can. One of the banes of my life is that of black jacks. These plants can be the goodies or the baddies, depending on your outlook. Some of the local rural people eat the leaves of the plant and say that they are nutritious; I've never got up the courage to try them. The plants are propagated by black stick-like projections that can stick to anything, they're nature's answer to Velcro. If a human walks through the bush, they get covered in nature's Velcro. If animals walk through, they too are covered. Our one cat has quite long hair and he's a nightmare to groom in winter. If we're a bit lax about combing him, our punishment is a bed full of blackjacks, and they can give a keen prick.

Once when I was unfolding a sheet to change the bedclothes, I noticed that it was full of blackjacks. We would have had an acute case of acupuncture if we'd tried sleeping on that at night. I couldn't understand how they'd all got there until I went outside to check the revolving washing line. The grass in the vicinity of the line was sorely in need of a cut and was choked with blackjacks. Normal washing would have coped, but large items like sheets would be a perfect target. So the mystery of the blackjacks was finally solved.

Our gardener Weighton has worked for us for the best part of thirty years. He has a secret supply of wild mushrooms on our land and it is a great source of amusement (to Weighton) and a great source of chagrin to Mike that he has managed to keep the location secret – until 2007 A.D! Not bad going for twenty-nine or so years! Earlier this year Mike was on an early, very early, far too early for me, walk to our boreholes one morning and he decided to take a shortcut. By chance, he came across an area that had mushrooms sprouting every which way. I am suspect of wild mushrooms, too many people in Zimbabwe die each year as a result of eating the wrong ones. I am never tempted to stop and buy them from the vendors on the sides of the road in areas such as Bromley. Mike picked a couple of the mushrooms to bring back to the house to ask Taundi if these were the good ones, on receiving assurances that these were indeed ok, he proceeded to cook them. I declined his offer to join him. I love mushrooms, but thought I'd wait for twenty-four hours or so, and if Mike was still on his mortal perch, then I'd reconsider. The critical period came and went, Mike was still alive, so I agreed to sample some. I was disappointed. The only way I can describe them is to say that they had a fishy taste and felt slimy. It wouldn't be a hardship for me to give them a miss in future, and I've also noticed that Mike hasn't gone mushroom hunting again. Weighton, I'm sure, heaved a great sigh of relief, as he makes quite a tidy sum from the sale of these fungi and I don't think he was too happy to have us cramping his style.

Weighton is quite an enterprising soul, albeit at our expense sometimes. We have caught him in the act while walking through the bush, of carrying a huge sack of our tomatoes for sale when we were doing one of our periodic checks of our fences for snares. He looked decidedly sheepish, but quite frankly, to survive in Zimbabwe, you have to turn a blind eye to a lot, and providing there are enough vegetables for our consumption, if the staff can benefit from the surplus, good luck to them. When the rains come Weighton has an added source of income, that of flying ants. He sets up traps made out of old sacking which he drapes over the ant mounds near the entrance hole, and he manages to catch thousands of the ants this way before they fly off. He fries them and reckons that they have a taste similar to that of popcorn. It's a cheap, readily available source of protein.

There are a lot of prickly pears dotted around our property. We didn't plant them, they just appeared. I've always thought that the best use of a prickly pear is that of a good burglar-proof hedge; they're ideal for our climate and don't need much in the way of watering. Most years we don't tend to see much, if any, of these fruit, but this year, 2007, for some reason, Weighton decided that we should have some, - maybe his market had declined and he had excess. I tried them in fruit salad, nothing to get excited about there. Then I had the idea of putting them in the blender with ice and making a kind of sorbet. Apart from the mouthful of pips at the bottom of the glass, they made a refreshing drink on hot summer days. I thought I was being so smart when I was cutting them up; I wore my rubber washing-up gloves so that I wouldn't be covered in the miniscule irritating hairs. Success. I was *not* so smart when I later decided to wear the same gloves to wash the dishes – and ended up with my hands covered in the tormenting hairs that had affixed themselves to the gloves! It took Mike and me ages to get the hairs out; we sat on the balcony in the bright sunshine with a magnifying glass and a pair of tweezers! The hairs seemed to insinuate themselves into dishcloths, tea towels – everywhere you went in the kitchen, you'd be sure to be attacked by prickly pear hairs, it was horrible. It is difficult to imagine that these minute hairs could cause so many problems. Next season when the pears are ready, I think I'll give them a miss, I'll stick to cool, refreshing, natural water to quench my thirst, and at least I won't have to suffer the painful side effects of the hairs!

MONKEY BUSINESS

Our menagerie grew with the arrival of two vervet monkeys, Tsoko and Susie, tsoko being the Shona word for monkey. A couple who lived on a smallholding on the way to Lake McIlwaine or Lake Chivero as it is now called had owned them, and were now emigrating to Belgium and thought that we might enjoy having some monkeys to add to our ever-growing animal family. Tsoko and Susie had never been caged and had always run free, so we decided that they would continue to live like that with us in Mazowe. We loved the monkeys and they gave us so much joy and entertainment, but oh boy, were they hard work. We could never leave a window or door open otherwise they were in the house in a flash and it looked as if we'd been vandalized! One time when they did manage to get in, they tore clothes to shreds, destroyed jewellery that had been on the top of my dressing table, knocked over dining room chairs and went on the rampage in the kitchen opening cupboards and sampling food.

Tsoko, butter wouldn't melt in his mouth

When we arrived back home from work each day the pantomime that we had to go through to get out of the car and into the house was ludicrous. We would get out the car, close the door, open the kitchen door, go through, and close the door. Then if we had groceries or parcels, the process was reversed; open the kitchen door, go out, close the door, go to the car, open the door, take out the package, close the door, carry the package to the house, open the door, go through, close the door. If we had been doing a big monthly shop, the food would almost be past its sell-by-date by the time we managed to get it into the house, and all this because of two cute, gorgeous, furry beasts, which were hell-bent on monkey business.

We had this little garage-to-house dance routine down to a fine art, but, naturally, our visitors didn't, and it was usually a mad dash for us to reach our guests before the monkeys did. Good friends arrived for a Sunday lunch, we had a great day and it was only when they were leaving did they realize that they hadn't locked their car and had left the keys in the ignition. Tsoko decided that it would be fun to play with the locks, and to this day, we're not quite sure how he managed it, but when we went outside to bid our friends farewell, we discovered their keys locked in the car, courtesy of Tsoko. It was no easy task for Mike and his friend Billy to get the keys out, they definitely won't be adding car theft on to their CVs, the length of time it took, we'd have been quicker getting a locksmith to come out from town. Needless to say, Billy was *not* amused! In 1983 we decided to build a swimming pool and were getting quotes from various companies. One sales rep arrived to give us a quote, he unfortunately didn't lock his pick-up truck, Tsoko and Susie decided to explore the inside of the cab and to turn all the quotes, contracts and other paperwork that he had in his vehicle, into confetti. We found out that this gentleman did not have a sense of humour and we never did receive a quote from him, in fact, we never heard from him again.

Tsoko was quite tame and would come and sit on your lap. One of his favourite past-times was to forage through Mike's moustache looking for any livestock that might be lurking in there. The disturbing fact was that it would appear that he did manage to find something alive – if not, he was putting on an Oscar performance. Susie wouldn't let herself be touched, but would come and watch us from a distance and occasionally take food from someone she knew and trusted. They had the most beautiful eyes and were so human-like, but they could be demons too. They were only doing what comes naturally but they could be so destructive. If we were sitting inside the house and Tsoko didn't feel that he was getting enough attention, he would pick up a flowerpot, tap on the window to get our attention, then fling the pot to the ground, smashing it. He'd sit and look at us again and repeat the whole performance if he still didn't think that we were paying him adequate attention. We had to buy flowerpots in bulk to assuage his appetite for them. Obviously Tsoko didn't have green fingers.

The kitchen window was always left open for the cats, but that also meant that the vervets could get in. The monkeys thought it was a great game to terrorise the cats and used to wait in ambush on the windowsill. Mike came up with a brainwave working on the monkey's natural aversion to snakes, so we put a rubber snake at the window, which worked for a couple of days until Tsoko figured out that it was harmless and sat and chewed it up. This was followed by a real snake that a gardener had killed. Tsoko again worked out that this reptile wasn't going to cause him any harm, and anyway, after a day or two, the stench of the dead snake wasn't very pleasant. We had to make a plan. The big guns had to be brought out now and we had to get down and dirty. My innovative husband went all out with his next device. He attached a battery operated cattle prodder to the burglar bars so that every time Tsoko and Susie attempted to come through the window, they would get a little electric jolt. This was effective, *but* it also meant that the cats received an unwelcome jolt of electricity, which rather defeated the whole purpose of putting the prodder there in the first place.

The crème de la crème of contraptions was finally placed at the open window. Again, Mike's mind figured out an ingenious idea, an electric bell was attached to the burglar bars, and the gap between the bars was only large enough to permit something the size of a cat or a vervet to get through, but it was impossible to pass through without touching the wire that caused the bell to ring. The idea of this was that every time anyone heard the bell, we'd tear through to the kitchen, and if it was a cat that had set off the bell, that was fine, but if it was a monkey, then all hell would be let loose. We didn't reckon with the cunning monkey mind. Tsoko worked out that if he sat on the window ledge and tapped the wire, the bell would ring and someone would come running. I think he took a special, sadistic delight in seeing us run into the kitchen, only to behold this little angelic face looking at us through the window, his big eyes staring at us in total innocence. And though he might only have been a primate, he was no stranger to human nature, he knew that we would soon tire of that game and we would eventually get bored with all the false alarms. Ultimately we had to admit defeat, the window was kept closed and we resorted to a sandbox for the cats.

I'm not a great lover of jam so wasn't in the habit of purchasing any. You can imagine my surprise on opening the kitchen door one morning to find a jar of an expensive brand of strawberry jam smashed on the back doorstep. I'm not great in the mornings; it takes me a while to come to. At first I thought it was blood, then I saw the fragments of broken glass glinting in the early morning sunshine. It didn't take a Sherlock Holmes to discover the solution to this mystery. The jam definitely could only have come from one of our long-suffering neighbours' houses when Tsoko and Susie paid an uninvited visit. We never did find out exactly who it belonged to, but just think how lucrative it would have been if we'd been able to channel the monkeys' inquisitiveness and enthusiasm, and had been able to teach them to steal more valuable items.

Oh well, it could have read like a chapter out of Oliver Twist with me taking the lead as Fagan, but it was obviously not to be.

Different cultures have differing views on peacocks. We never viewed them as unlucky with the 'evil eye', just an infernal nuisance. My in-laws originally kept the peacocks in their garden in Harare until their neighbours, rightly so, objected to the hideous screeching, and as a result Mike and I were subjected to the torment instead. These regal birds thrived at Mazowe and bred like wild fire. They were beautiful birds, I'll grant them that, and were also a topic of conversation, *but* they were *so* destructive in the garden, and the noise when they were mating was hideous. One Christmas both Mark and Heath had been given battery operated boats that changed direction at a clap of the hands, or some other such noise. The boys had great fun playing with the boats in the swimming pool, trying to ram each other or making the other boat change direction. Imagine how frustrated the boys became, when every time they clapped their hands, the boats changed direction, to be immediately followed by the peacocks' screeching, and the boats going off in the opposite direction usually under the fountain where there was a good chance that they'd be sunk! The peacocks never tired of this game, and both boys were totally fed-up with them.

I rather think that the monkeys shared our views on the peacocks in that they weren't overly enamoured with them either. They used to wait until the males were strutting their stuff to the peahens, and their tail feathers were fanned out in an exquisite display of stunning green and blue. At this point, the mischievous monkeys would dive onto the unsuspecting peacock's back and proceed to pluck the long, awesome tail feathers out one by painful one. The poor peacocks would run around in square circles, screeching at the top of their lungs and trying to dislodge the monkeys, but to no avail. It was quite a spectacle to watch, Tsoko and Susie resembled dwarf jockeys sitting backwards on their mounts. Every cloud does have a silver lining and the spin off of the peacocks' torture by their primate siblings, was that I had a never-ending supply of imposing, peacock tail-feathers to use in arrangements.

Monkeys are naturally inquisitive. While this trait was most entertaining, it was at times, most embarrassing! Well it was for me at least; I have a sneaking suspicion that Mike revelled in it. The fashion at the time for women was boob-tube dresses, and more than once, Tsoko would jump up on an unsuspecting woman who thought he was so cute and adorable, then proceed to pull her boob tube down and reveal all! We made it a habit of informing female guests of Tsoko's fetish with women's clothing, so that forewarned was forearmed. Probably the most disconcerting incident was when Tsoko, who took great delight peering innocently up ladies' skirts, one day decided that he wanted to live on the wild side, and reached up and pulled our guest's panties down! He obviously hadn't heard of 'How to win friends and influence enemies'. I don't know who was more embarrassed, our guest or us. He did it with such innocence!

Every month Mike would have to attend a board meeting at work, and one of the South African directors used to prefer staying with us than in a hotel. On morning, the two men looking very suave and business-like in their dark suits had just got into the car, which was parked in the garage. Unbeknown to them, Tsoko and Susie were sitting on the rafter poles of the garage roof and were directly above the car. Mike started the engine and at that exact same instant, a moist, brown, soft plop landed on the windscreen and slithered leisurely down the glass leaving a streak of brown excreta in its wake. The two men looked at each other each mentally working out how long it would take them to get out of the car, get a cloth and wipe down the windscreen. Great minds think alike. They decided that the quickest, most efficient way to solve the problem was to put on the wipers and hopefully flick the offending item far away. For the record, that method doesn't work, all it does is to leave a streaky, smelly, brown-smeared windscreen that is much more difficult to clean than it would have originally been.

One of the negative aspects of the monkeys was that they were aggressive towards young children and babies, I presume that this was a form of jealousy, but as I was by now pregnant with our first child, we had to make the heart-wrenching decision of getting rid of the monkeys as we just didn't feel that we could take any chances. We contacted various wildlife agencies, which although prepared to take Tsoko and Susie, said that they would be kept in cages. Mike and I talked and talked about what we should do, but we just couldn't bring ourselves to confine our pets to a lifetime prison sentence spent in a cage. We discussed the situation with our local veterinary training institute near our house and came to the sad, but realistic conclusion that we would have to perform euthanasia as it would be the most humane solution. The vet gave us the drug, which we injected into bananas. I sat on the front lawn and offered the spiked banana to Tsoko. He died in my arms, and it felt as if I was killing my own child. To this day, I can still see him looking at me as he slowly fell asleep in my arms. Susie ate a banana too, and she died. I cried. My body wracked with sobs. I knew it was the 'right' thing to do, but doing the right thing isn't always the easiest. They were both buried in the pet cemetery with Whitey and Zoe. I often wish I didn't get so emotionally involved with my animals. My life would probably be much easier, but maybe not as rewarding.

VICTORIA AND ALBERT

We acquired a pregnant dairy cow called Victoria. I've come to disbelieve those adverts depicting picture-perfect stout bovine cows with soulful eyes standing in fields of green on a beautiful summers day producing gallons of fresh milk and cream. They do not exist. They are a figment of some advertising guru's imagination. Victoria developed mastitis and by the time we had paid vets' bills and bought the required muti (medicine), it was cheaper for us to drive into Harare, buy our milk and drive back home again. That didn't mean that we stopped loving Victoria, and our affection for her increased after she gave birth to a beautiful calf, which we named Albert. Never having spent much time on a farm in my youth, I was enthralled to be involved with farm animals.

Albert behaved just like an over-grown dog and he used to lick my hand while staring up at me with those huge, beautiful eyes framed by six-inch long lashes. I learnt about cattle through trial and error. This was the case with Albert. As he matured, so did his nature, and not for the best. He also became a racist. If one of our black staff went near him, he tolerated them - just, but if he saw a white person, he went absolutely, stark-raving berserk, behaving like a caricature of a raging bull, snorting and pawing the ground. If we drove out of our security gate en route to our dam and Albert was in the vicinity, he would position his horns under the rear bumper and start jerking the car up and down. It was intimidating and didn't do much for the chrome bumper either.

Ricky was a good friend who lived on a farm nearby, and he told us that if we castrated Albert, it might calm him down somewhat. So, for our own safety, we decided to take his advice. Ricky and a gang of workers came one Saturday and together with Mike and our workers, proceeded to do the necessary deed. Albert's bellows could be heard far and wide, and even

Ricky finally admitted that he hadn't met a bull with such an attitude problem. I even felt for the poor beast when he cried out and after his treatment of me, I didn't think I'd have an ounce of sympathy for that psycho. Our neighbour's daughter, Fiona, used to have a horse called Toffee and the two of them would often ride through our land en route to neighbouring farms. We decided that we would have to do something drastic about our demented beast when we witnessed young Fiona and Toffee galloping for all they were worth, being chased by an incensed bull. If Toffee had been at Ascot, he'd have been a serious contender especially with Albert on his heels. There was nothing for it; Albert had to go. Ricky again came to the rescue and took our bull away to their farm to fatten him up in preparation for slaughter.

Any time we went visiting the farm, we would go to the barn and all would be quiet – until we walked in and Albert heard our voices! It always amazed me just how strong the bars across his stall were. I was certain he would snap them in thousands of pieces the way he charged and banged against them. When the time came, I can't say that we took any pleasure in eating Albert, but his demise did bring peace and quiet and a semblance of normality back into our lives. A dairy farmer we met later, told us that dairy bulls are amongst the most unpredictable of all bulls as they mature and can be incredibly nasty. We learnt from our experience, and to this day, we buy our milk from the shops, although we do cull our own cattle and cut up the meat ourselves. It really is so much simpler to jump into your car and go to your nearest supermarket, being self-sufficient isn't always easy.

RUWA

We have had many Dobermans over the years and they have all been lovely pets and not at all the vicious dogs as they are often portrayed. When naming our dogs, we had got into the habit of either naming them after the people we had got them from, or after the place they came from. Ruwa was no exception. We collected him from a breeder in a combined farming and industrial area just outside Harare called Ruwa, and thus, Ruwa came into our lives. We once had a magnificent Heinz 57 dog from a town called Macheke, so you can guess what the dog's name was. We had a 'Mary', a 'Barney', a 'Zoe' (an abbreviation of Mazoe), a 'Rinke' (the surname of the people who bred her, a lovely dog but as thick as two short planks), and a 'Roddy' after Mr. Rodkin. We did have the usual 'Prince' and 'Caesar' kind of names as well. We acquired a fantastic stray German Shepherd through our friend Denise who was working at a local vet at the time. Denise flatly refused Mike's offer of having a dog named after her, so we came fairly close by naming the dog Denva. The poor dog was totally confused for quite a while, as she didn't realize that she was 'Denva'. Heath tried out every name he could think of to see if she responded to any of them, but it was a lost cause.

Ruwa's young life was very nearly brought to an abrupt end through his delight in chasing cats, it must be pointed out that the cats did not enjoy being chased. By now our house had extended considerably, whenever Mike and I had a bit of spare cash, and a bit of spare time, we poured it into building our dream home. We had completed my sewing room; my sanctuary. I love that room; I can be in the middle of a project be it some craft, working on the computer or even sewing and if we have guests or I need to take a break, I can walk out, close the door behind me and not have to tidy everything away. The room is lovely and cool in summer, but in winter it's like a butcher's cold room! Our house is built of stone and is a lovely, solid building. The sewing room has two large windows that look out onto the enclosed courtyard that leads from the bedroom wing, it's lovely and secluded and in winter it's sheltered from the wind.

Our old friend Tom Bayley, gave us two stinkwood saplings to plant in the courtyard and they are not only a constant reminder of old Tom, who was a character in his own rite, but they are a wonderful source of shade. I could even write a chapter just on those trees – and before you ask, no I'm not an expert on perennial plants, but the ever changing aspects of the trees is fascinating. For a few months near the rains we have a remarkable happening that could take pride of place in any horror movie; the tree was one huge mass of skinny black worms hanging from every surface possible. They clung to the trunk and the branches, they hung from leaves and twigs, they landed on the earth below the trees, they were all over the nearby garden furniture, they landed on our heads and shoulders, we just didn't seem to be able to escape from them. Then as quickly as they had arrived, they seemed to vanish just as fast making us wonder if it had been all been a figment of our imagination.

The trees were a source of habitat for countless birds, pookies (night apes), a serpent or two, squirrels, meerkats (a sort of mongoose) and our own domesticated cats who used the base of the trunk to assist with their manicures, or is it pedicures? In the winter months the trees would lose most of their foliage creating an awful mess that constantly needed sweeping. With the advent of the rains, the dark green leaves would form a shady canopy over the courtyard, providing relief from the scorching sun. The courtyard was home to several tortoises, which had been rescued from the neighbouring farms en route to being the main course on the menu. As there was a constant source of food and water for these reptiles, it also meant that there was a constant source of nourishment for the other animal visitors which all had their varying seasons to come visiting. The squirrels usually made an appearance in winter and they'd torment the cats who were sunbathing in the sheltered courtyard, they'd sit just out of reach on a branch and chatter away at the cats knowing full well that the cats didn't have a chance of catching them.

When Mike and I later started our own little business, we tried to call this room the 'office' as it now housed our filing cabinets and other 'officey' bits and pieces, but none of us could get out of the habit of calling it the 'sewing room'. This room, which, as the house was cantilevered over a hill, was, built on ground level on one side of it, but the other jutted out over the hill. Mike had put a huge water drainage pipe running under the floor of the sewing room and it emptied into a drain on the other side, which led to the swimming pool terrace. Building a house on a hillside wasn't easy.

I bet you thought I'd forgotten that I was writing about Ruwa. I hadn't, I just got a bit sidetracked, which often tends to happen to me. The cats used this drainpipe as a quick get-away from the dogs and a shortcut from the front to the back of the house. If they were being chased, they would dive into the drain and would be able to exit safely on the other side of the house and I'm not sure if the dogs ever figured out where the cats disappeared! The look of complete and utter stupefaction on the dogs' faces was a picture, their heads would twist from side to side, then bend down and look in the pipe, turn and look backwards, then back into the pipe, but they never solved the mystery of the disappearing cats.

Ruwa was giving chase to one of the cats and as he was still a young puppy managed to get quite a distance into the pipe before becoming well and truly solidly wedged. His yelps were heart wrenching. Fortunately Mike was at home at the time, as I didn't know what to do and I'm not sure that I could have coped with situation. Ruwa was too far in the pipe to try and reach to pull out, so Mike and Weighton, our gardener, got an extra long pole, wrapped cloths around one end to try and lessen the effect of the harsh metal pushing against Ruwa's young body. Weighton then went to the exit of the pipe at the swimming pool end, inserted the pole and tried to push Ruwa out backwards. The puppy's piercing screams were awful and I was sobbing. Mark and Heath were with me and they too were distraught, Ruwa really was part of our family and the thought of him being in pain was distressing to us all.

I asked Mike to stop, as I couldn't stand it any longer. Thank goodness Mike is a pragmatist. He said we had three choices; the first being to continue pushing even though it was painful, the second being to leave him in there to die, and the third was to shoot him to put him out of his misery, but there would be no guarantee that the first shot would kill him. What a choice.   Mike and Weighton finally succeeded in pushing Ruwa out backwards.   The poor pup was in a lot of pain, most of the skin had been scraped off his chest, stomach and inner parts of his legs and he had massive raw bloody patches on his underside.   Medication, loads of T.L.C and extra special feeding soon put him back on his feet.   Needless to say, he never went near the drain again, but as an added precaution, Mike put a grate over the entrance to the drain so that water could get in, but not over-enthusiastic puppies.   The cats did not appreciate this new arrangement. They had lost their short cut and their bolthole, but if it meant that we would never have another repeat performance of Ruwa stuck in the drainpipe, then the ends most definitely justified the means.

Ruwa was a part of our lives for many more years, twelve to be exact. He wasn't anyone's dog in particular; he was everyone's dog. As a watchdog he was a joke, as a faithful, loyal, loving companion, he could not be bettered. The household had my strict instructions that Ruwa's place was on the floor, and it was a constant source of amazement to me how he managed to sneak up on chairs and beds without anyone seeing a thing! I wouldn't have minded if he was a small dog, but I'm talking about a fully-grown Doberman. Dobbies seem to have one flaw in their design and that's their hips and back legs. Virtually every Doberman we've had eventually suffers from this affliction and this was true of Ruwa. His long hind legs finally battled to cope with the weight of his body. We would carry him onto a blanket into the sun when he was cold, then into the shade when he was hot, we would make sure that he always had food and water within easy reach, but in reality, we were just putting off the inevitable. In our family I'm usually the 'softie' but in this case, I was the one who had to make the 'decision'. Mike kept saying that the dog looked a bit better and maybe we should just give him a day or two, but in my heart I knew the answer.

We lifted him on his blanket into the back of the truck and drove down to the veterinary training centre situated a few miles away from our house. Mike went into the office to make the arrangements and the vet was so caring and understanding; he suggested that instead of putting Ruwa under any more stress that we leave him in the truck with the tailgate down and that he could perform the euthanasia on the dog where he was. I held Ruwa's head in one arm and stroked him with the other. He looked at me with those tired brown trusting eyes and I'd like to think that he was grateful that he was no longer going to have to fight with the pain and indignity that daily wracked his body. He slipped away peacefully, I cried for my old friend, Mike had to keep clearing his throat and the vet said, "It's never easy saying goodbye to an old friend" which summed up exactly how I was feeling.

RUBY WEDDING CABARET

Our house has been built over the years, as and when we had the
necessary finance and also when Mike had the time, as he used to do a
fair amount of work-related travelling. The main part of the house was
finished in 1980 and we decided to have a roof-wetting party. As the timing
for this coincided with Mike's parents' Ruby Wedding anniversary, we
decided to combine both occasions and celebrate together. Never again! I
(foolishly) elected to do all the catering myself and if I'd had any inkling of
what this would entail, I'd never, ever, ever have agreed to it. We had a
guest list of approximately fifty and I'd asked my mother-in-law for a *small*
guest list to add to ours. Many of the family and friends on our list would
have also been invited to my in-laws' anniversary celebrations, so there was
a fair amount of over-lapping. Of course, I hadn't taken my mother-in-law
into account, had I? I'm not getting at her, we got along well, but she wasn't
the one doing all the hard work.

You can imagine my reaction when I was presented with a list of two
hundred or so people. At first I thought it was some kind of joke, but it
weren't no joke! Through putting a lot of pressure on Mike, I managed to
get his parents to whittle down their list somewhat, and in the end, between
their friends and ours, we had about a hundred and fifty guests. To this day,
I don't know how I coped. I was working full time, eight to five, five days
a week; my kitchen was minute, half the size it is now; we didn't have
luxuries such as microwaves and I didn't have the culinary experience that I
now have. A few close friends and my mother were a real help by
providing various dishes or desserts, but on the whole, I did the bulk of the
work myself. The planning that went into the evening was staggering. We
had to hire tables and chairs, crockery and cutlery, tablecloths and
serviettes; I had to organise floral arrangements for each table; we got a

local bottle store, Philips Central Cellars to run the bar and provide a barman, and I organised a disco and made sure that he had an assortment of music to suit all generations. I settled on a meal of cold meats and salads accompanied by various breads and pickles and had a variety of desserts ranging from fresh fruit salad, ice cream and chocolate sauce, trifle, mousses, cheesecake and meringues.

Another headache was that of parking. Although we do have a large property, it is mostly hillside, so trying to find a large enough area of flattish ground wasn't easy; when one was found, the next problem was that it entailed a fair walk to the house at night, on rough, uneven ground in semi-bush. In true Zimbabwean fashion, we made a plan. We bought candles and put them in little brown paper packets that were weighted down with sand. These were placed at close intervals along the road and leading down to the house and were most effective with the amount of light that they gave, and there were no mishaps that we were aware of.

Some of our friends had arrived earlier to help us get organized, and while Mike and Gordon, who had been our best man at our wedding, were seeing to the parking arrangements, there was suddenly a primeval scream followed by a gleaming, black, totally naked body which bolted past them. They were flabbergasted and literally stopped in their tracks. They wondered if they'd actually seen the apparition or if it was a figment of their combined imaginations. None of our staff knew who, or what, the mysterious spectre was. One minute he was there, the next he had vanished. The men carried on with their work and half an hour or so later, the vision re-appeared, groaning and grunting and disappeared just as quickly. A few of the guests had started to arrive and as they were being shown where to park their cars, were given the fright of their lives by a gleaming, naked, grunting, black man jumping out at the car and banging on the bonnet ferociously. The guests were in a state of shock.

This impromptu cabaret act had to be stopped. Mike, Gordon, and two other men valiantly rugby tackled the intruder, subdued him, tied him up and left him in an out building. That was a relief to all. Just when we thought the evening might go off without another hitch, some new, elderly guests arrived, visibly upset, saying that a naked man had accosted them. Somehow the 'apparition' had managed to free himself from his bonds. We were trying to play this aspect of our party down, it's really not done to have the cabaret act scare our guests witless; it's actually very bad business sense, it's more likely to make them drink even more than usual – and we were footing the bill!

Mike, Gordon and a couple of other men went out in search of the phantom, located him, again subdued him, tied him up again and left him locked up in the same room. All seemed to be going well and we were half way through the evening when the naked man rushed onto the patio, deftly made his way through the tables, reached the bar at the far end, grabbed a bottle of beer and rushed out the same way that he'd come in. He was never seen again. No one knew anything about him. It was a complete mystery. The case is still unsolved. The evening was a great success from all accounts, but I will never try and tackle something of this magnitude by myself ever again. At least I can say that I did it.

MOVING THE DEAD

My late mother-in-law Babs died when she was quite young, in December 1986. I never did find out where she got the name Babs and of course, those who would have been able to tell me have long since died. Her real name was Dorothy, and she had a beautiful French second name, Elixene. Babs was diagnosed with breast cancer in 1983 and fought a long, hard battle. Her husband Yvo, Mike and I were at her bedside on the morning of Wednesday 10th December 1986 when she died. For a couple of days before she died she was comatose, not eating, drinking or even being aware of those around her. On the morning of the 10th she awoke, ate a few spoons of oat porridge and when I took Mark, who was two-and-a-half at the time, and Heath, who was six months old, in to see her, she managed with great difficulty, to croak their names. It was wonderful that she recognized her grandsons, as within an hour she was dead. She had lived to see the birth of her two grandsons, but it was such a pity that they never got to know her. I think they would have enjoyed her company especially as she was fanatical about fishing and would sit for hours at our dam on her folding chair, with her rods and worms and all the rest of her equipment close at hand. One year we had an especially fierce bush fire and Babs was adamant that she was going to continue fishing, eventually Mike had to manhandle his mother into a car and drive like he's never driven before, just one step ahead of the flames all the way up the hill to the safety of our house.

Babs was buried in the family plot in the Pioneer cemetery in Mbare on the outskirts of Harare. She was buried along with her in-laws and we've often joked that it must have been purgatory for her, as she did *not* get on with her mother-in-law, who I would think, from reading between the lines, was quite a fierce lady. In its day, Pioneer cemetery was well maintained and many famous names are buried there, but six years into Zimbabwean Independence, the cemetery had become an eyesore. All the brass name plaques had been stolen, as had some of the marble headstones, apparently they made wonderful coffee tables! When the grass grew too long, the caretakers just put a match to it and burnt the whole area. Mbare had also become a dodgy part of town and there was every chance that your car would be vandalised, stripped, or stolen from the car park. Mike and Yvo used to own one of the largest engineering firms in the country and one of the services they did for the community was to cast bronze plaques at a very nominal rate and in some instances, even for free. Mike's grandfather, Walter, who was the founder of the business had a massive bronze plaque weighing close on half a ton. Thieves had managed to pry it free from its concrete plinth and get it as far as the boundary of the cemetery where they'd hidden it under some bushes presumably for retrieval later when they had transport.

On being informed about Walter's plaque, Yvo and Mike decided not to replace it at the gravesite as it was just asking for it to be stolen again, so for years it was kept outside Yvo's office next to his parking place. Years later in 1996 Yvo and Mike disposed of the company and we were landed with Walter's plaque. It's in storage in our shed with the myriad of other junk that Mike will not get rid of – 'you never know, it might come in handy one day'! I'm not talking about a little shed at the bottom of the garden, I'm talking about a stone building 50 x 30ft with aluminium IBR sheets for the roof, eleven sets of windows, a wooden door on one side and a lift-up 'laziman' garage door on the other side of the building. The whole structure is completely burglar barred and alarmed. Apart from all Mike's 'junk' we've had excess furniture, a land rover, a boat with a hole, a table tennis table – you name it – we've had it, and it's all been stored in the shed.

In 1998 Yvo, died. As he was very active in the Mary Magdalene Anglican church in Avondale, the church very kindly offered us a place for him in their Garden of Rest. We jumped at this opportunity, as it would be far more pleasant and convenient than Mbare. Not only was it the 'right' side of town and therefore safer, the surrounds were attractive and as that was the church that we frequented, it just made sense. Mike's sister, Yvonne thought that it might be a good idea if we dug up Mum's remains and buried her next to Dad in Avondale. The church gave their approval, so the next step was to the undertakers, Doves Morgans. We thought we'd have to go through yards of red tape, but it actually was all fairly painless. Isn't that always the way?

The main problem that the undertakers had was in locating exactly where Mum was buried as all demarcations had been lost or stolen. Mike and I went to the office at the entrance to Pioneer cemetery and were given free rein to go through their entire card index system trying to find the exact location. I could have spent days in that office. The history contained on those cards was extraordinary. There were names of people that I had learnt about in history in school, all either neatly hand-written or typed on little white index cards. The office is right off the main, busy road and there is no security, anyone could walk in off the street, vandalise the cards, or even just steal the metal frames that hold the cards just for the metal. History aside, we didn't have much luck in locating the exact site. Eventually a photograph that Yvonne had taken when the family had all been together at Mum's gravesite located her position, so this was shown to the undertakers.

Shortly afterwards, at noon on a Friday, we had a phone call from the undertakers saying that they had dug up Mum's remains, had put them in a new wooden casket and that they were ready for collection. We couldn't believe the swiftness and ease with which this had all been done, we were used to things being done in African Time, or not even being done at all. We drove to Doves Morgans premises and Mike collected the casket and when he returned to the car where I was waiting, we had a somewhat heated discussion. Mike didn't know what to do with his mother, as we were shortly due to meet with our accountant in a restaurant for lunch. I flippantly replied that we should just "bung her in the boot" and go for lunch. Car-jackings and theft from cars were endemic then, and still are now, and Mike was worried that if we put Mum in the boot, Murphy's Law would prevail: either the car would be stolen or broken into and Mum would disappear! As Mike said, "How would we be able to explain to Yvonne that we've lost Mum after all these years?"

I understood where Mike was coming from, but I flatly refused his suggestion that we take the casket into the restaurant with us! It would have fitted into a large shopping bag, but I had a dainty handbag! Mike then suggested that we go into a supermarket, buy a couple of items purely to acquire a carrier bag to put Mum into and then take her into the restaurant. By then I was speaking very slowly and deliberately trying to get through to Mike, "I - will - NOT - walk - into - the - restaurant - with - your - mother - in – a - TM – shopping - bag!" TM is the name of a chain of supermarkets in Zimbabwe. Finally we came to an amicable and very sensible suggestion, my mother would be at home, and we'd ask her to baby-sit Babs. Problem solved. We arrived at my parents' garden flat, which like the majority of homes in Zimbabwe, lies behind a huge wall and a big black, steel-cladded gate. I rang the gate bell and when my mother poked her head through the Judas gate to see who was there, she was a bit confused when I asked her to baby-sit, as she knew that school wasn't out yet, it was far too early for either of the boys to be visiting. I explained that it was Babs and that I was sure that she wouldn't be a nuisance or make a noise, and that we'd had a near divorce as I refused to go to a restaurant in the company of my dead mother-in-law. Being a true Zimbo, I've done a few weird things in my life, but even I do have my standards and draw the line at certain things.

We arrived at the restaurant a few minutes late and I made our apologies. "I'm sorry we're a bit late, but we were going to bring Mike's mum with us and didn't know what to do with her so quickly popped over to my mum and left the old girl there." Theresa, our accountant, had known us for many years and knew that Babs had been dead for ages. She said that she was a bit confused. I suppose people don't go around digging up their dead mothers every day. So I explained that we had dug Babs up that morning and I didn't fancy bringing her to lunch with us. Later, after lunch, when we went to collect the casket, my mother said that Babs had been perfectly well behaved.

Yvo's casket had been kept in our spare bedroom waiting for the arrival of Babs' one, so that we could inter them together. Taundi was very superstitious and would not go into the bedroom while Babs and Yvo were in there in their caskets. Saturday 10th October 1998 arrived and it was the day to take the late parents to their final resting place. Mark, being the eldest, was given Grandpa's casket to carry out to the car and Heath was given Granny's. Boys will be boys, and my sons are definitely boys. They were each shaking their casket to see how much noise it would make and who was heavier, and who would rattle around the most, granny or grandpa. With a bit more Latino rhythm the boys would have looked like members of a samba band each with their hand-held maracas, they could have given Ricky Martin or Santana a run for their money. Babs and Yvo were interred together in the church grounds, and Yvonne, Mike, Mark, Heath and I were all present.

UNDERTAKERS AND
AMBULANCE DRIVERS

Mike and I seem to have missed our vocation in life. Maybe when we grow up, we'll become undertakers or ambulance drivers! The first body was that of the old madala. Then there was Babs. Several others have followed. Don't worry, we're not morbid, it's just that we're Zimbos and we have to make a plan. It's not usually the kind of thing that one does, driving around with a dead body in the car, but hey, this is Africa, and sometimes we feel like we are the characters in the Mad Hatter's Tea Party. There was a government clinic about eight kilometres from our house, and although it was adequate for the every-day type of medical situation, such as children's immunizations, births of babies, any real emergencies were referred to the hospitals in town. Both Mark and Heath had all their baby jabs and weighing sessions at the clinic. When I talk about a clinic, I mean a rural clinic, no fancy equipment, no computers, no transport and only a temperamental party-line telephone for means of communication.

When we were at home, we acted as the ambulance or the hearse, depending on the condition of the patient. It is almost impossible to believe, at the time of writing this book, that in the 'good old days', we had landline, party-line telephones that worked according to the vagaries of the weather, and a health service in the major towns and cities that actually had roadworthy ambulances and fuel, which were able to make the twenty minute or so journey from town to us! It's unheard of now. We had a member of staff whose wife was having a difficult pregnancy and the situation became fairly serious. Our cook phoned for an ambulance one Friday when we were both at work. The ambulance arrived at our property, and made the treacherous journey from our house at the top of the hill, to the compound situated next to the dam in the valley, at the bottom of the hill. It was no mean feat driving up and down that boulder-strewn road with an incredibly steep incline.

The patient and her husband were loaded into the ambulance and survived the journey up the hill. What goes up has to come down and the road leaving our property is steep and as a result has several curves in it in order to assist with the gradient. There is one bend about half a kilometre from our house, which is deceptive, and has been the cause of more than one vehicle careering off the road into the bush. Most likely the driver of the ambulance was so relieved to have coped with our road from the compound, that when he got out onto this narrow, tarred road, he experienced a false sense of security. Whatever the reason, he overturned the ambulance at the corner! The ambulance was in quite a bad way and didn't appear as if it would able to continue with the journey. The patient, her husband, and the ambulance crew walked back the half-kilometre to our house where they phoned for a replacement vehicle, which arrived an hour later. This ambulance collected all concerned, set off back to town, and you're not going to believe this, but it too, overturned at the corner! The patient decided that life was too short for this and that she wasn't so ill any more and flatly refused to get back into the second ambulance which had by now been righted and was back on its wheels. To this day this corner is known as 'Ambulance Corner'.

Gray was a rogue, but a likeable one. He could fleece you with a smile on his face and you wouldn't be able to get mad at him! Well, not as mad as we should have anyway. He was our cook cum general factotum from 1977 until 1979. All during this time, he was robbing us blind and we were quite oblivious to the fact. A neighbour eventually pointed it out to us after her cook, who was concerned for our welfare, had told her what Gray had been up to, but by then it was too late. The deed had been done, and we put it down to experience. However before we knew of Gray's light fingers, we had a bit of drama. As is the RULE, if somebody is going to take ill, it happens in the middle of the night, and Gray's wife, Anna, was no exception. There was the usual knock on the door in the wee small hours, which we opened to find a distraught Gray imploring us to take his wife to hospital. Anna was writhing in pain and it was with great difficulty that we managed to get her in the back seat of the car with Gray. For the duration of the journey to the hospital in Salisbury, Anna was in agony. It is not a pleasant experience feeling so helpless and it was a relief when we arrived at Parirenyetwa Hospital.

Government hospitals in Africa are not renowned for their caring attitude, and it took Mike quite a while to try and find anyone who was interested in Anna's plight, let alone get a gurney or wheelchair so that we could move her into the hospital building!

Anna was kept in hospital for a few days and then died. No explanation was given; the death certificate stated 'cardiac arrest'. Your guess is as good as mine. Anna had been moved to the morgue at Harare Hospital and it was necessary for Gray to go and identify her prior to her burial. I accompanied him to the morgue; firstly, to provide transport, and secondly, to help with the paperwork as he wasn't literate. I can still recall the scene at the morgue. There had been a measles epidemic and the morgue was full to over-flowing. When the tray holding Anna's body was pulled out, she had five or six babies or very young children lying on top of her. It was a gruesome sight. Poor Gray looked as if was on the verge of collapse, and I didn't feel too good myself. The necessary paperwork was done, the required fees paid (always a problem in Africa), and Anna's body was released. Her family had arranged her funeral quite a distance away in the area that she had come from; and so I said my farewell to her in the morgue.

Gray had been stealing from us before Anna died, but her death seemed to exacerbate his habit until we had no choice but to dismiss him. It transpired that he was a consummate gambler and judging by his mounting debts, not a very good one. We contacted the local police as we thought they would just give him a warning and perhaps frighten him into changing his ways. The police were not prepared to do anything unless we laid charges, and we decided against doing that. We would never recover our property and it would just make life harder for Gray's children who were already suffering from the loss of their mother. We dismissed him and he found a job not too far away from our property, in Christon Bank.

The one thing you couldn't help but admire in Gray was his temerity! A few months after leaving our employ he came back and asked for a reference as he'd provisionally landed a cushy job, dependent on his getting a good reference! Needless to say he was sent packing, he didn't seem to realise that he was lucky he wasn't in jail! Our other staff kept us informed of his where-abouts for a while, but then he just seemed to drop off the face of the earth and that was the last we heard of him.

MANA POOLS

Anyone who has ever been to Mana Pools will know that I'm not exaggerating when I say that it's one of the most beautiful, natural spots in Zimbabwe, a true "Out of Africa", Meryl Streep, Karen Blixen et al, experience. Mana Pools National Park got its name from the pools of water that lie in the riverbeds during the dry season; the meaning of 'mana' is 'four'. Very good friends of ours, Denton & Pat, were going camping at Mana and had invited us to go with them. Our friends were well equipped for the trip and were going to be providing the gas frig and gas braai (barbecue), they also had a decent tent, lamps and other necessities. I had initially been a bit nervous about going on the trip as our baby Mark was six-months and it's a malaria area. Mana is isolated not the best environment for a young baby, but as Denton and Pat were bringing their two very young children as well, we decided to join them.

At the last minute Denton and Pat had to cancel their holiday due to unforeseen circumstances and Mike and I swithered about whether we should go. The campsite was booked and paid for so it seemed a waste not to make use of it, but we were horribly under-equipped for the trip. Our tent was circa 1908 and Baden-Powell would have been proud of it, we only had a small, one-ring primus stove for all our cooking, we had a Coleman cooler box and had to pack it with dry-ice and hope that it would keep our food cold for the time we were at Mana. This was very optimistic on our part as we were going to be in Mana in September, which is a hot time of the year.

We were young, we were adventurous, we decided to go to Mana Pools. It's quite a trek from Harare to Mana, the journey taking us past Karoi and turning off at Marongora. The scenery is indescribable. I am so often humbled by the sheer rugged beauty of the African bush. It's such a true

94

saying, that once you have Africa in your blood, you always have it. The National Parks in the Mana area are strict about the number of vehicles that are permitted in the area at any one time, it is also a requirement that visitors check in at various posts en route to the camp to enable the Park rangers to know their where-abouts and can go to their assistance if it is needed as the park is so massive and all the camps are miles away from each other.

We had arrived at the main gate, checked in and were on our way to our campsite, when Murphy's Law we got a puncture. It was midday, it was stinking hot, tempers were a bit frayed, the baby was fractious, and the mopani flies were driving us crazy. These disgusting insects get in your eyes, in your mouth, up your nostrils and are the most tenacious, annoying species you could hope to meet. Apart from the park rangers at the gate, we hadn't seen hide-nor-hair of another living being and it would have been quite easy to believe that we were the last three humans left on earth. The car was stopped and Mike set about changing the wheel. This was easier said than done, as the road was sandy and the car fell off the jack; the air in that shimmering African heat was blue with Mike's most descriptive expletives!

The inside of the car was like an oven, but there were no trees where we'd stopped, only long grass and a few shrubs. Mark was crying and every time he opened his mouth, he received another batch of protein in the form of mopani flies. I took Mark out of the car and tried to make a shelter for him under the shade of a towel draped over his pushchair, it wasn't great, but it was better than being stuck inside the roasting car. Finally we were ready to go and just as Mike was packing away the tools and I was getting Mark back in the car, we noticed a huge male lion in the grass just a few meters away from us! He'd obviously been there throughout the proceedings and seemed to be watching our antics with complete and utter boredom!

More miles down the hot and dusty trail and another puncture. We were *not* amused. We had tubeless tyres and had to stop every now and again for Mike to put air into them. By the time we finally arrived at the camp, we were fed up. Every cloud does have a silver lining and as compensation, our campsite was magnificent. We were under the shade of a huge tree right at the edge of a slope that led to the sandy banks of the Zambezi. Mike was unpacking the car and I had placed Mark in his pushchair and was giving him his belated lunch of a jar of Purity stewed vegetables, his favourite. The individual campsites at Mana are well spaced out, but sound does travel and you can imagine my feelings on overhearing the South Africans in the next spot to us rudely commenting "Imagine bringing a baby that age to a place like this, how irresponsible!" I just wanted to pack up and go home. I was close to tears.

As Mark and I were sitting under a tree in the shade I had my back to Mike and couldn't see what was going on. I said to Mike, "Let's just cut our losses, pack up and go home!" So many things had gone wrong already and I was also upset by the remarks of our neighbours. To which he replied, "Don't be silly, once we're organized we'll be ok." I reiterated my wishes to Mike in no uncertain terms and it was only when he replied very, very, slowly through gritted teeth, "We - can't - go - any - where - right - now", that I turned around and took in the scene. Mike had spread our tent out on the ground in preparation for pitching it, when a huge elephant came along and stood on top of it and proceeded to relieve itself. I had never fully appreciated the size of an elephant's bladder, I'd never had any reason to think about it – I mean, why should I? For the record they have an enormous tank. The liquid kept coming and coming and coming. The sound was spectacular. There was nothing we could do but hold our breath, not move and wait until jumbo deigned to move on once he had finished his business.

I suppose we should have been grateful that it was only urine the elephant had to release; it could have been a whole lot worse. It has been estimated that a thirsty elephant can drink approximately 160 to 250 litres (or 35 to 55 gallons) of water at one time. Supposedly a trunk load of water is equivalent to 9 litres. Daily an elephant can pass up to 100 kilograms (or 220 pounds) of dung. Now that would have given us something to think about! Sleeping in a urine-soaked tent was not one of my most memorable experiences, but it was a better alternative to sleeping under the stars in the African bush in an area frequented by unpredictable buffalo, elephants, baboons, honey badgers and the host of nocturnal beasts that roam around at night. We slept on stretchers on either side of the tent with Mark in his pram between the two of us. I kept a bucket of water in the tent in case I had to change nappies during the night, as I didn't fancy walking to the ablution block in the dark, not knowing what I'd encounter en route. I awoke one night thinking that Mike had serious tummy troubles, there were serious gurgling, slurping noises going on and I knew that they weren't from Mark. It was only when Mike switched on the torch that we realized that it was a honey badger inside our tent helping itself to our water! I don't know who got the biggest surprise, the badger or us!

Disposable nappies were a luxury when my children were babies. They were unobtainable in Zimbabwe and could only be bought at great expense, using valuable foreign currency in countries across our borders. I had hoarded a few disposables for this holiday, as it would have been completely impossible to take buckets in which to soak the towelling nappies before scrubbing and rinsing them. Some holiday that would have been. One evening, we had finished our dinner cooked on the dinky little primus; Mark was asleep in his pram in the safety of the tent, and we were relaxing in the cool evening air, watching the moonlight playing on the Zambezi, listening to the night, bush sounds. Every evening the baboons raided the dustbins in the camp. No matter how carefully the lids were replaced, the baboons managed to get in and made an awful mess. This evening, Mark had produced a particularly disgusting nappy which we had wrapped in a plastic bag, tied the top tightly and deposited in the nearest bin. A big baboon was going through the bin oblivious to the humans in tents around him; he came to our 'parcel', which he began to open with excited glee. He opened the nappy out, held it to his nose, sniffed – and the look of complete and utter disgust on his face was priceless! I've never seen a nappy travel such a distance and at such a speed. Not that I'm in the habit of seeing flying nappies, that is. Oh how I wished that we'd had a camera at the ready.

Mike is an avid fisherman and had caught a lovely, big tiger fish. Tiger fish aren't my favourite fish for eating, as they are so full of bones, but kudos to Mike for catching it. We have an arrangement that works well in our marriage, Mike catches, cleans and guts, and I cook. Quite frankly I prefer tinned John West salmon to the real thing – at least then I don't have to bother with the cleaning, bones and all the rest. I left Mike to do the preliminary preparation to the fish and I took Mark off to the ablution block to bath and change him for the evening. A young woman walked in while I was busy with my baby, we took one look at each other and it was great hugs all round. The young woman was Carol and we had been at senior school together and were, and still are to this day, very good friends. As you can imagine, we had quite a few years to catch up. Carol came back to our campsite to say hello to Mike and it was hours later when she finally left. Mike had done his best, he had tried hard – he'd decided to take over the culinary duties for the evening while I was otherwise engaged with Carol, but the greyish mush that he served up for dinner, turned my stomach and I couldn't even pretend to eat it. All these years later, Mike still tells Carol that he hasn't forgiven her for ruining his momentous meal, especially as he never caught another tiger fish that size the rest of our stay there.

Mana is a truly magical place.   It is unspoiled, it is the way people conceptualise Africa when they romanticise about it.   The sunrises and sunsets on the Zambezi are stunning.   We would rise early in the cool of the morning, and with Mark strapped firmly to my back, would go for long hikes through the bush and along the banks of the Zambezi. The abundant bird life was an ornithologist's dream. There were herds of buffalo that roamed at will through the camp and we had a healthy respect for these unreliable animals.   There were strict rules in existence in the Mana area stating that it was illegal to have citrus fruits in the park as the elephants found it hard to resist them.   If an unsuspecting park visitor did bring citrus with them, then it had to be left in the ablution block, as this was fairly elephant-proof, being made out of bricks and mortar. Some foreign visitors found it difficult to grasp the fact that the wild life in the Park was truly wild. There were some Italian campers and they made the disastrous mistake of leaving a pocket of oranges in the boot of their car – with devastating results.   The camp's resident old tusker felt that he wanted a shot of Vitamin C, and he sniffed out that there was a supply in their car. Undaunted, he used his massive, powerful trunk and tusks to implement unspeakable damage to the bodywork of the car whilst the hapless Italians stood and watched, completely helpless to prevent the destruction.   An expensive lesson.

THE BABY-RUN

Nearly every child that has been born to members of our staff, if they have been born at night, has been transported in their mother's stomach (almost!) in our car. So have some of the babies born in daylight hours, but most often by then, we were at work, so the women had to make their own way to the local clinic. The husband would come knocking at the door, usually when we were sound asleep. Mike would get up and open the door and groggily argue with the hapless expectant father. He always wanted to know why they couldn't wait until morning, and did they really think it was necessary for him to make the 'baby run' in the middle of the night. I had endless trouble trying to get through to Mike that these women were sometimes on their fifth or sixth baby, and that the more time he stood wasting arguing with the husband, the greater the likelihood of the baby being born in the back seat of the car! It must be a man thing.

What was even more infuriating, was that often, the pregnant women we transported, were not even members of our staff, but lived on neighbouring properties! We're talking about women who lived in grass huts and cooked over an open fire and walked for miles with a bucket to collect precious water form the nearest source. It was shortly after the first farm invasions in 2000, Tuesday 3rd October, when we were all suffering from a dose of paranoia and everyone was wary of neighbours and staff, not knowing who to trust, when the pregnant woman on the plot of land on our eastern border, decided that she had to get to clinic immediately. This was a much more civilised time of evening, seven o'clock. I decided that I would go with Mike, and told Mark and Heath to lock themselves in the house and not open the door for anyone. Our old Toyota Cressida deserves a medal for all it has done over the years, and this time was no exception.

The hut where the family lived didn't have a road leading to it, only a footpath. Fortunately there was a full moon, but even with the moon and the headlights, it was difficult making our way in the bush. The shadows were deceiving turning into rocks or shrubs or massive anthills or even worse, huge gaping holes. Mike drove the car as near to the hut as he could possibly get it, and with great difficulty, turned the car around so that we were facing back the way we had just come so that we could be on our way as soon as our passengers arrived. It's necessary to explain the mood of the country at that time. Mr. Mugabe had given the 'War-Vets' free rein to take whatever land they wished, and it was more often than not, taken forcibly. Some of the so-called War Vets weren't even old enough to have fought in the war, but they still demanded their 'compensation'. The nation was feeling very fragile; the atrocities were unbelievable; and in many cases, the police were unable or unwilling to intervene, as they deemed the invasions and the ensuing violence to be of a political nature, and therefore, not their jurisdiction. In cases where they supposedly did try and restore law and order, it was just a smoke screen of legality, just a bit of window-dressing, and nothing was really ever achieved.

I don't know whether it was mass hysteria, paranoia or just plain cowardice, or, the result of cleverly manipulated propaganda by the powers-that-be, but when we whites in the outlying areas saw a group of black people coming towards us, we'd get that heavy, sinking feeling in the pit of our stomachs and wonder whether they were a band of War-Vets bent on a mission to reek havoc and mayhem and to take our homes away from us. More often than not, they were complete innocents who had suffered as much, if not more, than the rest of us. The government's misinformation worked very well, trying to twist the farm invasions into a racial dispute. It wasn't. It was not a black-white issue; it was a ruling party versus the opposition (of all colours, creeds, beliefs) issue.

So with this in mind, you can imagine that Mike and I were feeling vulnerable, sitting in a car at night in the bush in a rural area that had seen its share of farm invasions, and a group of eight or nine Africans started coming towards us! It transpired that this was the pregnant woman and her entourage, but just for a few seconds, my heart was beating at the double and it felt like it was going to burst. What I'd been warning Mike about for years, had come to pass – nothing to do with politics and everything to do with Mother Nature. Don't waste time arguing with the husband when he knocks at the door; get the woman to hospital and argue later! The baby had decided that she wasn't going to wait and as the woman was placed on the backseat, the baby decided to make her presence known to the world! Do you have any idea what that does to material on the car seat. Mother and baby were still connected by the umbilical cord, father decided to climb in the back next to her and another male relative climbed into the front passenger seat, while an elderly female relative was filling our boot with suitcases and other belongings. It looked as if the woman was going to be away on a world tour with the amount of luggage that was being amassed.

I know I'm not a rocket scientist and that maths has never been my strong point, but three adult males (including Mike), and one recumbent woman with a baby attached, didn't leave a whole lot of room for moi! In fact, it left no room at all. I was adamant that I was not walking through the bush back to the road that led to our own property. Forget about War-Vets, I have a very healthy respect for snakes and all the other nocturnal creepy-crawlies that come out at night. So we made a plan. There was nothing for it but for me to sit, facing forward, on the bonnet of the car, with my fingers hanging on like crazy in the gap between the windscreen and the bonnet. Just for the record, there's not a whole lot to grip onto there and if I'd broken a fingernail, all hell would have been let loose. Only in Africa! The car started inching forward with Mike straining to see round me. That implies that I'm very wide. I'm not. I'm definitely not the width of the bonnet of a Toyota Cressida – no comments thanks. I'm not wide, I'm cuddly. It was extremely difficult not to slide from side to side across the bonnet, and every time the car hit a bump, or went over a mound of earth, it would bounce me up, and as I came down, I could hear the soft crunching sound of metal! I could mentally hear my husband groaning.

Mike has always taken pride in any vehicle he has owned, so you can imagine his chagrin the next morning, when he was examining all the little (and some not so little) dents on his car, at least I have a rounded derriere, it would have been far worse if I'd been all bony, just think of the gouges those bones could have made. We finally made it to the road. I'm not sure if the passengers in the car were expecting me to sit there like an over-sized emblem, all the way to the clinic, they didn't seem fazed by the sight of a middle-aged white woman sitting on the bonnet of a car driving through the bush at night. Enough was enough.

I slid down to the ground, not quite as graciously as I would have liked and for a few seconds my legs felt a bit wobbly. They were traumatized after their ordeal. I told Mike I'd be fine, that I'd make my own way home and wished the passengers good luck, and hurried them on their way. It was only when the car had gone off down the road, that my predicament hit me! White women don't normally walk around on their own at night in Africa. White women don't usually walk around on their own in the bush day or night in Africa; and white women certainly don't walk around on their own in the bush at night in rural Zim during the era of the land-grab! I wasn't that far from home, but it was far enough and up a steep hill to boot! I had the added problem in that we had locked our security gates on the way out of our property, and Mike had gone off to town with the keys. I started the climb up the hill to our house and just as I turned the final corner and was on the home stretch, in front of me on the road, was a group of about five Africans. My heart was in my throat. They were probably neighbours or innocent passersby, but I was a woman on my own at night and I wasn't about to try and find out whether they were friend or foe. With false bravado, I did an impressionable 'jolly-hockey-sticks', "Good Evening! It's a lovely night, isn't it!" whilst striding up the hill!

I think the group were in shock at suddenly seeing this loco white woman hoofing it up the road at night, greeting them like a sergeant major! They were struck dumb and didn't utter a sound. I don't think I've ever walked up that hill quite so fast before, or since. Our security gates are about seventy-five metres away from our house, which, if the boys had the TV blaring, meant that they would never hear me calling to them to unlock the gates. Luck was on my side. Usually our dogs, though the most lovable soppy canines, are as thick as two short planks, and under normal circumstances would just come to the gate wagging their tails like crazy, but not make a noise! For once they acted like the guard dogs they were meant to be, and with a little help from me, they started making a rumpus at the gate, and eventually Heath came with the key and let me in. I should have known it would be Heath; I'd have had to wait for the commercial break before Mark would come and open the gates for me.

On reflection, I realise what an irresponsible thing I did walking around at night on my own. In subsequent discussions with friends, they all reckoned that I was an idiot, to put it politely. If something had happened to me, it could have been hours before anyone discovered it. Zim was reeling from the 'invasions', the situation was volatile, there was no one in authority that could, or would have come to my help, and I put myself in a vulnerable situation like this. Ignorance is bliss! Mike was gone two hours and was not impressed with the state of his car on his return, my dents on the bonnet, and the bloody mess on the back seat. The next day he took the seat out of the car and spent hours cleaning it.

We had endless arguments with Mark and Heath for days after the incident as they both refused to sit on the stained part of the seat. No one from next door ever came and thanked us for the trouble we went to; it was expected – we had the car, so we should provide the transport.

CRISWELL a.k.a. D.D.

Kriswell Camudzi was known to all and sundry as D.D, which stood for Deaf and Dumb. Kriswell's father, Tommy, worked all his adult life for our friends and neighbours on Hidden Valley Farm, which bordered onto us. Tommy's family lived on the farm and the children grew up there. D.D. was one of many children in a large family. He was born with three afflictions, any one of which would be considered a serious handicap in itself, but having to live with all three, was a tragedy. D.D. was deaf, dumb and epileptic. I have no idea what he was like as a child, but as an adult, he coped so well with the hand that life had dealt him. He was well liked by our staff, they all had a very soft spot for him and when he was able, he worked like a Trojan. He worked for our family for twenty-two years and it was a win-win situation. He was able to live in the area in which he had grown up with his parents just a couple of kilometres away from him. He had regular employment, which he'd never had before and which must have given him a sense of achievement and independence.

Many times his epilepsy prevented him from working as it could sometimes take several days for him to recover from an especially serious fit. This was a major drawback to his finding employment. We lived in a farming area, and unless an employee had certain skills, he or she, usually worked as a farm labourer and as such, was only paid for the time that they worked. No work, no pay.

We had employed him as a contract worker for a short while and found that he was such a vigorous and willing worker, that we decided to employ him full time. This was a bit of a chance on our part as there were only certain chores that he could be given to do. I flatly refused to allow him to do any work in and around the swimming pool area. I had witnessed his epileptic fits before, and when they occurred, he was completely unmanageable and had superhuman strength. He was of medium height and build, but was strong. If he fell into the pool during a fit, he could quite easily not only drown himself, but could drown whoever was attempting to rescue him; I wasn't prepared to take that chance. D.D. never used formal sign language, but it was amazing to watch how he communicated. My contact with him was somewhat restricted, as I never quite grasped the concept of 'talking' with my hands and using arm actions, as Mike and the other workers did. But I made a plan, and we somehow managed to 'talk' to each other.

As very young children, Mark and Heath were terrified of D.D, as have nearly all the dogs we have ever owned. The exception is two of the dogs that we have at present, our male Doberman, Marka, and the female German Shepherd, Denva. D.D.'s 'speech' consisted of a series of grunts and other unintelligible sounds emblematic of a deaf mute, all of which petrified the boys and the dogs. It was such a pity, as D.D. was trying to be friendly, but they found him scary and they would bolt away as fast as they could go! It must have been a lonely world for D.D. to live in, yet, in his own way, he seemed happy. Apart from the days when he had had a fit and was suffering from the after effects, he had a smile on his face was cheerful and always ready with a wave. He was married to a woman, whose name was Fungai and who had suffered from polio as a child and walked with a bad limp, and he was the father of two children, Tawanda and Rutendo.

It was frustrating if he was working quite far away, especially if he had his back to you, and you wanted to give him instructions, it meant that we'd have to walk to where he was and face him, otherwise he'd have no idea that his presence was required. I was mainly concerned for his safety when we were experiencing our annual bush fires. Mike and the other men would try to shout instructions to him or to warn him of danger as he had no way of hearing the roar and the crackle of the flames as they raced up our hill. I always worried about him if we saw him out walking on the main road on his days off, he wouldn't be able to hear a vehicle coming. Yet he always seemed to manage. Our security gates were kept locked all the time, and many is the time when D.D. would be weeding the lawn with his back to the gate and visitors would arrive and sit with their hands on the hooter trying to catch his attention, not realising that he was deaf. It would only be when someone dashed out of the house to go and let the visitors in, that D.D. had any inkling that there was someone at the gates.

When our boys were young, we used to combine their birthday parties, as their birthdays were only two weeks apart. We had an Irish friend, Esther, who had come to the party with her two daughters who were both at nursery school with the boys. I loved listening to Esther's strong Irish brogue, I didn't always understand what she was saying, but there is nothing to beat the sound of an Irish accent. After one of the parties, Esther had to leave early to get home. She drove out of our top gate and instead of turning right to get onto the road, and eventually home, she turned left. This meant that she was still on our land and that she would arrive at our bottom gate lower down the hill. Both top and bottom gates led to the house. On reaching the bottom gate, Esther realised that she had made a mistake somewhere, and as D.D. opened the gate for her, proceeded to ask him for directions. Oh I'd have given anything to be a fly on the wall during this exchange! In the end, she angrily raced up the driveway to where we were standing watching the proceedings, trying *very* hard not to laugh, and she said, "I've been asking your gardener for directions and he doesn't seem to understand my accent and he's making fun of me!" D.D's grunts and groans were unintelligible to her. We've had many a giggle over this incident.

For many years our driveway consisted of grass and our garage was built slightly higher up the hill. I'm short, the car was high, my rear-view mirror was several feet off the ground and therefore a bit restricted so that when I reversed, I did not notice D.D. in my blind spot. He was weeding the drive behind me, and he didn't see me as he had his back to the garage, and of course, he couldn't hear me. Fortunately I'm a woman (wouldn't have it any other way!), and fortunately as such, tend to be a bit more sedate behind the wheel of a car.

Back to D.D. Well, it was more like back into D.D. I slowly reversed the car out of the garage (always mindful of animals and children who might be in the way) and was startled when there was a gentle thud. I switched off the engine immediately, jumped out the car and ran round to the back with my heart in my mouth. The thud was the connection of my rear bumper and D.D's back! He was not amused. He was unharmed, but not exactly overjoyed. He gave me a good ticking off, grunts and groans coming fast and furious, arms gesticulating wildly. The message was received loud and clear. There was no mistaking what he was inferring. After that incident, it added a further five minutes onto my journey each time I took the car out the garage, checking, double checking and even sometimes, triple checking that there were no gardeners, animals or other foreign objects in my way. It was a huge relief when years later we could afford to have the drive tarred and I didn't have to worry about a gardener on his haunches below my line of sight.

The epileptic fits were a terrible sight to behold, and if we, or the staff caught D.D. in time before he was well and truly into the swing of things, we usually managed to get him in a prone position away from danger such as the swimming pool or a fire. The local people did (and still to this day, do) their cooking and heating of water (for washing and bathing) on open fires. One day, what we'd all been dreading, came to pass, D.D. rolled into a roaring fire. He was lucky, it was mainly his arms that were burned and we quickly got him to the clinic in Christon Bank.

What a waste of time, they could do nothing for him as they had completely run out of stocks of medicinal supplies. So it was left up to me to do my Florence Nightingale act, and Florence Nightingale I definitely am not. Over the years I've built up quite a substantial supply of first aid requirements, but dealing with D.D's burns was out of my league. I did what I could with iodine and other burn remedies that I had, and if I say so myself, I must have done something right as he wasn't even scarred when the skin eventually healed.   Trying to work with the burnt flesh was something I'll never forget and hopefully, something I'll never have to deal with again. Our staff all came to me when they wanted a pill for a headache and other aches and pains, or a plaster for a cut; but I was loathe to give D.D. anything that was administered by mouth.   I had no way of knowing how he would react, whether it would spark off a fit, or what other effect it would have on him. This was harsh on him, but I always sent him off to the clinic even for minor aches and pains, I wasn't prepared to take the risk.

One time I was in the house with Kate, the maid, when D.D came to the back door. He was experiencing the onset of a fit, his eyes were glazed and his facial features looked totally different. Usually he was full of smiles, but this time he scared me. It wasn't D.D. who was on the other side of those eyes. I don't know much about epilepsy or of D.D's unique condition, but the person who came to the back door, wasn't the man that I had come to know. He was naked to his chest, and his body was finely honed after years of manual labour. He was powerfully built. Kate screamed to me to help her close the door. She and her husband lived in the compound in the cottage next to D.D, and she had obviously witnessed many more of these fits than I had, and knew what to expect. The two of us women were pushing the door closed from inside the house, while D.D leaned against the doorframe with one arm and with the other, pushed against us to try and get the door open. He appeared to have superhuman strength. It seemed effortless for him. Kate and I were pushing for all we were worth, and it was a battle for us. We finally managed, and as the door closed, I quickly locked it and shot the bolts.

We were both shivering and breathless from the effort it had taken, and I must admit, I was shaken. I don't know where D.D went after leaving the kitchen. I don't know if this was the after effects of a fit, or the onset of one. I don't know the reason he came to the house; he might have been trying to ask for help in his own way. I just know that I didn't want to go through that ever again. There is no way of telling what he would have done if he had got into the house, I was taking my lead from Kate who knew him far better than I ever would. After that incident, Mike and I made a decision that not only would D.D never be given work near the swimming pool, he would never work on his own without another member of staff being present. Our staff worked on a rotation system so that they could have days off, but there was always someone on duty to look after the animals. It was a system that worked well for everyone, but we had to make it that whenever D.D worked, we also had another member of staff on duty at the same time, even if it was only to watch the animals. One of our cows wears a bell around its neck to make finding them much easier, but D.D was unable to hear the bell.

As our sons grew up, they too came to like D.D and weren't scared of him any more, and miracle of miracles, we finally got a dog that liked D.D and even allowed him to pet it! Mark and Heath had each been given a Doberman puppy; Mark had the male dog, which was named Marka (at least Mark was never able to forget his dog's name .....). Heath had the female pup, and he called her Cassy. Marka loved D.D. Cassy on the other hand, who was our watchdog, hated the poor man with a vengeance. I don't know if she hated him or was terrified of him, but whenever he was in the vicinity, Cassy would disappear. D.D was overjoyed at finally being able to fondle a dog's ears and pet it, instead of having the dog rushing away.

In 2000 when the farm invasions took place, we had a gardener Peter, who was a rabid piece of work if there ever was one. Peter decided that he was a latent War-Vet and decided to throw his lot in with the War-Vets who had commandeered the farm in the valley below us, after first having 'visited' us saying that they wanted our place. The reason they decided to leave us alone was that we didn't make a living from our land, so it wasn't attractive to them, and technically we own a smallholding, not a farm. We're careful in our family not to use the "f" word – not the one you're thinking of, but 'farm'. One of the first courses of action these so-called new farmers embarked upon was to cut down nearly every tree they could. Talk about a fast cash crop. There is a great demand for firewood in this part of the world. It didn't matter to these new 'owners' whether the tree was an ordinary little indigenous tree, or whether it was one that had taken hundreds of years to grow. It was a definite cult of 'off with their heads'! It was no different with the War-Vets in our valley. The demand for wood seemed to be outstripping the supply, so they had to get help and Peter offered his services as a middleman in procuring employees for them. He sub-contracted D.D to work for them on his days off and after working hours. I'm sure D.D had no idea who he was working for or what he was doing. All that mattered to him was that he was going to get paid.

D.D was up a tree with an axe when he had a fit, fell out of the tree and in the process, broke his jaw. The rest of our staff was furious with Peter. He never was popular at the best of times, but his involvement with the War-Vets had put his shares at an all time low. D.D was liked and protected by his fellow workers, and they saw this as a complete and utter sell-out. To make matters even worse, D.D never did receive any pay for raping the farm of its trees and Mike and I had to shoulder the medical bills to get his jaw fixed. We took D.D to Concession Hospital on Sun 28th October 2001, but as they were unable to deal with his injuries, we were summonsed to collect him and had to transport him and his wife Fungai, to Harare Hospital on Tuesday 30th October. We were having to use our own very precious, at times, almost unavailable and very expensive, fuel, to help a man who had been a victim of Peter's greed!

Peter was sent to Coventry. The staff wouldn't speak to him; they even tried to force us to deduct the cost of the medical bills from his wages and didn't understand when we explained that it wasn't legal to do that. Post 2000 government hospitals in Zimbabwe aren't the most efficient places. Again, D.D's treatment had the added problems of his epilepsy, and of his inability to communicate with the hospital staff. It was a long, arduous recovery for D.D, and a financially expensive one for us. Recover, he did, and after many weeks was back at work. Peter decided not to grace us with the pleasure of his company any longer, and left our employ. Peter being Peter didn't leave quietly, but that is another chapter in itself.

In 2005, Mark, his girlfriend, now his wife, Vicki, and Heath, were home on holiday from the UK. Even though it was July and therefore winter in Zimbabwe, after experiencing winter in Britain, the boys and Vicki thought they'd gone to solar heaven. We have a balcony that runs along the whole front of the house facing our magnificent view, and each bedroom has a glass sliding door that opens out onto this. If you stand at the western edge of the balcony, you overlook the terrace where the swimming pool is situated. As a family, we spend a lot of time on the balcony, it's cool in summer, warm in winter and the view is stunning. We still had the rule in place that D.D was not permitted to work near the pool on his own, but whenever we were congregating upstairs, D.D just happened to be working by the pool as it meant that he could see us. We think it was his way of attracting our sons' attention as they'd been away from home for quite some time, he would greet them and they'd wave back. I guess he was making up for all the time they'd missed out on his company when they were younger and terrified of him. By this time, Mark and Heath too, had come to have a soft spot for D.D, you just couldn't help liking him. His smile was infectious.

Mark was leaning on the railing waving down to D.D who'd again materialised in the pool area. D.D was waving back, a big grin on his face and grunting away at a greeting for all he was worth. It's a family joke that Mark has a weird effect on people and animals. Once again, Mark's unique brand of charm weaved its bizarre effect, and this time the recipient was D.D. Mark shouted that D.D was having a fit – and he was right at the pool's edge! Mark and Heath are both runners, but I don't think I've ever seen them move that fast. You actually have to be pretty desperate for a swim in our pool, it's not that far from the house, but it's not that easy to get to. You have to get out the house, run down a flight of stone steps to the next terrace and open a wrought-iron gate that is deliberately difficult to open; we childproofed the pool area when the boys were young. A stonewall surrounds the pool area, and the gate is impossible for a child to open. Those sons of mine moved like they were possessed. Mike also joined them and between the three of them they dragged the writhing man away from the pool. It was no easy task. He was a dead weight and to compound matters, his canine friend Marka decided that D.D was playing a game, so he grabbed hold of one foot and started larking about and pretending to growl. By good luck, the helpless, prone man was wearing gumboots, so wasn't harmed, but his boots did have air vents in them where the dog's teeth had punctured them. I'm sure he must have grown an inch or two; it was like he was strung out on a rack, Mike and the boys pulling in one direction, and Marka in the other. D.D was gently laid in the shade of a tree and when he was able, was helped back to his house. The fits took a lot out of him, and he was usually off work for a couple of days, during which time he looked grey and ill.

Towards the end of 2005, D.D was ill. He went to the clinic and they *thought* he had malaria, but weren't sure. I did have 'muti' (medicine) for the treatment of malaria in my Aladdin's Cave of first aid supplies, but there was no way I was going to give it to D.D. If trained medical personnel wouldn't treat him, then neither would I. His condition deteriorated and we took him to hospital in Harare, along with Fungai to look after him. Even though it was a solemn occasion, Mike and I had a quiet smile to each other as we drove through the hospital gates and were stopped by the security guard who asked us if we 'had anything to declare'! We weren't sure if we were meant to 'declare' the near corpse in the back of our truck. Conditions are harsh in this country and there was wide-scale theft of bed linen and anything else that wasn't nailed down in hospitals necessitating the introduction of strict security measures. It never ceases to amaze me how naïve Mike and I can be at times; we gave Fungai money for the stay in hospital and bus fares to and from Mazowe, but we never appreciated the fact that in this time of economic collapse in Zimbabwe the government health services couldn't afford to feed their patients. D.D was in hospital for three days, during which time he wasn't fed, only given water. His wife didn't have enough money to buy food; she slept on the veranda of the hospital, as she had nowhere else to go.

Public telephones had long since been a thing of the past. With our crazy, spiralling inflation, coins were no longer a viable form of currency; no coins meant no public phones, so Fungai had no way of contacting us to tell us of her dilemma. To compound the situation, our landline telephone hadn't worked for over two years, so she would have to had to contact us via our cell phones which would have been atrociously expensive for her. The couple returned home, but D.D never fully recovered. He would work a few days, then take ill, and so the cycle continued. At the end of December he took a turn for the worse, and in January 2006, we took him back to Harare to hospital. Fungai and his sister accompanied him. On arrival at the hospital, Mike and I thought that he was dead; although his face had a serene expression, he was hardly breathing and was just a framework of bones with skin stretched over it. Mike went off in search of a gurney so that we could wheel him into the hospital. The mind boggles at the thought of how D.D's wife and sister would have coped on their own, one disabled from polio, and the other, elderly. This time we were prepared, we gave the women an adequate amount of money, and they had supplies of food. Mike and I lifted him out of the truck onto the gurney, and I was shocked at how light he was. I had a lump in my throat as we left, I knew that that would be the last time I would ever see D.D.

The two women returned from their hospital vigil and two of his young male relatives went to take their place. We gave the young men a lift into town so that they could go to the hospital and take care of their uncle, and gave them money for their return bus fares. You can imagine our surprise when they returned the next day saying that they hadn't been able to find D.D and no one at the hospital knew anything about him. We took them back to town again armed with money for bus fares, and told them to locate their uncle. They did. He had been removed to the hospital morgue, and with bureaucratic bungling his hospital records had gone walk-about.

Death in any community is a traumatic experience for those left behind, but in some traditions, it can be magnified. The husband's family laid claim to the property and depending on the relationship with the in-laws, the widow can have a pretty raw deal. D.D's family was no exception. Fungai had no say in the funeral arrangements and a rather obnoxious brother came to deal with us. He felt that the widow, his sister-in-law, was due far more money than we had given her, which he in turn would get from her. Fortunately Mike is good at dealing with these situations, I tend to blow my top and storm out! It was explained to Mr. Obnoxious that we had paid far in excess of the termination package due to the widow; we were allowing her and her family to continue living in their cottage on our property rent-free (two years on, at the time of writing this book, she and her family are still there); we were prepared to provide free of charge, vegetables from our garden for the wake; we were prepared to use our truck for transport for D.D and the family (which was a *massive* saving to the family especially as we were using black market fuel); we were prepared to pay a substantial amount for the coffin and other expenses; and still, the hard-nosed brother tried to get more out of us. He was a slimy character and I couldn't bring myself to talk to him.

The day came to purchase the coffin. Mike invited me to come along with him, Mr. Obnoxious and another 'brother' and a 'sister' – whether they were blood relations or not, is anyone's guess. What a learning curve this was to prove to be for me. No amount of reading, watching TV, or hearing someone talk about it, could ever replace the actual exposure I had to a side of life I had never witnessed before! I know that sometimes when I tell this particular story when we're overseas, that people downright don't believe me. They give me *that* look, as if to say, what's she on, been sniffing, or what planet has she just arrived from? I can assure you every word of it is true.

First stop was at the coffin makers in the township of Mbare, Harare. The number of whites who frequent Mbare is negligible. A few whites and tourists used to visit the renowned Mbare Market, which was a huge open-air flea market. The tourists went to buy curios and other knick-knacks to take back home, and we went to buy second-hand clothes. Here it was possible to buy clothing that was different to what everyone else was wearing and a fraction of the price, most of it having been donated by well-wishers in the Western World. The Mbare Market had been a landmark for as long as I could remember, but in 2005 Zimbabwe experienced its own manmade Tsunami when the government decided to do away with the informal trade sector, and razed the market and many, many other locations where informal vendors plied their trade. Structures that had been in place since I was a child were destroyed. Peoples' homes and their livelihoods were wiped out, their goods stolen or destroyed, all with the blessing of the government.

Our journey took us a bit further into Mbare to a workshop that was little more than a shack where the coffins were manufactured. The top of the range coffins were solid structures, but the one that was in the price-range of the D.D family, was little more than corrugated cardboard with handles. Mike went in to enquire the price as we were paying the lion's share for the coffin and was told that it was Z$28 million. That was before our currency went into complete free-fall, and Z$28 million was worth something. There was no way we could afford that amount. So we made a plan and Mr. Obnoxious went in, and the price for him was Z$2.8 million – just the matter of a decimal point depending on the hue of your skin. The coffin was so flimsy that I was sure that D.D would fall through it, but beggars can't be choosers. The next trip was to the hospital morgue to collect D.D. Perhaps the patients are lucky that they aren't fed at the hospital, the proximity of the kitchens to the morgue is scary. If I was a patient and the hospital did decide that I was worthwhile being fed, I'd become vegetarian in a hurry – goodness only knows what they put in the 'beef' stew!

We reversed the truck as close as was possible to the ramp outside the morgue and proceeded to wait while the family went inside in search of their deceased relative. I admit I have a weak stomach, but Mike usually has a cast iron constitution, he's the dustbin in the family; but even he eventually had to admit defeat. It was a stinking hot day building up for rain, we were parked near an open drain and the stench emanating from there was unbelievable. A hospital worker, clad only in overalls and white gumboots, but no protective gloves or a mouth mask, was emptying the repulsive contents from the drain with what looked like a wooden paddle, and he was just dumping them onto the ground next to him. I shudder to think what they were, but whenever I think of them, the smell and texture of cooked tripe comes to mind – but tripe that's been left out in the sun for days on end. We both sat in the truck which was like a sauna, with the windows up, and our hands over our noses and mouths, and with me swallowing for all I was worth to keep my stomach contents down.

It seemed like eternity, but was probably only half an hour or so, until the family reappeared with D.D in his fragile coffin on top of the gurney. Mike helped slide the coffin into the back of the truck, and therein my adventure started. Our truck is a double cab, so we can carry passengers. This means the rear of the truck is somewhat shorter than other pick-ups, and even though we had a canopy to cover the back, the coffin was longer than the truck, so we had to leave the tailgate down with about a foot or eighteen inches of D.D sticking out the back. It's not easy to disguise a coffin. A coffin looks exactly like what it is, a coffin. And there was no mistaking that we had a coffin in the back of our truck. The lid didn't fit very well, and I had visions of it sliding off and D.D's toes sticking out. If you are ever in Zimbabwe and see any vehicle driving around and it has bits of red tambo (cloth) tied to the wing mirror, door handle or some other part of the vehicle, it is a funeral vehicle. It's a makeshift hearse, which is also used to transport mourners. Mr. Obnoxious and family decorated our truck in red. There was no way than anyone could fail to know what the truck was meant to represent and what it was carrying.

I could have coped with driving around in a 'hearse' with the deceased and the mourners; it's not something that one does every day, but the chances of me bumping into someone I knew while transporting the body from the morgue to our home were slight. All I had to do was put on dark glasses and slide down a bit, and as our truck was a common one, we should be home and dry. Nothing against D.D, I liked the man, but it's just NOT the done thing! What I had not bargained for was the family announcing that they now wanted to go shopping for food for the wake! It really just isn't done. I mean, how many of you have driven around shopping centres with a dead body in the back of your car? To make matters worse, each time we stopped in the car park of a shopping centre, D.D's family jumped out of the truck to go off shopping and left us alone with him. I was hoping like crazy that his big toe wasn't sticking out! The final stop was Golden Stairs, an up-market garden centre, which also boasted a coffee shop and antique store amongst its attractions. This was the 'in' place to go, and when Mike indicated that he was turning right to turn into the centre, I tried to assert myself and put my foot down. Enough was enough. I was *not* going to drive in there with D.D, coffin and all. I shrilly said to Mike, "You can't go in there! You can't do this to me!" I should have known better, Mike doesn't care what people think.

I'm sure he gets a kick out of being 'otherwise' sometimes. The boys and I are convinced that he's 'Mr. Bean' personified, at least Rowan Atkinson is only *acting* the part. I was mortified. I slid down as far as possible in my seat, kept my sunglasses on and averted my face. I wish you could have been there to see the expressions on the faces of the patrons coming out of the coffee shop! When they saw the coffin, red rags, and hopefully, not D.D's toes, they'd do a double take, then take a very, very wide berth around our truck to get to where they were parked. They would furtively turn round and give us a quick glance then walk on trying to pretend that they hadn't seen anything amiss. The black staff and the security guards at the Centre were fascinated; this was most likely the first time they'd seen marungus (white people) driving around with a coffin in the back. I bet they were wondering if it was a member of our family. We, or more to the point, I, survived the mortification of driving around the various shopping centres and northern suburbs with our cargo intact and didn't meet anyone that we knew personally. The northern suburbs are usually where you find your four-wheel-drives, your Mercs, BMWs. The northern suburbs are where the 'mink and manure' set live. The northern suburbs are where most of our friends and my students live. The northern suburbs are not where you drive around with a corpse in a coffin in the back of your truck!

We had no problems going through the regular police roadblock, although I do think they were somewhat surprised to see whites driving around in a funeral vehicle. The compound on our property where the staff lives is in the valley next to our one dam. The road leading to it is treacherous. The gradient is steep, *very* steep, and as the road comprises of dirt and rocks, going downhill one's foot is on the brake pedal the whole time; but coming up the hill takes another kind of skill. Mike knows the road like the back of his hand, and so he should, he and his father surveyed and built it. We made it safely down to the compound with our precious cargo. I got goose bumps when we stopped the vehicle and a group of about twenty chanting women, led by Fungai, made their way towards us. Their heads were bowed and they were sombre. Four men carried the coffin out of the back of the truck and took it to D.D's house and the chanting women followed behind. I was worried that coffin would disintegrate and discharge its cargo on the dirt path, but D.D managed to make it intact back to his home.

The family had told us that they would bury D.D as soon as the grave was ready, and that they had already been given permission from the War-Vets or 'new' owners of the farm adjacent to us, that D.D could be buried on the farm next to his father, Tommy and other members of his family. Mike and I were concerned about the body decomposing. We fetched it from the morgue close to lunchtime on a Thursday and it was going to lie in the house and wait for the completion of the grave. It was an oppressively hot day with massive thunderclouds building up and it looked as if the heavens were going to burst open. We hadn't been on the adjacent farm for years and we knew that no road maintenance of any form had been carried out by the War-Vets. Even in the 'good old days' when we used to go visiting the farm, the road was bad. It was dirt and full of mounds of earth, supposedly to help with run-off in the rainy season, but a death trap to any unsuspecting driver who didn't come to an almost dead stop before going over the humps. There were also huge craters of potholes and a central ridge guaranteed to crack the sump of any low-slung vehicle. We were concerned that if the heavens did open before the funeral took place, that our truck would be marooned on the farm, as the ground would just become a sea of wet, sticky mud. The days when you could expect help to get towed out by a tractor were over. Any vehicle left behind on the farm was more than likely to be confiscated by the 'new' owners.

We had known that the funeral wake according to the Shona tradition was to take place on the Thursday night; we had bought the food, we all but emptied our vegetable garden to provide enough sustenance for the mourners and those paying their respects. We never got a wink of sleep that night. The singing, wailing, chanting and beating of drums never ceased the entire evening and continued right through to the following day. Our house is at the top of the hill and the noise from the compound carried straight up to the house, it was if we were at the wake in person. The next day, we were getting edgy and anxiously watching the build-up of thunderclouds. Finally at lunchtime, Mr. Obnoxious arrived at the house to tell us that the family was ready to proceed with the funeral. Twenty-four hours after we had collected the body and with the oppressive heat, D.D must have been ripe, but he was now ready to be put to rest.

We arrived at the compound to be met by the men carrying the coffin, with Fungai and the wailing women bringing up the rear. The one noticeable thing was that apart from young babies strapped to the backs of the women, there were no children around, even though it was school holidays, and this was really unusual considering the sizes of the families on our property, which made me wonder if the rituals of funerals were considered solely to be an adult domain. The coffin was reverently slid into the back of the truck and six men climbed in with it. Mike and I were in the front seats, D.D's wife and five other women climbed on to the passenger seat. The poor truck groaned at the sheer weight of humanity! The next obstacle was getting back up the hill and I had visions of D.D sliding out the back as we climbed the steep hill back up to the house. Sometimes it almost felt as if the truck was vertical coming up some of the steeper parts. The added weight of all the passengers actually helped the truck to get a better grip and we did make it to the top, collecting another passenger en route, Taundi, our cook who had remained behind to open and close the two sets of security gates for the truck. As we were driving along the road towards the entrance to the farm, a neighbour's gardener flagged us down trying to get a lift to the funeral! You have to be optimistic to live in Africa. Needless to say, Simon had to make his own way to the funeral.

The road on the farm was everything we expected it would be and worse. Mike had to concentrate on every inch; one false move and we would have been in one of the craters and encountering serious damage. D.D's family were buried in a beautiful setting, near the base of a hill, but the road ended about half a kilometre away from the hill and we were forced to drive through virgin bush. Mike was not happy. He did not want to go any further. As a hundred or so mourners who had congregated on the farm now surrounded us there was no going back. Fortunately, Weighton, who is Mike's second in command, knew how twitchy Mike was feeling about driving blind through the bush, with the grass in some parts almost as tall as the truck. Weighton and several men walked slowly in front of us pointing out the way and we followed the route they were taking.

We stopped at the base of the hill and D.D was carried to his last resting place. The women all congregated to one side under a tree and the men went up to the grave, which had been dug quite high up the hill. Mike with his engineering background was impressed with the grave and now appreciated why it had taken so long to prepare. The men had waited until we'd arrived back from the morgue with the body and then had worked throughout the night to prepare the grave. There were sturdy branches criss-crossed under the coffin so that it wouldn't rest directly on the earth and again on top of the coffin, so that the soil would do as little damage as possible. A new cup, bowl and a blanket were all placed on top of the coffin before the soil was replaced. One of the men said a prayer, all the while the women were singing, and when he'd finished he asked Mike to say a few words about D.D. We waited until the coffin was almost covered and then made our way home bringing D.D's wife and a few other women back with us.

It was the end of an era saying goodbye to D.D. What prevented me from feeling emotionally overwhelmed was the memory I had of D.D's face when Mike and I took him out of the truck and put him on the gurney at the hospital; he had a look of such complete and utter serenity and peace that it was difficult not to think that he was better off now. His must have been a hard life with an uphill struggle to communicate with his fellowmen and to cope with his epilepsy. And yet, for all his adversities, he was such a cheerful soul. At the time of writing, D.D's wife and family continue to occupy the house in the compound and his younger brother, Edmore now works for us, but he's not a patch on his older brother. We did have a few more problems with Mr. Obnoxious, which was what we expected. He tried to squeeze more money out of us, even though we'd paid the widow far in excess of what was due; the money he was angling for wouldn't have been for the benefit of D.D's wife and children, but would have gone into his own pocket! Mike eventually sent him packing. From where I'm sitting writing this on my balcony, I'm looking directly at the hill, the other side of which D.D is buried and no longer suffering.

TAUNDI AND LUCIA

Taundi was our domestic worker after Gray our previous employee left our company. Taundi (pronounced Town) is small in stature, big in heart, and one of life's gentlemen. He hailed originally from Mozambique, but he and his family had been in our area for many, many years working in and around Christon Bank. Taundi's brother, Paulus, worked for a friend of mine in Christon Bank, so he came from quite a close-knit family unit who all kept in close contact with each other. At the time of writing, Taundi has been in our employ for thirty years and is part of the family. He was with us well before the birth of our children and he had tears in his eyes when each of the boys left home to go to the United Kingdom to attend university. When Mark left for the first time, it was in 2003 and the majority of whites in the area had left as they had been evicted from their farms; my parents had left the country the year before and now our son was leaving. Taundi came out to the car to say goodbye to Mark and he turned to me with tears in his eyes and said, "Will I ever see my young baas again?" 'Baas' means boss or employer and as Mark was the eldest child, under normal circumstances he would most likely continue to employ Taundi or members of his family. Taundi always called our boys by their Christian names, but as this was a somewhat sad and rather sombre occasion, he chose to use the more formal form of address.

I couldn't answer him as I too had a lump in my throat and thoughts of a similar vein were running through my mind – would Mark ever see his home again? When Mark came home for the first time for a holiday, he walked into his room and then called for me. On the table next to his bed was the biggest floral arrangement I've seen in a long time – I didn't even know we had half those plants in our garden! This was Taundi's way of welcoming Mark home.

He and his wife Lucia lived on our property and over the years produced one daughter and five sons. It was always a source of amusement if we were in town, Harare, and for some reason I had to phone home to speak to Taundi. He always addressed Mike as baas and me as madam. The conversation would go somewhat as follows, "Hello Taundi (town), this is the madam."

"Hello. The madam is not here she is in town."

"No Taundi, this is the madam."

"No – the madam is in town."

"No Taundi, I AM the madam."

"Oh, hello you are the madam."

"Yes Taundi."

"Ah, you are the madam and you are in town."

By the time we'd got to this stage of the conversation, I'd usually forgotten what I'd phoned to speak to him about anyway!

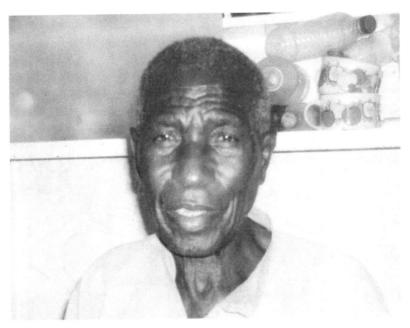

Taundi in the kitchen

In the late 1980s, Lucia developed diabetes which was kept under control by regular visits to the local clinic for check-ups where she was given the insulin she needed to take daily. We had the odd scare when for one reason or another, she took a 'funny' turn and had to be rushed off to the clinic by either our neighbours or ourselves. By and large she managed her diabetes well and lived a completely normal life. Some time in 2003 she came to me and said that she was having difficulty in obtaining insulin from the clinic, as they were not able to supply the amount she needed, and that she had often gone the odd day without any insulin at all. She said that she was worried about the erratic supplies of insulin and she knew she could die if she didn't take it regularly. When Mugabe had come to power in 1980, one of the catch phrases was free health and free education for all by the year 2000. Initially, the health and education standards had been extremely high and it did indeed look as if we were heading for the 2000 target. With the farm invasions in 2000, the situation deteriorated rapidly. Often, our local government-run clinic could not even provide the basic necessities, let alone something like insulin.

I went to my local private pharmacy and was told that I would be able to source Lucia's insulin from them, but at great expense, as she was not on any form of medical aid. They suggested that I contact the Diabetics Association in Harare, which I did. They were most helpful, and when Lucia was unable to get the insulin from the clinic, she could go to them. This sounds great in theory, but in practice, it was an expensive, tedious exercise – and definitely not in the category of 'free health for all by the year 2000'! Depending on the source of the insulin, it was not always free. The Zimbabwean economy was in free-fall with the highest inflation in the world, and the bus fares to the hospital in Concession, where Lucia usually obtained her insulin, or the bus fares to Harare to the Diabetic Association, were increasing daily, and quite often were out of the reach of domestic worker on basic pay with a wife and six children to provide for; so, as was often the case in Zimbabwe, our workers' problems became our problems.

At three o'clock on the morning of the 2nd July 2006, Taundi woke us up saying that Lucia was in a bad way. He wasn't joking, she hadn't had insulin for two days and looked awful. Mike tried to persuade Taundi to let him transport Lucia to hospital in Harare as hospitals in the city tended to be more efficient than those in rural areas. Taundi insisted that he wanted Lucia to go to Concession hospital in a rural farming area where she had been going for years and where they had her medical records. Mike drove, Taundi, Lucia and her sister to the hospital. To someone reading this living in a first world country, that statement might not mean much. We are talking of a time in history when the economy was hurtling out of control and commodities like fuel were a luxury. If you were one of the fortunate few who had access to foreign currency, then you could buy coupons for fuel using hard currency; some people also had the good fortune to work for a company that provided fuel as part of their pay package; some people went to all the trouble of driving to a neighbouring country, using precious forex to purchase fuel and bring it back into the country; but the majority of us mere mortals were at the whim of the extortionate black market prices and the precarious availability of fuel. So a comment such as, 'Mike drove .. (them) to the hospital' means *so* much more to us than the bland statement it appears to be.

July in Zimbabwe is the height of winter, and even in Africa, it can get decidedly cold at night. On arrival at Concession hospital, there was not a soul to be seen. Mike said that he had almost free rein of the hospital, walking at will into rooms and offices. Finally, closeted behind a closed door, with a three-bar electric heater hard at work, was a hospital orderly, fast asleep. He was alarmed on opening his eyes, to see Mike standing in front of him. Lucia was admitted to hospital and her sister stayed behind to look after her, a very necessary precaution in a post 2000 government hospital. Concession hospital did not have insulin. I subsequently heard from a friend who worked in the medical profession that insulin was in chronic short-supply nation wide. In my ignorance and naivety, I was certain that once Lucia was in hospital receiving proper medical attention, she would recover. I keep forgetting that this is Africa. On her third day in hospital, Lucia received some insulin, was told that she was fit to go home, and collapsed and died on the steps leading out of the hospital with her sister at her side. The day was the 6th July 2006. I was devastated, so I can't even begin to wonder what Taundi was going through.

Taundi did not have the money to pay for the funeral, so we paid for the coffin and for some of the food that would be consumed at the wake. Once all the arrangements had been made and the coffin purchased, Mike drove Taundi, his eldest son Shem, and Lucia's brother to Concession to collect Lucia from the hospital morgue. I really don't know how we, or our staff, would have survived living out of town if we didn't possess a truck. Mike was disgusted with the morgue personnel, they showed everyone into the morgue, pulled out the tray that contained Lucia and handed Taundi and his brother a pair of gloves each so that they could lift her out into the coffin – the staff had no intention of touching the corpse as HIV and AIDS were rife in Zimbabwe. Taundi is diminutive and by this time, quite elderly. He was also still trying to come to terms with his wife's death – and there he was, expected to lift her shroud-covered body into the coffin. Mike, Shem and the brother-in-law, between them, lifted the shroud containing Lucia and placed it in the cheap coffin.

The arduous journey back from Concession, past our property and further on to the farm where Lucia was to be buried followed. The salient point to remember is that at this time in our country's history, nearly all the farms had been taken over by the so-called War-Vets and as such, were not particularly welcoming places for a white person. The farm where Lucia was to be buried was no exception. The 'new' owner of the farm was a radically loyal ruling-party supporter and rabidly anti-white. It was for this reason that Mike would not allow me to accompany him and the funeral party to the farm. The road through the farm was appalling and obviously had not had any maintenance work done on it for many years. It was full of gullies and channels that had been gouged out by tractor wheels, and if our truck tyres went into one of them, the vehicle could be well and truly stuck there for a long time. There would be no help from the 'new' owner and he could quite easily be bloody-minded and not permit us back on to 'his' land to retrieve the truck. Mike is not a wimp, however he was anxious about continuing along the road, but he had no option. There was nothing for it but to keep on going. There was no means of turning around. One false move and the truck could be stuck fast in one of the channels.

It was with great relief that the makeshift hearse finally reached its destination. Hordes of Africans, mainly men, and the majority drunk, swarmed towards the truck to retrieve the coffin. An especially inebriated gentleman tried to persuade Mike to join in the activities, but Mike was more than a bit concerned with the situation in which he found himself, and even Taundi whispered in Mike's ear that he thought it would be safer for him to leave, and to leave quickly. That was easier said than done. The truck had to be turned round, no easy task given the condition of the road and the condition of the revellers; next came the nerve-racking journey back along the treacherous road and without the aid of passengers watching out their windows for hazards! It was an anxious wait for me and you can imagine my relief on hearing the truck coming down our driveway.

Lucia's was another needless death. In a normal, sane environment, her supply of insulin would have been available; she would have been able to grow old and enjoy her grandchildren. To survive in Zimbabwe, you have to have a pragmatism that extends far beyond normal boundaries; if you do not, you will be consumed with depression with every needless death, with the sight of AIDS orphans and other street-kids, with the abject poverty in which the vast majority of Zimbabweans live. It's not that we don't care, or that we're callous, it's just that we'd become swamped and overwhelmed with all that we see and witness, so we mentally switch-off and get on with life.

PETER

Peter has been mentioned earlier on in this book. He was quite a character, but characters can be difficult to live with. Peter, like all our staff, had been with us for many years, from the 1970s and had been employed by my late father-in-law as a general labourer before Mike and I got married. Peter then worked for us, finally ending up as a gardener. He had deformed feet. Neither we, nor our staff ever got to see what the deformity was; no matter what the weather, no matter whether he was working on dry land or wet (as when we were building our dams), he never went without gumboots. It was obviously something that he felt quite strongly about. Once when he injured his foot at work, he wouldn't let me take a look at it to see if I could help him in any way. Peter's wife was a small, petite woman, whom I felt desperately sorry for her after her first pregnancy; she gave birth to twins, I never did find out the cause, but both babies died shortly after being born. Peter and his wife did go on to have more children.

Peter was a very vocal person. Wherever he was working, if there was another person in the vicinity, he talked, and talked and talked. I have no objections to anyone talking, in fact, I could give them quite a run for their money in that department myself! But when Peter talked he often put on a falsetto woman's voice and it was infuriating to hear him chattering away for hours in this high, squeaky voice! He'd been with us at every stage of the building of our home; he'd helped Mike and my father with the various bits of building when he wasn't working in the garden. If we ever had some painting to be done inside the house, it was invariably Peter who came and did it. His work was all right. He was not the greatest worker, nor the worst; and he had quite a presentable personality. *But* it was most peculiar, every time after Peter had been working in the house, weeks or months later we'd find little things missing. Nothing important or particularly expensive, and nothing that you'd notice straight away. It was mainly things out of Mike's cupboard, things like the freebies that companies hand out at Christmas: cufflinks, golf balls filled with whisky, pens, miniature clocks, small things. They were such trivial items that it was hard to pinpoint when they'd last been seen or used. One day they were there, the next they were gone. As a result of this, I never fully trusted Peter and used to make sure that everything was locked up when he came into the house.

Peter was a radical. He would have made an excellent trade unionist. If we ever had any unrest among our staff, we always knew who was the instigator. For many years, employers have been guided by the government in the amounts they paid their staff. We've always paid above the minimum wage, but Peter wanted more and would incite our staff and we'd have a delegation at the back door. When it was pointed out to them that we were paying well over the minimum wage stipulated by the government, they usually accepted our word and left amicably. *Not* Peter though! He would argue the point and I can't count the number of times that he said he was leaving and looking for a better-paid job. He never did.

Every Christmas we gave each member of our staff a financial bonus, a food hamper, clothes and toys for the children; the staff all appeared grateful, but not Peter. He wanted more. He never seemed satisfied. As I mentioned in the chapter on Criswell or D.D, Peter embraced the farm invasions and war-vets with glee. Our first taste of his radicalism was on Friday 19th October 2001 at six o'clock in the morning, when we had a 'visit' from some supposed war-vets. At the height of the farm invasions, anyone who donned a ZANU-PF tee shirt could claim to be a war-vet and do what they liked with impunity. Our two war-vets arrived at the gate resplendent in their ZANU-PF tee shirts complete with pictures of Robert Mugabe on them. These two *gentlemen* said that they'd heard that we weren't paying our staff enough and demanded to see all our pay records.

This was at a time in our history where law and order had gone out the window, where the police would not interfere in 'political' matters and War-Vets were considered 'political'. We were fortunate that there were only two men and not two hundred. Even so, it can be quite intimidating. Mike refused to be threatened and refused to stand and discuss private matters such as wages, at the gate with two arbitrary men in 'party' tee shirts, who didn't have any identification. The discussion got quite heated and I must admit that I was concerned. Not that we had done anything wrong, but these men could have attacked Mike with complete immunity and I would have been completely helpless to intervene. Mike turned his back on them and walked back to the house. We were lucky. That was the last that we ever saw of them, but it later transpired that Peter had 'invited' them to come and talk to Mike! I got to the stage that I found it almost impossible to even greet Peter when our paths crossed. We have always been fair to our staff and tried to help in any way we could and this was the thanks we got. What did help me get through the day was, knowing that the rest of our staff felt exactly the same way about Peter as I did.

With hindsight, Peter did do us one big favour. At the time of the invasions, even though many of the farmers hadn't been able to actually work their farms for months, sometimes even years, they were still expected to pay their workers severance packages before the 'new' owners could take over. This was financially crippling to many a farmer. Some of the staff had lived and worked on the farm for years and years, and the packages were based on a percentage of the present rate of pay and the number of years worked. In some cases, this came to quite a large sum. Peter decided that he wanted his package – even though he wasn't going anywhere and neither were we. We could ill afford it at the time, but decided that if that's what the staff wanted, we'd pay them out, then they would all start as new employees with fresh contracts. We had four members of staff at the time, Taundi, Weighton, Peter and D.D. All of them, with the exception of Taundi opted to get paid out. When asked, Taundi said he didn't want to be paid out then and that he trusted us that if and when we did eventually leave, we wouldn't run out without paying him. Guess who's laughing all the way to the bank. With Zimbabwe's hyperinflation, the wages are possibly at today's rates, almost a thousand times more than they were when we paid out. Taundi is going to cost us a *lot* of money when either he or we, eventually leave. At the time, we thought Peter's timing was lousy, we were somewhat cash-strapped ourselves, but I think our remaining staff are now kicking themselves for listening to him.

His final fall from grace was when he subcontracted D.D's services to the war-vets on the farm in front of us. I can't remember the time frame, but it was after we'd had the visit from the tee-shirt brigade, that we had our next encounter with war-vets. It was a day that both Mike and I were at home, and for some reason, although our security gates were closed, they weren't locked. We heard a vehicle coming up the driveway and opened the door to see a rather fancy double-cab, four-wheel-drive coming to a stop, and two well dressed, youngish, African men alighting. Mike went outside to talk to them, and I hid just inside the house behind the front door to listen to the conversation. The men said that they were ex Zimbabwean soldiers who'd just returned from fighting in the Democratic Republic of the Congo and were looking for some land to 'take' and rather fancied the look of our place.

I felt sick. I was shaking. If they had forced the issue and decided they wanted our home, there wasn't much we could have done about it. Farmers had been given just a couple of weeks to vacate, some just days, and in a few instances, literally minutes. To leave a home that in some cases had been in the family for generations. I listened to Mike telling our uninvited guests that as we lived in a rain-shadow area, and even in the best of rainy seasons, had to be careful with water. I listened to Mike telling them that as we lived on top of a hill, any thing that we grew had to be grown on a terrace, which involved a lot of work. I listened to Mike telling them how vulnerable we were in a lightning storm, being at the top of the hill. I listened to Mike telling them that we've never been able to make money out of our land, and that we've only ever been self-sufficient. After listening to Mike, I began to wonder why we were living in this place if it was as bad as he'd been saying! We had a tame pair of pet guinea fowl called Tweedle Dum and Tweedle Dee, and they were milling around the men and Mike as they were talking. One of the men said that they'd enjoyed hunting and eating guinea fowl in the D.R.C and that he thought these two would make an excellent meal. I don't know if he was joking or trying to taunt us, but I got a knot in the pit of my stomach on hearing this.

The conversation was all fairly amicable all things considered – it's a surreal state of affairs when you listen to your husband being sociable and polite to the men who were possibly trying to force us out of our home. Shades of Alice In Wonderland! It was crazy. Mike must have done a good job at dissuading these war-vets, as they left us and went to the farm in the valley in front of us. This farm had already been 'taken' by war-vets, but obviously 'our' guinea fowl hunters were higher up the totem pole and ousted the initial group. I'm not sure which group of war-vets it was that 'employed' Peter to cut down trees, when he subsequently subcontracted D.D. Suffice it to say, this is where D.D was up a tree, had a fit, fell out and broke his jaw. This was the final straw as far as our staff was concerned. They had put up with all Peter's shenanigans over the years; the squabbles in the compound, the arguments at work, the constant bickering and complaining. D.D was popular and he was vulnerable, and his accident was a direct result of Peter's greed.

Peter was always having arguments with Mike and then threatening to leave. Usually Mike tried to placate him and persuade him to stay. He wasn't a bad worker and we worked under the premise that it was better the devil you knew. By now, even Mike had had enough. He called Peter's bluff when he said he was leaving, and said that he would get his severance package ready for him. As Peter had already been paid out, his present severance package was a mere pittance. We decided that we would give Peter an extra bonus of ten thousand Zimbabwe dollars, which in those days was a reasonable sum of money. We didn't have to give him a cent extra, but times were hard and he'd been with us for many years. Peter and his family hadn't lived in the compound. There were too many altercations. So Mike had built a cottage on our eastern border, far away from the compound. It was a pretty setting in a little valley near a small river, which flowed in the rainy season and dried up completely when the dry weather came along. We have to supply all our own water and as a result, have five boreholes, none of which is very good, we average about one hundred and fifty gallons an hour and that's in a good season. They are all grouped together in this valley and as theft is rampant in this part of the world, Mike had built strong little sheds to cover the motors with sturdy locks on the doors. The valley was fertile with virgin soil and Peter's crops thrived. The only drawback to living in this valley was that it was bitterly cold in winter as the sun took quite a while to reach there.

I think Peter was taken by surprise when Mike said that he would get his severance package ready for him, I think he thought it would be like all the other times when he was persuaded to stay. He must have thought that he was indispensable. Peter had a small crop of maize growing and it wouldn't be ready for another couple of weeks. It was our land, our seed maize that we'd given all the staff, and our water. We weren't replacing Peter but it was advisable to have a permanent presence near the boreholes, so we made a plan. We made an arrangement with a brother of Weighton's that he would move into the cottage as soon as Peter vacated it. We did not employ this brother, but again it was another win-win situation. He worked in the area and needed somewhere for him and his family to live, and we wanted a presence near our boreholes to prevent theft. Mike organised that Peter's wife could come periodically and collect the mealies as they ripened, thus ensuring that Peter and his family would not miss out on their crop. Why we bothered to be decent I'll never know, and Peter's parting gift to us was to ring-bark our flourishing avocado tree so that neither us, nor our employees, could ever enjoy the benefits of it. What a bitter little man.

Peter left, I heaved a sigh of relief and got on with life. Who was I fooling? I knew it had all been too easy. Our mail is delivered to a post box in the suburb of Mount Pleasant in Harare, and shortly after Peter had left, there was an extremely curt, demanding summons in our mail box from the Domestic Workers Union ordering us to a meeting the next day. Again, a bit of background is required. At the time that all this was taking place, during 2003 to 2004 period, there was a severe fuel shortage in the country. The queues at fuel stations were miles long. Some trusting people left their cars in queues overnight, hoping that they would still be there the next morning and that they would still be intact. During the school holidays, it was a way for youngsters to earn money, by 'guarding' cars in queues. There was a service station near the school our sons attended and that's where we did most of our queuing. We would join the queue at about four or five o'clock in the morning, not knowing if the service station was even going to get a delivery of fuel; sometimes these queues were called 'hope' queues.

I hated these queues. They tended to bring out the worst and the best in people. We were fortunate in that the queue near the school was fairly orderly, no one trying to force their way in, or jump the queue; but some of the other queues we've been in were an absolute nightmare, especially those who catered to the E.T's or emergency taxis. The E.T's were usually combi-type vehicles that carried in the region of sixteen or so passengers. They rule the roads. They are the most arrogant, inconsiderate, rude, dangerous drivers you could have the mishap to meet, and this behaviour continued when they were in fuel queues. There were also frightening reports of armed robberies in the queues. The thieves knew that people in the queue had a fairly large sum of cash (which was the only means of paying in those days, except for the few people who had accounts at service stations), usually a cell phone and perhaps jewellery.   We never encountered thieves, but know people who weren't so fortunate.

I preferred sitting in the queues in winter. In summer the temperatures would soar and it was like sitting in a sauna. Whenever we went in the car I was prepared, I always had water, something to eat and a book to read. We've been in queues for up to eight hours at a stretch and that's not exactly a whole bundle of fun. When I say the queues were miles long, I'm not exaggerating; this meant that the car could be miles away from the service station – and miles away from the nearest toilet! It's psychological, but the minute I got into a queue, I was bursting for the loo! Unlike a lot of the service stations in the Western world, ours don't all have toilet facilities, and some of them that do, would be better not to! Depending on your neighbours, it could turn out to be a fairly sociable event in the queue, or it could turn out to be an ordeal. I've actually made a couple of friends in 'our' queue, one in particular, Mary-Jane, apart from the fact that I like her as a person, she lived quite close by AND had a loo! Her staff was told that I was welcome to use the facilities even if Mary-Jane wasn't home.   You have no idea how frustrating, infuriating, annoying – all the negatives you can think of – when you've sat in a queue for hours and hours, and either the fuel depot didn't deliver the fuel, or the pumps ran dry just before you reached them. Many a time I've burst in tears of sheer anger and frustration.

So with this background in mind, you can imagine how we felt at being summoned to the Domestic Workers' Union, which was situated in Harare near the Queens Hotel. We had to use our own precious fuel to get there. The area around the Queens Hotel is a dodgy part of town. It took the two of us to go to this meeting, Mike, armed with his file with all his documentation and me to guard the car. It was oppressively hot, building up for rain and the only parking we could find was in the searing hot sun. I couldn't even sit with the windows fully down, as it wasn't safe; street kids, thieves and other unsavoury characters frequented this area. Mike was away for the best part of two hours and when he returned, I was dehydrated and had the beginnings of a migraine. I was ill and went straight to bed when we got back home.

From the moment Mike entered the office in the Domestic Workers' Union, the representative had been antagonistic. These representatives couldn't give a hoot about the worker and his grievance, but the more money they can squeeze out of the employer, the more they can claim as a percentage for themselves. Fortunately for us, unfortunately for the Domestic Workers' Union, Mike has always been fastidiously careful about doing things by the book and making sure that every 'i' is dotted and every 't' is crossed. Peter had told the Union that we hadn't given him his full severance package and Mike was able to prove that we not only paid him the legal package but also actually paid him far in excess of the requirement. Peter then said that he had worked as a 'night watchman' for twenty-six years guarding our boreholes and their precious motors, getting up two or three times a night to make sure that all was well, and had not been paid for all these years of extra work. Mike patiently explained to the belligerent Union representatives that Peter hadn't been living in the cottage near the boreholes for that length of time, as the cottage hadn't even been built. We had built the cottage in the vicinity of the boreholes as a deterrent, but have never had a night watchman per se, and even if we had, why had Peter waited for twenty-six years to claim his money!

The Union representative was racist and very antagonistic; nothing that Mike said was listened to, he was not prepared to listen to reason. Two hours later, even the ever patient Mike was at the end of his tether, he politely told the Union representative that he was not going to get another brass farthing out of us and that we'd see them in court if that was the way they wanted to do things. Needless to say, we never heard from them again. Outsiders to Zimbabwe have no idea the pressure and stress that events such as this can put on a person. We were white and our accuser was black, and supposedly a good party member. If it was an isolated case, that would be fine, but there are pinpricks like this every day for the population, and the worrying thing is that we have no back up in the form of the government. A few weeks went by and we thought that was the last we'd heard from Peter, how wrong we were.

On arrival at home one evening, we were greeted with another sharply worded summons to the local police post in Christon Bank the following day, Friday 4th April 2003. Peter was accusing us of deliberately herding our cattle into 'his' maize crop and destroying it! His crop was virtually finished and his wife hadn't been to our place for a few days to collect the maize cobs. In the interim our cattle had wandered into his crop, and as Weighton's brother who was living in Peter's old house had gone away for a few days, the outcome was that there wasn't anyone present to prevent the cattle going where they wanted, and the fence that Peter had erected around the maize was flimsy. The damage was negligible. The next day we duly went to the police post and once again I was left in the car in the stinking hot sun.

The minute Mike gave the reason for his presence, the policeman on duty verbally attacked him saying that Mike could go to jail for a crime like this, and what right did he have to do such a thing and that he was a racist. Once again Mike kept his cool and explained that firstly, Peter did *not* have an acre of maize growing, it was more like a few square metres; secondly, it was *our* land that he was growing his mealies on from seed that *we* had given him, and that he was using *our* water to irrigate his 'crop'. Mike also explained that Peter had left our employ of his own accord and that we had graciously permitted him to continue collecting his maize until his crop was finished. We had also explained the situation of the new incumbent of the cottage and that it was hardly our fault that this man had had to go away for a few days and therefore, the crop was basically unprotected. The policeman finally calmed down and apologised to Mike, we even offered to give him a lift to our place so that he could come and see the crop for himself and talk to our staff; but he said that it would not be necessary.

So finally, for once and for all, we had Peter out of our lives. The ironical thing is that while Peter was accusing us of all these 'crimes', he lost out financially. Every trip that he had to make into Harare to the Domestic Workers' Union cost him expensive bus fares; the Union would have taken a cut of the package that we had already given him and we worked out, that he probably had nothing left of the money by the time he'd finished his little vendetta. As luck would have it, he's now working as a gardener for friends of ours in Christon Bank. They didn't know the saga and dramas that we'd had with him, and even after being told, they said that they thought that perhaps he'd turned over a new leaf. For their sake, I hope it's true. However he couldn't have been all bad. Peter had taken a liking to one of our male Dobermans, Roddy, and was visibly upset when the dog died. Roddy was buried with the rest of our deceased menagerie in our pet cemetery and the stone cairn marking the grave was bigger than all the others. Peter went to the trouble of planting a pink geranium amongst the rocks and it's still there to this day.

VICTORIA FALLS

One of the natural wonders of the world and it is in the region of 150 million years old. It has to be seen to be believed. The Falls are 1708 metres wide, making a spectacular curtain of water, which plunges into the Zambezi gorge. The Falls and its surrounds have been declared a World Heritage Site. It's impossible to even begin to describe its majesty. Mosi-oa-Tunya, The Smoke That Thunders; what an apt name. David Livingstone was the first white man to set eyes on this wonder of nature in 1855 and he named the falls in honour of the then Queen of England. It is not only the Falls themselves which are known and appreciated, but the Zambezi river and its environs are equally fascinating, especially at sunset with the indescribable ochres, oranges and reds of the skies against which are silhouetted the palm-covered islands upstream before the waters plunge towards the gorges below. Livingstone himself was impressed with the area above the Falls, and he wrote of them: "The whole scene was extremely beautiful; the banks and islands dotted over the river are adorned with sylvan vegetation of great variety of colour and form. At the period of our visit several trees were spangled over with blossoms. Trees have each their own physiognomy. There, towering over all, stands the great and burly baobab, each of whose arms would form the trunk of a large tree, beside groups of graceful palms which with their feathery-shaped leaves depicted on the sky lend their beauty to the scene."

As with Mecca, Victoria Falls is the Zimbabweans' place of pilgrimage. It is watched over by Nyaminyami the serpent-like river god that is the bearer of both good and bad luck. It's a 'must', to be visited at least once in a lifetime. The drive to the Falls is an experience in itself through the changing topography and culminating in the town of Victoria Falls. Overseas visitors to Zimbabwe say that one of the reasons they appreciate the Falls is that it is so un-commercialised and unspoilt; although we locals agree with them and appreciate the fact, we tend to find the town itself as a tourist trap, offering everything from curios, tours and tribal dancing to drugs! Once away from all the tourist trappings and at the site of the Falls themselves, everything is put into perspective and the sheer power and majesty of the Falls is breath taking. It was a bit worrying walking along some of the paths especially when they veered quite close to the edge of the chasm of the Falls and having to keep an eye on two excited, boisterous young boys. One false step would be all that it would take and over they would go, never to be seen again.

We spent many enjoyable hours not only walking in the rain forest of the Falls themselves, but also exploring the bush in front of the famous Victoria Falls Hotel. This was a mine of trophies for the boys of skeletons of animals such as warthog, and it was soul-destroying to see the disappointment on the faces of the boys when we told them that as we were in a national park, they were not allowed to remove any of the skeletons. I had stayed at the Victoria Falls Hotel with my parents when my grandmother came out from Scotland one year on holiday, and twenty years later, it didn't look any different. I felt as if I was in a time warp. Understated genteel elegance. The hotel had an old-world, graceful ambiance, yet remaining truly African at the same time. It felt right to be sitting sipping rock shandies (a non alcoholic treat Mark and Heath were permitted on special occasions), eating dainty sandwiches and listening to a marimba band, all at the same time. Just down the road from the hotel is the small railway station and it's so easy to imagine chic, fashionable ladies in long dresses alighting from the train and making their way to the hotel.

We went on foot over the bridge that spans the border between Zimbabwe and Zambia and saw the Victoria Falls from the 'other' side, and I know I'm letting the side down, but I actually prefer the view of the Falls from the Zambian side. Before we made our way to the bridge we stopped for a while and watched the bungee jumpers plunging down into the gorge, and we also saw, way down in the choppy water, brave souls who were challenging the rapids whilst white-water rafting, definitely not for the faint hearted. The thought of rafting has never appealed to me, but what puts me off even more is that I've been told that the walk down to, and then back up from, the landing stage is a killer – worse than the actual rigours of the rafting. We were staying in the Sprayview hotel in Victoria Falls township itself, on a bed and breakfast basis, and this gave us the opportunity to try out the other hotels and restaurants for dinners; and there was always the Wimpy for the days we were hot and tired and just wanted a snack meal and an early night. There was a lot of fresh fish on the menu such as tiger and bream, and our family favourite was crocodile tail.

We had a family room at the Sprayview with an inter-leading door between the two bedrooms, and as all the rooms in this part of the hotel were on the ground floor we could park our car right outside the door. There were notices on the back of the door from the management requesting that we kept our outside door closed at all times – not because of thieves, but because of the prevalence of vervet monkeys! They were everywhere. On the whole our family were most circumspect about keeping the door closed and we didn't experience any mishaps – until the fateful day. Boys will be boys, and Mark and Heath, a.k.a. The Undertaker and Hulk Hogan were wrestling in the room. I was concerned about something getting broken, whether furniture or human, and also the noise level was getting past toleration point. I told the boys to stop. It's funny how kids think their parents are thick. The boys went into their room, closed the door and carried on the bout from where they had left off. Without warning, there was an almighty splintering of glass from their room, followed by complete silence. I felt sick in the pit of my stomach and it was all I could do to rush to their room fearing the very worst. I had visions of lacerated faces and bodies, of blood spurting every which way.

The sight that met me was of two extremely pale boys entangled in a curtain and still entwined around each other and the window, which reached down to floor level, smashed into a thousand pieces. Mark and Heath had a wake-up call. Neither of them even sported a scratch, thanks to the curtain; they could have been torn to ribbons and seriously injured. Of course, to this day, each blames the other, so they both received a spanking – if they had listened to me, this wouldn't have happened. The hotel was most understanding, but the next problem was that the glass couldn't be replaced for a couple of days until a replacement arrived, and the monkeys thought it was a great game to dive in and out of the window! So the management made a plan. Eventually they found a board and blocked the window temporarily much to the chagrin of the mischievous monkeys.

BUNTY

In 1984 together with my good friend and neighbour Sheelah, I attended a bible study class on Tuesday mornings at the Mazowe Citrus Club. Most of us lived in the area. Mazowe and the surrounding areas are mainly agricultural, thus we lived miles apart. They were a lovely group of women and I often wonder how many of them are still living in Zimbabwe now. Considering the fact that I was probably the only woman not living on a farm, the chances of the rest of the women still being here is extremely remote after the land invasions. They would have all had their farms taken from them and some of them would no doubt have endured the most horrific experiences in the process.

Not only did we study the bible, but we also had talks and demonstrations designed to help us to become better homemakers. It was through our bible study group that I made the acquaintance of Bunty. She was a missionary from England with an energy, fervour and faith that put many of us to shame. For a while she worked at Montgomery Heights in Mvurwi, formerly known as Umvukwes. Montgomery Heights was a Christian children's home that tried to place the children in a family setting as far as was possible. Bunty also travelled to many countries on the African continent preaching and when she returned to Zimbabwe, her good friend Denise would organise get-togethers so that we could catch up on all that Bunty had been doing. For a time I acted as Bunty's Zimbabwean 'secretary'; she would send me letters detailing her work, news, travels and future plans then I would type and print these and send them out to a mailing list.

I regret that I never really knew Bunty that well; she was quite an inspiration to us, but to me in particular. On Thursday 20th February 1992,

Bunty came to spend the night with our family on the return from a stint she'd had in one of the really remote areas where she'd been living in a grass and mud hut and had not had any of the amenities such as electricity and running water. I had decided that I'd do a roast for dinner with all the trimmings as a welcome for her. Early evenings were always a bit chaotic when the boys were younger both trying to tell me about their day at school, doing homework, preparing the evening meal, feeding pets and all the other chores that mothers around the world will recognise. I had prepared as much of the meal as possible before Bunty's arrival.

She was appreciative of the effort that I had gone to, but she asked if I'd really mind that instead of having roast potatoes, we could have chips! She said she was craving them and had been thinking of chips the whole time she'd been in the rural areas. To help me out, she insisted that she'd cook them while I got on with other things. She cut the spuds and put the fat on the stove to heat up. I had been in the bedrooms putting laundry away and smelt burning. I ran to the kitchen to be met with black clouds of billowing smoke and flames leaping from the stove! I screamed for Mike. Bunty had gone through to the lounge to chat to Mike and had completely forgotten about the oil heating on the stove. As we live in a rural farming area and have no access to emergency services such as fire engines, half the time we have no means of contacting anyone anyway, so we have to make a plan and be self-sufficient, and have a store of hand-held fire extinguishers.

We managed to put the fire out and apart from a blackened ceiling and walls; there wasn't too much damage to the kitchen. We had been extremely lucky. We were coughing and spluttering so much from the smoke that we couldn't sit inside the house to eat the remainder of the meal minus the potatoes, so we had our evening meal outside on the balcony. Just as well it was summer and therefore not too cold to sit outside. When I think of what a disaster the evening could have turned out to be! I must admit it put me off making chips for quite a while afterwards. Bunty was terribly apologetic. She was embarrassed. It was an accident, it could have happened to anyone.

Bunty went back to England and I did hear from her for a while, but as with the rest of our bible study group, we have lost touch. I know life moves on and that changes are inevitable, but we Zimbabweans seem to have had our fair share of changes and of saying goodbye to dear friends and family. I've got to the stage now that I don't actually say 'goodbye'. I use euphemisms such as 'We must keep in touch', 'Remember to email' and other such meaningless statements. It works, it makes me feel better, and as a survival mechanism, that's what counts, it's just a whole lot easier than going through all the emotional upheaval of prolonged farewells.

WHAT A PONG!

This is not exactly a pre-prandial, post-prandial or anytime prandial, topic of conversation! The topic being our septic tank. Oh yuk, I hear you say; and oh yuk, it is. The only amenity that we get from the rural Council in our part of Mazowe is that of paying taxes! We have to dispose of our own refuse and our own sewage. We have to source our own water. In years past, the Council used to be able to maintain our roads, but for the last three or four years, we, the residents have had to do patch-up jobs to enable us to make use of the road. The Council maintains that the rates go towards facilities like beer halls (which I don't use!) and clinics. Our staff prefers to come to me for minor medical ailments as half the time they make the trek to the clinic to find that it doesn't have any supplies! O.K that's my moan for today and it's only in latter years with the crazy situation in the country that the Rural Council has been so inefficient. Before I digress let me return to the delightful topic of sewage. It's not a pleasant subject, but it's a fact of life. A pretty basic fact of life.

As we live in a rural area, the disposal of our bodily wastes is our concern. So when building the house, Mike built a septic tank that is approximately two and a half metres deep. Although it's in quite close proximity to the front door, it's strategically camouflaged and I must admit that the plants around it are prolific, although Mike is convinced that the roots have never penetrated the tank. Through experience, we've discovered that on average, the septic tank will need emptying every fifteen years or so. The first time we needed to empty it, I wasn't sure whether to divorce or murder Mike! It was school holidays and we were expecting a family from South Africa to come and stay with us for a week. The father was a business acquaintance of Mike's and although I had met the wife once, I didn't really know them. They had two sons who were ages with our boys.

141

I had been working my little butt (maybe not quite *so* little!) off getting the house ready for them. The whole place had been blitzed and it shone. I made new curtains and a toilet seat cover for our bathroom and one for the guest bathroom. I baked and cooked until I nearly dropped and the freezers were full to the brim. I had done my part, there was nothing more I could do but relax and try and be the perfect hostess. I had *not* counted on my husband! The day before our guests were due to arrive, Mike discovered that the septic tank was full and there was nothing for it but to empty it immediately. I really hadn't given this subject a whole lot of thought. I mean, the realms of the mysteries of plumbing weren't my domain. If I had done a bit of lateral thinking I would have realised that whatever came out of the septic tank, would have to *go* somewhere. I just hadn't thought that the 'somewhere' would be where he put it! I left it all up to Mike after all he'd built the house.

Mike and two employees had the unenviable task of taking the sewage out of the septic tank, but *I could not believe my eyes* when I looked out of the front door and saw that they were dumping the contents on the front lawn! I rushed outside my nostrils firmly pinched together and hysterically screamed at Mike that he just could NOT put that disgusting gunk on MY FRONT LAWN! Sometimes I don't know why I waste my time and energy. When Mike has made up his mind, he's made his mind up. He was adamant that the sewage would be good for the lawn. When I asked him how on earth he thought we could explain this away to our guests, he said that we'd just tell them that we were top-dressing the lawn! Come on! There's top dressing and then there's top dressing. Fifteen years worth of the contents of a septic tank is quite a lot of 'top dressing'. We have a big lawn and it was well covered in 'top-dressing'. It wasn't difficult telling the boys not to play there. They would have preferred to sit quietly inside doing homework in the school holidays, they would have preferred being nice well-behaved little boys, - they would have preferred anything but play on the lawn.

Our main security gate and entrance is right where the lawn begins. The main security gate is where our guests would come through at the end of their tiring journey. And their first impression of our home would be when our excrement assaulted their nostrils. Mike made sure that our guests would have a holiday to remember. They arrived at the front door with somewhat wrinkled noses and said that they knew they were out in the country by the 'farmyard' smell! Mark and Heath nearly choked on their suppressed giggles, Mike and I couldn't even bring ourselves to make eye contact; but I was able, with a straight face, to say that we'd just top-dressed the lawn and we'd appreciate if people stayed off it. The silver lining in our cloud was that as the time passed, the 'farmyard' smell lessened, as did the chances of us blurting out the truth. I really don't think these people could have handled the truth. They were real townies from a big city in South Africa and I'm positive that they would never have top-dressed their lawn from their septic tank.

Another fifteen years has just come around and another emptying has taken place. I'll never understand men. This time, Mike could have put the sewage wherever his little heart desired. We were not expecting guests, we didn't have little boys who like playing ball games – and guess what, Mike came up with the innovative idea of digging a deep hole fairly near the septic tank and depositing the sewage in there! Why couldn't he have come up with this idea fifteen years ago? Why did he put me through all the stress of not only trying to keep up with the Joneses, but also having to keep downwind of them? Why, why, why? Men are different creatures. I don't care whether they're from Venus or Mars, but I was pretty close to pushing one into a septic tank fifteen years ago!

FRAGMENTS

The wife of the farmer next to us was a Canadian and always had the most delightful way of saying things. She would phone and say, "Elijah" – her interpretation of Eilidh, with a name like I have, I've got used to answering anything within reason running from 'eyelid' to 'alias', think I'd draw the line at alien, though – "would you and the fragments like to come for tea?" the fragments being Mark and Heath. Part of the reason that Mike and I put off having children for so long, eight years to be exact, was that there was a war on. I watched other women in the area fussing over the safety of their children in a war situation. To me, part of the joy of living out of town is to enable the kids to run wild in the bush. There were neighbours down the road with a boy of about eight and he was constantly dressed in red overalls so that his mother would be able to find him in a hurry if the need arose. Eventually the mother couldn't stand the strain of living in a sensitive area during the war with a young child and they left for the safer climes of Australia. By the time we did have children the war had ended and we were living under black majority rule. The country opened up and money was poured in, my children, unlike my childhood, were able to get the imported 'goodies' that were unavailable to us.

Lego was available. It was expensive, but we could get it. Over the years on trips outside the country as well as buying it locally, our sons amassed quite a collection of Lego and they took exceedingly good care of it. Mark, especially, took pride in his Lego and Mike found an old, small tin trunk with a padlock where Mark could keep his precious collection under lock and key. Before we had visitors if they had children with them, the Lego would be locked away and the key hidden. He did show us where he'd hidden the key, but we were sworn to secrecy. By this time, his younger brother Heath was mobile so the tin box was kept locked even more! I was driving through town with both the boys one scorching hot day, which was building up for rain. We were running late for an appointment and were in the middle of a traffic jam that wasn't going anywhere! To aggravate things, I was having a spot of car trouble with the car cutting out periodically and me having to keep the revs up to prevent us stalling. I was frazzled, snappy and the boys were fractious. A great time was being had by all.

Why oh why is it at times like these that children ask awkward questions? Ok, I admit, it could have been worse, it could have been about the birds and bees, I got off lightly, it was about Lego – but why in the middle of a traffic jam?

Mark, "Mummy, when I die, will I go to heaven?"

Me, "Yes dear." I didn't know what had brought this topic of conversation about, I didn't think my driving was that bad!

Mark, "Mummy, will I like heaven?"

Me, "Yes it's lovely there."

Mark, "Mummy have you been there?"

Me, "Not yet."

Mark, "Well how do you know what it's like?"

Me, "Because I'm a mummy."

Mark, "But how do you know?"

Me, "Mummies know everything."

Mark, "Mummy when I go to heaven will Jesus be there?"

Me, "Yes he will."

Mark, "Mummy when I go to heaven can I take my Lego with me?"

Me, "Yes you can."

Mark, "Mummy if I take my Lego with me, should I keep the box locked?"

Me, "That sounds like a good idea."

Mark, "Mummy, what happens if I forget the key?"

Me, "*Just make sure you take the damn key with you!*" I know that's not the perfect mummy-answer. But if you'd been in that sweltering oven of a car that kept cutting out, late for an appointment that we didn't have a hope of keeping and listening to that piping, whining 'Mummy' all the time, I reckon you'd say I acted with a considerable amount of restraint. By the time we finally got home and I could sit and discuss the matter rationally with Mark, he'd forgotten all about it and wasn't the slightest bit interested.

When the boys were young there was a sewing craze here, called 'Stitch Witch' and it was sewing with stretch fabrics such as tee-shirting. In the earlier days of our marriage I made nearly all my own clothes and those of the boys. I went for a course of lessons and then spent many hours making tee shirts, track suits and other items of clothing that were unique and individual. My speciality so to speak, were boys' underpants which my boys named, 'punky brewsters' after a show on television. I loved making punky brewsters and the more colourful, the better. They were made out of tee-shirting and would be in red, white and blue, or green, yellow and orange, or whatever colour combination I happened to like at the time. Mark and Heath's underpants were admired by their friends – when they were changing for sport or swimming, I think I should add here - and it got that their friends asked for punky brewsters for themselves. I had an assembly line of boys' knickers going and whenever Mark or Heath were invited to a party, the present was a couple of pairs of my underpants. I've never worked out whether our boys were inordinately popular, or whether the other kids just wanted fancy underpants, but whatever the reason, my sons seemed to spend their lives at parties and I seemed to spend my life at the sewing machine.

My horizons were to expand – to bigger bums, I mean of the posterior type. A friend Lyn had shown her husband a pair that I'd made for her son and the husband said he fancied a pair in red, white and blue to make him look like Batman! Who was it that said that all men are just little boys at heart? I made him a pair. I wasn't sure if I'd got the fit right, but it's hardly the kind of thing you can ask someone to model for you, I'm not that liberated a woman. Fit they did. They fit perfectly, he placed another order. By now, Mike was feeling a bit left out. His sons had punky brewsters, another man had punky brewsters and he didn't have any. So I made for Mike. My father then started making rumblings and he too was kept supplied. I would never have dreamt of even offering to make a pair for Mike's dad, he was of a generation that was staunchly attached to their 'aertex' grandpa-type white undergarments. He would have been mortified if I'd given him a pair of multi-coloured, tee shirting punky brewsters.

My sewing's a bit like me, not always consistent. I am human after all. I'd have good days and bad days. On one such bad day, the elastic and I had a bit of an altercation and when Mark donned his underpants, he was having trouble walking! With hindsight, I could have made a fortune making 'bad-day' punky brewsters for the opposition team from St. Michaels school when they were playing a soccer match against our school, St. John's Prep! We'd have beaten them hands down, or feet first, whatever, every time. The boys definitely grew out, and I don't mean literally, of the phase of Mummy's homemade broekies (pants)! When they started the rugby-playing phase of their lives, then it was time to move on to the real thing. Although I gave a great sigh of relief, it was a poignant moment, the end of an era.

My friend Coleen sews beautifully. Our two families were going up to Nyanga for a weekend and would be sharing a National Parks lodge at Udu Dam. Coleen's sons and mine were the same ages. I was still in my enthusiastic sewing phase of my life and I knew that Coleen had made new winter pyjamas for her boys and that they would be wearing them at Nyanga. I was not daunted. I would *not* be outdone. I made a pair of really snazzy, colourful p.j.s for each of my sons. Now we were equal. Mark had a blue and red pair, and Heath a bright fluorescent yellow and orange pair. I was up there with the best of mothers! It's always cooler at Nyanga and the evenings are no exception. Coleen and I insisted that we wanted a braai (barbecue), and her husband Zack, and Mike were outside muttering much better while they were getting the fire going. We ladies, meanwhile, were sitting in the lounge near the Jetmaster fireplace with its roaring fire while sipping our wine.

The men called us to join them outside, the meat was cooked and there were four ravenous little boys hovering near the braai. The two families were sitting around the fire eating and talking and generally having a pleasant time. Heath started fidgeting and complaining that he was being eaten by mozzies. I tried explaining to Heath that you didn't get mozzies in Nyanga and it was far too cold at that time of year for them to be out anyway. On an earlier trip to Udu, I had been bathing the boys one night and found them covered in tiny pinhead sized black specks. I'd never come across them before and I went tearing off to the Park's office to complain that there were bed bugs. I came away with egg on my face. The 'bugs' were in actual fact pepper ticks. These minute ticks were the devil's own job to get off the skin and seemed to attach themselves to the children more than they did us, I suppose because the children were shorter. The pepper ticks seemed to favour the groin area and if left, caused a nasty rash. With this in mind, the next night whilst bathing Heath, I checked for pepper ticks in case this was what he'd mistaken for mozzies. He was tick free.

Another day. Another braai. Another complaint from Heath about the mozzies. I couldn't ignore him this time he had tears in his eyes and neither of my sons were given easily to tears. Why did this have to happen to me? Why did this have to happen to **me** *in front* of Coleen? When they run these sewing courses, the instructors should remember to tell the participants to remove the pins. Poor Heath wasn't being attacked by mozzies, he was having mummy's home version of delayed acupuncture. Needless to say, my sewing prowess took a knock that day. Friend or not, Coleen hasn't let me forget it.

The rainy season and the schools' athletics seasons coincide. Many a time the fields have been a quagmire and on occasion an event has had to be cancelled. We had a good rainy season in 2000 and the beginning of 2001 and the school fields had suffered as a consequence. It was decided that the ground was just too waterlogged to entertain any hope of holding the final inter-house athletics meet, which was a real worry to the serious sportsmen of the school, two of whom were our offspring. The headmaster got permission from the University of Zimbabwe for the school to have their sports day there and be able to use the track. As with all government-financed institutions, the UZ was cash-strapped, this showed in the condition of the track and its surrounds. No problem. The school made a plan and provided a team of gardeners and volunteers on the Friday and by Saturday March 17th everything was ship-shape. Inter-house athletics is compulsory attendance and the stands were a sea of emerald green with the boys in their school tracksuits. The boys were seated on the left of the stands with the V.I.P section in the middle and the parents on the right. This would be the last year that St. John's College would be a boys only school, as from January 2002 the school was offering the International Baccalaureate as well as 'A' level and as such, they had to be co-ed for the I.B. syllabus and so they admitted girls to the lower sixth. Initially this did cause a few headaches, as with the school song, 'We are the men in green', but every problem's solvable. But no, I don't know what they've substituted for 'men'; maybe twenty or so in skirts sing 'women'.

Back to sports day. Things were going well. The runners were finding it easier going on the tartan track instead of the sodden grass at school. The events got underway about nine in the morning. A trickle of UZ students came as spectators and sat on the grassy bank opposite the stands. Then a few more arrived and a few more. They started to heckle some of the competitors, especially if they were white. One particularly despicable UZ student tried to interfere with the athletes as they passed him. In Mark's one race for instance, he was streets ahead of the others and the student made to grab him as he passed, but missed. Fortunately Mark was completely oblivious to all this until his fellow athletes told him all about it after the race. Another student was riding his bicycle on the track hindering athletes. We, the spectators were getting a bit uneasy. We had just come through a hideous year with the farm invasions and several of the parents were farmers who had been evicted from their homes. Amongst the black parents we had supporters of the opposition party and they too had suffered horrendously. To top it all, we were all parents, very concerned parents, of school-age sons and we didn't want them to get mixed up in riots.

The U.Z students were growing in numbers and were becoming more disruptive. It was difficult to know what to do. A few of them, who appeared to be drunk, came up onto the stands, sat in the V.I.P seats and heckled the headmaster and his wife. Other students sat amongst the parents. There were racial taunts. We white parents were told that we were 'white pigs' and that we should all go 'back home to England', even though half the parents there had no claim to British ancestry anyway. The black parents were taunted for being 'sell-outs'. I was impressed with the body of parents, but in particular, the men. No one uttered a word in retaliation. It took an awful lot of restraint to sit there and listen to these louts. I felt like standing and screaming at them. I felt like going up and hitting one of them. None of us dared move. Someone muttered about calling the Riot Police – who'd spent enough time at the university in the previous months. However, the safety of the boys was paramount. There were also a lot of young siblings who'd come to cheer their big brothers on, amongst the spectators. It was a volatile situation and had to be handled with extreme care. The headmaster, VIPs and staff showed great dignity, totally ignoring the louts. Many of the black parents were embarrassed and a couple tried to talk to the unruly students and explain that this was merely a school sports day and it included boys of all races. A few families did leave taking their sons with them, but only a few.

Somehow, the rest of the events were completed without too much mishap, but it was wisely decided to leave the presentation of the various cups and awards until another day. It was sad that this had to be so. It's a proud moment for both the athlete and the parents to have the presentation done on the day and in front of everyone, but in this case, discretion was definitely the best part of valour. The athletes, staff and parents left the university in a rapid but dignified manner, ensuring that no one was left behind. This event was the final nail in the coffin for some people, as was the case with the family sitting next to us. The wife had been extremely agitated during the unpleasant incident and within a few months, they'd sold up and moved to safer climes.

Zimbabwean school children have had quite an interesting time. Take for instance, on Sunday 4th July 1999 we were having tea with friends when a member of the family who had been watching the television news in another room came in and announced to us that the government had declared the following day, Monday 5th July, a day of national mourning for the funeral of the late Joshua Nkomo, the Vice President. Just like that. No warning to the public or business sectors. What about those citizens who hadn't been watching television or listening to the radio? What about people who'd had long-standing appointments? What about patients destined for operations or other procedures? The list is endless. Our family enjoyed an unexpected day at home. Monday 2nd July 2001 saw us at home again as the

Zimbabwe Congress of Trade Unions (ZCTU) had organized a national stay-away in defiance of the government. It was compulsory for all employers to give their staff the day off on Saturday 9th March 2002 to enable them to go and vote; Monday 11th and Tuesday 12th of March 2002 again saw businesses and schools closed, again to enable people to vote.

2002 saw the fun and games with the government saying the private schools couldn't write the Cambridge exams locally, then rescinding their decision. The final straw as far as the headmaster of our school was concerned and many other heads, was when the government arrested the headmasters over the school fees, in essence, arresting them for doing their job! One of the reasons that the privileged few, my family included, send their children to private schools here is so that they will get an internationally recognized education with internationally recognized qualifications. The parents bear the brunt of the private school fees, although we always complained, we knew we had no choice in the matter. I've never understood why the government was so against private schools as the children of government ministers all attend these schools. When you think about it, private schooling takes the burden off the Ministry of Education having to provide funds for these scholars, but for whatever reason, the private schools appeared to be a thorn in the government's side.

Every year our board of governors would convene a meeting of parents and invited representatives from the Ministry of Education to discuss the increase of fees and to answer any questions pertaining to the school's budget. The school's financial records were available in the bursar's office to anyone who wished to peruse them. The proposed fees would be announced and a show of hands asked for. As much as we all grumbled and moaned, we all agreed with the expenditures and we all wanted the best for our children. Our school had the added disadvantage of being comparatively new compared to some of the more established schools, as a result, our needs were for expensive capital items such as buildings and we didn't have an old established 'Old Boys' association to help fund raise on our behalf. At the meeting on 29th March 2004 there was a unanimous vote to increase the fees. The school board duly informed the government. It was our money after all and if we were prepared to pay for our children to receive a first-world education where was the problem. Alas, the powers-that-be didn't see it that way.

The week of Tuesday 4th to Friday 7th May 2004 was a dog's breakfast and the private schools were summarily closed by the government for 'illegally' increasing school fees. When school resumed on Monday 10th May, the parents and pupils were shocked to find out that our headmaster had been arrested. The government decided that the headmasters of the private schools had broken the law by increasing the fees above those stipulated by the Ministry of Education. So the headmasters were arrested. Zimbabwean jails are not pleasant; believe me that is an understatement. With usual Zimbabwean resilience, we can always squeeze a smile out of even the bleakest of situations. When the police arrived to arrest the hapless school heads, they would not permit them to make a phone call to let at least someone, anyone, know what was happening to them. A very young constable had walked the considerable distance from the Borrowdale Police station to one of the long-established private boys' school to arrest the headmaster. For some reason, Zimbo police and 'transport' do not seem to be synonymous.

The green young constable was perspiring heavily when he confronted the elderly head of the school. The headmaster said that he'd gladly accompany the young man arresting him, but where was the transport? When it was explained to the headmaster that he'd have to walk the ten kilometres or there-abouts to his holding cell, he advised that there better be a wooden casket waiting for him at the other end as the distance and the heat were wont to take their toll. He made a plan. He then suggested an alternative, he himself didn't have a vehicle, but he could phone a friend who would willingly take them to the police station. Two birds with one stone. A phone call was made so that people knew what was happening to the headmaster, allowing the young policeman to effectively carry out his arrest with the added comfort of a lift back to the police station.

More governmental interference continued. Our sons have been fortunate that we were able to have them as day scholars as Mike went into town for work every day and could therefore take them in and collect them. The majority of children around us in Mazowe were boarders. They would come home at half term and on certain exeat weekends, but for the rest, they remained at school. When I saw how uptight the boarders got the day before they had to go back to school at the beginning of a term, I was eternally grateful that our family didn't have to go that route. For some obscure reason in May 2004, the government decided that the boarding schools could only have weekly boarders, even though at the private schools, the parents paid for everything, this meant that children had to be taken out on a Friday afternoon and returned at the crack of dawn on a Monday. For many parents of boarders, this was a complete impossibility; some came from as far away as Zambia.

Our good friends and ex-farming neighbours were in a dilemma. Their daughter Tracy was a boarder at Arundel School for girls in Harare. If things had been sane and normal, they would have still been on their farm next to us and the weekly boarding wouldn't have been a problem, the opposite, they would have welcomed it and the chance to see more of their youngest daughter. Things were not normal and sane. The family was no longer on their farm and were now living five-and-a-half hours away from Harare on the Mozambique border. Between them and us we coped with taking Tracy out at weekends. If we'd lived in town, it would have been so simple. But we lived out of town and had the added headache of sourcing enough fuel to get to and from school and we were also having to go between two schools with differing schedules. Somehow there's always an added complication to life in Zim, but we made a plan and coped.

PEER PRESSURE

Mark has never been overly concerned with what others think of him, whereas with Heath, it's a different story altogether. Both the boys are runners and have enjoyed considerable success especially with long distance running. The first school term of every year, from January to April, was the athletics and cross-country season. The school had various routes that they used to use for training in and around Borrowdale, Harare. One of the routes was along the road where we have our second home so that we have a place to stay when in Harare. While the boys were at school we had a maid working for us, Adlet. She was a large lady. An extremely large lady. I don't know if there's such a thing as a double 'Z' cup in a bra, but I reckon that she was a size fifty double Z. There was plenty of bounce per ounce there. It was Adlet's custom to sit on the concrete culvert at the roadside outside our gate at lunchtimes and play with her children and entertain her mates. Adlet loved talking. Adlet had lots and lots of mates and lots and lots to talk about. It's really *not* the done thing in the northern suburbs to have a maid, a pile of squalling kids and a crowd of maids from neighbouring houses all sitting outside one's gate, but we thought of it as added security. No one would be in a hurry to try and take on Adlet.

Adlet hard at work

The school athletic squad used to run at lunchtime as soon as lessons were over. When Mark ran down the road and saw Adlet, he'd wave and say 'Howzit' to her. This was NOT the case with Heath. As he ran past, he'd look the other way, it just wasn't cool to acknowledge a bunch of women and kids. I've never considered myself cruel, not deliberately so, just maybe a bit thoughtless sometimes and that's what happened on this occasion. I would never deliberately embarrass my offspring, would I?! I had been rushing out on an errand and needed to get a message to Heath. I didn't see how I was going to do it and then had one of my rare brainwaves, I'd ask Adlet to pass on the message to Heath when he was running past the house. I know, I know. I wasn't thinking. It would have been ok if it had been Mark, but this was Heath we were talking about.

As Heath was running down the road with his head turned most intent on the conversation of the boy next to him, - yeah Heath, we all believe you, - Adlet shouted out, "Heafy!" How absolutely humiliating. Heath ignored her.

"Heafy!" Louder this time. She was again ignored. It wasn't easy to ignore Adlet's dulcet tones. This was a bit of a problem for her, she had to pass on a message, it was important. She got up and started a bit of a trot after Heath. With her size fifty double Z cup, this was quite a feat.

"Heafy, mummy wants you!" This was too much. Heath said the earth moved for him. He could feel it wobbling behind him. He sped up a bit.

"Heafy! Mummy wants you!" She sped up. He sped up. The road seemed to tremble even more.

"Heafy!" A bit more breathless this time. Heafy went faster. Adlet went faster. Heafy went even faster. Adlet went even faster. With Adlet's running we're talking about a 2.3 on the Richter scale. This was serious stuff. Heath reckons he broke a personal best in his efforts to get away from the diligent maid.

"Heafy. Mummy wants to tell you she will be late!" This was gasped out. Adlet had reached her limit. She was worn out. When Heath finally got home, I was persona non grata. How could I *DO* that to him! According to him, the WHOLE school had heard Adlet. EVERYONE was mocking him. He'd be the laughing stock of the school. But, he was impressed. He had no idea that Adlet could run that fast. In admiration he said, "You know mum, if we had her in the team, we'd cream the other schools, boy that woman can move!"

All's well that ends well. By the next day, the 'whole' school had totally forgotten the speeding maid, and had moved on to other heady matters. The message had been delivered in a most energetic manner, and Adlet hadn't done herself irreparable damage with her size fifty double Z's bouncing every which way. There's a challenge for Playtex or Gossard, design a sports bra for Adlet. The earth tremor didn't even register on the Richter scale and I'd wager that Adlet even impressed all her shamwaris (friends) with her sprinting ability. She impressed Heath. That was a real test. I have learnt not to pass messages via the ready-maid (sorry, couldn't resist that) method and have had to devise other ways that don't include sprinting maids. Just wish she moved that fast in the house. Suppose you can't have it every way.

We had some tortoises that were rescued from a neighbouring farm after our friends had been evicted during the land invasions. One extra large tortoise was named Bayley after her previous owners. Bayley was quite a character and if we were sitting in our courtyard she would come up and inspect us, well our feet anyway. I often wondered if she'd actually take a bite out of our toes, but I never left mine anywhere near her just in case. She'd spend hours digging up the courtyard flowerbeds and then lay her eggs in the holes. Out of the hundreds of eggs that she laid, only four ever hatched, perfect little miniatures. Heath and his friend Mike enjoyed pottering around in the kitchen experimenting with different dishes, not always producing something that was edible, but every now and again, they'd surprise themselves and us. The two boys had been visiting the proud mamma and her new bambinos when they found one of her eggs lying abandoned on the path and they decided to try cooking it. The cost of our electricity doubled that month. The egg was put in a pot of boiling water. It boiled and boiled and boiled. The boys replenished the water a couple of times and even then, when they shook the egg, it still sounded liquid inside.

The egg was then cracked open a put in a frying pan and this time it did appear to solidify and cook, sort of. Why do we never have a camera present when we need one? The look on Heath and Mike's faces was priceless. They looked like a combination of a wizened old man, a wrinkled prune and a cabbage patch doll. Some of the gunk slid down their throats before they were able to spit out what remained in their mouths inducing a gagging reflex. They both decided that they'd have to be stuck on a desert island for a few years without any food before they'd ever be able to appreciate eating a tortoise's egg. I'd love to know what other people thought when the boys said that they had tried cooking a tortoise egg for breakfast – they must have believed that we were down on our luck and that we had to resort to eating reptile eggs! Heath took great delight in telling all his mates about their egg eating experience. Funny thing was, this didn't seem to embarrass him, *but* I could see people looking at us and thinking, "Poor people, they really must be on their bones, imagine having to eat tortoise eggs". How come it's ok for kids to embarrass their parents, but it's not ok for parents to embarrass their kids? As it's almost impossible to gauge what's embarrassing to kids and what isn't, it doesn't make parenting any easier. Parents should be provided with 'How to' manuals when babies are born.

Two tortoises that we've had for many years are Fred and Rosie. We rescued Fred when Mark was a baby for the princely sum of Z$10 (which was a lot in those days) from a roadside vendor. We acquired Rosie and Jason a few years later from a youngster whose family was emigrating to Australia. Rosie was and still is, a lovely little tortoise with her own personality. Maybe it was her diminutive size that made handling easier for the boys, but she was everyone's favourite. She was the 'sample' that was taken to nursery school and then to big school to show to the other kids and she was the one whose life was very nearly brought to an abrupt end. The tortoises were kept in the courtyard off our bedroom and everyone and his dog used this as a shortcut to get to the swimming pool. So far from being a quiet spot where I could find peace and solitude, it was a busy thoroughfare for little feet. Mike built the exterior door of the courtyard out of steel, it weighs a ton and even I have trouble opening and closing it, this was another of our many security devices around our home. Mark and Heath and their friends, battled closing the door from the outside which led to the pool terrace, not only was the weight of the door a factor, but also the fact that it didn't have a handle …. another security measure. Many a time the door was left ajar, and many a time the dogs used to sneak into the house by that route.

I went into the courtyard one day to find two Dobermans lying on the grass in the shade of the tree and playing Frisbee with Rosie! The poor little thing was thrown from one mouth, caught, then thrown back again. If the dogs had been playing with a real Frisbee, I'd have been most impressed, but as it was, I was most distressed. I grabbed Rosie and threw the dogs out. Her poor shell had teeth puncture marks around the sides, but the worst part was at the top of her shell, which was cracked and had a big gaping hole in it. I could see right inside her. In those days we had a phone that worked, so I got onto the vet only to be told that a tortoise without a shell is a dead tortoise. I wasn't prepared to give up on her. I poured copious amounts of Teramycin antibiotic powder into the hole. It was amazing just how much of the powder went in. I used up a whole bottle. I was worried about ants and other undesirables getting into the hole and causing problems and of course I was really concerned that the shock might kill the poor little tortoise. When Mike came home, he put a covering of plastic putty to cover the hole, which enabled the shell to knit together underneath. This must have happened about sixteen or more years ago and Rosie's still going strong. She has a 'scar' on the top of the shell where the plastic putty had been and there are indentations along her sides where the dogs' teeth had penetrated. She's one tough little tortoise.

Must have been my frugal Scottish ancestry, but when the boys were little I didn't see much point in their having separate birthday parties. Mark's birthday is at the end of March and Heath's in the beginning of April, so I used to give the boys a combined party the week between the two dates. When they were very young, the boys' parties took the usual form with me going over-board baking for the mothers who stayed – and who were invariably on a diet! When I look back, I could have saved a fortune and many hours of hard work, all I needed to buy was a few packets of Korn Kurls or Chicken Flings and a few dozen Freezits (which used to be called penny cools in my day, however with our rampant inflation, you can add a whole lot of zeroes to the price). Freezits are so simple and so popular with the kids and it's just frozen flavoured juice wrapped up in a plastic tube. The kids never seemed to tire of the antics of Jo-Jo the Clown who seemed to be hired for nearly every party we went to. We even had him to one of our parties and Heath, who normally loved him, was terrified out of his wits at the sight of him in our home! Heath clung to me like a frightened animal and wouldn't let me out of his sight. However, the next Saturday my youngest child just couldn't wait for the time to come to go to the meeting of the Jo-Jo Club, we were counting the number of 'sleeps' he was going to have before he could see Jo-Jo again! Just can't win with kids sometimes.

Life was much easier party-wise as the boys got a bit older. Well it was easier for me anyway; finally the onus was on Mike. We now had camping parties and these were extremely popular. The first campsite was in the bush on the way down to our dam. Everything had to be taken there although there was a tap not that far away so that the boys could get potable water. Mike had a couple of large tarpaulins that he rigged up as shelters for the kids and they had a braai and cooked boerewors (type of sausage), chicken and steak. This was easy entertaining for me. Nyama (meat), bread rolls and juice. What could be easier? Mike's job was to camp with the boys and stay with them for the night. One of the first camping parties another dad, Zack, very kindly offered to help Mike out. It very nearly ended a good friendship. That was his first and last offer, clever man decided that life was too short and more fool Mike if he was daft enough to subject himself again to this kind of torture. The night that Zack camped with the partygoers, neither of the dads got a wink of sleep. The next morning they both looked worse for wear, they looked awful.

As an ex girl guide, or even just as a multi-tasking woman, I would have been organized enough to have taken a torch with me, but the non multi-tasking dads forgot to take one. Under normal circumstances this wouldn't have been a problem but this night when the men heard a violent retching (food combining doesn't feature much with party kids and it's obvious that vast quantities of boerewors don't go too well with cream soda and ice cream), they didn't want to wake up the ten slumbering little bundles of joy. The only way they could find out who'd been vomiting was to follow the smell. Rather them than me. I've done my share of cleaning mess from both ends, babies and young kids tend to be like camels in that respect and talking from experience, it's not a whole bundle of fun. When they did locate the unfortunate child by carefully stepping over young bodies spread every which way, it turned out to be Zack's eldest son, Stuart. Mike and Zack cleaned the boy, sleeping bag and surrounds to the best of their ability under the conditions. They'd just all settled down to a fitful sleep when they were woken by a blood-curdling yell which made the hair on the back of their necks stand up. It transpired that young Nigel had had a nightmare – shades of vors, cream soda and ice cream again? The men calmed him, he immediately went back to sleep and Mike and Zack decided to cut their losses and sat in their chairs next to the dying embers of the fire.

Future camping parties were held at our new campsite. This was much better organized. It was closer to the house; there even was a proper loo, which was quite a work of art. We had an old toilet in our shed (Mike throws *nothing* away) and he dug a deep long drop, placed the toilet on top and then our gardener built a grass hut around this. We even had a door that closed; it was almost like the real thing. I always opened the door very gingerly and never entered immediately just in case a passing nyoka (snake) had decided to take refuge in the little hut. Mike had acquired ("You never know when it's going to come in useful" kind of acquisition) some aluminium sheets and used them to build a stone rondavel (round building) with four slit windows, a concrete floor and a sturdy door. This enabled us to leave folding chairs, camping stools and other camping equipment in there in safety and made our camping trips much more uncomplicated. There was a water tap next to the rondavel and the view was stunning. We named our little building 'Craster Castle'. We had small 12volt fluorescent tubes about nine inches long that Mike plugged into the cigarette lighter of the car, this was five star camping compared to our facilities at the previous campsite.

Actually we had cleared the land and built up a large area which was held up with massive stone retaining walls about four metres high and half a metre wide as Mike and I were planning to build a small cottage here for use in our dotage. We spent many hours at the new site sitting on folding chairs sipping cold wine and enjoying the view and planning our new home. We were on the point of ordering building materials and making a start to the cottage when the land invasions took place and all our plans were put on hold – as were our lives, for the foreseeable future. The boys preferred sleeping under the stars at the new site and Mike didn't have to bother with erecting tarpaulins and, as luck would have it, never once was a camping evening rained out. At the time, we had the soppiest of all the Dobermans that we've ever had, Ruwa. What a lovely dog, but the biggest wimp out. He used to be taken on camping trips as a means of protecting his human family, mainly from wild pig. What a joke. Ruwa used to sleep on one of the stretchers and if there was even a rustle of a leaf forget about a wild animal noise, he'd dive under the duvet with his head under the pillow and lie there shivering until the coast was clear.

The birthday camping trips usually took place on a Friday afternoon after school and the parents came to collect the boys late on Saturday afternoon. By then the boys were filthy, smelly, exhausted and their digestive tracts were taking strain from the vast quantities and weird combinations of food that had been consumed. To try and add a bit of spice to the parties, Mike made a plan and took the boys on 'game' walks after their braai at night. 'Game walk' is said very tongue in cheek. Many, many years ago there were leopards in the area. We still have our fair share of baboons, wild pig, duiker and members of the reptile family, however, as you can imagine, ten or so excited little boys crashing through the bush was certain to chase away anything alive that could possibly move. Mike thought that it might be entertaining on one such walk to surreptitiously throw stones into the bush and then pretend that the ensuing noise was the result of a 'wild' animal moving. This form of entertainment backfired on him. All it did was to frighten the kids and had them all anxiously clamouring to hold his hand all the way back to the camp and even reduced one little boy to tears. So that act was subsequently dropped from Mike's party repertoire.

ELECTRIFYING

Ever since I can remember, electrical appliances, especially the smaller ones, have been a luxury item in Zimbabwe. You can imagine our excitement, when, shortly after Independence in 1980, we could just walk into a shop and buy a toaster or kettle or pressure cooker instead of having to make the trek to South Africa and use precious forex to do our shopping. Sure it was more expensive to buy the appliance locally, but it almost made us feel normal like the rest of the world. Roundabout 1992, our trusty toaster was eventually laid to rest. It had served us well and Mike had repaired it so many times, but this time, it decided that enough is enough, and died. I went to a new and rather swish electrical shop in Borrowdale Village in Harare and bought a new toaster. We were proud of our shiny new toaster. We'd only had the toaster a week and it broke. Mike took a look at it and the element had broken, it was easy to see that it only needed a bit of fuse wire. He could have repaired the toaster in a few minutes, but as it was under guarantee, I took it back to the shop. The shop assistant was amenable to changing the toaster and said that they had been having problems with that particular model and replaced it with a new one.

The following week, same story. The toaster went on the blink, Mike looked at it, the element had gone and once again, I went off to the shop and duly had the toaster replaced. The following week the same thing happened. You have no idea how embarrassing it was for me going back to the shop to exchange the toaster, and the shop assistant was giving me a funny look every time I walked into the shop. It happened for the fourth time and I just could not bring myself to go back to the shop. I had been telling my friend Coleen the whole toaster saga as it had been unfolding, so she knew the history. Coleen and I had boys the same age at the same school, so we helped each other out on certain days, fetching and carrying

163

the boys. On the day of the fourth burnt-out toaster, Coleen had been giving her eldest son Stuart and Mark a lift back from school. She said she didn't want to be telling tales, but knowing how I was feeling about having to go back to the shop with the latest toaster, she felt that she had to tell me what she had overheard.

Both boys had been in the back seat of her car, and Mark's piping little voice said, "Hey Stuey, do you know how to make sparkles?" To which Stuart replied in the negative, so Mark said, "Well, you switch on the toaster, stick a knife in it and boy there's thousands of sparkles!" Mike and I didn't say a word to Mark that night, but next morning at breakfast, Mike casually asked, "Mark, how do you make sparkles?" Mark's face fell. He *knew* that we knew, and knew that I was fed-up with the whole toaster episode. He asked how we had found out. We didn't want to 'drop' Coleen in it, so Mike said, "It's easy Mark. You talk in your sleep." The poor kid was too scared to go to sleep at night for ages in case any other deep and dark secrets were revealed.

You would have thought that that was the end of our toaster woes, but nothing could be further from the truth. We now had a working toaster and it no longer suffered from mysterious bouts of damaged elements, but we didn't bargain for Abby. This wasn't a 'she' it was an 'it', a grey tabby cat who, with her sister, Mega, came to us from the SPCA just about the time that Mike gave me an ultimatum – him or pets. Not an easy decision, but Mike is kind of cute as well and as we by now had seven cats and seven dogs and the chances of me getting seven husbands were slim, so I chose Mike. Although Abby was a scrawny little thing she was full of character and I think in another life she and Mark must have been related as they both seemed to have a fetish about toasters. All things considered, Mark's obsession with sparkles was infinitely more preferable to Abby's obsession! We never caught her in the act, but being an agile, supple feline, she somehow managed to squat over the toaster in order to relieve herself. Believe me, you *never* want to experience anything like this. The smell of toasting cats' wee is indescribable; it brings tears to your smarting eyes; it's great for clearing sinuses and your teeth feel as if they're almost curling in on themselves. Even with every window and door open to get rid of the smell, the stench permeates the whole house for hours.

I didn't think I'd ever be able to eat toast ever again. The boys and I wanted to cut our losses and throw the toaster away – after all, I'd had plenty of experience in getting new toasters just recently. Mr. Fix-It Mike thought otherwise, he looked upon it as a challenge – not eating urine-flavoured toast I mean, but of getting the toaster clean enough for our use again. Abby was chastised and changed from using the toaster to one of the ring plates on the stove. I think this was even worse. The stove obviously can get to a higher temperature thus creating a stronger smell. Long story cut short. Abby was shown the error of her ways and finally we convinced her that the great outdoors provided a greater selection of environs in which to do her daily ablutions. Once again I digress. We still had the stinky toaster to deal with. Mike took the toaster into his workshop for quite a time and on its return, we were assured that it was perfectly clean and fit to use for human consumption. Be that as it may, the boys and I decided that we'd give toast a miss for the foreseeable future.

It was shortly after the return of the newly cleaned toaster to the kitchen that one of the South African directors of our family business decided to come and stay with us for a couple of nights instead of staying in a hotel, which he found too impersonal. On these visits, I used to get up with the sparrows and prepare breakfast – the family loved when he stayed with us – we started with grapefruit, then onto the cereal followed by a cooked breakfast, then scones fresh from the oven. This gourmet delight was an absolute feast compared to our normal breakfast fare. Shortly after the toaster fiasco, Brian was staying with us again. Our oven was in a work-to-rule mode and I didn't trust the outcome of any baking that I did; it's a whole lot easier to blame the stove than my baking! However, if I say so myself, the one thing that I do excel at, is making scones. We could not have these delicacies on this occasion, and Mike said that I was being silly and I should just make toast. I was horrified. Mark and Heath were ecstatic. They had bets to see if Brian would a) notice an 'unusual' flavour in the bread and b) survive eating the toast. The boys and myself abstained from toast that morning; but Mike and Brian had some.

Our two sons watched the men with rapt attention. It was as if they were watching Wimbledon in slow motion. Their heads would turn in unison to watch their father bite, chew, masticate, swallow; then, in unison, they'd turn to watch Brian go through the same process. Neither man gagged.

Neither man clutched his throat in horror. Neither man fell to the ground in agony. The jinx of the wee toaster (not the Scottish use of wee) was over. It did take a while for the three of us sceptics to return to our morning toast, and the first time I did, I slathered the bread with extremely liberal helpings of Marmite that would mask any underlying scent that may be lingering. It must be a good thirteen or more years since we bought the toaster and it's still going strong; Abby is no longer with us, she's in the big cattery in the sky, actually she's in the pets' cemetery at the back of our property and our two surviving male cats are true male Zimbos – they prefer urinating outside. It must be a male thing.

SIX FOOT UNDER

Mike's sister, Yvonne had remarried a man called Gabriel, who died suddenly in July1994 as a result of an aneurysm. As he was Greek, his family decided to have a full Greek Orthodox funeral, which seemed to us, who were not used to things like this, to last for hours. On receiving the news about Gabriel's death from Yvonne, I left our young sons with my mother and went and stayed with her, as I didn't think it was right that she was left on her own after the death of her husband. It was a bit of a stressful time all round for our family. Just prior to Gabriel's death, Mike's father, Yvo had been in hospital for an operation and was only released on the day of the funeral. Mike and I collected him from the hospital en route to the funeral. Yvo was a staunch Church of England believer and didn't agree with the use of candles and the other trappings of the Orthodox Church, and so, flatly refused to light a candle as we entered the Greek Church saying that he didn't 'hold' with that kind of 'thing'! He was a proud and somewhat stubborn man of the 'old school' and insisted on standing the whole way through the funeral service. We kept entreating him to sit, as apart from his obvious age, he was still weak and should have been at home in bed, convalescing. As it was July, it was winter and it was cold, and Yvo was shivering as he stubbornly stood next to me. No one would have criticized him for sitting through part of the service, but we were wasting our breath.

Yvo survived the service and allowed us to help him into the car in order to follow the funeral cortege to the Pioneer cemetery, the same one in which Mike's mother was buried. We parked as near to the gravesite as possible to make it a bit easier for Yvo, but it was still a fair walk for him. More standing ensued while the priest said the last rites swinging the incense around and the coffin was finally lowered into the ground. I was feeling tired from all the standing and I wasn't elderly and I hadn't just come out of hospital; so I know Yvo was feeling the same way, although he wouldn't admit it. The throng of mourners filed past the grave each stopping to scoop up some earth and throw it on top of the coffin and to say their farewell. Yvo was in front of me in the file and it seemed to take forever before our turn came. The old man was exhausted and as we neared the grave and he stooped to get some earth, he started, ever so gently, to slide down the mound of earth towards the waiting coffin and his late son-in-law! Any other time I would have had a fit of the giggles and seen the funny side of things, but this was a solemn occasion with a lot of distraught people. Most un-ladylike, I grabbed hold of the collar of his jacket and hung on for dear life. Then, horror of horrors, I too, felt myself being dragged down into the vortex by my unsteady father-in-law! That'll teach me. If I'd been wearing sensible shoes I might have had more 'grip', but my fashionable, frivolous footwear was worse than useless.

I don't think I've ever felt quite so helpless. If I let go of the collar to save myself, Yvo would land up on top of the coffin, and if I continued to hold onto him, there was a very good chance that we'd both land up in the grave. It was like a slapstick comedy. I really didn't fancy torn stockings, scratched legs, broken fingernails. Mike came to the rescue. He clutched on to his father's collar and pulled him back away from the gaping grave and the momentum carried me away from an incredibly mortifying incident! I wouldn't have been able to face anyone at the wake after the funeral, let alone give my condolences. I rather hope that not too many people noticed our predicament. It was just as well that Mike made a plan and came to our rescue.

We made it to the wake in one piece and were able to comfort Yvonne and give our condolences to the rest of Gabriel's family. We eventually managed to get Yvo home and into bed where he belonged and he slept the sleep of the dead, and for once, he was prepared to listen to reason and took life easy for the next few days. I know that he felt bad as if he was shirking his responsibility, as he wasn't able to be of more help to his grieving daughter. He was of the 'old school' where one didn't let silly little things like recuperation get in the way of family responsibility. Yvonne was in complete agreement with us when we tried to get the 'Old Man' as he was known to take it easy and to sit in the church, but he could be as stubborn as a mule when he felt like it. There was no budging him.

PARAGLIDING

On one of our holidays in Nyanga in the eastern part of Zimbabwe on our border with Mozambique, we were in Troutbeck Hotel having the traditional feast of tea and fresh scones saturated in thick cream. I say 'tea' although I always have the wonderful coffee, which is grown in the area. Mark and Heath had taken themselves off for a wander, and in their travels read an advert on the hotel notice board for tandem paragliding rides, and being adventurous young teenage boys, wanted one. My mother said that Nyanga always reminded her of Scotland, and with a bit of imagination, you could forgive yourself for thinking that you were north of the border in the UK. The topography, the rounded, barren hills and the sometimes bleak-looking landscape, do have a hint of the northern climes. It's a beautiful, rugged area. It's definitely colder in winter, and that's part of the enjoyment of going to Nyanga, is that it is expected to be cooler. It's bliss for trout fishermen with several dams and rivers. Long walks and hikes are another attraction. It's a wonderful place to be to unwind and recharge your batteries.

There are hotels in the area, but many visitors tend to stay in the National Park lodges, which, while not five star, are adequate and affordable. Each set of lodges is built around a small fish-stocked lake in picturesque settings. There are also many privately owned cottages that are sometimes rented out to holidaymakers. We've spent many happy holidays in Nyanga. Sometimes we would come for a weekend, travelling from Harare on a Friday afternoon and leave on Sunday night, but if we came in the school holidays we'd usually make a week of it. We'd always go to the same viewing and picnic sites and frequent the same hotels for teas and lunches; somehow we never got bored of the place. Unfortunately that part of the world has had its tranquillity shattered, as it too has not been immune to the government-backed land grabs, and the ensuing unpleasantness.

At the time we were there, none of us had the slightest inkling that anything was amiss and that our futures would be indelibly changed by the land grabs. We were just an ordinary family having a break away from the hustle and bustle of everyday life. That's where the scene was set for this chapter on Para-gliding. Mike and I relaxing at the hotel and the boys excitedly running back to us with a cell-phone number that they'd copied from the bulletin board, to ring to book a tandem ride. The ride wasn't cheap, so it was decided that only Mark could have a ride, as I also felt that Heath was a bit young – the scourge of being the youngest in the family keeps rearing its ugly head! I used to refer to Mark as my favourite first born and to Heath as my favourite second born. This went on for many years until Heath complained that he was tired of always coming second! So I changed to my favourite eldest, and favourite youngest, son, Heath seemed to think he could live with that.

On Saturday 28th April 2001, we had to get up at the crack of dawn on the day of the ride and phone the organiser to see if it was still all on, depending on the weather conditions. It was all systems go. Mark was so excited that we arrived at the take-off point before anyone else. The ride was to be from World's View, an aptly named mountain with a view of the world for as far as the eye can see. I never get tired of going there and just sitting and staring out and communing with nature, it's awe-inspiring. One word of advice for any mothers of young children, seeing your child running off the top of a mountain attached to a complete stranger, with just a few pieces of nylon cord and a few metres of material between him and his maker, is not the kind of thing that you should watch if you're at all faint-hearted! Mark was attached in tandem with the organiser of the ride, a Kiwi, Mark. He was also the trainer cum organiser of the para-gliding club in Harare. The ride wasn't a great success as the wind died down at an inappropriate moment and cut the ride short. It was enough. Our Mark was hooked. He wanted to learn to para-glide and had his first lesson on Saturday 5th May 2001.

It's Murphy's Law; the para-gliding club was miles away from us. We had to travel the twenty-five kilometres into Harare from our side of town, go through town, and then another twenty or more kilometres out towards Enterprise. Kiwi Mark had been a paramedic in New Zealand and was a stickler for safety, for which I was grateful. As he said, it was his reputation on the line if any mishap was to happen. The club met on

Saturdays and we had to fit this in around the boys' school sports schedule, as there were often fixtures on Saturday. More often than not, Mike would go out to the 'club' with the boys. I use the word club in inverted commas as I actually mean a mealie field, surrounded by bush on a farm. There was no loo, no facilities of any kind. The para-gliding club did make use of the facilities of the Enterprise Club which was run by the farmers but this was a few miles away and was usually only frequented at lunchtime or after the last ride of the day.

Mark loved the training. He studied the manual assiduously. I wish he had put the effort he did in studying the theoretical side of para-gliding into his G.C.E 'O' Levels! He practised and practised his ground handling, and finally Kiwi Mark said that Zimbo Mark was ready to take to the skies. He was the youngest qualified para-glider in Zimbabwe and stayed that way until usurped by his brother, Heath, a year later. Kiwi Mark was good to Mark and looked out for him. Mark was invited to all the socials even though a lot of them he had to miss due to school, those that he did go to he enjoyed and he was made to feel part of the group not like a kid who was hanging around. There were many trips away to Nyanga, Mutorashanga and other mountainous regions. In the school holidays we approved Mark attending some of these camps, and again, he was well looked after by the adults. It was a daunting decision to make to allow him, at fifteen years of age, to go away with strangers on these camps in pursuit of a dangerous hobby. We had to trust him and trust our gut-instinct. He loved every minute of it.

The following year, like every red blooded sixteen-year-old male in Zimbabwe, Mark got his driving licence. It's almost a rite of passage for the boys in this country, the day they turn sixteen, they start making plans to get their provisional learner's licence. I suppose it comes about as there is almost no public transport to speak of and it's not the done thing to have Mummy be your taxi driver forever. Kiwi Mark then used Mark as his gofer in the school holidays driving to the airport to collect consignments of supplies and other mundane tasks. Mark wasn't paid in cash for this but he loved driving so it wasn't any hardship and it was a sort of barter system, he was 'paid' in that he was able to get rides, so he was more than content.

When the club went to mountainous regions, it was a case of getting to the top of the mountain, getting into all your gear, waiting for the correct wind, and you were away. When the club met on the field at Enterprise, they had to use Kiwi Mark's truck to winch the rider and glider up until they were at the correct speed and height and could undo the harness. Driving the truck required skill. It couldn't be too fast or too slow, it had to be smooth, not jerky – lives were at stake. Kiwi Mark's truck owed him nothing. It looked as if it had given him many years of faithful service and had had a hard life, it was on borrowed time and was just a dead truck waiting to go to the truck cemetery, but it did the job, and that's all that was needed.

Life was made a bit easier for us the following year when Heath took up paragliding. I say this with tongue in cheek, one glider and two boys does not a good scenario make. Apart from the 'sharing' aspect that we drill into our kids when they're small, there was the added complication of suitable weather, and that was out of everyone's hands. When the weather was right, Mark would go up first and inevitably by the time it was Heath's turn, conditions weren't suitable and he'd miss out. However it did mean that Mike and I felt a lot happier when the two boys went off together on camps, they would be able to look out for each other. I went out with Mike and the boys to the club one day to watch Heath, as I hadn't seen him do a proper ride. Every time he came down, he seemed to make a beeline for a patch of mealies growing near the runway, I was sure that he was going to get a broken leg, but me of little faith, I should have known to have more trust in him, and once again, he proved me wrong. He didn't break a leg, only the mealies.

Mike had been out with the boys to the club on Friday 6th June 2001 in the afternoon and came back like an excited little boy. One of the members an American from Boston called Tony, had given him a tandem ride. It was quite a hair-raising experience for Mike as Tony had decided to practise 'spiralling'; this is where the 'pilot' deliberately puts the glider into a spin to simulate what would most likely happen if there were a problem. Thus the pilot is able to practise getting out of the situation and not to panic if ever faced with the condition. The 'g' force is quite something and although Mike and Tony were most likely only airborne for about five minutes, Mike said he felt as if the skin was being pulled taut on his face. I reckon I'm fairly laid-back, however seeing someone you know and love, spiralling at speed out of the sky is not a pleasant experience.

I decided to go and watch the gliding on Saturday 7th June 2001 and had just made myself comfortable with my folding chair and my book, when energetic American Tony bounded up to me and said, "Hi. I'm Tony. Would you like to come for a tandem?" Naively I thought it was very kind of Tony to offer me a freebie as usually tandem rides were expensive. It was only later that I realised that Tony had only just acquired his tandem licence and had to fly with a 'passenger' for a stipulated number of hours, and I was the only mug available at the time. I like flying – in proper planes. A few metres of nylon and cord do not constitute my idea of a suitable means of flying. It was just as well that Tony didn't give me time to think about things, as I'm sure I would have declined his generous offer, except that if I had said no, I'd possibly have regretted it later. At least I can now say that I've done it and add it to my résumé of experiences.

I hadn't even given the actual flying or gliding part a thought, what was of concern to me was how we got up into the great blue yonder. The club used a dirt airstrip and Kiwi Mark, or who-ever was the designated driver, would drive down the airstrip getting up to a speed of thirty-five kilometres an hour while at the same time winching up the para-glider. Once airborne the pilot would release the clip that connected the glider to the winch cables. I panicked. There was no way in the world that my little legs with my size three feet (big size three mind you) have ever moved at a speed even remotely close to one kilometre an hour, let alone thirty-five! Tony helped me into my harness and explained the "do's" and "don'ts" of para-gliding. I didn't hear a word. I dumbly nodded my head, but I wasn't taking anything in. I just kept thinking of my little legs going round and round at that speed. I know, I know, it wasn't one of my brightest moments. If any of the members of the gliding club could run at thirty-five kilometres an hour, they wouldn't be taking to the skies, but would be heading for the next Olympics. I just wasn't thinking clearly. I was in panic mode.

Suddenly there was a jerk on the cable and we were on the move. My little legs were saved. They only had to run a few steps and then we were off the ground, it wasn't the humans that had to do the thirty-five 'k's an hour, it was the truck. When we were still on the ground, Tony had shown me how to release the clip when the truck had reached the end of the runway and we were up, but I couldn't manage it, so he had to do it for me. It was only when I was up in the sky that I realised just how flimsy a para-glider actually is. It seemed incredible that such a little piece of material in the canopy above us could keep the two of us adults aloft in the sky. Tony was pointing out landmarks to me and I even saw Mark landing on a cricket field at the Enterprise Club some distance from the airstrip. The problem with being a passenger in a tandem ride is similar to that of being a passenger in a vehicle, it tends to be more bouncy and if you have a tendency to travel sickness, it's not the best place to be. I suffered horribly with carsickness for many years and it was now manifesting itself in airsickness. A piece of advice to any would-be tandem glider passengers, I wouldn't advise eating a packet of cheese and onion chips before being airborne. They were right in my throat and I had to swallow like crazy to keep them there. They oh so nearly came back up and out. That would have been *so* embarrassing.

One itsy, teensy, weenie little thing that Tony had omitted to mention was that for this particular 'flight' we would be going cross-country! Why me? If it had been Mike, he'd have thought he'd died and gone to heaven. He'd have appreciated it. He'd have enjoyed it. He wouldn't be battling to keep a packet of chips from being regurgitated! Tony kept giving me the GPS thingy to hold so that I could see where we were going. Didn't Tony know that I couldn't see a dickey bird without my reading glasses? That I wanted to keep my head up and not look down at the ground way, way below us. Anyway, I was absolutely terrified that I'd drop the thing! It's not exactly as if I could just hop out and fetch it if I let go. So between swallowing as if my life depended on it – can you imagine if I hadn't been able to contain the chips and they came out and the wind blew them straight into Tony!! – and wondering exactly how long a cross-country would entail, I can't really, in all honesty, say that I enjoyed my ride.

We flew for eleven kilometres and came to where the Enterprise and Mtoko roads branch off from each other in a "Y" shape, with a triangular patch of grass where the three legs of the 'y' all meet up. As we were nearing the grass, Tony pointed it out to me and said that that was where we were going to land. I thought that he'd taken complete leave of his senses, or he was making a sick joke. It looked about two square inches big and to make matters worse, the roads were busy with buses and trucks and cars going in all directions. I envisioned landing on the top of a bus with all the luggage, furniture, bicycles and other katoonda that Zim buses have on their roofs, and eventually finding ourselves out at Mtoko. One minute, we were above the grass, the next I heard Tony telling me that I could release my harness. I hadn't even felt the landing and I was sitting on my behind on the grass triangle. It was such a smooth landing that I honestly hadn't realised that we were down safely. The recovery vehicle was there in a couple of minutes and we were whisked back to the airstrip. I must say that the three men in my family were quite envious of me that night, but they thought I was a bit of wimp when I admitted to being scared. Maybe I should have kept that to myself.

Both of our sons take after Mike and are slim. Their weight is also kept in check by the amount of long-distance running they do, and this caused a bit of a problem when we eventually relented and decided to buy Mark a glider of his own. We could not just walk into a shop and buy one, this is Zimbabwe, and like everything else here, we had to 'make a plan'. How I hate that expression, but it is a fact of life here. Kiwi Mark sometimes had second-hand gliders for sale so we approached him. The smallest glider that he had for sale was a 1993 Profile 27, lilac in colour, designed to carry a weight range of 75 to 95 kilos. That was all very well, but Mark was only 50 kilos and would not be able to control the glider. Ever inventive Mike made a plan and came up with the idea of having a seat made out of lead to make up the difference in weight, so he designed a seat that weighed 16 kilos. It still didn't take Mark up to the required minimum weight, but any heavier, and Mark would not have been able to carry the airbag, canopy, harness *and* a lead seat.

Mark had a few trial runs with this lead seat, and it did the job perfectly in the air, but it was a dead weight to carry on landing especially with all the other equipment and considering that sometimes, the pilot would have to walk quite a distance before meeting up with the recovery truck. Then Mike had a brilliant idea, which not only did the job to perfection, but also kept me happy as well. It was definitely a win-win situation. We bought South African wine in five litre cellar casks. It was the perfect solution. The adults had the pleasure of imbibing the boxed nectar, and when we had finished, Mike would remove the foil innards of the cask and fill them with water. It made the perfect ballast for Mark, and also would be much safer for him on landing than a chunk of lead and would also provide drinking water if needed while awaiting the arrival of the recovery team.

On several occasions in the school holidays Mark went with the club to various spots around the country to practise his gliding. One such time, he had landed, and as he was hot, thirsty and slumped at the side of the road in the shade of a tree, he decided to have a drink of water out of the innards of a wine cellar cask, just as his headmaster and family drove past! The school that the boys attended had a strict code of conduct. Strict discipline: no alcohol, no smoking, no drugs; and there was my little boy lying at the side of the road supposedly swigging back litres of wine! Explanations were given and there were no repercussions.

Like nearly everything else in our beautiful land, the para-gliding club had a sad ending. The airstrip the club used on the farm was the only other available runway for emergencies if a plane got into trouble at the Harare International airport. With the lawlessness that was prevalent in the early years of the new millennium, war-vets, more aptly, squatters decided that it was their right to take up residence along the airstrip and they even started growing their crops right up the middle of the runway. The mind boggles to think what would have been the outcome if there ever had been an emergency at Harare International and a plane had to be diverted to this airstrip. Kiwi Mark decided that he'd had enough of an uphill struggle trying to keep the club going. It was a constant battle sourcing fuel, it was a constant battle trying to keep prices affordable but realistic, it was a constant battle with the new 'residents' on the airstrip, so he gave up fighting and went back to his native New Zealand. It was sad that things had to come to this, but I was secretly relieved. I didn't worry so much about Mark and Heath having an accident while gliding, that's life and it could happen anytime, anywhere; but what did worry me sick was the thought of them landing in a restricted area, or amongst a group of rabid, so-called war-vets, the outcome might have been nasty.

On one of the club's trips to Nyanga, a young woman paraglider who was a visitor to Zim, had taken off from World's View and had had a good ride and a safe landing. She thought it a bit strange that none of the local residents came to greet her when she landed, the local kids were normally present in their droves, offering to carry the glider, asking questions, just being kids. She thought it unusual that there was absolutely no one about. She was completely alone. The recovery vehicle arrived at great speed. There were none of the usual niceties and discussions about the flight, the wind conditions, the thermals and all the other technical jargon. The recovery crew literally bundled her into the truck with her glider and drove away as fast as they could go. Unbeknown to this woman, she had landed in a restricted military area, hence the lack of local residents, and the outcome, had it not been the club's recovery truck that got to her first, could have been quite unpleasant.

SPUDS AND FOOD

I cannot remember the last time that we ever bought vegetables or fruit; we are so lucky that Mike is a keen gardener and has green fingers. Our first vegetable 'garden' was huge. It was almost an acre in size and was situated near our dam. Apart from the vegetables, we had established fruit trees: pecan nuts, litchis, custard apples, citrus and bananas. We also experimented with pineapples, but it was a losing battle with the moles, taking a bite out of each one. On the whole the pineapples didn't do well and were tart. Mike's also battled with growing melons of various types, but again, he was waging a losing war against the insects. We love watermelon but so often they'd be 'stung' and have holes all over them and they'd be vrot (rotten). The problem with the location of the vegetable garden was that it was a fair trek from the house. It was fine going to it as it was downhill, but coming back up was different especially if we were laden with produce. It was difficult to control and keep a finger on the pulse of things when it was such a distance from the house. We had to allow for the normal 'shrinkage', but there's shrinkage and there's *shrinkage!*

So we made a plan and in the early 1990s Mike decided to set up an orchard and vegetable garden much nearer the house and within the confines of our security fence, which encircles four acres of our land. We told our staff that they could have the original garden for their own use to help supplement their food supply. They have never availed themselves of this offer. The terraces that were built for the vegetables are overgrown and choked with weeds, the fruit trees have never been watered and the whole garden has been left to rack and ruin. It is a crying shame, but it wasn't our decision. The second garden is now well established, as is the orchard and we're completely self-sufficient. In 1992, Zimbabwe experienced a crippling drought and we were forced to reduce the size of our garden as a result, but we still had enough for our own consumption.

We've always been great vegetable eaters and I reckon there's nothing better than the taste of vegetables and fruit straight out of the garden. Our homegrown produce may not always look so good, but it's the taste that's important. When either of our sons went to stay with friends, we always sent along a basket of vegetables as a means of thanks. Whenever we went visiting, we took a basket of fresh vegetables. We used to provide produce for both sets of parents as well and one time this caused quite a laugh. Mike and Weighton had grown a local cucumber, not the nice smooth green-skinned ones that you buy in shops, these were prickly and no one in our family, apart from Mike, liked them. We took a pile in to my parents one day and said that they should pass them out amongst their friends and neighbours in the complex where they were living, we often did that with any excess vegetables we had. Most of the residents in the complex were elderly like my parents and were surviving on pensions. Surprisingly enough they enjoyed these cucumbers – it was not long after this that we were told that the blacks use these cucumbers as aphrodisiacs!

Weighton taking a rest

I always have a deepfreeze full of frozen seasonable vegetables and I do quite a bit of 'pickling' of cucumbers, onions, bell peppers and cauliflower. I also squeeze the citrus fruit and boil it up to make juice. Any excess of grapefruit, naartjes or oranges, is made into marmalade and the granadillas have the pulp removed and frozen in preparation for granadilla cake, one of Heath's favourites. A glut of tomatoes and onions are rendered down into relish that is so useful for all sorts of dishes, I make huge batches and keep it in jars in the freezer. A surplus of pumpkins becomes pumpkin soup and the pumpkin seeds are roasted with salt and chilli powder to make the most incredible snack full of potassium and magnesium. The chillies grow like weeds. I dry them out on plates for a few weeks, then put them in my blender and make my own chilli powder – it's potent stuff! It's a sure-fire way to clean out your sinuses. Mark's girlfriend, Vicki, showed me how to lightly fry spinach leaves, and these proved to be so popular as snacks with our guests, that I always made sure that I had a container full of them in the freezer, ready to produce at any time, and they're a great source of iron.

We had eagerly been waiting the maturation of our potato crop. Mike had checked it and said that it looked as if we would be able to lift the spuds soon. The day arrived. I was drooling at the thought of baked potato drenched in some outrageously decadent sauce for dinner. The gardener had just started lifting the potatoes and turned to Mike with a perplexed expression on his face. There were *no* potatoes! Someone had entered the vegetable garden some time earlier, dug up all the potatoes, and then painstakingly replaced all the stalks and leaves back in the holes to make it seem as if the spuds were still growing! It was thoroughly done. It was a work of art. We never did find out who stole the potatoes, but they must have spent hours putting the plants back, it was so realistic that it fooled both Mike and the gardener. There was no baked potato for dinner that night, or for many, many nights to come until the new crop was ready. Whoever took the spuds deserved them just for their brilliance if nothing else.

There are quite a few baboons in the area. They come and go with the seasons and cause havoc when they get into the garden. I have no objection to any living creature eating to keep alive, but I do object to the baboons coming en masse and being so wasteful. They love mangoes, but instead of taking one, eating it, finishing it and going onto the next one, they'll take a bite or two out of the fruit, throw it on the ground and start on another one. This is infuriating. We also like mangoes. A young friend of ours showed us how to take the flesh off the mango, add a dash of vodka, and mix it with crushed ice – add some ice cream - and voila, you have a decadent (and healthy?) dessert. In 2004, we had trouble with one lone male baboon coming to our vegetable garden, climbing the security fence and going on the rampage.

Baboon thief!

Not only was he helping himself to our fruit and vegetables, but he was quite aggressive and he'd frighten Taundi's two youngest children. Taundi's house overlooks the vegetable garden so the children were often in the vicinity. We'd know he was visiting when we heard the kids screaming as they high-tailed it back to their house. This was one cunning baboon! He started coming at ten o'clock when the gardeners went off for their morning tea, so Mike thought that he'd outwit the baboon, so he staggered teatime. Not to be outdone, our intrepid visitor started coming at lunchtime. Lunchtimes were then staggered. So it started coming at five o'clock.

There's a limit to how much you can stagger knock-off time. The gardeners do have to go home sometime and the baboon would just wait them out.

One blistering, hot day Mike and Heath decided that they were going to sort out the baboon once and for all. The balcony of the house looks down onto the terrace with the swimming pool, which is surrounded by a low stonewall, and this terrace in turn looks down onto the terrace where the orchard and vegetable garden are situated. My two men were crouched down behind the stonewall awaiting the arrival of the baboon. They must have been boiling in the searing heat. They were in the direct sunlight. They were there for the best part of an hour and I'm sure the onset of heat stroke and delirium must have been kicking in. I was sitting on the balcony with a nice, long, cool drink, reading my book watching these two twits in the sun and in a big, shady tree near the swimming pool terrace, sat the relaxed baboon. It was also watching the two macho, desperadoes with delighted amusement. I eventually called to Mike and Heath and told them what was happening. They felt like complete fools. I'm convinced the baboon winked and waved to me before he sauntered off, never to come back and bother us again. I imagine the rest of the troop had a good laugh when he told them how he'd outwitted the two Homo sapiens and given them heat stroke into the bargain.

ANIMAL FARM

Over the years our place has resembled the proverbial farmyard although we are not farmers and our property is not a farm, it's a smallholding, which in essence is basically a mini farm. Living on the top of a steep hill in an area with little or no water, isn't exactly conducive towards farming. It's funny, even our farming friends (well, the ones we used to have who lived in the area before they were evicted from their farms) refer to our place as 'the farm'. They'd phone up and say "Are you on the farm, can we come and visit?" Our place never has been and never will be, a farm. As much as it annoys me when people refer to our property as a 'farm', over the years I've got used to it and learnt to accept it – well, that was until the farm invasions started in 2000. Now I suffer from paranoia and when asked where we live, I say 'Christon Bank' and not Mazowe. Christon Bank is a residential area of smallholdings and plots, whereas Mazowe is a farming area. If we tell a white that we're living in Mazowe, they want to know how come we're still there and all the other whites have been evicted .... and you can just see it going through their mind, "What kind of bribe did you pay?"; if we tell a black where we live, I'm always afraid that if they're 'good' party supporters, they may come and 'relieve' us of our land!

I have tried to make it clear to family, friends and neighbours, that in our house, we don't use the 'f' word – no, not the rude one you're thinking about, I mean the 'f' as in 'farm'! That way I don't have to go round making excuses for where we live and feeling either guilty or afraid about the fact. So now that I've cleared that up and you know that *we don't live on a farm*, I'll continue with my 'farmyard' story. We have tried keeping chickens, ducks, sheep and goats, with varying degrees of success. It was after our donkeys were tragically killed, that we realized just how useful

183

they had been in keeping the grass short, which in turn, reduced the damage done by the annual bushfires. Mike was, and still is, most diligent about cutting firebreaks every year, but with the long, dry, winter months, the parched grass was just a fire waiting to happen. This prompted us to buy five head of cattle from a neighbour and thus our own supply of beef was assured as well as being instant lawnmowers. The cattle, or mombes, as they are known locally, were much easier to control than sheep or goats, which, because they were that much shorter, were always getting out of our property, just nipping under the fence. No matter how often Mike and Weighton would go round the fence replacing stolen standards, repairing holes where the wire had been stolen to make snares, it would just happen all over again. They were fighting a losing battle. They took to weighing down the strands of barbed wire by means of a large stone or rock tied onto the fence by wire, this was reasonably effective and there's not much attraction in stealing a stone.

The original mombes were indigenous cattle that had never been treated for ticks and other parasites, they'd just been left to their own devices, all they had to do was eat and provide nyama (meat). Shortly after we bought the mombes we noticed that they had problems with screwworms and Mike asked me to phone up and get and get the price of some 'muti' (medication) to sort it out. The man I spoke to on the phone was trying to give me the details of quantities needed, prices, and all the other relevant information. He then asked, "What is the size of your herd?" To which I replied, "Five." He said, "Yes, madam. But five what?" I seem to attract weird conversations.

Me, "*I have five*".

Him, "But is your herd five hundred or five thousand?"

Embarrassingly, I replied, "Five mombes only!" The hapless salesman then directed me to another company that sold the muti in considerably smaller quantities. He must have thought that he had the last of the big spenders on the other end of the line! Now we had not only a healthy, screwworm free, effective, living lawn mower for the bush grass, but also, a source of meat. I am grateful that it is always Mike who has to do the necessary with the mombes when we needed to replenish the freezer. There is no way that I could do it and I know that Mike does not enjoy it either. As he says, the animal has done us no wrong and it stands there looking at you with big, brown trusting eyes and then we put a bullet through its brain. The staff round up the beast to be slaughtered and get it into the sturdy stockade made out of branches. Mike then shoots the animal at point-blank range. The staff skin the mombe, decapitate it, cut off the hooves and tail, take out all the entrails and drain off the blood, all of which they kept. The skin alone fetches a tidy sum, which they share among themselves.

The carcass is cut up into four big chunks and hung overnight on wire from the rafters of the garage. We have a metal, roll-up door to the garage, similar to the roll-up doors that shops use for security. It's not everybody that has a cow hanging from the rafters of their garage. We have to make sure that the door is closed at all times while the mombe is hanging, otherwise the dogs, especially Marka, think they've died and gone to the big butchery in the sky! Next morning, we are up at the crack of dawn so that we can get the work of cutting and packaging the meat done before it gets too hot and the flies become too active. To package the meat, I also save every plastic bag of every shape and size that I can lay my hands on: old sugar bags, the bags the bread comes in, the bags that the mealie meal and dogs' biscuits come in, you name it, I make use of it.

I used to buy proper clear plastic bags, which certainly made life a whole lot easier. Then they became too expensive and the size that we needed wasn't always available, so we changed to using supermarket carrier bags. These did the job fine and we used these for years, until once again, the Zim situation reared its ugly head and the supermarkets started making customers pay for the carrier bags. In Africa there is very little that goes to waste. Apart from the usual uses of the bags, i.e. for carrying purposes, these bags are put to myriad of other uses. I've seen the most attractive bath mats made out of them, even hats - the bags are torn into strips and either knotted or crocheted together. Young boys make a serviceable football out of them by tightly rolling bag upon bag until the required size and then they're all kept in place by string, it's not quite up to the standard that David Beckham is used to, but it does the job.

As you probably know, AIDS and HIV are endemic in our land, and not too long ago there was an appeal through our email server for carrier bags for a local woman who runs a 'hospice'. The reason I've put this in inverted commas is that the woman concerned lives in a mud hut and out of the goodness of her heart cares for the AIDS sufferers and orphans in her village. She has no recompense to funds public or other, and has to rely on the generosity of the local villagers. The reason she needed the plastic bags was that she couldn't afford gloves to wear when dealing with the patients if they'd messed themselves, so she'd tie a bag around each wrist and try and carry out her work that way. She wasn't concerned about contracting the virus herself, her main concern was of not only passing on the infection to others, but if something did happen to her and she became ill, who would look after the sick and infirm?

I know, I know, I was talking about cutting up mombes – it's the association of ideas: meat, bags and that led me to think about the AIDS carer. Over the years, we have acquired from the Cold Storage Commission, Colcom (the association that deals with pork products), and cookery books, several charts showing the various cuts of meat. It would really make life so much easier if God would number the parts of the animal when he created them, then it would just be a case of 'painting by numbers', except we'd be 'cutting by numbers'. As it is, we'll look at the hunk of meat in front of us and Mike will state that it's 'number eleven' which is, for instance, steak. I'll look at the same piece and be insistent that it's number twelve, which is stew! We have certainly improved over the years and we seem to get it right most of the time now.

We have an old table, which is kept solely for cutting up mombes, and we have Taundi and Weighton helping us. These two members of our staff, Mike and I, now have it all down to a fine art. Mike and I decide how each piece is to be cut. The three men then cut it accordingly. This sounds easy, but we don't have a band saw, so they use hacksaws and a lethal-looking, sword-like blade with a handle made out of plastic putty that Mike made up just for this purpose. It's hard, laborious work. I package and label the meat. The dogs lie close by and are rewarded with bits of gristle and finally with a huge bone each, it's almost like a scene out of the Flintstones with Fred and Dino. It takes us a couple of hours or so to do all the work and when we are finished the dogs are so replete that they just lie there like bloated ticks. They can't even be enticed with any more titbits. The cats go wild for the liver and they even brave the dogs and come into the garage looking for more. There are piles of meat: one for us, one for the staff, one for the dogs and cats. Between Taundi and I, we mince the meat that is intended as 'mince' with an old hand-mincer similar to one that my grandmother used. The freezer works hard when we deposit all the meat in there, it doesn't switch off for about a week, sometimes longer, depending on the number and length of the power outages that we have.

Mike takes a couple of kilos of silverside to make biltong, which is the same as American jerky, and no matter how much he makes, it's never enough – especially if Mark and Heath are at home. He cuts the meat into strips, liberally sprinkles it with salt and pepper; sometimes he even uses chilli powder. He's devised a 'cage', which used to be a chinchilla cage from the days we kept these rodents. A slight diversion this time; we didn't want the chinchillas, I'm using the 'royal' we here, what I actually mean is that Mike didn't want the chinchillas but the cages were a bargain and he wanted the cages – who knows what for, so we landed up with about twenty-five chinchillas just so that we could get the 'bargain' of eighty cages! The chinchillas were cute looking, bad tempered rodents that tried to bite me every chance they could get. Fortunately for us they were quite elderly when we got them and didn't live that long. All for the cages which have sat up in our glory hole of a shed for the best part of thirty years or longer! At least one cage has been put to use, that of drying the biltong. Mike puts the wet biltong in the contraption, which is covered with gauze to prevent flies and other insects getting at the meat. The cage is then hung from the rafters of the roof that joins the kitchen to the garage. This is a perfect position for drying the meat as it acts like a wind tunnel and also remains dry in the rainy season. Unfortunately the meat usually shrinks to almost half its original size, which means less biltong. You can never have enough biltong. It was a way of life in this part of the world, but due to our hyperinflation, it's sadly become a luxury item now.

We're beginning to wonder if it's the air out our way that's affecting our mombes, or if we've just acquired a *most* unusual strain of cattle. Basically they're of the Heinz 57 variety, but they do tend to do the weirdest things. A month or so ago we had a visit from a rather irate neighbour. The old adage about the grass being greener seems to be taken as gospel by our mombes. No matter how much green grass we have, they make it their mission in life to break through the fence and go onto neighbouring property. Most of the land bordering us is in the hands of the so-called new farmers, and they do NOT take kindly to cattle, most especially, white-owned cattle, paying them an uninvited visit. Our irate neighbour was of the friendly variety and is a brother several times removed (yes, those kinds of relationships do exist in Africa) to our gardener. Seemingly our herd had negotiated the barbed wire fence, gone onto his land and had decided to add a bit of variety, or perhaps it was roughage, to their diet and nibbled on the washing hanging on the line next to his hut.

They devoured a couple of babies' nappies (hope I'm never that hungry), a pair of underpants and a shirt. This was a bit perplexing for us. We didn't know how to deal with clothes-eating cattle. Did this mean that something was lacking in their diet? If so, what was it? We're still trying to figure that out. In the interim, I had some towelling nappies left over from Mark and Heath's baby years, they make wonderful dusters, the nappies, I mean. We were able to replace the noshed clothes, and judging by the wide grin on irate neighbour's face, they were of a superior quality to those that he had lost. Problem was were we opening a can of worms? Would there suddenly be a spate of mombe-eaten washing? What a novel way of revamping an old wardrobe. Not so long after the first incident, our mombes decided to bulk up on a couple of towels and a washcloth. Again, replacing the items wasn't the dilemma. Were our cattle experiencing psychological problems? What was making them behave in this irrational way? Presumably it really, really is, genuinely, the mombes that are being so destructive? We haven't had any more funnies, so we're keeping our fingers crossed that the curse of the hungry mombes has come to an end.

Charger was a scapegoat, or more precisely, an escaped goat. He was being ferried to his fate on the roof of a long distance bus when he fell off. He was unharmed. The local people believed he was bewitched. I reckoned he was just plain evil! Adding to this belief was the piece of tambo or string that he had tied around his neck with a $10 note wedged under the string. We were completely ignorant of the significance of this. We thought that it was strange that none of our staff was prepared to handle the animal, but he was dirty and smelly. Admittedly he didn't get his name as a result of his docile nature, his name was a true reflection of his character. He was an exceptionally mean-spirited, cantankerous, evil-minded goat who loved attacking all and sundry. On more than one occasion I've been on my hands and knees cowering behind a tree, a rock, anything that would afford protection after that cantankerous idiot had sent me flying. Maybe if I'd been transported on the roof of a bus under the blazing African sky and had just fallen off, I wouldn't be the most serenely natured person either.

Our farming friend and neighbour Rob, explained that in local lore, if a person had some bad luck or other similar problems, if they put some money on the neck of a goat, the misfortunes would be transferred to whoever took the money. Rob further explained that the local people would now consider Charger to be 'possessed' and would not handle him in case they too suffered bad luck. He was possessed all right. Possessed of a foul temper! Rob said that if we ever wanted to get rid of Charger, he'd pay well for him as if the goat was put amongst his goats, the chances of poaching would be greatly reduced. We didn't have goats at the time, we had sheep and Charger was put in charge of them. Our staff watched with great trepidation as Mike removed the offending piece of tambo from around the goat's neck, I never did find out what happened to the ten dollars, it vanished mysteriously. When the staff saw that nothing untoward happened to Mike, they too were able to handle the animal.

I'd like to say that Charger became another of our beloved pets. He did not. He was too bloody-minded to be loved and his mean-streak was constantly in evidence. He seemed to go on forever; admittedly towards the end he was only a shadow of his former magnificent self. He was a smelly, tatty, scraggly old thing – but he went to his grave with his volatile personality still very much intact. To give him his due, he did take good care of the sheep. No living thing, human or animal, in its right mind would dare to take him on and so the sheep were able to live to a ripe old age as well. I can't in all honesty say that I was sorry when Charger went to meet his maker, but I do have a clear conscience in knowing that he had a good life with us, better than what he gave us.

MICE OR MEECES

Fortunately I like rats and mice. The time came when Mark decided that he wanted pet mice. Whatever Mark did, Heath did exactly the same. So two little boys wanted pet mice. We tried to talk them into keeping hamsters or guinea pigs, but the boys were adamant that they wanted mice. I hadn't realised just how difficult it would be to obtain mice in Zimbabwe. There has never been a surfeit of pet shops and those that were in existence, seemed to specialise more in aquarium fish and caged birds. I contacted every pet shop in the Harare area, to no avail. Someone suggested that I contact the veterinary department at the University of Zimbabwe as they breed mice for use by various other faculties, such as the faculty of Medicine.

I phoned the veterinary department and after the usual being put through from extension to extension, then being put on hold, I finally got through to a lady who was most helpful and said that she would keep the mice for me and that they would be the princely sum of fifty cents each. In those days, in 1993, Mark and Heath were getting around a dollar each a week for pocket money, so they were able to pay for their mice without having to save up. On Friday 17ᵗʰ September 1993 I went to the university armed with a Bata 'Tommy-Tacky' shoebox to collect the mice. In Zimbabwe nearly every child has at one time or another, worn Tommy-Tackies, they come in white, brown and black, and are also available in adult sizes – I even have a pair of white ones. Tackies (tennis shoes) are an institution in Zim.

I managed to find the Veterinary department without too much trouble, but it took a while to wend my way through the maze of buildings, long corridors and courtyards with paths leading off in every direction before I finally found the office I was looking for. The lady I had spoken to on the phone wasn't in her office, so I was directed to another office where a most attractive young woman sat behind the desk. She seemed to know my name and about my phone call but looked at me in consternation when I produced my little shoebox. She said, "I think there's been a misunderstanding here," and she lent down under her desk and pulled out a cage which contained an enormous cane rat! I could have saddled this thing up and ridden it back home. I looked at my tiny shoebox, then at the rat, and I thought, 'this isn't going to work'. The young woman assured me that cane rats make wonderful pets and she thought the boys would be delighted with it. The rat was so big it would have terrorized the cats and dogs, possibly even the boys. I declined the offer. So back through the various mazes until I found myself in another part of the veterinary department where the mice were housed. I chose two pairs. Okay, I can hear you all say, how could she have been *so dumb*! We can all be experts with hindsight. I did know that mice breed like rats, if you'll excuse the pun; and I did know that two pairs of mice would produce many, many generations of mice; but I just didn't think they could breed quite as fast as they did.

Another piece of advice for would-be mice-keepers, don't use a cardboard shoebox in which to transport the mice. Their cardboard-eating capabilities are nearly as amazing as their breeding ones. I did manage to get them home. Just. They'd almost eaten their way through the box as I drove through the gates. The boys had originally planned to keep the mice in an old budgie cage that we had, again, a word of advice, not a good idea. I didn't realise how mice have the incredible capability to elongate themselves into a long sausage-shape and squeeze through the seemingly impossible narrow bars of the cage. While Mike had to 'make a plan' to try and sort out another habitat for the mice, they had to spend their first night in their new abode, in the bath, after I first checked that they weren't able to climb up the sides. If you're intending keeping mice in your bath, remember first to wrap the chain for the plug up around the taps, mice are very adept at climbing chains, again I discovered this from experience.

Mike used to keep tropical fish and had quite an array of aquariums. One in particular was about four feet long and one foot wide, it was decided that this would make an ideal mouse house. Mike made a very nifty top to the tank with chicken mesh to enable the mice to have a constant source of fresh air and he made a big enough trapdoor to enable the boys to get to the mice and to also clean the tank. This arrangement worked well and the boys kept the mice in the garage. I was fascinated with the newly born babies, they were pink and curly and looked like shrimps. They kept coming fast and furious. It's amazing. When you want mice, they're none available, and when you want to get rid of them, no one wants them. The novelty of keeping mice wore off, and we were eventually able to get rid of them.

A phone call to the university and another trip later, I came home with Pinky and Perky, female white rats. I had learned my lesson by now. Short of immaculate conception, there would be no babies. Pinky and Perky were definitely better pets than the mice. They were kept in the same fish tank, but this time it was kept on the balcony so that it was more accessible to the boys. I could never tell the difference between the two rats, but Mark and Heath swore they could. None of our cats gave the rats a second glance, the only thing the rats had to fear, was an owl, which used to come periodically and sit on the balcony rail at night and stare at the rats in their cage. Each rat had its own 'bedroom' and there were walkways and tunnels all over the place for them. At first we used newspaper in the tank, but the rats were turning a funny greyish colour from the newsprint, so then we managed to source sawdust for them and they seemed much happier with that.

They loved chips (crisps) and also had a sweet tooth. I had to make sure that the boys knew how to feed them properly and that the rats got their quota of sunflower seeds, maize kernels, greens and Willard's Pronutro. Every Zimbabwean will know what Pronutro is. It's a household name. It's a breakfast cereal derived from soybeans and which comes in different flavours such as natural (my favourite), banana, honey and chocolate and I can't imagine living in a country that doesn't have it. Children, especially growing boys, will eat bowls of it for breakfast, lunch and dinner. Adults also eat it. It's great with hot or cold milk. It's wonderful for kittens and puppies before they can manage adult food. It's great for sick animals. It's the perfect meal to take when you're hiking through the Chimanimani Mountains of Zimbabwe, all you have to do is add powdered milk to it before you leave home and then mix it with pure mountain water and hey presto, you have an instant, substantial meal. I hope a representative of Willard's Foods is reading my personal endorsement of their product.

Pinky and Perky thrived. When Mark and Heath were at school, I'd often take the rats out of their cage and have them sitting on my shoulder, they were great company. The only design flaw I can find with a rat is its tail. The boys discovered that quite a few of our friends didn't like rats – ninety-nine point nine per cent of whom were women. I think my mother was the main one and Mark and Heath learnt at an early age, that if they dared to bring Pinky and Perky anywhere near granny, they could laugh off their inheritance. I didn't have the heart to tell the boys that there wasn't a whole lot there to inherit in the first place, but it did seem to keep them on their toes and the rats in their cage when the grandparents were visiting.

I can't remember whether it was Pinky or Perky who died first, whichever one it was, was buried in our pet cemetery up behind the house by the reservoir. The remaining rat didn't appear to pine for its companion, and lived for several more months until she too, died of natural causes, and she went to join the rest of the menagerie in the pet cemetery. By this stage the boys weren't so interested in keeping pets, as they had been when they were younger, which was a relief.

MAMA HUKU

Mama Huku was saved from a fate worse than death – which in fowl terms, means being eaten. Huku is the Shona word for chicken. We were spending the night at our house in Harare and had risen fairly early one morning. I'm not a morning person and it was confusing to hear 'chicken noises' shortly after dawn when I'm most definitely not at my best. I don't do mornings. I couldn't understand it. At first I thought it was Mike making silly sounds, although I couldn't fathom why anyone would like to sound like that before their first shot of caffeine had kicked in. I thought I'd better go through to the kitchen to check that Mike was all right. On my way through the entrance hall I was astounded to see a Peeping Tom in the form of a hen sitting on the windowsill staring in at me. She was rather a splendid-looking bird with feathers the colour of burgundy and gold, streaked with black stripes. This was one hen with an attitude problem. I don't suppose I could blame her as she most likely had recently escaped from being the main item on the menu. A lot of the animals that have come in to our lives seem to have had attitude problems. She could have been a whole lot worse I suppose. So we made a plan. Mike went into the garden and she permitted herself to be caught without too much trouble and to be put in a cardboard box in the garage until it was time for us to return to Mazowe later on in the day. We never did find out where she came from, so we took the view that possession is nine tenths of the law.

On her release from the box when we arrived back home, she, in no uncertain terms, made sure that the rest of our menagerie knew that she was at the top of the totem pole. The dogs were even a bit cowed by her stroppy attitude, but worse than that, was the look of complete and utter dejection on the face of our resident cockerel. He came from good stock. He was blue blood. He used to be a show Bantam and had regularly won prizes on the annual Harare Agricultural Show. It was a big comedown for him coming to live with us, but his original owners were finding it difficult to source and pay for, the feed for the birds, so we became the proud owners of the Bantam and his harem. The minute Mama Huku made the acquaintance of Family Bantam she decided to get the pecking order sorted out immediately and to show who rules the roost. She was all out for female emancipation.

She eventually mellowed and peace was restored in the chicken run. Our fowls are free-range during the day but tend to lay their eggs in the run, which is open throughout the day, so that they can come and go as they please. We excitedly waited for eggs from our chickens. No such luck. Every time we enquired, we were told by the staff that snakes had got the eggs, or the chickens weren't laying because of the change in the weather, or Mama Huku and Bantam weren't compatible. You name it, we got an excuse for it. Mike and I happened to be walking through the bush near Taundi's house one day and we chanced upon his huku and her splendid brood of chicks all resplendent in burgundy and black stripes. I don't lose my temper easily, but when I do, it's not very pleasant. We'd been taken for a monumental ride. On our arrival back at the house, I threw my toys out the cot and had a little tantrum. I demanded to know from our staff why marungu's (white people) hukus didn't have eggs and / or chicks, but theirs not only did, but were clones of Mama Huku!

Lo and behold, a few days later we received a couple of eggs. It was a start. Then a short while later we were the proud grandparents of two rather splendid chicks. I think Mama Huku was getting fed up with her eggs being stolen, so she has found herself a secret nesting location near the workshop and judging by her broody attitude, we'll be grandparents again, providing the snakes, dogs, humans et al, don't get the eggs before the chicks hatch. It's quite a sight at lunchtime when the dogs are being fed, not only do the two Dobermans and the German Shepherd eat out of their own dishes, but they share with the chickens and the pigeons! It must be galling for the dogs. We do give the birds food in separate containers at the same time as we feed the dogs to try and stop this train of events, but they much prefer to eat out of the dogs' bowls. The dogs have a huge water dish just outside the back door under the roof, but we have a problem with hawks killing the pigeons, so they and the chickens use the dogs' water dish as a semi-indoor swimming pool that the hawks can't reach. Problem is, when they're finished, the water is covered in a greasy film from the bird's feathers and we constantly have to change the water.

Waiting for breakfast

We have had many different kinds of tame birds over the years, but without a doubt, Mama Huku is the most destructive one we've ever had in the garden. I thought the dogs had been going wild digging up flower beds and destroying plants, but we discovered it was Mama Huku who became progressively worse when her chicks came along and she was showing them how to fend for themselves. Mama Huku isn't quite 'top drawer' but she's certainly a character in her own right though.

LAKE CHIVERO

Lake Chivero, or Lake McIlwaine as it was known before Independence in 1980, has always been a popular resort with Harare residents. It's only thirty kilometres away from Harare and boasts several boat clubs, angling clubs, picnic grounds and the National Parks have lodges and a game park on the shores. In its heyday, it was quite the place to go to and was always busy, in fact, packed, on public holidays. Times have changed; the availability of fuel is always an important criterion, and with our hard earned money being eroded by rampant inflation, which at the time of writing this book is now at the 5000 per cent mark, there is precious little money left to spend on entrance fees to National Parks, or to the boat clubs and other resorts. It was a popular place to go for a drive at the weekend and there were several 'Ma and Pa' type places that served light lunches and cream teas, or one could go to the Hunyani Hills Hotel and order a meal that ranged from hamburgers to roasts. Church and Women's groups used to book rooms for their members at the hotel for weekend retreats and conferences. Those days are a memory only. The tearooms closed many years ago. The hotel may still be operational, but I wonder if it gets enough patrons to warrant keeping it open.

Lake Chivero

On Saturday 14th August 1999, our family and my parents went to the National Park lodges at Chivero and stayed in Fish Eagle Cottage. This cottage had the prime position on top of a hill with a magnificent view overlooking the lake. The surrounds consisted of indigenous plants, massive boulders and balancing rocks that we climbed up to explore and which were brimming with squirrels and dassies (rock rabbits), which were quite tame and very entertaining. The lodge had recently been tastefully refurbished and we were delighted with it. The lounge, dining room and kitchen were to the right of the building, and to the left, in a long row were three bedrooms and the toilet and bathroom. All these rooms led on to an open veranda, which ran along the front of the house. That evening, after dinner, Mike had had a bath and as it was such a lovely evening, he decided to sit outside in the garden and listen to the night sounds. He had been sitting quite still for the best part of half an hour when he noticed a shadow moving near the lounge bay window. At first he thought that it might be either Mark or Heath playing a trick and trying to sneak up on him, so he said nothing and sat stock-still. Then as the shadow stealthily moved towards the veranda and some light fell upon it, Mike realized that it wasn't either of the boys, but a young African man.

One of the lodges at Lake Chivero

Mike suddenly said, "Can I help you?" The young man was obviously startled, but recovered enough to blurt out that he was the night watchman and was there to guard us! Try pulling the wool over the other one! He was no more a night watchman than Mike was Elvis Presley. Heath had heard the exchange of conversation and came out to see who is father was talking to. This was too much for our so-called night watchman who took off like a thoroughbred. Mike and Heath gave chase, but the man was gone, just melted into the night, hopefully never to be seen again. Whenever we stay at a National Parks lodge, or in any guest cottage, I always enjoy reading the comments in the Visitors' book. Earlier in the day I had been reading out to the rest of the family different comments from previous occupants who had been bothered by thieves and were warning future residents to be on their guard. I hadn't wanted to upset anyone, but I'd been feeling uneasy the whole afternoon.

Mike and I tried to play the situation down so as not to frighten the boys or my parents, and a short while later, Heath and I were sitting at the dining room table playing a game of cards. My mother was having a bath, so we'd left the lounge door open as it gave a full view from where the two of us were sitting of the veranda, the bedrooms and the bathroom. We could make sure that Mum would be all right. It was Heath's move with the cards and he hadn't put one down, I looked up at him to see what was holding him up. The look of sheer, speechless terror on his little face made my heart lurch. I turned and looked out the door to see what he was looking at, to see two men in mufti and each of them carrying AK rifles. It was my turn to be speechless and terrified. I managed to get a strangled 'Mike!' out of my mouth and he dashed to the door. It turned out that these were the 'good guys'. They were the genuine night watchmen employed by National Parks and they'd heard the rumpus and had come to see if we needed assistance. Probably they weren't in uniform due to the financial constraints of the Department of National Parks, we never did find out the reason. They informed us that robbery was rife in the lodges as there was a massive squatter camp just on the other side of the game fence, and these people were making life unpleasant for visitors to the lodges and the Parks' employees as well.

That night I insisted that everyone sleep with bedroom doors locked and that if anyone needed the loo in the middle of the night, they had to call for either Mike or me to accompany them. I made a plan and I also took the bath mat, toilet seat cover and cistern cover and all the other furnishings that weren't nailed down into our room for safekeeping, because if these things went missing, we'd have to pay to have them replaced. I was grateful that we were only spending the one night there, our nocturnal visitor had put a bit of a damper on what was supposed to be a relaxing get-away. Next morning we were up at the crack of dawn and went on a game drive. No matter how long I live in Africa, it is still always a thrill to see a rhino, giraffe, wildebeest, duiker, ostrich and other animals in their natural setting and it makes dragging myself out of bed worthwhile.

Rhino in Lake Chivero national park

Kudu at Lake Chivero

We'd just finished our huge brunch, when the Park's warden came to see us. He was making a report on the incident the previous evening and wanted to make sure that we hadn't been harmed in any way. It must have been a mammoth headache for him trying to deal with the desperate squatters. I didn't envy him at all. Two weeks after we had been at Chivero, farming neighbours of ours went there for the weekend and by coincidence, were staying in Fish Eagle lodge as well. They arrived at lunchtime on the Saturday and decided not to unpack their small pick-up truck with all their provisions carefully locked away in it. They thought it would be nice to first have a quick siesta and then get down to the unpacking later. They were sleeping in the same room that Mike and I had been in and Nan put the truck keys in her handbag, which she placed next to her bed. A short time later, they awoke to find that not only had the handbag 'walked', but so had the truck and everything in it! We got off lightly in comparison.

Sunset, Lake Chivero

Bushmen paintings, Lake Chivero

MURDER MOST FOUL

Our neighbours had a maid who came to an unpleasant end. She was brutally murdered. The neighbours were away on holiday and had left their maid in charge of the house and had asked that if there were any problems, the maid or the gardener could come and call on us for help. It was during the school holidays, so both our sons, who were young teenagers at the time, were at home with me and just as Mike came home from work, the neighbour's gardener, Moses, arrived at the back door with a long rambling tale about the maid being drunk and running amok in the house. Mike would have preferred to sit down with a cup of tea and relax. Instead, he changed out of his suit into shorts and deciding that he could do with the exercise, chose to walk down the hill to see what the fuss was all about. Mark and Heath went with him for the walk. I guess holiday boredom was getting to them.

Mike said that he's never seen the two boys so speechless and pale before! The maid was not drunk. The maid was dead. She was lying semi-naked, face down in the dining room in a pool of blood and her throat had been cut. It was like the scene out of some voodoo movie. There were little mounds of burnt ashes and artefacts around her, not arranged haphazardly; instead they seemed to be in some weird sort of order. The floor and walls were covered in her blood. The blood had flowed down the steps into the lounge and saturated the carpet and there was blood in the entrance hall leading off the dining room. It was a slaughterhouse. It resembled a ritualistic killing. It was horrific. Mike went into the entrance hall to use the phone to call the police, but decided against it, as there was blood all over the floor and around the telephone stand.

He locked the neighbours' house and with the boys ran back up the hill to our house and I phoned the Mazowe police. At first I couldn't take-in what

Mike was telling me. I kept asking him if I should call for an ambulance (in those days we still had the luxury of municipal ambulances that were reasonably road-worthy and did have the fuel to enable them to go on call-outs). It took a while for it to sink in that the maid was past help. The boys decided to stay at home with me, they were both very subdued. Mike returned to the neighbour's house to await the arrival of the police. All the evidence seemed to point towards the gardener who had first contacted us. He said that he had seen the maid making a rumpus in the house and as there are French doors in the dining room leading outside, it would have been easy for the gardener to look through and see what the maid was doing, or what someone was doing to her and he would certainly have seen her lying dead on the floor. He never wavered from his story and was adamant that she was drunk and making a noise when he last saw her. The weapon that had been used to slit her throat was never found.

Mike was with the police for quite a time while they were carrying out their investigations. The following day once the police had finished with their investigations and removed the body, some other neighbours came to help us to clean up the house and remove all the grizzly details. It was fortunate that the floor in the dining room was quarry tile, so that was easy to clean, as was the entrance hall. The walls and the lounge carpet were a different story and took a bit more cleaning. What was also amazing was that there didn't seem to be signs of a struggle. The dining room furniture was neat and tidy, there were crystal glasses on the sideboard, none of these had been knocked over or broken.

There were several phone calls from the police in the ensuing days clarifying certain points, then the C.I.D in Bindura phoned and told Mike that he had to come and make a statement. Bindura is a town about sixty kilometres north of our house and as I keep harping on throughout this book, fuel is a very scarce, very expensive commodity! Mike argued with the detective about driving all that way, but he was told in no uncertain terms, that he would find the fuel and would present himself to the Bindura police ASAP! I can really understand why people don't want to get 'involved' any more. If your life's not in danger, then your bank account is! While Mike had been making his statement he mentioned that he'd come home, changed out of his suit and walked with Mark and Heath down to the neighbours. The C.I.D pricked up their ears. Why did he drive up to our house, change clothes and then walk down to the neighbours? Did that mean that he stopped off at their house first, murdered the maid, had blood on his clothes and therefore needed to change them? Mike said that it was quite tense in the interview room and for a while it looked as if he was the prime suspect. The detectives were going round and round in circles. As there didn't seem to be any motive and also (thank goodness for small mercies!) Mark and Heath were also witnesses, Mike was finally believed. It just goes to prove that you can be in the wrong place at the wrong time and everything can go pear shaped *very* easily.

No arrests have ever been made. My money was on the gardener, but obviously the police couldn't get anything to convict him on, so he was never arrested. There was no forced entry to the house, nothing appeared to have been taken and it was most unlikely that the maid slit her own throat. Mark and Heath never mentioned the incident again. I think that seeing a dead body made quite an impact on them. The case has never been solved.

2003 AND THE DANGEROUS MAIL

I have stated in the introduction to this book that I am not going to discuss politics per se; but the problem with that is that so much of the political upheavals in Zimbabwe are such an integral part of our lives, that we can't disassociate them. There have been and I'm sure, will continue to be, many turbulent years in Zimbabwe's history. The incident, which I am about to describe, took place in 2003, which was one of the many tumultuous years of the new millennium. There was a chronic shortage of fuel for starters. It was in this year that we as a family started spending nights in Harare instead of going back home to Mazowe every day in order to try and save on fuel. We were (and still are) fortunate that we have a house in Harare in the suburb of Borrowdale that over the years has served as offices and a pied-a-terre in town for us. I have mentioned in a previous chapter about the frustrations of fuel queues. We would often get into a 'hope' queue at five or six in the morning, even at this time of the day, we wouldn't be anywhere near the front, and I'm talking of queues that were kilometres long! Sitting in a queue for six or more hours is the not most productive way to spend your time.

There were also shortages of basic commodities such as milk. It was virtually impossible to walk into a supermarket and find milk. On the rare occasions when the shops did have milk to sell, it was rationed to the public. I used to be infuriated by this. We lived twenty-five kilometres from the nearest shop and we didn't go into Harare everyday, people who lived near the shops were in a position to buy milk when it was available. In March of 2003 there was a postal strike, and later on in the month on the eighteenth, there was a mass 'stay-away' organised by the Zimbabwe

Congress of Trade Unions, (ZCTU). The stay-away had been coordinated to protest the high unemployment and the high cost of living. It's just as well that no one then knew how much worse living conditions would become in Zimbabwe.

The schools were shut on Wednesday 19th March as a result of the stay-away, which if nothing else, gave us an extra free day at home. Going through my diary for March of 2003, it seems like an endless list of: looking for milk; finding milk from a 'source' who had a 'contact' on a dairy farm, and having to go to this person's house on specific days to collect the milk, and of spending endless hours in fuel queues. That's all we Zimbabweans seem to do, is spend our lives in queues for one thing or another. Another commodity that was in critically short supply was mealie meal, which is the flour made from ground maize kernels. This is the staple food of the masses.

In the days of virtual sanity before the farm invasions, farmers grew the maize and sold it to the government controlled Grain Marketing Board, GMB. After the land invasions, not a whole lot of maize was grown, and of that which was grown, farmers (whether they be the true owner of the farm, or the 'new' farmer) quite often found that it was far more lucrative to sell their crop to private millers than to the GMB. As we lived in a rural area, it was sometimes possible for our staff to obtain mealie meal from the GMB. It was not as simple as that statement makes it out to be – this, after all, is Zimbabwe. We had to write a letter to the GMB giving the names and identification details of all our employees, their spouses and children. This letter was hand delivered to our nearest depot of the GMB in Concession, which was about thirty kilometres from our house, which meant that more very precious, virtually unobtainable fuel was wasted. Also to be taken into account was the complete waste of man-hours involved.

The letter was then stamped. Zimbabwean bureaucracy love rubber stamps. Zimbabwe could not survive without the rubber stamp. The tattiest, old, dilapidated piece of paper will be accepted for all sorts of business dealings as authentic, provided it is endorsed by a rubber stamp, even if sometimes the lettering on the stamp is illegible. The GMB letter also stipulated the day and time that we had to make the return journey to Concession to collect the bags of mealie meal. More fuel and man-hours wasted. At the beginning of 2003 we still had a landline telephone in our house that worked. I say 'worked', rather tongue-in-cheek. We still had the privilege (ooh the sarcasm!) of using a party-line telephone. At one stage there were fifteen households on our party line. You do the maths, maybe on average six people in a household (remember that a lot of Zimbabweans tend to have large families) that would come to ninety people all trying to use the one telephone line.

That also supposes that the telephone line was operable, which a good twenty fiver percent of the time, it wasn't. You would also have to factor in inclement weather; the slightest whiff of rain or a storm, the phone would go on the blink. A strong wind bringing a branch down over the lines, the phone would go on the blink. A desperate thief stealing the phone cable for the copper wire it contains, the phone would go on the blink. An antiquated system that came out on the Ark with Noah and was in desperate need of upgrading would go on the blink for the slightest little hiccup. It was technically illegal to try and do emails on a party line, actually, it was meant to be almost impossible, but if you knew the 'special' plug that was required for the wall socket, and the 'special' code that had to be dialled, it was meant to work. I don't know of anyone who had success on our line doing emails. What they did manage to do was to jam up the line for the rest of us.

Right, you now have a brief history (a very brief one) of the telephone system in rural areas – oh, I know what I forgot to mention, was that we all had our own individual ring, for example, our personal ring was a short and a long ring; another household might have one short, three long, and so on. If anyone received a call in the middle of the night, it disturbed all of us. We couldn't even leave the phone off the hook, as it would interfere with the rest of the line. If someone else was on the phone, we could hear their entire conversation, which meant that they could also hear ours! Sometimes, even when the phone was back on its cradle we could hear the conversations of others, it was quite spooky. Our party line died a quiet death in September 2005, and is still not working!

Right, back to the GMB saga. We would phone, if and when the phone wasn't busy, and if and when it was working. The number of times that we would phone and be assured that our order was ready and waiting, only to find once we had trekked all the way out to Concession, that either they'd never heard of us, or there wasn't any maize, or we'd have to wait sometimes for hours for our order to be made up. I have never worked out if our treatment by the GMB staff was all part of a power game or just sheer incompetence. I don't know how we would have transported the maize if we didn't have a truck as sometimes we were coming back with half a ton so that we had sufficient for all the staff and extended families. I don't know how the families who lived on our property and roundabout us (we did 'pad' our list of employees to include friends and relatives in close proximity to us) would have survived had we not been there to help them. They would have had to make a plan as the vast majority of them live in huts with no running water, no electricity, no phone and no transport.

Sugar was also conspicuous by its absence on the shelves of the shops. Sugar always seems to be in short supply. If you didn't have a black market 'source', then you didn't have sugar. On Wednesday the 9th of April 2003, my emotions were roller coasting. I had sat in a fuel queue from seven to eleven in the morning. As I had managed to get fuel and the pump hadn't run dry by the time I reached it, I was on a high. I then went to my milk 'contact' to be informed that she didn't have any milk and wouldn't have any for another couple of weeks. I was on a low. I had just got back to our house in Harare and was full of doom and gloom when Mike met me at the gate, we were chatting when a young black man walked down the road past us carrying a twenty-five kilogram bag of Sun Sweet sugar, which is the light brown, unrefined sugar.

Mike greeted the man, asked him if he was interested in selling the sugar and making a quick buck and after a few negotiations, we were the proud owners of a huge bag of sugar. I don't know where the man got the sugar. I don't care if it fell off the back of a lorry. All I knew was that we now had sugar. I use a fair amount of sugar in my cooking and preserving. I don't do nearly as much baking as I used to as flour is quite often in short supply too. Then if I did have sugar and flour, more than likely there wouldn't be any cooking oil or margarine, or eggs would be scarce, or we would have a power cut and no electricity.

The ZCTU organised another stay away for Wednesday and Thursday the 23rd and 24th of April 2003; so again, businesses and shops were closed in protest to the government's policies. We were extremely lucky to have friends who access to a houseboat on Kariba, that's another story in itself.

In this year of shortages, trying to cater for the trip was a nightmare. It was impossible to walk into a shop and buy the provisions we required. Mike and I had been tasked with buying the soft drinks for the trip. Winning first prize in the lottery might have been an easier undertaking. At the beginning of June on Monday the 2nd, the ZCTU arranged yet another mass stay away which was to last for the whole week until Friday the 6th. An old family friend, Uncle Bill, had died and his funeral had been arranged for the 2nd June. As a child I had a lot of 'aunties and uncles' in Zim, they weren't real family, but as my parents and so many of their peers were six thousand miles away from home and therefore, quite often away from family, we all seemed to acquire a whole extended non-family family.

Mike and I attended Uncle Bill's funeral at the Highlands Presbyterian Church on the Enterprise road in Harare in the morning, and the family and close friends had all been invited back to the house for the wake after the funeral. As Uncle Bill had lived in Mount Pleasant and our post box was at the Mount Pleasant post office, Mike suggested we make a plan and collect our mail en route to the wake. Every now and again, I get 'feelings'. Nothing like being clairvoyant, more like women's intuition. The boys and Mike tend to scoff at my 'feelings', but more often than not, something comes of them, it's the Celt in me. I said to Mike that I didn't feel happy about going to get the mail and we should just leave it. Mike said that it made sense to collect it when we were in the area, as it would save precious fuel, especially as we didn't know when we'd be back in town with the stay-away.

Mount Pleasant Post Office

The Mount Pleasant post office, the library and a community hall are all built around a large parking area. As we approached the car park, we saw hundreds of people, mainly young black men, armed with broken branches and other debris which was scattered all over the place. I again said to Mike that I did *not* want to go into the car park. I had one of my 'feelings'. Again Mike disregarded my pleas and we went in. Our car was the only vehicle there amongst the seething mass of humanity. As soon as Mike got out of the car he was accosted by some of the men. He could do nothing right in their eyes. They criticised him for not supporting the stay away as he was dressed in a suit and they thought that he had been to work. They spoke to him in Shona and criticised him when he spoke in English. If he answered them, they criticised him for talking back to them, if he remained silent, they accused him of ignoring them. Nothing would please them.

I was sitting in the car and I was panicking. The men circling the car brandishing their branches appeared menacing. I felt completely powerless. Mike had to run back to the car as the men around him were beginning to push and shove him and some of them were carrying hefty branches. I was desperately praying. If anything happened to Mike, there was nothing I could have done to help him and nobody that I could have called on for help. Mike made it back to the car before his pursuers caught up with him, the car started first time, and although the mob tried to prevent us from driving out, we were able to leave the car park without incident. I was shaking violently. I screamed at Mike that I would never ever allow him to put us in such a dangerous situation ever again. I can't even begin to describe the utter fear and helplessness I experienced. The irony was that there wasn't any mail in our post box after all that.

We arrived at the wake and we were both fairly shaken. Mike apologised to me and agreed that he should have gone by my gut instinct and just driven past. We later found out that had we been an hour earlier at the post office, the situation would have been even worse. The riot police and the university students had clashed in the car park. The police had used water cannons and tear gas and the students had tried to retaliate with branches. We had encountered the tail end of a mob of infuriated students who wanted to vent their anger on whoever was available at the time. We happened to be at the wrong place at the wrong time.

OLD KEN

Old Ken was born old. Ok, maybe that's not being fair and maybe we never really got to know him. As far as we were concerned Ken was a cantankerous old man. I suppose he wasn't really. We never got close to him and he was one of the 'old school' and we tended to find him a bit intimidating. I admit I was a little bit scared of Ken. I'm sure if we'd taken the time to get to know him better we would have found a different side to him, but as it was, that side of him remained an enigma to us. Ken was a neighbour of ours who had come to 'Happy Valley' as some were wont to call the Mazowe valley, many years before Mike and I ever did. He was ex British Army, very proper, very correct. He had a strong opinion on most matters and I could imagine him sitting writing vociferous letters putting the world to right, to the editor of a newspaper. We both liked his wife Helen, and in the early years of our marriage, I would occasionally go down to their house for coffee, or Helen would come to our house. They had no children and their house definitely wasn't geared for babies. Neither of them was fond of young children, so when our family came along, our socializing with them came to a virtual standstill.

Ken wasn't shy about phoning up and asking to borrow tools and equipment. Mike has always been a bit chary of lending and borrowing. Apart from these infrequent occasions we didn't see much of the couple. Helen was seriously ill for many years and had been confined to a wheelchair for quite a while. Life must have been lonely for Ken once Helen died. They had been used to doing a lot of entertaining and with Helen's illness their social life must have taken a severe knock. Fewer and fewer people were prepared to drive out of town using up their fuel. The standard of driving and the conditions of the roads had deteriorated so badly that some people weren't prepared to drive at night, especially older people. Ken's good friend and long time immediate neighbour was widowed and a couple of years later, left the farm and moved into an old age home in Mvurwi a good distance away. Then the land-grab of the early years of the new millennium hastened away many remaining whites from the area. Our immediate neighbours, Alan and Hilary made a point of visiting Ken every Friday night, so that he not only had some social contact, but they could check up on his welfare as well. One of his employees, Daniel, who had been with him for years acted as his chauffeur when Ken was no longer able to drive, so he wasn't completely cut off from friends and neighbours – it's just that there weren't that many left!

On the evening of Friday 16th April 2004 Ken went to bed and died in his sleep. Daniel found him on Saturday morning and raised the alarm. Well, he raised whatever alarm he could. As was the norm, none of the landline phones in the area were working. Alan who was one of the executors of the estate was on holiday in Cape Town. To compound matters, the 18th of April is Zimbabwe's Independence Day and therefore, it was a holiday weekend. Ken's driver had driven into Harare and informed one of Ken's acquaintances about the death. They in turn contacted Alan and Hilary in Cape Town, who in turn contacted Mike and me. This all had to be done by cell phones. Zimbabwe's mobile phone networks leave *much* to be desired at the best of times and the situation wasn't made any easier by the position of Ken's house which was in a valley and the signal was intermittent.

It was eight o'clock at night by the time we'd received the call about Ken. We went straight to his house. Saturday night and a public holiday to boot didn't do much for the standard of driving at night on Zimbabwean roads with vehicles with no lights or reflectors, cattle wandering on the roads, drunken pedestrians and cyclists. These would have been bad enough on their own, but add to the melee the fact that there was a shebeen that was doing a roaring trade virtually opposite the turnoff to Ken's house and there had been a terrible accident involving several vehicles, meant it was complete and utter chaos. We safely manoeuvred our way to Ken's gate, to find it locked with a chain and padlock.

Ken's smallholding was on the western edge of a farm completely surrounded by bush.   He was isolated. The nearest neighbours were also on a smallholding surrounded by a security fence, as we all were. We were out in the bush. It was evening in an area that had seen some extensive nastiness with the farm invasions by War Veterans. Memories were still fresh. There were no authorities one could call upon for help. Not the most comforting thought especially when you are a member of an ethnic minority. We sat at the gate and hooted and hooted. We could see lights on at the house, after about ten minutes an exceptionally drunk domestic worker came to the gate. Mike explained that we had come to see what we could do to help. The worker said that he would go and find the key for the gate. He disappeared and we didn't see him again that evening. There was nothing for it, Mike had to make a plan, he climbed over the gate, which was topped with some ancient barbed wire, and he made his way to the house.

He was probably only away fifteen minutes finding someone sober enough to provide the key for the gate, but it seemed like an eternity to me. Sitting in a car in the pitch black of night in the African bush, with the cacophony of drunken beings vying with beating African tom-toms, can do wonders to a fertile imagination. I was not happy. The relief in seeing Mike returning to open the gate just flooded through me. Somewhere along the way Daniel had collected an elderly lady friend of Ken's, who had come back to the house and was prepared to stay there guarding the house contents and to await the imminent return of Alan and Hilary from South Africa. I can't remember the woman's name, but we felt sorry for her. She was in a house in which her friend had died. She was surrounded by three members of staff who had drunk to console themselves. They'd been with Ken for the best part of thirty years, but they were now past being coherent. The only means of communication that this woman had was Ken's cell phone, which had died as the battery needed recharging and no one knew the pin code. Add to this the racket coming from the shebeen, it was no wonder that the poor woman was a nervous wreck. We did what we could for her. I offered to spend the night with her, but (thankfully!) she declined saying that she would lock herself in the house and the drunken staff outside and she wouldn't open the door to anyone.

The funeral undertakers had come earlier to remove the body. That was another saga altogether. They couldn't remove the body without a death certificate. No one could locate a doctor who was prepared to travel out to Mazowe on a Saturday night of a holiday weekend. The police were worse than useless, it was the same old, same old "We haven't got any fuel to come out." Hilary managed to solve the dilemma from South Africa. She contacted a gynaecologist in Harare who was prepared to sign the death certificate, sight unseen of the deceased, who just happened to be a male, until he could be transported to Harare where the paperwork would be done properly. Don't know that Ken would have approved of these methods, – at least the gynae didn't give him a check-up! Only in Africa.

Hilary had asked us to try and contact Ken's nephew, the heir, who was somewhere either in Europe or the United States, as she didn't have his contact details with her in Cape Town. It is almost impossible to describe the mechanisms of the antiquated telephone system in a third world country. It's not a case of picking up a receiver, dialling a number and making contact. After about an hour, Mike and I decided that life was too short and we gave up. The nephew was contacted eventually, but not by us in Mazowe. Hilary had also asked us to organise a security guard for the property as Ken had some extremely valuable silverware and a several pieces of very good furniture. Ten o'clock on a Saturday night is not the best time to try and secure the services of a security guard. Trying to secure the services of a guard in a rural farming area that was still reeling from the aftershocks of the farm invasions was also not easy. Trying to secure the services of a guard, who had to travel about thirty kilometres out of Harare at night on a public holiday in a country where the public transport was either erratic, or nonexistent, was well nigh impossible.

Many of the security guard companies had closed down as a direct result of the farm invasions, there was nothing left for them to guard. Lots of farmers had used the services of these companies to guard their crops, workshops and buildings and as the farmers had been displaced, there was no longer any work for these guards to carry out. Talk about letting your fingers doing the walking. I was getting cramp in my index finger from dialling, but did eventually find a company which was prepared to let us hire a guard, but he couldn't start work until the following day, Sunday. There was nothing we could do about it, we just had to hope and pray that the vultures would stay away from Ken's house and the old lady staying in it, until the guard arrived. Early on Sunday morning we went down to Ken's house to check up on things and to inform the woman and the staff (who had by now recovered apart from severe hangovers) that a guard would be arriving later on. Even that didn't go simply. After organizing things to the best of our ability, we went into Harare for a farewell braai (barbeque) for old family friends who were emigrating to the United Kingdom. While we were there Mike received three or four phone calls from the guard and his company saying that they wanted to 're-negotiate' the price! Mike was not amused, but he eventually got it sorted out. Alan and Hilary subsequently arrived back from South Africa, so it was no longer our problem.

Ken's wife Helen had been buried in the cemetery in the little church in Glendale, which is a further twenty or so kilometres past where we live. That's where Ken wanted to be laid to rest, next to his wife. Ken's nephew had arrived from Europe, so the funeral was arranged for Friday 23rd April 2004. Arranging a funeral in this country is not that straightforward either. If one decides on cremation, the body could be waiting for weeks until gas becomes available for the crematorium. I jest not. Christians have had to resort to becoming honorary Hindus in order to use funeral pyres to cremate the deceased when there was no gas. Even burial in a grave is not straight forward either as Ken's mourners were to discover. The so-called, self-styled War Vets had 'taken' over the church and its grounds in Glendale, saying that it now belonged to them. There was a group of about fifty or so of them. They also decided that they were not prepared to let any more 'marungus' (whites) be buried in their 'hallowed' ground.

You can imagine what was running through the nephew's mind! He was a high-powered businessman from Europe and here he was being dictated to by an unreasonable rabid mob. Some of the older mourners were ex farmers who had had unpleasant experiences of their own with War Vets and were understandably nervous. The 'townies' who hadn't had first-hand experience with War Vets, were nervous of all that they'd heard, read about and seen happening in the farming areas. They too, were understandably not happy with the situation. It took a while, during which time some of the mourners decided that they would say farewell to Ken in their own way and in their own time and own place, so they left. Hilary made a plan and managed to negotiate with the War Vets to allow Ken's coffin to be placed in the grave. She bargained with them and they finally agreed on a price of Z$50 000. For that amount they also threw in a couple of hymns and two pall bearers to replace the mourners who had left. The nephew just watched the proceedings and wondered when he'd stepped through the Looking Glass into the Mad Hatter's Tea Party!

This is Africa. Placing a coffin in the ground is one thing. Being allowed to cover it incurs extra costs and negotiations. With a pandemic such as AIDS and HIV in Zimbabwe, coffins, even those that have had one previous careful owner, are greatly sought after, as are the clothes and personal affects that the deceased has been buried with. To get around this little glitch, it is necessary to hire the services of a guard to watch over the coffin for a period of about six weeks, depending on the season of the year and the heat, to make sure that the body is fast on its way to decomposition and therefore fairly yucky and not so attractive to would-be coffin and clothing thieves. This all of course, incurs added negotiations and expenses. Once all these little hiccups have been attended to, through negotiation and bargaining, it is then, hopefully, time for the deceased to rest in peace. Life in Africa is interesting. Once Ken was safely in the ground next to his beloved wife, the few surviving mourners went back to his house and gave him a send off that I'm sure he would have been proud of.

There was a little postscript to all of this. When the farm invasions had first started, Daniel, Ken's employee, had asked Ken for his 'own' piece of land, that is, a piece of Ken's land! He had seen people all around him getting land for free, so why shouldn't he climb on the bandwagon. To which, Ken answered, 'Over my dead body!' Several months after Ken died, Daniel died. Daniel was much of an age as Ken, so it was more than likely old age that got him in the end. Our neighbour Alan had quite a performance obtaining a coffin for Daniel. There were just none to be had. He was eventually offered a second hand one from a dealer in Bindura, a town to the north of Mazowe. It doesn't do to dwell on these things. It was to be hoped Daniel wouldn't be too concerned about the condition of his casket. A coffin was eventually found. Daniel was placed in it. The next problem was where to bury Daniel. You can't dig a hole in the back garden and drop a body into it. Daniel had been living in the area most of his adult life and therefore wanted to be buried there. The War Vets, or 'new' farmers in the area weren't exactly forthcoming in giving their permission to bury Daniel on 'their' farms. A solution had to be found. A solution was found. A plan was made. Ken's estate was still being sorted out and as Alan was one of the executors, he sought permission from the heir, the nephew, to have Daniel buried in Ken's rose garden. So over Ken's dead body, did Daniel get 'his' piece of ground. May he rest in peace.

LET THEM EAT CAKE

Bread is taken for granted in so many parts of the world. It's not considered a luxury. Zimbabwe used to be known as the breadbasket of Africa we had so much going for us, but thanks to our land-grab, farm-invasions, whatever you want to call them, the Zimbabwe of the first part of the new millennium is more like the basket case of Africa. We go through shortages of the most basic commodities like cooking oil, wheat, milk, eggs, sugar and yet the supermarket shelves are bulging with imported biscuits, cereals, wines, whisky and things that the ordinary man in the street has absolutely no need of. The bakers have to pay for the wheat and in turn have to pass the cost onto the consumer. That's business. The government keeps introducing price controls to try and protect the ordinary man, but often these controls just cause shortages and then things are only available on the black market at a much higher price, so it's just a vicious circle especially with the economy in meltdown and rampant inflation, which is the highest in the world.

The bakers retaliate by saying that they won't produce standard loaves of bread at the controlled prices, they'll produce 'fancy' loaves, give them a different name, then they do not fall under the price control policy. So they make a standard loaf, stick one or two raisins in it (which the consumer hopes to goodness are genuine raisins and not a couple of deceased flies) and can ask whatever they want for the loaf. These little bread 'wars' have been going on for years and it's not unusual to find the shelves that should contain the bread, like Old Mother Hubbard's cupboard, completely bare. When that happens, there's also a very good chance that flour is unavailable, so we can't even be enterprising and make homemade bread. I must admit that I've never found the bread queues quite as long and tiresome as the sugar queues, but they're still not a whole bundle of fun either.

Mike and I were in TM supermarket in Borrowdale in Harare one morning in the bakery section and we were first in the queue waiting for the bread to be wheeled out on the metal stands. The queue built up behind us. We were the only whites except for one little old white-haired lady just next to us and we were all laughing and joking and just generally being pleasant to one another. As the swing doors from the bakery opened and the bread was wheeled out, all hell was let loose and within a split second, from being first in the queue, the next thing I knew I was sent sprawling and I was on my hands and knees on the bottom tier of the bread racks and I was being trampled underfoot by the masses behind me! With some difficulty Mike finally managed to extricate me. You should try it sometime; it's not as easy as it sounds. I felt a like a contortionist! Reversing out of the bottom tier of a bread rack that had been laden with bread is not very elegant or ladylike. All was not lost. We did succeed in getting a loaf of bread each. We couldn't have taken any more as the store was rationing a loaf of bread to one per customer. I felt I should have been given an extra loaf as payment for the trauma that I'd just endured. All for a loaf of bread! I never did see the white-haired old lady again.

This crazy situation in our country tends to bring out the worst in us sometimes. Same shop, another occasion, another sought-after commodity, milk. Milk and milk products can sometimes be like hen's teeth, forget about the price going up weekly, sometimes even daily. It was lunchtime and I was on my way home, so I just stopped into TM to get a few bits and pieces and as I always do, I made a bee-line for the cold counter to see if they had any milk. They did. I thought I'd won first prize in the lottery! There were three two-litre bottles left and I put them in my trolley. A TM employee came up to me apologetically informing me that we were only permitted two bottles per customer – talk about the employee being in the wrong place at the wrong time! I hadn't been able to buy milk for a week, I lived out of town and miles away from the nearest shop and here I was being told that I could only take two bottles! When milk is available, I decant it into smaller bottles and freeze it. I took the third bottle and *threw* it back into the cold counter, while at the same time uttering some most unladylike expletives! Call me childish, call me immature, call me what you want. I was fuming and I was NOT AMUSED!

I got the rest of the groceries that I needed, waited my turn at the checkout and started putting my purchases on the counter. The last two items were the two bottles of milk. Supermarkets really ought to consider paying their employees danger money. The cashier looked at me apologetically and pointed to the milk. The ensuing conversation went like this with the cashier saying to me, "I'm sorry madam but you're only allowed one bottle of milk per customer."

"No. The lady by the cold counter said that we could have two bottles of milk each."

"No madam, it's only one per customer."

"The other lady said I could take *two*."

"Sorry madam, it's only one."

"I'm – not – leaving – this – store – without – two – bottles – of – milk!"

It's a pity that the cashier didn't know me better. When I talk *very, very* quietly and emphatically, it's usually because I'm in a seething, cold rage and am at my most dangerous and therefore, my most unpleasant. The hapless cashier continued to argue with me. I went from cold and quiet, to hot fury and screaming in a nano second. I was almost up on the counter with my hands around her throat and for a woman of my small stature, that's quite an accomplishment, all the while screaming like a banshee. I must say that it's a tad undignified getting back down off the counter though. A friend of ours passed by while I was attempting to murder the unsuspecting cashier and he was so embarrassed that he turned his head away. He did have the decency to phone me later to see that I was all right and not in prison or the loony bin. When the manager finally managed to calm me down, he let me leave with THREE bottles of milk! Why does it have to be like this? That's the one thing that the majority of Zimbabweans of all races will agree about, we're all so stressed with the situation in our country, that we all have very, very short fuses. Nearly trampled to death for a loaf of bread and having to have a complete and utter tantrum for a bottle of milk. Until you've lived through these conditions and experienced them, there is no way anyone can understand what it's like.

TO SEE OR NOT TO SEE

I'm sure Shakespeare won't mind me borrowing one of his well-known lines and putting a slightly different spin on it. It is quite easy to have a dim view of life whilst living in Zimbabwe. Not because we're pessimists – in fact, far from it, we've got to be either optimists or crazy to live here – no, the reason for our jaundiced outlook is because of the constant, *most annoying*, power outages. It is so difficult to even begin to explain how debilitating the outages can be. To put it in a nutshell, the Zimbabwe Electricity Supply Authority or ZESA, as we know it, is flat broke. Embarrassing finances aside, the equipment is ancient and sorely in need of being upgraded and to compound the situation, a lot of skilled manpower has joined the rest of the brain drain leaving our beautiful land.

Initially when ZESA started 'load-shedding' it did follow a sort-of-a, kind-of-a schedule. Depending on which area you lived in, your days and times for load shedding would be published in the local newspapers and you could try and plan your life around them. 2006 and subsequent years have been abominable for the supply, or lack of supply, of electricity to homes and businesses. Zimbabwe is unable to supply all our power needs so electricity is imported from our neighbours, namely South Africa, Mozambique and Zambia. South Africa is having its own problems in supplying its internal needs and as a result places like the Cape Province quite often have power outages. All of which does nothing to improve our situation here. The times when the most power is being used is in the mornings between six and nine o'clock, just when everyone is trying to start the day, get ready for school, work or whatever the day ahead holds. The next busy time for power usage is about four in the afternoon until eight or nine in the evening. Guess what, that's just when you're returning from a hard day, young children are fractious, evening meals have to be prepared, geysers have to heat water for baths, - that's right, you guessed it – those times in the mornings and the afternoons are the ones when ZESA is most likely to flick the switch and plunge us all into darkness.

Ah, but I can hear you say, hasn't this woman heard of generators? My answer to that is, you're thinking like a first world inhabitant! Yes there are generators and a few people in this country do have one. Forget about the initial financial outlay to purchase a generator, what do generators use to run on? What have I been harping on throughout this whole narrative that's a very precious, very expensive and sometimes unobtainable commodity in this country? That's right, it's fuel. And it's fuel that's required to run the generators. We know several people who own generators, but they can no longer afford to run them.

Instead of going the 'full Monty' of a generator, people who can afford to do so, are buying 'inverters'. This is, in reality, a converter. An inverter converts 12volts from a battery to 230 volts and will run a light or two and the TV. It's not powerful enough to run the stove or the frig, but it beats sitting in the dark. Before we got our inverter, Mike rigged up a Heath Robinson type of 'inverter' by using an old car battery which sits in our entrance hall and he set it up so we can run an emergency light on it and also by using a plug similar to a car cigarette lighter, we can plug in a Discman for music and also charge our cell phones. So we haven't totally gone back to the dark ages. The inverter runs our TV for about three hours per battery, an energy-saving light in the lounge, or a light in the dining room or a light in the kitchen.

The problem we've experienced is that we've only been having on average eight hours of power a day and we find that it's not always enough to fully recharge the batteries. It's the uncertainty that's so infuriating. There's no pattern to the power outages. The power can be off for just a few hours or it could be for a couple of days. The longest we've been 'out' at our house is for 10 days. Admittedly that was a fault, but it's still one long, very long time to be without electricity. If we knew that the outage was only going to be a certain number of hours or so, then I wouldn't mind opening the frig or freezer quickly, but since we have no way of knowing just how long it's going to last, I'm always loathe to do so. At least with the inverter I can use the laptop, so it has made quite a difference in our lives.

We were getting tired of having a banana and a glass of water for breakfast and a sandwich for dinner, so Mike built an 'outside' kitchen. Basically it is a braai (barbecue) in the back garden and he's put a tin roof over it so that we can even cook in the rain. How's that for progress. When we were building our house we had the foresight to install solar heaters. With the African sun it more or less ensures that we have hot water most of the year round without having to use the electrical element. It must be awful for people who are out at work and come home to cold water as the power's been off all day. Some people don't have water in their house when there's no power as their water comes from boreholes and needs electricity to pump it, some people's telephones only work when they have electricity. I even find that trying to write this book is proving tricky. When the power is on and I'm at home and not at work, then there are all sorts of other things that require electricity that need doing! It's a bit of a feast or a famine. The washing needs done, cooking – and I tend to cook double batches of things so that I've got something available for when we have unexpected visitors or there's no power – and all the other household chores that require electricity.

Just try sitting without power for eight to ten hours and you'll begin to understand what I mean. The novelty of having candlelit dinners has worn off, and I long ago stopped thinking that bathing by candlelight was romantic. Fortunately for me I'm an avid reader and have access to a library, so the evenings aren't too bad, especially on nights when there's not enough juice in the batteries to run the TV, but there are millions of people in this country who must experience a very bleak time chiefly at night and in winter. I have sat many an evening preparing lessons by candlelight. Mike has made some nifty candlestick holders that resemble a paraffin lamp. He's enclosed the candle in a glass structure so that we can take them outside and the flame won't be blown out. The constant blackouts have meant that candles are added to the list of luxury items. I have boxes of matches squirreled away all over the house, as it's a Zimbabwean phenomenon that whenever you open a box of matches, there's only ever one lone match left! Every Zimbabwean household has match thieves, but no one knows *anything* about the missing matches. I wonder if it's anything to do with the fact that the majority of the domestic workers also use fires and candles?

An added concern for us personally, is that nine times out of ten, whenever the power is off, the cell phone signal on our network goes! There is meant to be battery back up at the cell phone mast, but it hardly ever works which means that we are *completely* without any means of communication since our landline phone last worked in September 2005 and this is unsettling. You're not going to tell me that the thieves don't also know that we have no way of calling for help – though exactly who we'd call, I really don't know. At night time it's easy to see if the outage is a general one or just a fault on our property, all we have to do is look out a window and look down the Mazowe valley and see if there are any lights on there. We know the places that have generators and those that don't. Sometimes though Mike will have to go and check our mains box to see whether the fault is ours or not. I hate when he goes out at night. The mains box is outside our security fence about a five-minute walk away from our house and the box is quite low so that a child would be able to reach it. It would be so easy for thieves to throw the main switch plunging us into darkness and then wait for Mike to go out.

I have got fairly laid-back now about having guests for a meal and the power goes off. Before I used to get into quite a tizz. We were having a couple for Sunday lunch and the power had gone off on the Saturday afternoon and didn't come back until about three on Sunday afternoon. I had a complete wobbly, and to give Mike and Taundi their due, between the two of them, they cooked a roast and all the trimmings on the fire in the 'outside' kitchen! It wasn't bad. It was reasonably edible. Imagine how frustrating it is to get a cake, a soufflé or something, in the oven, it's half way through cooking, and the power goes off! When using the desktop computer I've also learned to back up after *every* line! I've learned my lesson the hard way. Some days, the power doesn't go off completely, but it's a bit like living in a discothèque. The power goes off, the power comes on. The power goes off, the power comes on. This damages electric motors.

We also have problems when the voltage is reduced as a phase has been dropped. We have three phases of power coming into the house, and it's not unusual for different parts of the house to have power, while others have nothing. Mike knows a lot about electrics. He built our house. Even more damaging to our appliances is when ZESA either put the voltage too high or too low – both of which are treacherous for any electrical appliance. Even having surge protectors on plugs doesn't help when a massive surge is sent racing through the wires. It's for this reason, that we never leave any plug in the plug socket, let alone switched on. Another reason for our over-the-top precaution is that on New Year's Day 2004, our house was hit by lightning. Even though every single appliance was unplugged, we lost TVs, music centres, the swimming pool motor, the stove, security lights – the list is endless – so now, it's just second nature to unplug everything.

I've spoken to people from other parts of Africa who think that the infrastructure in Zimbabwe is wonderful compared to their countries and I cringe. If that's the case, what's in store for us in the future? Our staff have solar panels that can run a TV or radio. During a recent thirty-one hour power outage, we had to wait for the cell phone signal to come back on, it always goes out the minute the power goes off and once the signal was back, Mike phoned our local branch of ZESA to find out what was happening. He was told that the technicians had gone out the previous afternoon to locate the fault, but that they'd had to stop working when night fell, as they can't work in the dark because they haven't got any light and the company can't afford torches! The following morning Mike at about nine o'clock, again contacted ZESA to see what progress had been made. This time he was told that the technicians had not left the depot yet as they were awaiting the arrival of the transport.

We were understandably miffed at this news, we thought that as the power had been off for about twenty-one hours, the technicians would had least make the effort to get things working again. Subsequent phone calls revealed that the truck didn't leave the depot until eleven in the morning, when the power had then been off for twenty-three hours.

Great excitement when at four-fifty in the afternoon, the hum of frigs and deepfreezes permeated the air! Again, we were not counting on Africa Time combined with ZESA logic. Our short-lived euphoria dissipated into much wailing and gnashing of teeth, when *fifteen* minutes later, we were again plunged into darkness for our 'scheduled' load shedding of electricity! Surely someone could have had the savvy to realize that we had been without power for the best part of a day and a half before they decided to pull the plug. The weekend of Saturday 2nd to Monday 4th May 2007 was another shocker. The power went off at five o'clock in the morning on Saturday. We weren't able to phone the power company as there was no cell phone signal and it was only mid-afternoon on Sunday when we could use the phones again. ZESA informed us that they knew about the problem and were looking for the fault, but as other areas such as Christon Bank, were experiencing load shedding of power, the technicians couldn't work on the line. A subsequent call to ZESA at six in the morning on Monday, said that they still knew about the problem, but that they didn't have any transport for their technicians. Power was eventually resumed at about nine in the morning, after having been off for forty hours. This is not an isolated case; we've just sat through another forty-five hour outage. Believe me it's not fun.

If nothing else, it was a good test to see how the deepfreezes coped without being opened. The outage wasn't as a result of a storm or some other catastrophe, but was a fault. If transport had been available, we could have been turned back on much earlier. These outages are causing havoc with the water supply on our property. We have five boreholes, none of which are prolific, but they provide enough for our needs if we're careful. All of the boreholes are down in the valley. The water is pumped a quarter of a mile uphill to a reservoir which is higher than the house, thus allowing the water to be gravity fed into the house. This reservoir can hold approximately two or three month's water for our staff, our vegetable garden and us depending on our consumption. Mike is finding it extremely difficult to pump water with all the power outages. The boreholes are on time switches timed to go on and off at certain times, but with the erratic power supply, it's virtually impossible to utilize these in the correct way as we never know when we'll have power.

I can't explain the varying emotions that are experienced when the power goes off. We vacillate between resignation, rage or tears of frustration. I never quite know how I'm going to react. Occasionally I amaze myself by being cool, calm and collected, but at other times, I am getting expert at having little temper tantrums.

BUREAUCRACY, RED TAPE
AND ALL

A frica has its own time. Why do today what you can easily put off until tomorrow. Africa Time is not just a concept of time; it's the rhythm of life here. It's not deliberate procrastination. It's also being sociable and polite. For instance, the vehicle licence plate furore, which took place in Zimbabwe in 2005 - 2006. It was at a time when the country was spiralling downwards in economic meltdown. For the vast majority of Zimbos life is extremely difficult. So you can imagine that we weren't impressed when a new ruling came into place that every vehicle must have a new set of number plates. Whoever owned the company making the number plates was laughing all the way to the bank.

Mike and I put off getting the new plates for as long as we could. We had four vehicles and these new plates were *not* cheap. For a while we all thought that the scheme would come to a grinding halt as apart from a small Zimbabwe Bird embossed on the plate, the lettering and numbers were the same as those on Zambian vehicles and was causing headaches at the border posts especially with the police and Interpol trying to sort out the legit cars from the stolen ones. No go, the government doggedly carried on with the issue of the new plates. There were horrific queues to get police clearance for the vehicles at Southerton police station and then other queues at the municipal offices to get the plates and to pay for them. The price of the number plates was going up almost weekly. As it took so long, sometimes days, to get everything done, certain service stations and individuals with contacts were acting as facilitators, for a nice fat fee of course. Mike was a bit hesitant to use a facilitator, as apart from the cost of using one, they required your ID and the vehicle's papers .... neither of which Mike was

228

prepared to let out of his possession. This is a country where you can be arrested for not having your ID in your possession!

In June 2006 we decided that we'd put it off for as long as we could and as the price was just constantly increasing, we'd better get the new plates. Mike had a 'contact' who appeared to be honest and wasn't too expensive. So he reluctantly handed over the documentation, money and waited...and waited and waited. The contact would tell us every day that he'd been to Rowan Martin Building, the municipal headquarters in Harare and that there were no plates available. This went on for the best part of a week when Mike finally decided to cut our losses and do it himself. The contact had done all the spadework doing the lousiest part, that of getting police clearance for the vehicles. Mike took himself off to Rowan Martin to do what he thought was going to be the easier part of the process. We live and learn.

The queue was long. The queue was very long. The queue was so long that it snaked almost back on itself. The queue was working to Africa Time. Mike was one of only two whites in the queue, but the derogatory comments concerning the changing of number plates transcended race. Everyone was on the exact same wavelength. Mike was in the queue from eight in the morning until ten o'clock. Then again from just after ten until midday. Why did he join the queue again? Well, after patiently awaiting his turn, he finally arrived at the cashier. He put the documentation down on the counter and asked for four sets of number plates. The story went a bit like my milk narrative. The cashier told him that there weren't enough sets of number plates available, so she would only issue him with one set. Mike does tend to have a slightly longer fuse than me and he patiently explained. "I have four vehicles and I need four sets of plates. I have been standing in the queue for hours and have used precious fuel to get here"

Cashier, "We don't have enough plates for everybody, so you can only have one set."

Mike, "I don't care about everybody else. I'm only interested in my cars. I need four sets."

Cashier, "You can't have four sets. We haven't got enough."

Mike, "I don't *want* new plates. I *have* to get new plates by law. I have wasted a whole morning and am going to be spending a lot of money for something that I don't want, but have to have! I am not leaving here without four sets of plates."

Cashier, "I am *not* giving you four sets. I will give you two only."

Mike, "Then I'll just join the queue again for the other two."

Cashier, "You can't."

Mike, "I will."

Cashier, "O.K."

Mike got his two sets of plates and went to the back of the queue to start the whole process over again. I don't know if I could have handled it as well as he did. Talk about bungling bureaucracy. The public had until the end of December 2006 to change their number plates otherwise they would be fined. Add to this the extra incentive of getting it done earlier, that of hyperinflation.

While Mike joined the queue for the second time, the woman who had been in front of him in the first queue came up to him and asked him if he'd noticed the young man who'd come and spoken to her and there had also been two others hovering in the background. Mike said that he vaguely remembered the men, but hadn't taken much notice. It transpired that these three men were not queuing customers like everyone else, but were thieves. They had targeted the woman and the "man" who'd approached her had already targeted her. She wasn't quite sure how the system of changing the number plates had worked. She didn't realise that she had to hand over the old number plates before receiving the new ones. The cashier who had dealt with her had explained this to her and posing as a Good Samaritan, the young man had kept a place in the queue for her whilst she went outside, removed her old number plates and rejoined the queue. On her return the young man left. She was grateful not to have to go to the end of the queue. She got her new set of plates and went out to the car park to discover there was no car! The car park was teeming with municipal police but no one had noticed anything. To make life easier for the thieves, they were now driving a car with no number plates, so it would be much more difficult to identify. Mike said he felt so very sorry for the woman. She was distraught.

Mike was by now not that far away from the cashier when a security guard wandered down the queue informing the public that there were no more sets of number plates left. The long-suffering public accepted the news with a typical Zimbo shrug and dispersed. Not Mike and the other white man in the queue. They both refused to budge until they had been provided with sets of new number plates. Talk about the squeaking wheel getting the oil. Lo and behold, miraculously, the required number of sets seemed to appear out of thin air and it was mission accomplished. This is just one example of the constant red tape that we have to endure.

In November 2005 Mike and I submitted applications for duplicate Zimbabwean driver's licences to replace ours that had got lost. The odd time that Mike was in town he'd pop into the Vehicle Inspection Depot, V.I.D, to see if the licences were ready. Or when he'd remember, he'd give them a call. May 2006 came. June 2006 came. We were getting a bit tired of waiting. Again Mike went into see them and was told that for a price of $2.5 million we could legitimately 'fast-track' the licences, so we agreed. We hit our next hurdle. Our file showing that we'd both been driving since we were sixteen and our applications for duplicates, was nowhere to be found. There was no record to say that we'd ever sat driving tests and passed. Did this mean that we'd have to re-sit our provisional licences and then do the actual driving test all over again?

Our file had been taken out of its storage place and had disappeared. Mike was taken to offices that were strewn with cardboard boxes, papers and files and told to look for the file himself. To no avail. He spent the whole of a Tuesday afternoon grubbing around in boxes that were on desks, under desks, roundabout desks. He went into offices strewn with paper work, radios were blaring, desktops were covered with Coke bottles and sticky buns. Office workers were chatting to each other, no one seemed to think it odd to see a middle-aged white man scrabbling around on his hands and knees. It was just accepted. It was organized chaos. He was finally given the name of the woman who was the supervisor and the next day he went and queued for an hour outside her door to be told that she'd look into it for him.

We thought we'd give her a week and then we phoned. No go. Our file still hadn't been located. We were getting a bit twitchy by now. We wanted our new licences as were going on holiday to the UK and wanted to be able to hire a car. The next week we both went in to see the supervisor. We queued outside her office for the best part of two hours until our turn came. Queuing is not my favourite past-time, at least when there's a bench or a seat it makes life a bit easier, but standing in a bleak corridor for ages tends to make me have a sense of humour failure. When the supervisor eventually deigned to see us she said that she'd send a policewoman to go with us and look for the files. Mike explained that he'd done that already, but she insisted. We followed the young policewoman through the labyrinth of offices to the archives for what turned out to be a fruitless search. We could have told her it would be a waste of time.

Back to the supervisor's office. Another wait. Not too long this time. She told us that we'd just have to wait until our file was found. Mike tried to explain that she was jeopardizing our ability to hire a car in Britain, to which she replied that she'd give us a letter stating that we did have licences. Mike then said that if she was prepared to give us the letter that was tantamount to her admitting that we did already have licences, so why wasn't she prepared to issue us with a bit of tin with our name on it! We didn't think that a piece of paper with the ever present 'official' rubber stamp from a third world country would carry much weight with the car-hire firms in Britain. Mark had taken an International driving licence from Zim when he went to the UK and he said that it wasn't worth the paper that it was printed on and no one accepted it on the odd occasion that he'd had to produce it. She would not budge.

We went on holiday without our driving licences. We did not hire a car. On our return to Zimbabwe we again enquired as to the status of our licences as it was now exactly a year since we had submitted our applications, it was November 2006. Still no go. The last enquiry we made was in April 2007 and we were advised that the V.I.D were only working on the October 2005 applications, so we'd have to wait a couple of months to see if our file turned up when they were working on the November 2005 ones, and if not, then we'd have to 'make a plan'. *I am so sick and tired of making plans.* However, this saga did end on a positive note. I received my duplicate driver's licence on 24th May 2007. Mike's licence did not materialize until a month later.

In June 2007, according to the news, the government had a backlog of over 300 000 passports and had ceased issuing them as they didn't have the paper with which to print them. The same has happened to personal I.D's – and it is compulsory to carry this on your person. We've had shortages of actual bank notes. Now, that's a fun thing to experience in a country that's going spiralling out of control with inflation. Firms won't accept cheques for payment. With hyperinflation by the time the banks have cleared the cheques, they are no longer valid. It didn't matter if you were a millionaire or billionaire (both an easy status to reach in Zimbabwe with all the zeroes we have on our currency), the Reserve Bank would only permit the banks to give individuals a certain paltry amount of money daily, which was hardly even enough to buy a bottle of milk. Eventually in July 2007 the Reserve Bank, bowing to pressure, increased the daily withdrawal amounts of cash, for private individuals it was increased from Z$1.5 million to Z$10 million a day, and businesses went from Z$3 million to Z$20 million daily, all of which is indicative of the rate of inflation, but certainly made life easier for us. In 2008 the limit was raised to Z$1 billion a day.

Why don't we just use a credit card? Even if you do have the privilege of a credit and / or debit card, many shops don't have the facilities for them. One morning in July is a case in point. Mike had business in the industrial sites in Ruwa and on his way back to Harare, stopped at the big TM supermarket there. Their wine was cheaper, as were a few other grocery items although they didn't have basics such as flour and margarine, there never seems to be a shortage of the imported luxuries. Mike was prepared to do a reasonable shop there, but they didn't have a machine for his Standard Chartered Bank debit card and that curtailed his spending power considerably as he didn't have the mounds of cash on him that he required. There's even a black market for local currency bank notes as so many people are scrabbling around like mad things trying to find enough cash to make payments or pay wages. The Mad Hatter didn't fly over this cuckoo nest, he landed right smack in the middle.

In July 2007 a friend of ours was in the process of winding up her affairs in Zim as her family had persuaded her to go and live in South Africa, as conditions were getting almost impossible here. She'd done all her necessary bank clearances, tax clearance and the only outstanding item was the police clearance on her car. She made several journeys to Southerton

Police Station where the clearance had to be done and in the process was using up her precious supply of fuel. Time was getting short and she was getting nowhere. Our area Mazowe is renowned for its oranges and one policeman quietly suggested that a pocket of oranges might speed up the process. It worked. My friend walked into the police station with a pocket of oranges and walked out with all the necessary documentation. It's a way of life here. Many times at police roadblocks we're asked, "What have you got for me?" It's useless trying to buck the system, not if you want to get things done.

DO YOU LIKE YOUR FATHER?

A fact of life in Zimbabwe is that a lot of people own guns. I don't like guns. My father had a small gun, a .22 revolver that he gave to me when my parents returned to the UK in May 2002. Dad had written a letter giving me ownership and his licence was still valid for a few months. I immediately put in a change-of-ownership application to have the gun changed into my name. The woman who dealt with me at the gun licensing office in the Morris Depot police camp, was not particularly pleasant. She was evil. It's just as well Mike was with me, he's so much better at handling these situation, otherwise I might have blown a fuse and I'd probably be behind bars right now.

I do understand where the woman was coming from. I already have a .22 Beretta pistol issued in my name. I was now applying for a second weapon. Makes me look like an Annie Oakley wannabe. All this from someone who isn't particularly fond of guns. I just wanted to get Dad's gun into my name and then I could legally sell it. Mike thought it might be an idea if we hung onto the weapon as it would be registered for use in Harare and we could keep it in our gun safe in Borrowdale in Harare. All our other weapons are registered for use in Mazowe only. Instead of explaining the laws about holding two weapons, this woman wanted to know why I needed the second gun. I explained that as Mike did a fair amount of travelling in his job (which some times entailed spending a night or two away from home) I had a weapon in Mazowe for self -protection and now one in Harare for the same reason.

She belligerently asked why I didn't bring the gun from Mazowe into Harare with me. I patiently explained that as I did not have a permit enabling me to travel with a weapon, it would be illegal for me to remove the gun from the property. Then she asked why I was scared to be alone at night. I'm not, but it's none of her business. Anyway, we've had a couple of nasty experiences in Mazowe. She then asked me who I slept with when Mike was away! All this in front of a crowded waiting room. That was it! I nearly exploded. Mike came to the rescue, told me to go and wait outside and that he'd deal with her. He managed to get her to accept our application for change of ownership and he was told to come back in a few weeks to see how it was going.

In the interim, we went to our local police station to arrange for a policeman to come to our house in Borrowdale and check that we had an adequate gun safe for storage. We made a couple of trips to the police station before we finally managed to liaise with a young member of the C.I.D who was available to come to the house. As he didn't have transport and the police were short of fuel, we collected him and took him back with us. What a nice young man. He inspected the gun safe and agreed that it was adequate and agreed to write a letter to that effect. He looked a bit awkward and said, "I'm a bit embarrassed, but please could you give me some paper to write the letter, we don't have any stationery at the police station." I gave him several sheets of paper. Not that I didn't think that he was capable of writing a letter, but anyone can make a mistake and he didn't have the luxury of using a computer or a word processor or even an electric typewriter, it was the old manual typewriter for him. We took him back to the station and waited while he typed out the letter for us.

The months went by and still no word about the change of ownership. Mike would phone or pop in and enquire how it was going. I didn't trust myself to keep cool. By now Dad's licence had expired and I was worried. I know I sound a bit paranoid, but I didn't fancy my odds in the event of a police raid for whatever reason, of being a white woman in an independent black country with an unlicensed gun. So we took it to a suburban police station and handed it in for safekeeping. This is a community service that the police carry out for people who are going on holiday or for whenever they are not going to be at home. Nine months later, I still hadn't received a change of ownership, but we were back at Morris Depot, as Mike's gun licence needed renewing. So I went with him. The place was its usual chaos, but we only had a short wait and were called into an office by a fantastic C.I.D officer.

When I say office, you've got to see this place to believe it. The licensing part of the building is a rabbit warren of inter-leading wooden buildings, built along the lines of garden sheds. One office leads into another, which leads into another, and on, and on. It was a scorcher of a day, building up for a thunderstorm and precious little ventilation in the 'offices'. The smell of old paper was almost overpowering and in one office there was a two-bar heater going full tilt – with some meat being cooked in an enamel dish on top of it! That whole complex is just a fireball waiting to happen! The C.I.D officer was great. He was helpful, pleasant and efficient. He dealt with Mike's renewal of gun licences and when that was completed, we asked him what was happening about my change of ownership with my father's gun. It took him a while to find the relevant file. I was amazed that anyone could find anything in that place, but there obviously is a system and it obviously works. Everything is done manually.

According to my file, my application for the change of ownership had been rejected. Quite frankly, I couldn't give two hoots about keeping the gun or not, it was the principle of the matter. The application had been rejected on a technicality, basically, the wording of my father's letter giving me ownership of the gun. Three or four words had made the difference between a yeah and a nay. The C.I.D officer said that I should just get my father to write another letter changing the wording and that all would be forgiven and I would be the official proud owner of the gun. Problem was, father was six thousand miles away. In May 2002 my parents left their home of fifty years and returned to Britain. It was not through choice that they went; it was through necessity. Both my parents had worked hard all their lives here in Zimbabwe. They'd paid their taxes, made it their home and put fifty years of their lives into this country. They had become Rhodesians and then subsequently, Zimbabweans, totally embracing this nation. My parents had paid into pension funds all their working lives to enable them to survive in their old age and not be a burden on anyone; all of which in a sane, normal environment would have been laudable – *but* they were living in Zimbabwe. The land-grabs started in earnest in the early 2000s, and with that, the spiralling cost of living. My parents had their pride and they were struggling financially. We were able to supply fruit and vegetables from our garden, but that doesn't exactly pay the bills. Birthdays, anniversaries, Christmas, Mother's and Father's days saw the presents in the form of a food parcel with the little luxury items that were way out of the reach of my parents - there'd be a slab of chocolate for Dad, Nescafe for Mum, maybe a jar of marmite or a bottle of HP sauce and if we could afford it, a tin of tuna.

My father once joked that he was becoming a connoisseur of toast. Never a truer word was spoken in jest. My parents were the lucky ones, they had family here to see that they never became destitute; they owned their home and had a few savings for a rainy day. They also could go back to the land of their birth and my father had had the foresight fifty years ago to keep paying into his British pension all the years they lived here. This must have been quite a strain on my parents financially over the years, but thank goodness they persevered. They, as we all were, had been getting fed-up with the quality of life here. The constant power outages, the ever increasing cost of living and the apprehension as they watched the farm invasions and the apparent lack of law and order. This was the time of their lives when they should be comfortably enjoying the fruits of their hard-earned labour; instead, they were seeing their standard of living dropping dramatically.

Good friends of ours, Rob and Val, lived on a farm a few kilometres from us. Val had grown up in the area and her parents owned the next-door farm where they had lived for sixty-six years. Our families usually got together at Christmas and with all the in-laws, outlaws and extras, there were about thirty-five of us at any one time. The 'wrinklies' would be put at one end of the table going down to the young sprogs at the other end. We'd put a bottle of whisky in front of Val's Dad, Tom Bayley, a character and a legend in his own right, and my dad, and the two old men would put the world to rights. Val's mum, Bobs, and my mum would sit and discuss knitting and crocheting. The rest of us would get on with having a great time. With the advent of the farm invasions, Rob and Val and their family went to hell and back – and have survived, but, without their farm. The ordeal that the so-called war veterans put old Tom and Bobs through is a book on its own, but suffice it to say, it made headline news around the world. The short version of a long, ugly story is that Tom and Bobs were kept 'prisoner' in their house on their own farm for five weeks and only left when the old man fell and broke his leg. I'm talking about a man who was in his late eighties and his wife was not a whole lot younger.

He died a few weeks later, most likely of a broken heart as opposed to any medical complications. If memory serves me correctly, he was eighty-nine when he died. I think this was the final nail in the coffin where my parents were concerned. Tom Bayley died on May Day, a public holiday here in Zim, May 1st 2002. My parents went into the travel agent on 3rd May and booked a ticket out of here for the 30th May. At first I was relieved that my parents were getting away from this madness for a while, I thought that they were only going on an extended holiday to the U.K for about six months. You can imagine how I felt when Dad clarified the situation and dropped the bombshell that he didn't think that they would ever come back here. We were, and still are, an incredibly close family. I always got on well with Mike's parents, as did he with mine. My father even worked for Mike and his dad for many years. My parents came to Africa on their honeymoon in September 1952 and left here four months before their Golden Wedding anniversary, on 30th May 2002. We couldn't even celebrate this momentous occasion together as a family. We have always made a point of being together for important times like birthdays and anniversaries and it broke my heart not to be able to do anything to make the day special for my parents. Being a long-distance family isn't any fun. I can't even begin to describe my feelings when we said goodbye to Mum and Dad at the airport. I was extremely grateful that Rob and Val were there for a bit of moral support.

I was still reeling from shock the following day when Mike and I went around to my parents' flat. They had left with a suitcase each. They left behind fifty years of their life in their flat. Wedding albums, photographs, other mementos, jewellery, clothing, furniture, in fact every thing that they couldn't carry in a suitcase. In the three weeks before they left Africa, they had put the flat into my name, changed ownership of the car, given me power of attorney over all their affairs here. It was as if they had died. I felt as if a part of me had died. So this was where the dilemma came about with the hiccup of the wording in dad's letter giving me ownership of his gun. Dad wasn't here to change the letter. I wasn't about to let on that he no longer lived here. Paranoia ruled the day.

The officer saw that I was a bit hesitant and asked what the problem was, so I answered that my father was 'away' for a while, I did mean physically and not mentally (though sometimes Dad, I do wonder about that!) and that it would take time to get the letter with the necessary changes. I didn't know if it would cause difficulties with the 'owner' being out of the country and I admit I was worried. I was a white woman with an unlicensed gun in a black independent country. The officer looked at me thoughtfully, and said, "Do you like your father?"

To which I answered, "Of course."

He asked, "Do you get on well with him?"

"Yes, very much."

Another hesitation, "Why don't you just sign your father's name for him?"

Was this a set-up? Was he trying to catch me out? Or was he doing me an enormous favour? I took the bit between the teeth, decided it was the latter and that 'father' would in due course 'sign' the letter and the change of ownership could be processed!

A few days later we were back in the same office with the letter 'signed' by 'father'. While the officer was making out the new licence in my name, Mike noticed that there was a discrepancy in the serial number to the one that was shown on the invoice of the purchase of the gun. A couple of the digits had been transposed at the end of the number. All the years that dad had owned the gun the licence had displayed the incorrect number. Mike pointed this out to the policeman. Again he went out of his way to help us. He made the licence out showing the serial number that had been written on the previous licence. However he warned that if the serial number was incorrect as Mike suspected and if the gun was ever used or reported stolen and there was a discrepancy with the number, there could be serious ramifications for me. He suggested that we take the licence, go to the police station where the gun had been lodged for safe-keeping, check the serial number and if we found it was wrong, then to bring the gun back to him and he would organise for someone in the police armoury to rectify the things by writing a letter stating the correct number, thereby allowing the C.I.D to issue a licence with the correct number.

Mike was ninety-nine point nine per cent sure that the serial number was incorrect. So it was with a bit of trepidation that we arrived at the police station. The country was in turmoil. There was a tenseness that permeated every aspect of life. Those with positions of power such as the police, could, on a whim, make one's life hell. It's always the uncertainty of not knowing. Of watching your tongue in case you said something that could be misconstrued. Of talking in code with family and friends. We waited fully five minutes at the desk in the police station before someone deigned to serve us, yet we were the only members of the public there. There were three or four policewomen and men in the room all chatting and they made us wait. They put us in our place. Or maybe it wasn't that sinister, maybe it was just 'Africa time'. That's the problem with this country, are we reading too much into a situation, or isn't it nearly as dark and threatening as we thought? It's almost impossible to tell and you don't want to find out the hard way.

A policewoman sauntered over to us and we said that we'd come to collect my gun. I had butterflies in my stomach. If the serial number did prove to be wrong, the policewoman would be well within her rights to refuse to give it to me. That would then necessitate us going back to Morris Depot, arranging for an armourer to accompany us back to the police station, collect the weapon, go back to Morris Depot! Apart from the complete waste of time this would take, it was using up our very precious supply of fuel. The policewoman told us to follow her into an office. It was bleak. A shelf on the wall, a desk and a chair either side of it made up the furnishings. The telephone was attached to the plughole in the wall by two wires in the plug socket. It did not emanate a feeling of efficiency. The policewoman asked to see the receipt that I'd been issued for the safekeeping of the weapon, collected the gun and came back to us saying, "I will have to work out how much you owe us."

Mike said, "No. You've got it wrong. The gun has been kept by you for safe-custody."

"Yes, I know that. Now I want to see how much you must pay."

"We don't owe anything. The safe-custody of weapons is a free service to the community."

"No. Things have changed. We have a new ruling. It now costs $500 a day."

"You've got to be mad! The gun's been here for nine months. It wasn't our fault that the change of ownership took so long. It's going to cost a fortune."

"O.k. but you must pay."

"I don't have that kind of money."

"O.k. let's discuss things. How much can you afford?"

At this point Mike took out his wallet. He had had a surreptitious look at the gun and he was right, the last two digits of the serial number were transposed. We were still very aware of all the complications this could cause, so most reluctantly, Mike took out all the money he had on him, which was ten thousand dollars and showed it to the woman. She smiled. She took it. She put the money straight into her handbag. There was no receipt issued. I was given the gun. She didn't even check the licence. She didn't ask me for any identification, I could have been anyone for all she knew. We had the gun and with great relief we left the police station.

Back to Morris Depot to see the C.I.D officer. Again, he performed over and above his duty. He checked the serial number and ascertained that it was indeed incorrect. He then phoned the armoury and arranged for us to be met there. It was a surreal experience to be two whites walking through a black police camp carrying a weapon, albeit an unloaded one. The armourer who met us said that he would do the documentation for us while we waited if that would be more convenient, but that we would have to wait outside the building, which was fair enough. I can walk for miles, but I cannot stand for a long time. I must have been looking a tad uncomfortable as the young constable who was on guard duty came over to me and invited me to sit on the bench in his guard hut! I could have kissed him. Half an hour later we were given the correct documentation, back to our friendly C.I.D officer, who issued a new and finally, correct licence. Then it was 'home James, and don't spare the horses'. This is what makes life so interesting or is it stressful, in this country, you have a situation in which one minute you've got a senior policeman going the extra mile for you, the next you're being fleeced by a junior. If it's not the police, it will be someone else. It can get a bit confusing at times.

A white woman who lives in Christon Bank near Mazowe, was on her way home and had just turned off the main Mazowe road and turned onto the Christon Bank road. To preserve her privacy, let's call her Rosie. There are always hundreds, well, not hundreds, but lots, of people standing at this turnoff ever hopeful of getting a lift. Rosie was on her own, so wouldn't normally have give anyone a lift, but she recognized two of the men standing there and as she was in a pickup truck and they could climb in the back, she stopped and gave them a lift. Unbeknown to her, a pregnant woman also tried to climb into the back of the truck, but didn't make it in time before the white woman drove off. Rosie arrived at her house; the two grateful men thanked her and went on their way. The next thing was the arrival of an officious policeman at the door accusing Rosie of purposely trying to kill the pregnant woman! Rosie was not even aware that this woman had allegedly tried to climb into the back of her truck. The preggy woman said that Rosie had watched her trying to climb into the back and had deliberately driven off before she was safely in the back. It was a blatant lie. It was a racial issue. The policeman demanded that Rosie take the 'injured' woman to a private doctor. We are talking about a third world country where a visit to a doctor, any doctor, private or otherwise, is a luxury and extremely costly.

Rosie stood up for her rights. She refused to take the woman to a private doctor, but said that out of the kindness of her heart, she would take her to the Concession Clinic, which entailed a round journey of the best part of eighty kilometres. The policeman was rude and officious. The pregnant woman was ungrateful. The upshot of this is that Rosie was going to write about her ordeal in the Christon Bank newsletter, which goes out to all the ratepayers in the area and was going to warn other unsuspecting motorists about the hazards of giving lifts. So one policeman on a power trip and not prepared to ascertain the facts and one selfish, ungrateful woman, will be the cause of suffering for many innocent people who would have been extremely grateful for a lift.

Yvonne, Mike's sister had an unpleasant episode with the police in July 2007. She was driving home from work one Tuesday at about 4.45p.m when she and fourteen other motorists were stopped for allegedly driving through a red robot by a human barrage of police across the road. Yvonne is adamant that she didn't go through on red, but as she pointed out, how could fifteen cars all have gone through at the same time? Our roads aren't wide enough for that volume of traffic. A young, very young, policeman came up to Yvonne and said that she'd gone through on red. She said she hadn't. He said she had. It went like this for a while, all the time the policeman was becoming more and more hostile. He said that Yvonne had two choices. She could pay an on-the-spot fine or go to the main police station, where he intimated she might not be treated very nicely. She was a woman on her own. She had no back up. She didn't have enough money to pay the fine. Not that everyone has a lawyer, but even threatening to contact a lawyer wouldn't have made much difference, in May 2007, Zimbabwean lawyers were beaten up and put in jail just for doing their job!

Yvonne burst into tears. The cop forced his way into her car and told her to drive around the block. She had no choice. They went a short distance. He told her to pull over and empty out the contents of her bag. She had Z$90 000 in her purse. He pocketed it and told her that he was going to get drunk on it that night. She then had to drive him back to where she'd collected him. When we visited later that night, she was both visibly shaken and fuming. This had happened on a busy road in broad daylight. I won't drive at night on my own and, even during the day, I am ever vigilant against car-jacking or having my windows smashed at the robots.

CRIME BUSTERS

Africa is, if nothing else, an exciting place to live. I don't mean exciting from the point of view of lions and elephants, dictators and unstable regimes. I mean exciting from a criminal point of view. We tend to be a bit blasé about it all and just accept it as a fact of life. The one thing that tends to cause most problems is that of hard currency. For the best part of my life it's been impossible to walk into a bank and buy foreign currency. There was a small window during the early heydays of Mugabe's reign when it was possible to visit a bureau de change and purchase forex, but by and large, forex could only be obtained on the black market at exorbitant rates.

The Reserve Bank controlled the country's forex and if you needed external funds for medical reasons or tertiary education, you had to apply to your own bank first, which would make application on your behalf to the Reserve Bank, which would in turn decide the fate of the application. There was no guarantee that the money would ever be forthcoming. In 2004, we put in an application for forex to our local bank in Borrowdale for university fees in Wales for Mark. I filled in all the necessary forms with the help of Jennifer, the foreign currency teller at the bank. She was efficient and helpful. If I happened to be in the neighbourhood, I'd take the opportunity to pop in to the bank and ask the status of our application. One day, Jennifer took great delight in letting me know that the bank had approved the application and that it had been forwarded to the Reserve Bank. Whilst this was all going on, in order to pay the university fees, Mike was in the process of selling a house that his father had left to him. The sale went through without a hitch and the money was paid into one of our accounts that we had with the bank and, which we seldom used.

Things were looking up; on a subsequent visit to our bank Jennifer said that the Reserve Bank had approved our application for Mark's university fees.

Things were going well and I was getting excited, as Mark was due home for a holiday from the U.K. So with all this excitement in my life, the hours spent in fuel queues and days going without fresh milk, and days without any water at our house in Borrowdale, paled and didn't seem nearly so bad.

On Tuesday 17th August 2004 I went to see Jennifer to finalise the forex formalities. I completed the necessary paperwork, I signed on the dotted line and was given my copy of the telegraphic transfer of the sterling equivalent of one hundred and eighty-nine million Zimbabwe dollars from our account to that of the account of the University of North Wales, Bangor. What a relief. I also got a mini statement showing the transaction for our own records. It was with great excitement that Mike and I were up at the crack of dawn on Wednesday 18th August to meet Mark's flight from the U.K at the back of six in the morning. Not only was it great seeing him after a year, but I also was able to give him the good news that the money was on its way to the university. Our first port of call before going out to Mazowe was Borrowdale Village shops so that Mark could go into Bon Marche and buy a packet of biltong (dried meat) and I could go to the bank to make sure that there had been no hiccups with the forex transaction. All I can say is that if Mark hadn't been with me every time I went to see Jennifer in the bank, either I'd think I was losing the plot and not firing on all cylinders, or I'm sure Mike would have bought me a white jacket with Velcro fastenings at the back and put me in a padded cell!

You have to have an African mindset to fully appreciate that what I'm going to tell you now is *not* so far-fetched. I would email the university to see if they'd received the funds and the accounts office would reply in the negative. Mark and I would go and see Jennifer in the bank and she'd say, "Oh the money couldn't go today because the computers were down." Power outages, computers down – there's nothing unusual about that. Happens everyday here. I'd email the university a few days later and receive a negative reply again. Mark and I would go and visit Jennifer who there and then, in front of us, would phone someone in the Reserve Bank to see what was happening. As Mark later so rightly pointed out, Jennifer was speaking in Shona (the local language) and as neither of us is conversant in the language, she could have been swopping recipes for all we knew.

Then we'd be told that the Reserve Bank didn't have all the money available so they were going to send half one day and half the next day. I'd email the university and advise them of this. The university would email back that they hadn't received any money. It was getting a bit embarrassing for me and Mark was getting a bit concerned, time was getting short before his return to the UK. Jennifer asked me for the phone number for the university and said that she'd phone as a bank representative on our behalf and explain that the funds were on their way. I was *impressed!* I never thought that a bank would go to this much trouble for a customer. She later informed me that she had got through to the university, but it must have been too early (at that time of the year we're two hours ahead of the U.K) and that all she got was an answering machine saying that there was no one available in the office to take her call. It all sounded plausible.

On one visit to Jennifer she mentioned that she'd be taking a few days leave and would like to come and visit me – I thought it was a bit odd, Mike thought it was downright dodgy! I'm a people-person, so I thought that perhaps Jennifer was taken by my charm and wit. O.K I know, one day I'll grow up, but it's still nice to dream now and again. On Monday 6th September 2004 there was an email from the university saying that they had not yet received any money from us, so Mark and I made our way back to the bank. The teller who was standing in for Jennifer looked at us blankly when I said that I wanted to know if the money had gone, she went away and looked at our file and seemed totally confused. I still wasn't too concerned at this stage and alarm bells hadn't gone off in my head. Jennifer had phoned and asked if she could come round and see me in the afternoon, so I thought I'd wait until she came to the house and see what she could tell us of the status of the forex, as this other teller didn't seem to have a clue as to what was going on. Jennifer phoned in the afternoon to cancel her visit stating that she had transport woes. I was secretly relieved. Apart from the times I'd seen her in the bank, I've never socialised with her and didn't know if we'd have anything in common. Mike thought she was up to no good.

Wednesday 8th September, I phoned the university to see if they'd received any money. I'm talking about phoning long distance from Africa to Wales. You really have to live in a third world country to appreciate just what a valuable and expensive commodity a telephone is! The bursar was most apologetic and said that they had still not received any money. The panic was beginning to set in. I was trying *awfully* hard not to show it to Mark, but I was WORRIED. Mark was flying back to Britain at the end of the week and was due at the university the following week. It's not an ideal situation for an international student to arrive for Fresher's week at university when not a cent has been paid towards your tuition. Mark was decidedly distressed! I decided to take the bit between my teeth, take all the paperwork, bypass the forex teller and go direct to the manager. Enough was enough. I'd been patient but my son's future was in jeopardy. The manager, Patricia sat and listened to my tale with an expression of utter disbelief on her face. When I'd finished my narrative she said, "I don't know what to believe. Firstly, our staff does not have the authority to make international calls, it would have had to come through me. Secondly, the Reserve Bank does not send funds out in dribs and drabs, they send out the entire amount in one transaction."

She looked through my paperwork and seemed distinctly puzzled by my duplicate copy of the telegraphic transfer form. She called up our account on her computer. She turned to me and said, "I don't know how to say this. But there never was any approval from the Reserve Bank and there never was any transfer of any funds to the university." I felt like someone had kicked me in the stomach. I thought I was going to be sick. The long and short of it was that Jennifer had 'borrowed' one hundred and eighty-nine million dollars from our account for her own use. She had stopped the telegraphic transfer somehow and redirected it for her own use. I really don't know how long she thought she could string us along. Surely to goodness she knew that she'd be found out sooner rather than later. I really don't know what made her tick. Mike was furious. He went to the very top of the bank and he let rip! He threw his toys out the cot! Fortunately for us, unfortunately for the bank and Jennifer, I always have kept a detailed diary of my daily doings; so I could give the chief executive of the bank chapter and verse of the whole dirty little saga. The chief executive was wonderful and pulled all the strings he could, but as he pointed out, even if they as a bank had the forex that we required, they could not send it out the country without the approval of the Reserve Bank. As Jennifer had been pulling the wool over our eyes and no application had been made to the Reserve Bank, we had to start from scratch! And that would take time.

You can imagine how Mark was feeling. He was leaving home (and he's a true African, his heart is here) going to the unknown, he'd never even visited the university and had no idea what to expect. And then he had this added complication of funds, or the lack of! My heart went out to him when he went through to the departure lounge at Harare international airport. He should have been excited about the prospect of going off to university, instead here he was going with this entire 'Jennifer' saga hanging over his head. He arrived at the university on Sunday 19th September 2004, for 'freshers' week and then to officially start lectures on Monday 27th. It doesn't matter whether you're a millionaire or not, in Zimbabwe if you haven't got forex then the only avenue open to you is to go through the official channels of the Reserve Bank, or pay through the nose for black market forex. The branch manager phoned and said that she wanted to bring Jennifer around to our house to apologise to me. I know it's not particularly Christian, but I said I never wanted to see her again. I just wanted the money paid to the university. Wednesday 24th November finally saw the university receiving the payment of the fees. I do not know what action the bank took against Jennifer, but neither she nor the manager, were ever seen in that branch again. Mike and I were well known in the bank after that. We were treated like royalty and everyone knew who we were – what a price to pay for five minutes of fame!

CRIME ABOUNDS

My late father-in-law Yvo, was an extremely independent man and even in his old age refused to come and live with our family, preferring to remain in the house that he'd lived in since the early 1950s. It was a constant worry for us. He was old and therefore he was a target for criminals. To live in most parts of Africa is to live behind burglar bars, steel security gates, alarms, security guards and all the other trappings that are supposedly meant to make us feel protected in our own homes. They're all very well and good if they are used correctly, but if you forget to lock the front door when you go to bed at night, then all the security in the world won't help. Yvo had done a few silly things like leaving doors unlocked – haven't we all! – and fortunately, although expensive financially for him, the robberies that he did incur did not harm him physically.

We also worried about his driving which was pretty hair-raising in his latter years. Driving in Zimbabwe is a bit like playing Russian roulette. It's so often difficult to find traffic robots that work. If they do, the bulbs are so dim that it's a guessing game as to what colour they are. Drivers in this country are either incredibly daring, or they're Kamikaze pilots in disguise. They will be in the right-turning lane and at the last minute, turn left. The robots might be on red, but if they're daring enough, drivers will take their chances sailing through in the face of on-coming traffic. If you see your best mate in the whole world and want to stop and have a chat, don't bother being considerate – or prudent – by pulling over to the side of the road, go for it, live life in the fast lane – or in the middle of the road actually, and just expect everyone to go round you, or to sit patiently behind you. We're so used to the state of affairs on our roads that we're actually quite blasé about it all; it's such fun to watch foreign visitor's reactions when they're in the car with you!

You now have a better understanding of our concern when Yvo took to the streets as not only was he nearly ninety, but he was also quite deaf. I used to worry sick that he'd be out driving when the President's cavalcade came along with the outriders on motorbikes and military vehicles with men armed to the hilt. These presidential guards and outriders shoot first and ask questions later if hapless civilian drivers don't get out of the way in time ......and sometimes drivers are literally only given seconds to move. Yvo shared his house and his life with a Heinz 57 variety mutt from the SPCA, Chippy. His lineage might have been a tad suspect, but his heart was great and he was a wonderful companion for Yvo. As soon as Yvo went to get into the car, Chippy would jump into the back and go along for the ride, fortunately his canine brain didn't get the implications of the danger that he was placing himself in. He was with his master and that was all that mattered.

We were constantly nagging Yvo that when he came back home, he should lock the car when he got out to open the gate. I know it's a maddening performance. Drive up to the gate. Switch off ignition. Get out car. Lock car. Get to gate. Unlock padlock on gate. Unlock car. Drive through. Get out car. Lock car. Close and lock gate. Unlock car, drive off. The reason we were pressurising Yvo to do all of this, was that two elderly lady friends of ours, on separate occasions, had each had their cars taken away from them at gunpoint while they were opening their gates. Not only were the vehicles taken, but also so were their handbags with their driver's licences and I.Ds. You might not think that this is such a tragedy, but wait until you live in a country where it can take a year or more to replace these valuable documents and then you'll fully appreciate how serious their loss can be.

Needless to say, Yvo did not always listen to us. On Sunday 12th July 1998, he'd been out with Chippy in the car, stopped at the gate and left the keys in the ignition. While his back was to the car and he was unlocking the gate, someone jumped in and drove away with the car – and far worse, they drove away with Chippy. Neither the car nor the dog was ever seen again. Frankly we were relieved when the car went, it was a blessing in disguise. Other people take annual holidays, but Yvo used to have an annual accident and these were getting progressively worse as the years went by. Luck was on his side, as yet, he hadn't maimed or killed himself or anyone else, but it was just a disaster waiting to happen. The loss of his beloved companion hit him hard. It hit us hard. Chippy was a part of all of our lives. We're convinced that Yvo died as the result of a broken heart. I know that sounds trite. I know he died as the result of a heart attack on Saturday 29th August 1998, two days after his eighty-ninth birthday. Not only had his independence been taken from him, but also his anxiety over Chippy's whereabouts was a constant heartache for him and he never stopped blaming himself for being careless where his beloved companion was concerned.

Zimbabwe can be a warm, vibrant, wonderful land, but it also has a darker side that unfortunately slithers insidiously into so many lives. In April 1994, our neighbours' beautiful daughter was brutally murdered at the bottom of our road. In July 2002 one of the boys in Mark's class was shot and killed in his home in front of his family, the thieves then departing without taking anything. In December 2003, the accountant on a tea estate where we were spending Christmas was beaten, forced to drink acid and left to die tied to a tree miles away from his home. Several members of his staff were also forced to drink acid. His memorial service was on Christmas Eve, what a constant reminder for his wife and daughters. In February 2004, the father of one of the boys in Heath's class was shot and killed in his home, in front of his family and on his eldest son's eighteenth birthday. The mother was also shot. She survived. Again, the thieves left taking nothing. The list could go on. These are people that we as a family personally knew. Thousands if not millions, of Zimbabweans would be in a position to tell similar stories.

There are of course the smaller, non-violent, but still invasive crimes. We have been blessed to have a man like Taundi working for us, as he is honest. There's always a 'but' isn't there? Someone or something is getting into our locked pantry and nicking the brandy! It was going down at such a rate, that Mike was seriously considering signing me up for A.A and, in turn, I was wondering when Mike was sneaking all the drinks. We don't think Taundi's taking the hooch. He's always been teetotal. If he is taking it, then he's selling it, not drinking it. When we are not at home, the pantry is always locked, and when we're at home we're always in and out of the kitchen and if it is Taundi stealing, then he must have an incredible slight of hand. BUT the brandy is going down. So is the whisky and other bottles of alcohol that we have in the pantry. Honey and peanut butter are disappearing. Precious, essential, unavailable things like cooking oil, sugar and soap aren't being touched! Because of the kinds of things that are 'walking', we feel that the thief is a person with a younger palate than old

Taundi, and that more than likely one of his teenage sons has acquired a duplicate key. Mike's trying to beat them (whoever 'them' are) at their own game and has changed the lock on the pantry.

You learn to live with funnies like this. It's a way of life and it could be a whole lot worse. Then there was the most curious incident when Taundi went out of the house for quarter of an hour or so, forgetting to lock the steel security gate on the back door on his way out. On his return to the house, he was bewildered to see the scullery in total disarray with vegetable baskets, the broom, floor mop strewn all over the floor, but the worst part was that someone had tried to jimmy or crowbar the handle and lock off one of the deepfreezes. They made a mess of the handle. They didn't manage to open the freezer, but they did manage to destroy the lock. Thank goodness Mike is a regular Mr. Fix-it. The irony of the situation is that in the scullery we have two 12 cubic foot deepfreezes which are locked, and two frigs packed to the hilt standing side-by-side, neither of which is able to be locked. Why go to all the wanton destruction on the freezer handle and lock, when it would have been so much easier to open either of the frigs and just help yourself?

Life for the majority of people, who live in a country where the unemployment rate is 80% and one of the highest inflations in the world, is not exactly a bed of roses. There are a lot of desperate people. People with families who need to eat. People with families who need clothes. People who need medical attention. So they turn to a life of crime. Our house would give Fort Knox a run for its money. I'm not sure if it's because we built during the war years, or if we're just both obsessed with security; whatever the reason, I have always felt safe inside our house. On the outside of both our front and back doors, we have hardened steel security gates.

We built our house during the war years when thoughts of security were uppermost in our minds. The alarm is on all the time. It's second nature that if we want to open a door or a window, we have to switch off the alarm first. There are panic buttons strategically placed around the house, the number of times that unsuspecting visitors have pressed these thinking that they are light switches is unbelievable. Every window is barred, not the twee little bars that you can buy ready-made, these are big, heavy-duty ones. Every door leading outside has at least a couple of bolts. The enclosed courtyard off our bedroom has a ten-foot wall with bits of broken glass cemented to the top of it. The house is built cantilevered over the hillside, so one side, the back, is at road level and the security here is extra strong. The rest of the house is way off the ground and therefore not easily accessible from the ground level at the front of the house.

One thing that I have learnt in this country, never say never. Nothing is impossible. We usually spend a night or so in our house in Borrowdale, Harare every week. It's a really weird, nomadic existence, but we've become accustomed to it. We started staying several nights in town out of necessity when the lack of fuel became especially serious in 2003, Heath still had to get to school. Friday 23rd May 2003 was one such night when we decided to stay overnight in Harare. It was a cold, winter's night and we had a fire roaring away. The peace and quiet of the evening was shattered when the phone rang at eleven o'clock. My stomach always goes into a knot when we receive late night phone calls. Invariably it's not good news.

The very first cell phone we ever owned was a Nokia 6110, an old brick. When I look at it now, I don't know how I managed to fit it into my handbag. Telephones are a bit of a luxury in third world countries. Roundabout 2000, Mark was pestering us to purchase a cell phone and we were adamant that we'd never have one and that they were invasive and totally unnecessary. Mark was like a stuck record, but we gave him as good as we got! We were not going to get a cell phone. They were far too expensive. Mark looked at us and we could see the little cogs going around in his grey matter. Some time later he came home from school quite excited and proudly informed the three of us, "I've got a cell phone!"

Mike, "Where did you get it from?"

Mark, "School."

Mike, "Well, you're just going to have to give it back."

With that, Mark proudly produced the cell phone. We still have it to this day. He made it in pottery class and it is an exact replica of the real thing, it was beautifully made. He reckoned that I could sit in the car when I was waiting for him and Heath to come out of school and I could have pretend conversations on my phone without the added worry that it might ring while

I was supposedly talking! Now I could be the typical 'northern suburbs' mother. A few months later we decided that it would be prudent to have a cell phone for emergencies especially as our party-line land line phone was temperamental at the best of times and hence the purchase of the 'brick'.

This 'brick' was eventually left in the house for Taundi to use in emergencies, as our landline hasn't worked since September 2005. This particular Friday evening the burglar alarm in the Mazowe house went off at nine o'clock. Taundi went into the house to see what set it off. He went into every room and could find nothing amiss. He thought that perhaps a nocturnal animal had set if off, it does happen from time to time. So he decided to wait a bit and a short while later, he heard a loud rustling of leaves. The patio below our balcony is covered in creeper, which grows on a trellis that is connected to the balcony railing. It is quite a substantial structure and our cats quite often use it to walk out on and take a siesta there in the hot weather – it must be paradise lying out there, cool breezes above and below and shelter from the sun in the form of dense foliage of the bignonia creeper. I would never have thought that the creeper and the trellis would have taken the weight of a man, but once again, I found out that you're never too old to learn something new.

The rustling of the leaves stopped. Taundi reset the alarm and silence prevailed. About an hour later the alarm siren shrieked through the quiet of night, the dogs went berserk. This time, Taundi made his presence known as he went from room to room trying to find what had set off the alarm. He couldn't find a thing. He decided to phone us in Harare as he was worried and frightened. All the while Mike and Taundi were talking on the phone in the background the siren was wailing and the dogs were barking. Mike jumped into the car and headed out to Mazowe. He didn't realise that our old Mazda 323 (which was actually my parents' car that they had left behind when they went to the U.K) could go so fast. He made excellent time back home. He went straight to our bedroom as the alarm siren is situated in a box just outside our window. As he drew open the curtains, he and Taundi were flabbergasted. The sliding door from our bedroom onto the balcony was wide open. We had always thought that our house was impregnable especially from the front. We learnt a valuable lesson. We had been *so* lucky! The thieves had cut two holes in different places in the security fence not only for entry but also to facilitate a quick getaway. They had managed to climb the four metres from the ground onto the downstairs patio and then a further three metres from the patio to the balcony by way of the creeper.

Whoever they were they had detailed information of the layout of our house, more so of our bedroom and of the alarm system. It must have been an inside job. We knew it wasn't Taundi as he'd been working for us for thirty years and we'd never had occasion to question his honesty. The person who immediately sprung to mind was Peter. Rarely do any of our staff see the inside of our house except for Taundi, but Peter was always seconded to do any painting and would be in a perfect position to give know the lay of the land. Maybe I'm doing poor Peter a disservice, maybe the thieves just struck lucky. The thieves had deliberately targeted our bedroom as the alarm could be disconnected from here. The intruders removed the panel of mosquito mesh from the outside of the louver windows, doing severe damage to the panel in the process. They were then able to manoeuvre the louvers open enough to reach the key that we always left in the lock. It was then a simple task to open the top and bottom bolts and hey presto, entry to the entire house. We will never know the reason for their hasty departure but we were grateful that Taundi was not harmed and that none of our possessions were taken.

Mike decided that we'd make it even more difficult to gain entry to the house from the front. We have two metre buttress walls at intervals to strengthen the patio terrace. These buttresses were now given a severe cement slope and had six inch steel nails cemented into them. Steel nails were also cemented all around the top of the retaining patio walls and any other surface that might provide purchase for someone trying to climb onto the patio. Barbed wired was then tightly wound all around the bottom of the balcony rail and also around the wires and poles of the trellis supporting the creeper. Anyone trying to gain entry to the house through this way would have a painful experience. The alarm wires have been painted the same colour as the wall to try and camouflage them and even in bright sunlight they are quite difficult to spot. As an added precaution none of the keys for any of the sliding doors are left in the locks. Judging by the various footprints in the soil around the holes in the security fence, there were five men. Not a pleasant thought. We were so grateful that our dogs hadn't been poisoned. In Christon Bank and surrounding area, there had been a spate of dog poisonings with some dogs dying in excruciating pain. As a result some residents now carry their own antidote to the poison.

Many residents especially in the more affluent northern suburbs organised their own Neighbourhood Watch and out of their own pockets paid for security guards to patrol certain streets, put wooden booms across the roads and liaised with the local police. Many people not only live behind walls topped with barbed wire plus an electric fence, electric gates and inside an alarmed house, but they also employ the services of a security firm. This is just a fact of life in Africa. It's far more difficult to organise a residents' security scheme in rural areas, the distances are just too vast, communications poor and it's not always practical. We do have each other's cell phone numbers in case of an emergency, but half the time there is no cell phone signal and we all live behind security fences and padlocked gates so it's difficult to get in to the grounds.

Monday 3rd January 2005 we were driving down our road in the early afternoon on our way into town when half way along the road we encountered a land rover full of heavily armed police. It was a frightening sight, after the land invasions we were still a bit wary of putting our trust in the police. We had know way of knowing if these police were coming to arrest us on some trumped-up charge. Oh yea of little faith. They were only doing their duty. The driver signalled to us to stop and then proceeded to warn us that there had been sightings of armed men in the area and that the police were going around to all the smallholdings to warn the inhabitants. We were grateful to the police but a bit uneasy about spending the night away, especially as our neighbours were away in South Africa at the time. We had to go into town for a prior arrangement, but we phoned Taundi to warn him to be vigilant. He said that the police had already been to our house and explained the situation to him. It was with relief that we arrived back home after lunch on Tuesday 4th January to find that our staff, animals, house and possessions were all intact.

Just as we were beginning to relax, the domestic worker from a house further up the hill, Vasco, came to see us and he was frightened, his employer was out of the country at the time and we were looking after things on his behalf. According to Vasco, the land rover came to the gate, which is always kept locked and the police became belligerent when Vasco refused to open the gate to allow them access to the property. He informed the police that he had not seen any armed men and that he would be on the lookout for them. We've never discovered why the police were so adamant that they wanted on the property, but Vasco had been at the wrong end of too many robberies and attempted robberies, and as the owner, Tom, was not present, Vasco was just as determined that as there was no discernible reason for the police to enter and as they refused to give a valid reason, they were not getting through the gate!

The situation turned verbally nasty. The police threatened Vasco and said that if he didn't allow them through the gate, the next time that he went out of it would be in a body bag. He was unrelenting. Short of breaking down the gate, which had been made by Mike, and which was fabricated from steel, and was in the region of two-and-a-half metres high, there was nothing the police could do but leave. We swithered whether we should try and do anything about the situation, but as it was supposedly the police who were involved, we decided that it would be prudent to leave things be. That night we went to bed and in the wee small hours of the morning my cat Ditch awoke me. He sleeps on the bed curled up next to me and he started growling, well a cat's sort of growl. He was not happy.

I woke Mike and said that something wasn't right. He got up, looked round the house, everything seemed fine. The dogs were barking but became quiet when Mike called out to them. To give the dogs their due, we're not always that fair to them. There's a lot for the dogs to bark at and it's not all sinister. They howl at the moon. They bark at the nocturnal animals like the night apes, or pookies, which sit in the trees making hideous screeching noises. They bark at the duiker running through the bush outside the security fence. They bark at the rabbits that are tantalizingly just out of their reach. They bark at people walking through the bush in the night. They bark at other dogs that roam the area scavenging. We usually can tell by the tone of their bark whether we should investigate or not.

The dogs were quiet for a while, but that didn't last for long. To add to the upheaval, Ditch had started growling again and then things came to an ear-shattering crescendo when the alarm for the outbuildings started its ear-piercing wail. This time we knew for sure that something was going on. I always hate when Mike goes out at night to check up on things. I personally think he should take a weapon, but he feels happier without. This night he again went out weapon-less. Up the hill behind our house we have a massive shed and anyone else's junk that they are getting rid of, we take, 'just in case'. If an object is at all repairable, Mike can repair it. The shed is full of borehole pipes, lengths of wood, old furniture, bags of cement, old fish tanks, an ancient land-rover, a boat with a hole in its side, a trailer – you name it, we've probably got it!

The glass in two of the shed windows had been smashed and the bars cut with bolt cutters – but obviously not enough to allow a person through. The padlock on the security gate had been forced with a crow bar, but that appeared to be all the damage. Mike, with the aid of Taundi who had come from his house when he heard the alarm, made a plan and did a quick temporary repair to the shed windows and rejoined the alarm wires where they'd been cut. Mike found a spare padlock to put on the security gate and as he was in the process of putting it on, something white in a bush a couple of metres away from him, caught his eye. Our big male Doberman, Marka, was also there but didn't seem concerned. Mike went out the gate towards the bush just as the white 'thing' rose up and hared away after first crashing through a barbed wire fence near the gate. The white thing was a white tee shirt on a black body. It could just as easily have run towards Mike as away from him. Could just as easily been carrying a weapon.

We both found it hard to get back to sleep and were both up long before the alarm clock went off in the morning. The amazing thing was that Heath was able to sleep through all of this. He had no inkling of the nights' drama. His bedroom is nearest the kitchen and by proximity, nearest the shed and its alarm, but he still managed to sleep through and was blissfully ignorant that anything had happened. It was only when he and Mike went out of the house in the morning that we discovered the full extent of the damage. Somehow the thieves had managed to jimmy open the kitchen window and had had a go at the burglar bars. Unbeknown to them, there are double sets of bars on that window. Mike wasn't happy with the original bars that were on the window as he felt that they were too flimsy so he put another heavy-duty set of bars in front of the existing ones.

Our Mazda 323 was parked outside the kitchen door, as there was no room for it in our garage. Heath noticed that the front window had been smashed and the back passenger door was open. The interior was full of spent matches – obviously used as a source of light – and the car had been ransacked for anything movable. We're convinced that the thieves were going to try and take the car; it would have been easy to push it down the driveway and out of the security gate. We decided against calling the police as nothing was taken and half the time the phones don't work so you can't get the police and when you do, they don't have the transport or the fuel to attend to a crime.

Just after breakfast, Vasco came to see us as he too had had problems in the night. Tom's electric fence had been cut and somehow the energiser had been immobilised. The attempt to break in to the house had been ineffectual and nothing had been taken. Vasco had seen the face of one of the intruders as they ran away. We thought that perhaps it would now be sensible to call the police and wonders of wonders, our home phone worked. We were even further amazed when the police arrived within thirty minutes, this was definitely a first. The land rover the two men arrived in was in such a state of disrepair that it had to be left on the road with rocks behind the tyres acting as brakes. They were not going to chance the hill down to our gate. We later wondered how they knew about our steep driveway! The doors on the vehicle had no handles and were operated by bits of wire.

We sat at the dining room table giving our statement. Both policemen were unusually taciturn and there wasn't a whole lot of small talk, which was unusual. I produced glasses of Mazoe orange juice and watched as both men sullenly listened to Mike saying that next time he'll go out with his gun and shoot first and ask questions later. I couldn't put my finger on it, I've learnt over the years to take heed of the 'feelings' I sometimes get, but there was something not quite kosher about these two men. They finished their orange juice and finished with the statements. Mike took them to kitchen window and the shed to have a look, but their inspection was cursory. Then they took their leave and supposedly went up the hill to Tom's house to interview Vasco.

Not long after this, Vasco again arrived at our backdoor in quite a state. He demanded to know why Mike had sent those police up to him! Mike explained that we hadn't been going to bother calling the police for our break in, but as two houses in the area were affected, we thought it was best. Vasco said that he'd taken one look at the police when they arrived at his gate and refused to let them in or give them a statement – he said that they were two of the men in the land-rover who had threatened to kill him the day before and that he recognised the face of the taller one as one of the night's intruders! No wonder those two men had been so prompt in their response to our call out. They evidently didn't want anyone else finding out about their nefarious activities. We never followed it up, but I'm certain that no report was ever made and no statements filed. To think that they were sitting at our table with us!

Tuesday 15th May 2007 we were again spending the night in Harare. At ten thirty in the evening, Mike's cell phone rang. I knew it wouldn't be good news. Taundi was using the brick cell phone, and once again he'd had fun and games. He'd been going back to check up on our house at nine o'clock after a five hour power outage and just as he reached the back door, he realized there were two men standing in the shadows. He had the presence of mind to dive into the kitchen while pulling the steel security gate shut. He said the intruders looked and sounded fairly young and both had hats pulled low over their faces which made us suspicious that they were known to Taundi. One of the men said that he had a gun and started to put his hand on the security gate. Nothing to our intrepid Taundi, crime buster of note, he always carries a big knife that's verging on a panga with him at night and he told the thief that if he put his fingers on the gate, he'd chop them off! At the same time, he pressed the panic button right at the door. We'll never know whether it was the idea of a samurai wielding Taundi, or the noise of the alarm, but the two would-be thieves took to their heels, leaving behind a few lengths of rope that they'd brought with them, obviously to restrain their victims.

Mike asked if Taundi wanted us to come back to the house, but the answer was negative. Taundi and his son plus our gardener had done the rounds of the house and the outbuildings and the only thing that was damaged was the broken padlock on the gate leading into our property. What amused us was the behaviour of our dogs! Seemingly our German Shepherd Denva, was sitting by the back door when the intruders were there, wagging her tail and giving them a warm welcome intimating, 'Welcome to our home'! I know our dogs are not the world's greatest guard dogs, but surely they're not *that* useless! I think our dogs are undercover guard dogs posing as benign pets. Under deep cover. Very, very deep cover. Their cover is so perfect that they've even fooled us and themselves to boot. Although it was late at night, I decided that it would be best if we phoned our neighbours and warned them that there were undesirables in the area. The undesirables decided to wait until about three in the morning of Thursday 17th May 2007 to make their presence known, this time at our neighbours, Alan and Hilary's home.

The neighbours have two dogs and I have to admit they are far better watchdogs than ours! Shumba is a lean, mean, killing machine of a Ridgeback. His adopted brother, Tiger, is an extremely handsome Heinz 57 variety with leanings towards the St. Bernard family. I love Tiger, but he knows how to use his teeth when he has to and I am very, very wary of Shumba. I would NEVER dream of walking into our neighbour's house in the dead of night with those dogs around. That is just what the intruders did. They jimmied open the back door and had a party in the kitchen. Thank goodness Alan and Hilary keep the inter-leading door from the kitchen to the rest of the house locked, as this had also tried unsuccessfully to be forced open. The thieves went away with full bellies and an assortment of electrical items that they stole. The footprints outside showed that there were four intruders. This little party could have ended tragically. Who knows what four men who'd been free with Alan's beers would have done had they managed to get through the inner door?

It didn't end there. Within a two-week period, Alan and Hilary were broken into four times, presumably by the same gang. On the last encounter, Alan was just about to unlock the door leading from the bedroom wing of the house when he heard the noise of someone in the lounge. He shouted to Hilary to bring the guns. As Alan unlocked and opened the door they were just in time to see the thief escape through the French doors where he'd partially removed the burglar bars. As the thief's backside exited through the door Hilary took a shot at him. Shooting's not one of Hilary's fortes, she shouldn't give up her day job anytime soon – apart from the fact that she's retired of course. The bullet went through another pane of glass (more expense!) and lodged itself in the water tank outside creating a little fountain of water. I know Hilary would seriously have loved the bullet to have lodged itself in the intruder's backside, but with all the complications that that would bring, it's just as well she missed. To make sure he got the message, she then went outside and shot a couple more rounds into the air. Don't think he'll be back any time soon.

ROADWORTHY OR NOT

Vehicles of all kinds have a hard life in this part of the world and when they finally go to the big scrap yard in the sky, they go knowing that they have given their all and have nothing left to give. They carry loads that they were never designed to carry. They go places that even the hardiest of four by fours would blanche at going. They perform tasks that would normally be unbelievable. Public transport in Zimbabwe is virtually negligible. There are far too many people for the numbers of transporters available. Rural passengers can wait hours even days for a bus to pass their way. The most common form of public transport is the commuter omnibuses popularly referred to as E.T.s (emergency taxis) not to be confused with alien E.Ts who 'phone home'. The E.Ts are usually sixteen-seater mini buses. They are quite often worked to death and concern as to their roadworthiness by their owners is not high on their list of priorities.

Typical sight on Zimbabwean roads

Saturday 27th December 2003 we were in a convoy of three four-wheel drive vehicles travelling back to the Honde tea estates in the eastern districts of Zimbabwe on the Mozambique border. This is a part of Zimbabwe like no other. It is lush, beautiful, verdant, and isolated. I admit to a feeling of slight unease when I am in the Honde if anything amiss were to happen, you are miles, many miles, away from civilisation. The Honde too, has not been spared from the political upheavals that have beset our country. This particular day we were coming from the Kairezi as it's now spelt, before Independence it was the Gairezi, a hauntingly beautiful and wild river. Our good friends and ex-neighbours, Rob and Val, who had been savagely kicked off their farm and were now working at the tea estates in the Honde, had very kindly invited us to spend Christmas with their family. Their son Doug, and our Mark, who were both working in the U.K would be home for Christmas and though it wouldn't be a Christmas like we used to share it would be the next best thing. This Christmas was to prove to be like no other.

On the 18th of December, the accountant of the tea estates had been brutally murdered and his memorial service was on Christmas Eve. Other members of the accounts staff had been forced to drink acid, but had survived their ordeal. To try and make life fractionally more manageable for the accountant's two distraught daughters and the other families on the estates, Rob and Val organised an outing to the Kairezi River where those brave enough could go tubing down the rapids. There were seventeen of us driving in convoy, with the six of us 'oldies' together with three youngsters in the lead vehicle, an Isuzu double cab. The group comprised of farmers who'd had experiences that you wouldn't wish on your worst enemy, of grieving relatives and of ordinary folk. Emotionally we were all a bit fragile while trying to put on a brave face. The horror was still fresh in everyone's minds and we were still feeling a bit raw. A friend and colleague had been murdered which jarred the concept of the festive season. The gang that had perpetrated this brutal attack on the accountant and his staff was still unaccounted for. Although it was highly unlikely that they were still in the area, it was felt best to take nothing for granted. We were probably the only whites in the area, we felt vulnerable. As a precaution we thought it best to keep in touch by means of walkie-talkies in each vehicle. In our vehicle we'd been discussing what call sign we'd use and finally agreed on "Dream Team". You can imagine our consternation when the youngsters in one of the following vehicles made contact and called us "Sparrow Fart"! Not quite what we had in mind.

The tubing and ensuing picnic hadn't been quite as successful as we'd hoped as the rain decided to come down in torrents. However it was still a good day and a lot of laughs and just for a few minutes we could switch off from reality. We were wending our way back home and had turned off the main road onto the road that leads down to the Honde escarpment. This must surely be one of the most beautiful parts of Zimbabwe. The road takes a steep, winding descent down into the valley and sorely tests the capabilities of vehicles' brakes. Our Isuzu had just begun its descent and in the distance we noticed an E.T parked at a lay-by ahead of us. Luckily Rob was driving slowly and just as he was about to pass the E.T it pulled out in front of us. A few expletives were muttered and we stayed where we were. It was obvious that the offending vehicle was experiencing mechanical problems.

Clouds of foul-smelling smoke were billowing out of it and there was a stench of binding brakes. What subsequently transpired took place in slow motion. The E.T slowly slid across to the other side of the road, it was a gradual and graceful slide, it was almost artistic. It reached an earth embankment on the far side of the road and gracefully mounted it and just as gracefully rolled over until it came to a gentle stop on its roof. As we drove past we had a vision of sixteen or so bewildered passengers hanging up side down like motionless bats. Again, as if in slow motion, the first bat clad in a bright red shirt slowly extricated himself and sat on the ground next to the E.T. We were in a dilemma. Do we stop or not? Under normal circumstances the thought wouldn't have entered our minds and we automatically would have stopped and rendered assistance.

These were not normal circumstances. Two of the occupants of our Isuzu had been viciously thrown off their farm. My own family had been threatened with expulsion from our home. My parents had had to leave their home of fifty years. The other couple in the truck had lost two members of their family as a result of the land invasions. Every occupant of the Isuzu was still raw with grief from the latest murder. If we stopped would we somehow be blamed for the accident? We came to a virtual halt and discussed the pros and cons. We watched a few more of the E.T. passengers getting out and no one appeared injured. There was no blood, no gore. The accident had happened so slowly that not much damage human or mechanical, had taken place.

We made a plan. We made the decision to continue with our journey. The 'Sparrow Fart' team was in contact with the two trailing vehicles and, as each of these passed the over-turned E.T, they reported in. It soon became apparent that all the passengers had managed to get out and appeared to be unharmed. If there had been serious injuries, there would have been no question that we would have stopped. As it was, an unworthy road vehicle had had a minor accident. We were worried that somehow we would be blamed for causing the accident. None of us were proud of the fact that we drove away. Unfortunately the prevailing circumstances in our country had affected our thoughts and therefore our actions.

Easter 2007 we went to Kyle National Park on a fishing trip with our good friends Debs and John. There were five of us in John's double cab truck, which was absolutely laden with our provisions for the weekend and we were also towing a speedboat. It would have been far more convenient if we'd been able to go in two trucks, but not only was the fuel difficult to source, it was also extremely expensive, so we decided to pool our resources. Mike and I managed to buy forty litres of diesel as our contribution. Although we would be passing several service stations en route to the camp, there was no guarantee that any of them would have fuel. This made long-distance travel so much more difficult. We also took drinking water with us, another precious commodity in Africa. There was running water available in the lodges within the park, but there was no assurance that it would be potable. The truck strained towing the boat and carrying the load – and what a load it was! We had to take everything that we would require for the Easter weekend. There were no shops for miles and miles, so if we forgot anything, it could have been a bit of a disaster. We ensured that we had all the essentials including Easter eggs. What else could we possibly need?

We left home early in the morning as it would take us about seven hours travelling and we couldn't go fast towing the boat. We were just near the town of Chegutu when we came upon a bus accident, which had only recently occurred. It transpired that the bus had crashed into a cow and we later learnt on the news that ten people had died in the collision. Zimbabweans are pragmatic. The uninjured passengers were already in the process of butchering the mombe (cow) while the dead and injured were still in the damaged bus! You've got to admire our resilience as a nation. Meat, actually food in general, had become such a luxury in many households that it would be insanity to miss out on this opportunity.

Another incident that we witnessed on another occasion was when one morning we were following a pick-up truck (sometimes called a 'bakke') laden to the hilt with passengers. They were in the cab. They were in the back, which was so full that they were hanging on to the sides. They were everywhere. Mike had thought about overtaking the bakke, but somehow the opportunity never presented itself. We were stuck behind it. We were plain just stuck behind it for the major part of our journey into Harare. As we were nearing the outskirts of the city, the bakke started producing an appalling smell like that of burning brake-pads and it started getting slower and slower. I suggested to Mike that now would be the time to overtake, I'm the expert back-seat driver. He was still a bit hesitant to do so as the bakke was not behaving normally and we were coming up the bridge over the Gwebi River.

The events of the next few minutes were fascinating. Filthy smoke started streaming out from the rear, passenger side tyre, followed by some incandescent orangey red sparks. The bakke got slower and slower. The driver and passengers seemed to be singularly unconcerned. Gradually the tyre eased further and further off the axle until it gently plopped onto the tar, genteelly bounced a couple of times and came to rest against the concrete railing of the bridge. Whilst this little drama was playing out in front of our eyes, the axle decided to give into the forces of gravity and again, most genteelly, dropped onto the tarmac and the lopsided bakke continued its slide ever so gently towards the verge.

No fireworks. No blood and gore. No histrionics. No alarm. Quietness and calm prevailed. The passengers in the back sat and grinned from ear to ear at us notwithstanding the precarious slant of the bakke. The stoic driver serenely and unhurriedly exited the cab to investigate. They all seemed to be unflappable and to be getting great enjoyment out of the proceedings. The fact that had they been going faster, or had they veered across the road in the face of oncoming traffic, or had they overturned, the consequences could have been tragic did not seem to phase any of them. Fact. Transport in Zimbabwe is a luxury for the masses. Fact. If you are fortunate to find a means conveyance from point A to point B, the passengers don't query its roadworthiness. Fact. Any mode of transport beats waiting for hours, if not days to get to the journey's end. Mike was impressed by the axle's capacity to carry the weight of the load for as long as it did before it sheered off. He was impressed by the bakke's capacity to come to a halt under those conditions without mishap.

For those who are not accustomed to driving conditions in Zim be aware that if you see broken branches, twigs, leaves, piles of grass on the side of the road in the direction in which you are travelling, they have been put there as a warning by a conscientious driver of a broken down vehicle ahead of you. This acts in the same way as a red triangle to denote a stopped vehicle. A few vehicles here do have red triangles, but unless you are prepared to guard them if they're out on the road, the chances are exceedingly high that the triangle will 'walk' in your absence. They make wonderful decorations in huts and houses. They can be used as a reflector on the back of a scotch-cart and have a myriad of other uses. So the use of natural, replaceable 'triangles' is most practical. A few drivers have the use of a cell phone and someone at the other end who is prepared to help, but the average stranded driver could quite easily find himself spending a considerable time next to his vehicle while awaiting help. Forget about the AA or other road services, this is Zimbabwe.

These broken-down drivers, sorry that came out wrong, I meant the drivers of the broken-down vehicles, are enterprising. They put out their warning foliage, quite often they put huge rocks under the wheels to act as brakes, and quite often leave the rocks in the road for unsuspecting drivers, and then they make themselves at home. They make a small fire on the dirt shoulder of the road to keep warm at night and to cook food. Many of the roadside vendors in the suburbs have huge bonfires going at night in winter and there is often quite a congregation around it of either customers who are waiting for mealies to be roasted on the fires, or of those passengers waiting for an E.T. to take them home.

LOCAL AFFAIRS

The community in our area comes under the Mazowe Rural Council. As with the vast majority of councils in the country it is cash-strapped, flat broke. Previous mismanagement of funds, rampant inflation, dwindling numbers of ratepayers all of these have contributed to the predicament. Zimbabweans are constantly looking for the light at the end of the tunnel and our tunnel just seems to get longer and longer. The local ratepayers association held its Annual General Meeting on a Sunday morning in May 2007, at a time of year when we are way beyond autumn and on a serious slide towards African winter. There are approximately one hundred and fifty-eight ratepayers in our area and, as is usual with events of this kind, possibly only twenty-five bodies decided to attend the meeting. The meeting was held in the local community hall within the school grounds in Christon Bank. 'Hall' is a bit of an exaggeration. At present it consists of a concrete slab approximately thirty by twenty metres, which is breaking up in places between some of the joints, a few metal supports and an asbestos sheet roof and no walls. This hall would not even be present if it hadn't been for the hard work, fund raising and generosity of previous ratepayers. The surrounding bush gave an explicit African ambiance to the proceedings.

Those of us who didn't have the foresight to take folding chairs, perched our derrieres on rickety, wobbly wooden benches, which were unusually patterned by the industrious workings of white ants. A nosy mama hen and her brood took an interest in the meeting. Mama upstaged the chairman on several occasions by walking along the low wall behind him, stopping, surveying us the interlopers into her territory with a beady eye, then letting forth with a most unladylike raucous cackle. The scrawny chicks didn't share mama's enthusiasm for the stage and they stood and watched from the wings – of the stage that is, not their own. The setting was given more

African authenticity from the smell of wood smoke that permeated the air. A few metres away from the hall stood, that's even an exaggeration, maybe I should say precariously tilted, a shack. Perhaps the caretaker lived there, perhaps the night watchman, perhaps a squatter, whoever it was, lived in abject poverty. I suppose they were just grateful for a roof over their heads. They can't be choosy about the quality of plastic sheeting used to cover the holes in the roof and the walls. They can't choosy about the size and shape of the rocks they use to hold the plastic sheeting in place.

They are grateful for whatever protection the shack offers. They are grateful that they have the facilities for keeping hens. The occupants of this dwelling *did* have the immense luxury of a nearby tap with running water. They also had the use of the hall's toilets. You note that I couldn't bring myself to use the word 'luxury' when discussing the loos. These consisted of long-drops, one for each of the sexes. Long-drops have their uses, but I am always apprehensive using them with thoughts of nyokas (snakes) being present. I also have in my mind the picture, actually it should have been censored – the picture I mean, not my mind – of Mike speedily exiting a long-drop at the foot of Mt Nyangani, in Nyanga, Zimbabwe's highest mountain at a height of 2,592 metres, with his knickers around his ankles being pursued by a *furious* swarm of bees that had taken great exception to the sight of his bare backside.

Digressing somewhat, it's the association of ideas. It was when we were staying at Rhodes Nynaga National Park in Nyngaga one school holidays that our family had the rare privilege of seeing a pangolin, no I'm not confused, this has absolutely nothing to do with loos or ratepayers association meetings, I just wanted to mention it. One of the game rangers had found the pangolin in the bush and called us over to have a look at it. What a magnificent creature and what a privilege to see one as they are not common. Pangolins are nocturnal anteaters and are believed by the local people to be the bearers of good luck. Nyanga is possibly my favourite part of the country. The name is derived from the headman Sanyanga, and means the place of the witchdoctors. Cecil Rhodes' attention was attracted by Nyanga (the old spelling before Independence in 1980 was Inyanga) in 1897 when he proclaimed that the area was the 'sanatorium of Rhodesia' because of its higher altitudes. He purchased an 82 000 hectare farm there, which was bequeathed to the people of Rhodesia on his death and subsequently became a National Park.

Right, back to the A.G.M, which is what this chapter is actually about, I apologise for my wanderings. No comments about wandering minds. Not that the proceedings of the meeting were boring, far from it, but I found my attention being caught by the inspiring surrounding scenery. Apart from mama hen's antics, we had flocks of birds that warbled loudly as if trying to drown out the voices of us mere mortals. There was the gentle wind rustling through the long, dry grass making a soothing swishing sound. There was the warmth from the sun. There were the dappled shadows where the sun shone through the indigenous trees. There was the faint rustle when an errant leaf would drop onto the floor. Dusty black children were playing in the dirt. A few ragged items of washing were pathetically hanging from a makeshift washing line. I loved every minute of being at the meeting. I *knew* I was in Africa. I was amongst good, hard-working people who wanted to do the best they possibly could for their community with extremely limited resources in incredibly difficult times. It made me proud to have the privilege of living amongst them.

The chairman explained that he had made various trips to the council offices to try and resolve several issues. Big deal, I can hear people say. Well, actually, it was a big deal. The council offices are approximately thirty kilometres away and I've gone on ad nauseam about the fuel situation in Zimbabwe. The chairman had used his own vehicle, his own fuel, his own time. It was a big deal. Each time he had gone to the council, he'd ask for the accounts to be made available for perusal and each time it was a wasted trip. The councillors worked to Africa time. It wouldn't have really made a whole lot of difference, the bottom line was that the council was stony broke and their equipment in such a state of disrepair, that they weren't in a position to do anything for the community. This situation was not peculiar to our particular council. It was the same state of affairs throughout the country. As a community we were on our own. It was up to us to 'make a plan'.

The local residents had formed a 'reaction stick'. In case of emergencies there was a list of telephone numbers of men in the area who were prepared to come out and help – of course that supposes that the phones worked. ZESA, the Zimbabwe Electricity Supply Authority was also broke. The

ZESA employees in our area were great and did (and still do) the best they possibly could with limited resources. There had been reports in the national newspapers that ZESA customers in Harare were having to source and pay for their own electric cable if it was necessary for repairs. We were told at our meeting that if we ever had the misfortune to have a transformer problem, we would have to pay for the cost of a new transformer ourselves! Unlike towns, where a transformer would service several houses, or perhaps and entire street, quite often in a rural area, it would be one transformer to one property. There was no way the majority of residents could afford the cost of a new transformer.

Power outages have been a way of life for so long in Zimbabwe that we should be used to them. We're not. And I'm not. I was being self-centred in my needs. I couldn't watch TV. I couldn't make a cup of coffee or use the stove. I couldn't use the computer. I couldn't use my hairdryer. I somehow was so wrapped up in my own needs that I didn't get the bigger picture. It was only at this meeting when the nursing sister in charge of the local clinic was giving her report and was explaining the difficulties *and* dangers of delivering babies in the dark, that the full implications of these outages hit me. The difficulties were those concerned with the safety of the mother and the child. The dangers were that so many of the mothers were H.I.V positive the nursing staff had to take extra precautions when dealing with them. This is difficult enough under normal circumstances, but in darkness, or by candlelight, the position was a whole different ball game.

The prevailing circumstances meant that the rural council was unable to fulfil its role so we as a community had to take control of our own affairs. The Zimbabwean Diaspora is far flung, and according to economists, the money that they send back home to family and friends, is keeping our economy afloat. We have our share of political refugees, but we also have a vast quantity of financial refugees. The latter would much prefer to be living in the land of their birth, but the crippling cost of living and the harsh conditions, have denied them that choice. There are so many of us here who are living in a state of limbo. We love our country, we don't want to leave, but daily it's getting more and more difficult to stay here. Many of us are at the age when we're past our 'sell-by-date' and it's a daunting thought to move to a new country where we would have to start from scratch to establish ourselves.

FLING FLANG FLUNG

My parents left Zimbabwe in 2002, followed by Mark in 2003. Heath was due to leave in 2005, and I was going to have to face the prospect of the empty nest in a contentious country. In one of my emails to Mark, I said, "When your boet (brother) leaves home, your Dad and I are going to be doing our 'Derby and Joan' act." It's at times like this that you tend to wonder why on earth you ever wasted money on school fees. Mark's answering email said, "These people, Derby and Joan, who are they, have I ever met them?" I didn't know whether to laugh or cry. I decided on the former, as I wasn't wearing waterproof mascara at the time. Then Heath did join his brother and grandparents, six thousand miles away and we were doing our Derby and Joan act in a country that wouldn't be out of place in at the Mad Hatter's tea party.

I'd had the privilege of being a stay-at-home mum for the best part of twenty years and although I'd done the basic bookkeeping and secretarial work for our little company, I hadn't gone out into the workforce. I needed *something* to do. A relative's daughter had just returned from a stint of teaching English in China and she made it sound easy and fun. She said that all you had to do was to stand up and talk. If there's something I excel at, it's talking. I like people. I like talking. Teaching English sounded as if it was tailor made for me. So I thought, why not?

Speciss college in Harare offering the ESOL (English for Speakers of Other Languages) course and I enrolled. I hadn't really thought it all through. I hadn't really given much thought to what the course entailed. My biggest concern was where I was going to be able to park my car when I was on the course! How simple could I be? I am so pleased that this was the case. If I had fully realized what the course required, I'd have probably said, "I can't do it." That would have been the end of that. Fortunately, I saw the course through. I wrote the exam and I passed. I also had no problems in parking my car you'll be pleased to hear. I loved every minute of the teaching and still continue to do so. I have met some wonderful people, who, in the normal course of events, I'd never have done. I get a thrill out of seeing a piece of language fall into place, or being able to share a joke (in English!) and be understood. I have learnt so much about the lifestyles, cultures, politics and tourism of my students' countries and with every single lesson, I learn something new myself. The students come from all over the world and from all walks of life. I never cease to be fascinated with the similarities and the differences between languages and between cultures.

It's sometimes a fine line trying not to be patronizing, albeit unintentionally. It's difficult to know when a student does know the meaning of a word, or they think they know. In one lesson, I was teaching advanced students and we were reading an article on 'Egyptology'. The class all seemed to be fairly clued up on the reading and the vocabulary, but I thought I'd better just check to be sure. I asked, "Does anyone know what a 'mummy' is?"

Henri, a young man from the Democratic Republic of the Congo answered, "It's a mammal with mammary glands." He wasn't wrong, just a different context. Another unknown word that came up in our reading passage was 'limp'. I explained what it meant and gave the different ways in which it could be used for example in a medical sense. I demonstrated the way in which it is masculine to give a firm handshake and a sign of weakness to give a 'limp' one. At the end of that lesson, the Angolan student came up to say farewell to me as he was returning to his country. I think he wanted to make sure that I fully appreciated his masculinity; I was lucky that he didn't do permanent damage to my hand.

By this time, I had stopped teaching at the college and had started teaching privately from home. I have come to the conclusion that Colombian women must be amongst the most beautiful in the world. I have had two as students and they were both stunning. Margarita became more than a student, she became a friend. We were both interested in natural and alternative health remedies and would walk around her garden discussing plants – all in English of course. We had a lesson in giving my fingernails a French manicure. We had lessons on cookery. We had lessons on the normal grind of the English language. In one reading passage the phrase 'far flung' was mentioned. Margarita asked me to explain it to her, which I did. I then expanded and taught about 'fling' as to throw and she said, "Oh, is it like the verb 'ring'? Ring, rang, rung. Fling, flang, flung?" We both burst out laughing, even Margarita could see that this wasn't right, and I said, "This is meant to be an English lesson, we're not learning Chinese!" When she left to go back to Colombia, we both had tears in our eyes and I treasure my farewell present of a pair of earrings.

Sexy Suzy had a different sort of beauty to Margarita. Margarita's features were classically beautiful. Suzy had sex appeal. Drop-dead sex appeal. There was just something about her. She was bubbly. She was alive. She was attractive. She never took the lessons too seriously, they were a fun time, and although she didn't realize it she was speaking in English so they did constitute a lesson. She would come to lessons in the most outrageous outfits that looked wonderful on her. She had a body to die for and a lot of visible body. She was a Latino in the 'Dirty Dancing' genre. Her clothes and makeup on anyone else would have looked cheap, not on her though. She looked a million dollars and with her personality, she could have got away with wearing anything or nothing as the whim took her.

She had never asked about the cost of the lessons before starting and when after our first session, Suzy asked whether the price was in U.S dollars or Zimbabwean, I thought, I *like* this woman. Sadly for me my fees were Zimbabwean dollars. If I could have been paid that number of US dollars, I probably would have treated myself to a world cruise on the Q.E II. Usually when we had our lessons we were alone in the house, but this particular afternoon, Mike was there. Suzy wasn't aware of this and when she heard a noise (Mike rummaging around in a cupboard) in the entrance hall next to the dinning room where we were sitting, she nervously asked, "What ees that noise? Who ees here?"

I replied, "It's only Mike." On cue, Mike poked his head around the corner and said hi. Mike enjoyed saying hi to Suzy. He never needed any excuse to say hi to Suzy. I can't imagine any red-blooded male not enjoying saying hi to Suzy. She really was very pleasant on the eyes. During this particular lesson, Mike had wanted to go into the kitchen, but didn't want to interrupt us further as he would have had to go through the dinning room where we were sitting, to get there. He went out the front door, around the house and in the kitchen door. As I was facing the window, I saw him go round. Suzy didn't. There was a noise in the kitchen. She nervously asked, "What ees that noise? Who ees here?"

"It's just Mike," I replied.

"Wot! You hav' two Mikes?" she asked in utter amazement.

"No Suzy, one is enough for me thanks."

Suzy often had to attend functions at an embassy in Harare and she said, "Every time I go there, the ambassador he drop something on the floor and he ask me, Suzy pleez you pick up. I pick up, and the ambassador, his eyes they are down here," she demonstrated his eyes being out on stalks, "and he look here," and she pointed to her very ample, delicious, Dolly Parton eat your heart out, bosom. Another time she went to a function, she said, "My husband, he very cross with me last night. What I do wrong teacher? The ambassador he sitting, I kiss on top of head and his nose eez here," pointing to her sensual cleavage. Only she could do something like that and get away with it. She was a breath of fresh air. She brightened up the day and I wish her well in the Caribbean where she's living now and I hope her new acquaintances find her as entertaining and likeable as I did. Go well Suzy.

Chilean Maria has also become a friend and we too have some good laughs. One lesson we had covered wild animals, hunting, culling, poaching and other related vocabulary. The next time I saw Maria she was spitting mad. She said that she and her husband had gone to one of the top restaurants in Harare and when she had read the menu, she became furious and she had started shouting at the staff and the manager, in her anger, she'd forgotten all her English and had been spouting at them in Spanish. She said that she would never go back to the establishment and that she was going to tell all her friends not to go. I told her to calm down and tell me what was bothering her.

"Do you know what they have on the menu?" she said.

"No?" I answered perplexed.

"They had poached fish." She replied.

It took me a few seconds, and then I clicked. Now I include the other meanings of poaching as in cooking by a method of steaming, as well as the illegal killing of animals. I'm not sure if Maria did go back to the restaurant, she looked a bit sheepish when she left me. It also reinforced for me the responsibility I have towards each and every student to try and prevent the pitfalls of the vagaries of the English language.

Wang Lee was a pleasant young man and a wonderful ambassador for his country, China. He was quite shy and diffident, but we did manage to share some jokes. I took him to a friend's house for tea at Christmas and he had his first ever taste of Christmas cake – I don't think he was overly impressed, we were at my friend's for one hour and twenty minutes and he hung on to his cup of coffee and took minute sips from it the whole time we were there, I think he was terrified that he'd get a refill, it just wasn't his cup of tea – sorry, couldn't resist that. I don't think he'd rush out and order a cup of coffee any time soon. He wasn't overly enamoured with the Christmas cake either. As he had a legal background quite a lot of the vocabulary we covered was based on legalese. We had discussed crime, theft, murder, manslaughter and other related words. When the word 'rape' came up, he asked me what it meant. I prefer that the students try and work things out for themselves, so I told him to look it up in his nifty electronic dictionary. He did. He looked at me and said, "What's wrong with rape?"

"It's wrong. It's not good. It's illegal."

Another glance at his dictionary. Another puzzled glance at me. "But, teacher, I don't understand what's wrong with it?"

"Wang Lee, you can't force someone to have sex. It's just not right."

Now his puzzled look turned to one of consternation. "But teacher, I rape every day."

Oh boy! I'm a woman alone in a house with a young man who's just admitted that he rapes every day! Did I panic? No. One of my brainwaves kicked in. Did I ask him to let me look at his dictionary? Yes. The only definition he had in it was 'green leafy vegetable' and he enjoyed *eating* it every day! Can you imagine the young man's panic? He's alone in a house with a middle-aged woman who's going on about having sex while he's discussing green, leafy vegetables. The look of absolute relief on his face when we cleared it up was worth a picture. I didn't get off so lightly; I still had to explain the meaning of 'rape' – and not the vegetable one.

Sandrine from Benin had the most fantastic sexy French accent and loved cooking. As a result, a lot of our lessons were based in the kitchen and she'd give demos to my other students. She showed us how to make the national fish dish and also how to make ginger beer from scratch – I mean literally from scratch. She brought her massive wooden pestle and mortar that she travels round the world with, won't leave home without it. It was so heavy being carved out of solid wood that I couldn't even lift the contraption. I'd bought some fresh ginger and Sandrine showed us how to wash it and pulverize it into a pulpy mass. The finished drink was wonderful and when I'm able to get sugar (which is not all that often) I make the ginger drink. I enjoy it warm as a tea or on a hot day, it's a refreshing cool drink. It was quite an experience for me to have a Beninese, two Mexicans, a Colombian, an Italian, and moi, the lone Zimbo, all in my kitchen at the one time.

In another of our lessons, Sandrine and I were discussing roasting chickens. When you buy a chicken to roast in Zimbabwe you have to remember to take the plastic bag containing the gizzards and feet out of the chest cavity. I'm talking from experience. Roasted plastic bag isn't going to help you get into the Michelin guide. From chickens, our lesson wandered onto cooking utensils and we finally arrived at Sandrine's kettle, which had just gone on the blink with the element giving out. The lesson further progressed from the smaller utensils containing elements to larger ones such as geysers. I was happy with the way in which the lesson was progressing, as it wasn't always the easiest thing to keep Sandrine focused. She'd flit from one subject to another and although it was all in English, and after all that's what she was trying to learn was conversational English, I liked the lesson to have at least some semblance of structure. We were almost winding up the lesson when Sandrine looked at me with a perplexed expression, she thought for a while, groped around for a few unknown words, and then asked why in Zimbabwe did we put geysers in our chickens? I then, was the one to look perplexed. Sandrine loved the fast-food places in Harare and I thought that perhaps Nandos or Chicken Inn had some new way of doing chickens – I thought perhaps she meant chickens cooked on rotisseries. She said, "Non. Non. Not dee cheekens you buy that are already cook-edd, dee ones you buy in Bon Marche and TM." Again I thought she might be referring to the delicatessen counter. "Non. Dee ones that are freezing that you cook at home." Finally it dawned on me. Sometimes it does take a while for me to see the light. It wasn't 'geysers' inside the chickens, it was the 'gizzards' – no wonder she thought us Zimbos were an odd bunch.

It's quite a responsibility helping foreign visitors to this country to try and understand the complexities of English. Take the case of Natasha from Serbia who wanted to enrol her young son in a nursery school and was relieved that there was one practically next door to where her family was living. Only when she went to make enquiries, did it transpire that it was a *plant* nursery. Natasha was also a slave to the latest fashions in footwear. It didn't matter if the heels were so high that she had to hobble along, if that's what was in vogue, then it was all worth it. I loved her shoes. She would have given Imelda Marcos a run for her money. I would have loved to know how many pairs she possessed. She phoned me on her return from a holiday in Serbia and invited me for coffee. She was excited and wanted to show me her latest donkeys that she'd brought back with her.

O.k. I did think it was an odd thing to bring back from holiday, but after all she was foreign, so who was I to question her. I asked her what size the donkeys were, her reply was that they were the usual size. When I enquired how many she had brought, she said two. I was by now, extremely curious. All was revealed on my arrival at her home, the 'donkeys' turned out to be a beautiful pair of sparkly gold-coloured high-heel 'mules' .... of the shoe variety and not of the ass family! Natasha thought we English speakers made life difficult for ourselves. Why, when we put on trousers did we put our legs into the trouser legs, if, when we were putting on blouses, did we put our arms into sleeves – and not into the 'arms' of the blouse? She could have a point there.

Italian Martina wanted the name of a good doctor, so I gave her the name of mine. She registered and when she came for her next lesson, she said, "That is a nice family practice."

I was a bit confused. "Yes," I replied, "many families do go there."

"No" she answered, "No, I mean that the doctor's sister is working for her."

I then had to explain the differences between a nursing sister and a sister who's a sibling. With every lesson that I prepare, I learn something new. With every lesson that I teach I learn something new. With every new student, I learn something new. My horizons have broadened although I haven't travelled to Mexico, Peru, Libya, Serbia and other such countries, I now have a more in-depth, first hand knowledge and understanding of them. I enjoy seeing the amazement on the face of the Angolan student who was chatting to the Brazilian student and who found that his country had so much in common with Brazil and their shared Portuguese heritage.

007 SHAKEN NOT STIRRED

So many Zimbabwean families have been torn apart and are in the four corners of the earth. Communication with other countries is not always easy. I deeply miss the family get-togethers that we used to have. I am not alone in my feelings, thousands, probably millions, of Zimbabweans are in exactly the same situation.

At first when my parents left Zimbabwe, my mother and I used to religiously write to each other every week. My letters were in the form of a diary with all the bits of gossip we'd normally chat about in person. Invariably our letters would pass each other's. We'd each ask questions and say that we'd answer them in the next letter, but it didn't always happen. In 2002 when my parents left inflation was negligible compared to the astronomical heights it later reached, but it was still present. The cost of postage was creeping up and even though I've always been an ardent letter-writer, I was feeling the pinch of the cost of the correspondence. I finally succumbed to using emails. I had no choice. Inflation was guiding my options. Problem - my parents didn't have a computer, so emails weren't an option for them. Mark helped to solve that problem. He got them a device that was attached to their phone and could send and receive emails. It was adequate for their needs.

I was impressed with Mother at her age mastering the intricacies of emailing. The first emails confused us. We thought they were in code. We thought mother had joined James Bond and the secret service and had gone into deep cover – because the emails needed decoding. We couldn't answer them because we didn't know what they said. I used to try and decipher them letter-by-letter, word-by-word. I'd look at my own keyboard, look at the surrounding keys and try and see if it was just a glaring typo on Mum's part, or a really complicated code that I'd have to crack. The situation was compounded as we and countless other Zimbabweans, use code words in our correspondence and on the phones. We had to be careful in case it was 'Big Brother' in the form of the authorities having a good old eavesdrop into our lives. Herein lay my dilemma. Was this a new code that we'd have to decipher? When I later visited my parents and saw their emailer, I had every sympathy and admiration for my mother. I'm a touch typist. I type fast. I cannot type on my mother's keyboard! It's four by six inches big. No wonder she kept hitting the wrong keys. The precision it takes to make direct contact with the correct key is quite an art. Her emails did improve when mother remembered to wear her glasses!

Mum reckoned that one of the worst things she's ever done was to have a cataract operation. When she got back home, she looked in the mirror and there was a wrinkled old woman staring back at her. That may well be, but it was the best thing for her emailing skills and we started receiving emails in English. On one of his visits to his grandparents, Mark taught his granny the marvels of how to use the '&' button. We now have an inordinate number of '&'s in our emails, sometimes even long lines of them. Then miracle of miracles, we started receiving the odd email from Dad. I was impressed. Most impressed. You can imagine my let down when I mentioned to dad how impressed I was with his new skill and he replied, "Oh I don't type them. I dictate them to your mum and she types my name at the bottom." Funny thing though, the dictated emails are almost error free.

I would love to be able to share some of our code words with you, except that would defeat the purpose of having a code. When the boys send us emails with attachments that for various reasons they don't want the Zimbabwean Big Brother to nose through, they send them with a password. The details of the password are sent in a separate email and I have to be extra vigilant to not delete these. As long as Mike and I are able to work out the coded email, it's actually all quite fun. It adds a sense of excitement and intrigue to our lives. We feel like we're 'nickesy, nickesy, seven', which is a Wrex Tarr rendition of 'double oh seven'. You have to be a southern African to know and fully appreciate, Wrex Tarr.

WHERE DO YOU SHOP?

We do have supermarkets. We do have shops of all sort, shapes and sizes. Shopping in Zimbabwe can be a bizarre event. Imported whisky. Imported skin moisturizers. Imported wines. Imported butter. Imported cereals, biscuits, coffee – you get the idea. No flour. No sugar. No margarine. No cooking oil. No milk. No salt. It's the local items and the basic items that are more often than not, unobtainable. It makes entertaining challenging and we have to make a plan. Flour is plentiful at the moment, it's at times like this that shoppers get taken unawares and are lulled into a false sense of security, and tend to forget the months that it was a memory and that it just wasn't there.

We've been through this with bread, sugar, rice, milk, pets' mince, toilet rolls, tampons, just about anything you can mention. When an item comes back into stock, if we're lucky enough to have the cash, we stock up. There's a subtle difference between stocking up and hoarding. There's usually a cupboard or pantry where there are a few bottles of cooking oil, a few packets of sugar. You can't afford to run out of these items, there's no guarantee that these things will be available the next time you go shopping, or for weeks or even months. There those who have the money, buy up everything in sight, wait for the shortage and then fleece the rest of us. That's life. That's the black-market. Many ex Zimbabweans who go to live in other countries find it difficult to get out of the 'Zimbo mentality'. My parents were amongst them. They were like kids in a candy store when they first went shopping in the U.K. The variety. The availability. It was difficult to comprehend that the store would still have the essentials tomorrow and that most likely, the price would be the same and not have doubled or trebled overnight.

In July 2007 the Zim government decided that all manufacturers, shopkeepers and other businesses had to halve their prices. Just like that! There were some unscrupulous entrepreneurs who were charging highly inflated prices and making astronomical profits, but not all businesses were like that. We have the highest inflation in the world. Loping three zeroes off the end of the currency and forcing shops to sell commodities at prices cheaper than it will cost them to replace the items, wasn't going to solve anything. For several days there was a feeling of euphoria amongst the hardest-hit those people who had really been living a hand-to-mouth existence. They went on a spending spree even if they had to borrow the money. Many shops had to limit quantities that customers could buy, there were long queues snaking to get to shops like Bata, where shoes had previously cost more than a couple of months salary. At the other end of the scale were customers stocking up on brandy and imported cosmetics, furniture and electrical goods. Everything that goes up has to come down. The euphoria was short lived. The result was that the shelves of many supermarkets were bare. The shops were completely empty. We could go to seven shops before finding eggs or bread. Not one of these shops had any meat, milk, cooking oil, salt – the basics.

Mike and I were browsing in the shops of the Metro Centre in Newcastle, England, when we were there in 2006 and we were both struck, firstly by the numbers of young people around – it's only when you leave Zimbabwe that you realize just how many youngsters of all races have left their home. Secondly, we were amazed at the number of people carrying not just one but several shopping bags. Zimbabweans tend to do shop for the absolute basics.

Where do you buy your loo rolls? We don't even have to leave our cars. There are vendors at the traffic lights selling bags of toilet rolls. It is a bit awkward trying to barter with them when the lights (if they're working) change to green, but it's not impossible. Traffic light vendors sell pay-as-you-go phone cards; plants; newspapers; sets of knives; sets of spanners; toys; wooden carvings; paintings; brooms; feather dusters; fruit and vegetables. It obviously pays the vendors to work where they do, but can be annoying when customers don't have the courtesy to pull over to the side while carrying out their transactions.

The vendors are even more prolific in the car parks at shopping centres, where they do NOT take no for an answer. On days when it's scorching and you're hot and bothered and have had a lousy day, it's extremely difficult to not lose your cool with the vendors. I know they have to make a living. I know life's difficult for them. It's the same with the street kids who come begging at the car windows when you're stopped at the lights, or the women with babies on their backs who are begging, or with the men and women coming to the gate begging for work or food. I feel desperately sorry for all of them, but the sheer numbers are overwhelming. Then the guilt trip kicks in. There's no simple solution.

Living under these conditions with hyperinflation, certainly helps to change your priorities. There are a fortunate few who have access to hard currency and for them life in this country has a standard of living second to none. They have generators to combat the daily power outages. They most likely are on an international medical aid scheme ensuring peace of mind in a medical emergency. They frequent the coffee shops and restaurants. They can afford to travel locally and stay in luxurious game lodges. They can go for a relaxing break to Mozambique or South Africa's inviting beaches. They are the minority. For the majority life is a never-ending grind.

Many pensioners are destitute now. My father's pension has just been increased eight hundred percent and at today's prices, he could buy himself three-quarters of a toilet roll, or one and half loaves of bread – A MONTH! I can't begin to imagine the plight of many of the elderly here who have similar pensions. There are organizations such as 'meals on wheels' and S.O.A.P (Save Old Aged Pensioners) and various churches, but the size of the task they have to do is daunting. It must be impossible to budget with ever increasing prices. For instance, Mike wanted to change the oil in my car. He priced the oil at our local service station on a Wednesday afternoon after having been to a couple of other establishments to check on prices. Our local had the cheapest price, 'only' $950 000 per tin whereas the others were well over the million dollar mark. Many companies refuse to accept cheques with the inflation, by the time they've been cleared through the bank the price has almost doubled. Credit cards are not a way of life here yet. He didn't have enough cash on him, and as the government limits the amount of cash individuals and companies can withdraw daily, he'd had his day's quota, which didn't even cover the cost of the groceries, therefore he would have to wait for the following day.

Thursday arrived. Mike was at the bank as soon as it opened, withdrew the cash and made haste back to the garage. Why the hurry? The hurry is because prices not only change weekly; it can also be daily and hourly. I jest not. He had been at the garage just before closing on the Wednesday, was back there an hour after opening on the Thursday and the price had gone up $50 000! What happened overnight to cause that increase? Your guess is as good as mine. Some companies give quotes that are only valid for twenty-four hours. We were given a quote for repairs that was valid for TWO hours! It must be next to impossible for firms to budget under these conditions. In 2006 the government lopped three zeroes off our currency in an effort to try and curb inflation. The outcome of this exercise was that you had a lot of *very* confused people, me being in the forefront. Imagine shopping one day and the price of an item is $1 500 000 then the following day it's $1 500 *BUT* you know that it's not really this price. Imagine having $1000 in the bank, and on waking, finding that you now only have $1!!!!

I really, really have to study the bank notes carefully. For a long time I kept converting from the old to the new currency. What makes it more confusing is that we've passed the position we were when the three zeroes were dropped, so that something that was a million is in actual fact a billion, but is it the old billion or the new billion? We had a week or thereabouts to surrender the old currency to be replaced with the new, not the easiest exercise for Zimbabweans who live in the rural areas and most likely only see a bus once a week if they're lucky. Many entrepreneurs had a stash of money so you can imagine there was a fair amount of panic when these people had only a few days in which to spend their old currency. So what's the problem with that? The problem was that that the central bank limited the amount that customers were allowed to spend at any one time. There were a lot of people who made numerous trips to the shops lots of times during this grace period. It was fine for those who just wanted to stock up on grocery and liquor items, but the difficulties arose with the more expensive purchases such as furniture – where did you get your money from, did it go through official channels, did you pay tax on it? This entailed frequent smaller purchases.

Far from alleviating the inflation, the dropping of the zeroes if anything, aggravated it. Those with money went on a buying spree. They had to. They had to get rid of the cash in a short space of time before it became worthless. They stocked up on cases of whisky. They stocked up on non-perishable food items. They stocked up on cleaning materials. They stocked up on toiletries. They stocked up. This led to empty shelves in the shops. It also fuelled the growth of the black market. It also meant that when the shelves were legitimately restocked, the prices would reflect those of the replacement value, which basically is the black-market value, so you were back to square one.

A prime example (and there are many others) which makes a mockery of deducting three zeroes from the currency is highlighted in our personal case when Mike was filling in our annual returns for our company to the Registrar Of Companies. Every year he completes a form giving the details of the company. After the dropping of the three zeroes, all cheques and financial statements had to carry the wording 'revalued' to show that the 'new' currency was being used as opposed to the 'old' currency. The completion of our annual returns caused much consternation. In the section, "Summary of Share capital and debentures", our nominal share capital was shown as Zim$20,000 as this was in the 'old' currency, we now had to show it as Zim$20. That wasn't too bad, where the confusion arose was with the section on dividends. We had 20 000 shares of Zim$1 each, but with the 'new' currency, we now had 20 shares of Zim$0.001 each! Instant paupers.

Forex is divided into the government's official rate, and the realistic and used rate the black-market or parallel rate. The privileged few with connections are able to obtain forex from the Reserve Bank of Zimbabwe for an 'inth' of the cost on the black market, thereby making massive profits. The rest of us have to obtain our forex on the black-market, the rate not only goes up daily, it can go up hourly. When my parents left the country in May 2002, they paid Zim$2000 for one US dollar. We were horrified at the rate! When I started writing this book the rate was about Zim$52 000 to a US dollar and in July 2007, it reached Z$400 000 to US$1. At the end of May 2008 it was Z$600 million to US$1. Having access to forex can be very profitable.

Even though it's technically illegal, prices and quotes are given in American dollars, but payable in Zimbabwean dollars. It's a crazy system. We received a sterling dividend cheque for the grand sum of four pounds, eighty-two pence. The next time we receive a cheque for such a paltry amount, we'll file it in the waste-paper-basket. The country is desperate for forex, so we did the right thing – and it's cost us! We deposited the cheque in our account. At that time, if we'd been able to dispose of it on the black-market (which we couldn't as it was in our company's name and therefore had to be paid into a bank account) we would have received in the region of Zim$250 000. We received our monthly bank statement which showed that we'd only been given Zim$2 000 by the bank, but to add insult to injury, they deducted charges of Zim$40 000! So it COST us Zim$38 000 to deposit a cheque.

Living through these times in Zimbabwe can certainly be character building.

BAMBI KILLER

A houseboat trip on Lake Kariba is an 'Out of Africa' experience. Over the years, we have had the fortune to be invited as guests on several houseboat trips, with our maiden voyage being in August 1995. It has to be experienced. Words hardly do justice to the haunting beauty of Kariba, the sights and sounds of the wildlife and the camaraderie of those on board. Kariba got its name from the Shona word 'Kariwa', meaning a little stone trap, which is used for catching birds and mice, or a traditional fish trap. Never has there been a more apt name. It's a fisherman's paradise. Kariba is a man-made dam and its making is a story on its own. It is built at the gorge where the Zambezi River narrows from some 650 metres to a mere 100 metres or less. In June 1954 the Federal Power Board was established to co-ordinate the generation and supply of electricity and work commenced on the construction of Kariba in June 1955.

Houseboats in Kariba

It was fraught with difficulties from the forced resettlement of the Batonka tribe who inhabited the area in 1956, to the eighty-six people who were killed on the construction of the dam and culminating in 'Operation Noah', led by Rupert Fothergill which rescued thousands of wild animals of all types from certain death as they were marooned on islands formed by the rising waters. An Italian firm of constructors, 'Impresit', built the dam and they also built the little church of St. Barbara on the Kariba Heights. This church was built in memory of those killed while the dam was being built. It is a circular building with no outside walls, but a number of archways formed the entrance to the building. I don't suppose there are many churches in the world that can boast of having the presence of wild elephants sauntering through their car park – which is also shared with the few shops in the vicinity.

I love the drive from Harare to Kariba. I love driving over the Great Dyke, which is a mineral-rich range of volcanic hills that run diagonally across Zimbabwe. I love the changes in vegetation and get excited when I spot my first baobab tree, that's when I really know that I'm on holiday, but the sight of my first elephant is definitely the cherry on the top. For many years, good friends, Graham and Denise, kindly invited us to join them on Kariba. Their son Adam and our Mark had become friends when they both attended Pooh Corner Nursery School in Avondale. The houseboat was an old tub. It was basic. No frills no fuss. It was great. There were cabins downstairs, but these were cramped so we used them for keeping our luggage. They also acted as a magnet for mosquitoes in the evenings and could become unbearably hot in summer. We all slept on the top deck, half of which had a roof but the sides were completely open to the elements. There were canvas awnings that could be let down in the event of wind or rain, in all the years that we went on board, I only once remember these being down.

Denise was expert at organizing the catering. She'd done it for so many years that she was almost able to a potato, to know the required quantities. She always made the chicken liver paté for the lunches and no matter how much she made, it was never enough. She could double, even treble the quantities and we'd still finish it well before the end of the trip. Packing for these trips was an art. We had to remember everything. Once you were out on the lake, there was no turning back for the salt that was sitting on the kitchen table back home. Every year we had different challenges with the catering. One year we battled to find minerals like Coke and Fanta. Another year beers were like hen's teeth. We had to take our precious horde of sugar and keep it hidden in our cabins and almost spoon it out spoon-for-spoon. We've taken cooking oil that we've had to ration and kept the bottle locked in our case in the cabin. Somehow we always managed. We made a plan.

We've encountered engine problems. We've had problems with the steering. We've had mechanical problems with the tender boats. We've always had a good time. It never ceases to amaze me how much I could eat, drink and sleep in a twenty-four hour period on the houseboat. Thank goodness we only went for five days and four nights. There were three members of crew, the captain, the cook and the deckhand. It was bliss. Nicky the cook could produce wonders in a miniscule galley that rose to temperatures worse than an oven in the summer. The table was always attractively laid and Nicky always had to give the women passengers lessons on folding serviettes to look like swans or fans. We provided the food. Denise gave Nicky the menu and le voila! Denise's forte was the paté. Mine was rusks for early morning tea. The deckhand would come to the top deck with the tea tray at six in the morning. I'm not usually a morning person, but it is a delightful time to experience the peace of the African bush. It is still cool and clear. The birds are busy with their daily chores, the hippos are grunting lazily to each other, the fish eagles are calling to each other and it's a time to make you feel grateful that you're alive.

The fishermen would have their tea and rusks whilst preparing rods, sorting out worms and filling cool boxes to take out onto the water with them. Depending on the variety of fish would depend on whether worms or kapenta were used. The rule of thumb was that kapenta were used for tiger fish and worms for bream. Kapenta are tiny whitebait-like fish that abound in the waters of Kariba. They were introduced to the lake in the 1960s ostensibly as a source of protein to supplement the staple food of maize meal for the majority of the population. They can be bought frozen or dried and I've tried cooking them in different ways, none of which has been successful. We've bought them dried for the pets. The dogs love them, the cats are fussy. A word of advice, don't keep them too long they get the most disgusting, foul, ugly-looking cross between a worm and a maggot creatures all over them.

Procuring fishing worms was another interesting activity. You would find it hard to believe just how seriously this is taken. The town of Chinhoi (its pre-Independence name was Sinoia) is located just the other side of the Dyke, this is where Mike prefers to buy his worms. Being an avid fisherman he used to have a worm 'farm' in our garden. The quantities of worms he needed could not be met by just digging around in the vegetable garden. A trip where there would be several fishermen necessitated buying worms commercially. Worm sellers can be found on the sides of the roads. Some will have crude homemade signs advertising their wares; others are discernable by a few poles protruding from the ground with a bit of tambo (cloth) tied around one. The advertising signs are quite a source of entertainment in themselves, there are 'Red Warms of Note' – yes, I'm aware of the spelling; there are signs saying 'Help me to get to England'; but there are also other signs, that to the uninitiated, appear fairly innocuous, but to those in the 'know' (and I have to discount myself at this point) advertising various forms of drugs for sale. It's all in the wording! When you know what to look for its pretty obvious. A few enterprising worm vendors have expanded their trade to include dagga. We stuck to the fish bait.

It could be a hazardous exercise stopping to purchase worms. Several vendors would come racing up to the car with their small makeshift containers in which they insisted were a thousand worms. I wonder if anyone's actually attempted to count to see if there really were a thousand worms? The vendors would almost upend the containers in the open windows to show their merchandise and more than once I've been showered with soil or errant worms. The haggling begins. I'm useless at this. It's a way of life in Zim. Mike's good at it. Finally a price is agreed upon and we are the proud owners of a container of 'nyongorosi' or worms. These containers come in all sorts of shapes and sizes and are made out of a variety of materials. Cardboard cartons are made out of old packing cases, plastic milk bottles have their tops chopped off to make sturdy containers, mini sacks are made out of old hessian sacks. The vendors are enterprising.

Back to the houseboat. The fishermen go off in the early morning and depending on their success, wend their way home about nine or ten. This is the time for a huge breakfast. More fishing or relaxing ensues. Lunch is partaken nearer three in the afternoon and usually consists of cold meats, salad and pickles, *and* Denise's paté. A houseboat trip without paté isn't a houseboat trip. A lazy afternoon either reading or snoozing in the shade. Enthusiastic fishermen may go back out to try their luck when the temperatures abate a bit. Pre prandial drinks whilst admiring the stunning African sunset on Kariba, taken on the top deck with snacks to keep the hunger pangs away (oh I can hear my poor over-loaded stomach groaning). Sometimes the snacks would be chunks of freshly caught fish cooked only as Nicky could cook them. Downstairs at about eight o'clock for the wonderful dinner that Nicky had produced. After-dinner coffee and post prandial drinks.

There is no special time of the day on Kariba. Each has its own beauty. Houseboats, by law, have to be moored to the shore overnight. There is nothing to beat sitting outside at night under an African sky where the stars appear so close that you swear you could almost reach out and touch them. There are the grunts of the hippos, the trumpeting of the elephants, you might even be privileged to hear lions roaring. There are often bangs and crashes in the bush around us, it's anyone's guess what they are. The creature that is in all likelihood the most morbidly fascinating one is the flatdog, or the crocodile. They are not always visible, but everyone is aware of their presence and everyone has a healthy respect for the danger they represent. No matter how sweltering the weather, how tempting it would be for a quick dip in the lake, few people are prepared to take that risk, unless they are right out in the very middle of the lake, even then there are no guarantees. Another concern is that of contracting bilharzia a parasitic disease, which can be serious if left untreated. The schistosoma haematobium is the most prevalent form of bilharzia in Africa; schistosoma masoni is another form, also found in Africa. Put simply, bilharzia is contracted from snails that abound in the shallows in the heat of the day. I've had bliharzia, it's treatable.

It is easy in the daylight hours to believe that the crocs do not present a problem.   There's usually the odd one or two on the banks sunning themselves or sliding into the waters for a dip.   Night-time is when that myth is quickly dispelled. Shine a powerful torch or searchlight out over the waters and you will be astounded by the number of red crocs' eyes shining back at you. It's certainly a wake-up call. One trip we had moored in a narrow bay in an attractive setting in Gordon's Bay. We'd had dinner and were relaxing when there was suddenly an almighty crashing and racket on the opposite shore. Mark grabbed the searchlight and shone it across the water to spotlight a terrified impala being chased by four or five aggressive hyena. The opposite shore ended in a narrow spit of land and there was nowhere for the impala to go but into the water, which it did, with a mighty splash.   The hyena stood and watched their prey escaping from their clutches. They did not follow it into the water. Maybe they too had seen the red eyes of the patiently waiting flatdogs.

We followed the distressed impala's passage across the water by means of the searchlight.   It was abreast of the houseboat and so close to our shore and safety, when suddenly there was a swirl of water and the impala disappeared from view. We had no means of knowing whether the impala had been taken by a croc or not. We were upset by what we had witnessed. We'd all been rooting hard for the impala to make it to safety. When the impala had gone under the water, someone had shouted that it was all Mark's fault as he'd focused the light on it and thus disorientated it. Someone also shouted that he should jump into the water to try and save the animal. Over my dead body! There was nothing anyone could do for the poor impala. It was gone. Mark was quite upset for a while until he came to terms with the fact that it would more than likely have happened anyway, searchlight or not. It did give him a bit of notoriety and he was given the name 'Bambi Killer'.

We had again kindly been invited on the houseboat in May 2003. This time it would be a much smaller contingent, consisting of six adults and two teenagers. Catering for this trip was a test of our ingeniousness. Cooking oil, sugar, margarine, salt and flour were some of the staples that were nowhere to be found on the supermarket shelves. We women each had to provide some out of our very precious stores from home. The best policy was just not to run out of an item. I have two twelve cubic deepfreezes, one is for the storage of foodstuffs that are normally kept in a freezer such as meat, the other is for dry goods that are so often not in the shops such as, flour, rice, powdered milk, margarine. Another reason for keeping dry goods in the freezer is to prevent weevils getting into the packets. I know that weevils aren't harmful and as someone once pointed out to me, they're an added source of protein, but I'd rather get my protein elsewhere! Once when we'd bought a bag of rice and opened it at home to find it alive with weevils, we took it back to the supermarket, the manager couldn't understand what all the fuss was about, although he did exchange it for us.

On previous houseboat trips Denise, our hostess, had ascertained from us approximately how many drinks we were likely to consume, then she'd place the order with the marina where the boat was moored. The crates of drinks would be awaiting our arrival. It beat transporting crates from Harare. Any unused drinks could be returned to the marina for a credit. This particular year we couldn't follow our normal routine, as there were no soft drinks on the shelves. Mike and I were given the onerous task of sourcing these drinks. It took us the best part of a day going from shop to shop. If a supermarket had any drinks they were rationed to one or two bottles per customer. Mike and I would make the journey in and out of the shop with each purchase for as many times as possible using a different check-out till on each occasion to try and make us look less conspicuous. Then we'd move on to the next shop.

Finally we had procured the necessary drinks and the holiday was under way. Mike and the two youngsters on the boat took themselves off fishing one afternoon in one of the two tender boats belonging to the houseboat.

Our hosts, Graham and Denise, myself and our farming friends, Rob and Val, all decided that we'd take the other tender boat, 'Sue' out for a sunset, game-viewing 'booze cruise'. Graham was affectionately known as the 'commodore' and was one of life's gentlemen. He was a stickler for safety when on Kariba and that suited me fine. He always made sure that we were back on deck before it grew dark. Kariba can be treacherous in daylight with the stumps of the petrified trees that are still present in the water, many just below the water awaiting unsuspecting hulls and motors, and there is also the added danger of submerged hippos. At night, Kariba can be a death trap. It's virtually impossible to see these dangers.

We set off puttering slowly out of the bay where the houseboat was moored at Elephant Point. It was idyllic. The searing heat of the day was dissipating to be replaced with a lovely cool breeze. The huge orange ball that was the sun was low on the horizon, surrounded by the red and yellow of the sky. Everything was still and quiet except for the odd call of a bird or the grunt of a hippo. The elephants on the shore were silhouetted against the crimson sky. It was paradise. We'd putter on for a bit hugging the shore, switch the engine off, and gently drift while communing with nature, each of us enveloped in our own private thoughts and in the solitude of a Kariba sunset. We'd gaze almost in reverence at the elephants, some so close that it was possible to make out individual features, but the 'commodore' always made sure that we didn't go close enough to disturb the pachyderms or to endanger ourselves.

We'd been stopped like this for quite some time. We chatted in a desultory fashion while sipping our sundowners. We marvelled at the splendour of the African wilderness around us and at the sheer privilege it was for the five of us to be experiencing this phenomenon of nature with not another human in sight. With a sigh, Graham suggested that as the sun was almost below the horizon, we'd better start wending our way back to the houseboat. He turned the key and tried to start the boat. Nothing happened. None of us was concerned, tender boats aren't a whole lot different from petrol lawnmowers – they quite often don't start the first time. When four or five attempts were unsuccessful, Graham was now looking a bit concerned. He was an accountant and not mechanically inclined. Rob, being a farmer and therefore used to tinkering with motors, pulled the motor up out of the water to see if he could get it going. His attempts were fruitless.

For the first time in all the years that I'd been on houseboat trips, Graham hadn't checked the tender boat before we set out to make sure that it had oars. We had precious little with us. We didn't have a torch as we'd expected to be back long before darkness fell. We hadn't taken jerseys, as it had been so hot when we left. We hadn't taken any insect repellent with us and the mozzies decided to visit us in their hordes. We had one beer and one lemonade between the five of us.

My concern was how to cope with the call of nature! Where we'd stopped wasn't exactly on dry land, we were next to a small floating island of mud and reeds, it would be difficult to get to the shore. There was a pod of hippos not that far from us and when you're in a tiny boat just a few inches above the water, hippos tend to look big! There were also a couple of jumbos on the shore mooching through the mud with their trunks. What was uppermost in our minds was unseen crocs. We knew that they were most definitely present. Darkness comes quickly in Africa. The sun appears to fall down below the horizon and almost in the blink of an eye night arrives. We thought that if we could get a message to the captain of our houseboat, he'd be able to send Mike out to rescue us.

The captain had a cell phone and by chance, Val had brought hers. That was all very well, but we didn't have the captain's number or the numbers of anyone we could contact in Kariba. I knew the numbers of two friends in Harare so we decided to give them a go. The battery on Val's phone was a bit low. It never rains but it pours. I tried the first number, my friend Coleen wasn't home but her son was. It is difficult to be clear but concise on a phone when you're very aware that the battery may die at any moment. It's also difficult to ask a teenager to phone 'someone' in Kariba – we weren't sure if there was such a thing as a 'Lake Authority' and to explain the situation to them. Just in case this youngster wasn't able to pass on our request (although he managed admirably), I phoned another friend in Harare with the same request. Sally, my friend, phoned the Lake Authority, she phoned hotels, she phoned every 'authority' she could think of bar the police – after all, it wasn't a matter of life and death, we only wanted to pass on a message. Bottom line, if you're ever going to have an emergency in Kariba, make sure you do so during working hours, as after five in the afternoon, you're basically on your own!

Something made Graham decide to give the starter one more try – and you guessed right – two hours later, it coughed into life. Waves of relief swept over us – especially over my full bladder, which had had waves washing over it for quite some time. We had to make our way back slowly, very, very slowly looking out for submerged trees, hippos and even sandbanks. As fate would have it, the night sky was black. Not a star, forget about the moon, to guide us. Denise and Val leant over the front of the boat on the lookout for hazards, whilst Rob and I leant over each side as an added precaution. It seemed to take an eternity. We had one close shave when we very nearly beached ourselves on a sandbank, which in the darkness was invisible. In the distance we saw lights and surmised that it must be those of houseboats. We weren't sure if it was the bay in which we were moored, but decided to make for it anyway. Just as we were slowly turning into the bay a small boat was making its way towards us and nearly blinded us with a spotlight. It turned out to be Mike, the two youngsters (one of whom was Heath), the deckhand and the cook.

The three fishermen had got back to the houseboat just as it was turning dark, and Mike immediately realized there was something amiss when we weren't there. He knew that there was no way Graham would be out after dark unless there was a problem. So they had come out to search for us. The relief of getting back was immeasurable. All the phone calls were a waste of time and money, it transpired that the captain's phone was on the blink and wasn't working, so nobody would have been able to get hold of him anyway. There were many laughs around the dinner table that night. It was certainly a night to remember.

MADAM, SHUT UP

I wasn't looking forward to Christmas 2002, as it would be the first one without my parents who would be on their own in the U.K. It was doubly poignant as Mark, who was eighteen at the time, was leaving Zimbabwe for Britian in mid January. I wasn't handling it very well, but life goes on. 2002 was a busy year with the death of a dear friend, my parents leaving, Mark writing his Cambridge 'A' levels and Heath writing 'O' levels.

Bindura is a town to the north of Harare and for various reasons we had been there several times in the later part of that year. Friday 21ˢᵗ December 2001 saw us at the Bindura passport office at five in the morning to join the queue to submit our application forms for the renewal of our passports. This was an anxious time for us. We were without passports for nine months waiting for the new passports and 2002 was a year of turmoil. This meant we were without passports if we had to get out of the country in a hurry. The farm invasions reached a climax. Zimbabweans with dual nationality had to renounce one or other nationalities and stand in endless queues to do so. People were joining the queues as early as four in the morning. We joined the queue to renounce our dual citizenship at half past five and it was already miles long. Every family had a 'Justin' – Just In case – this was a small bag that contained vital documents: passports, birth, marriage, death certificates, title deeds, gun licences and anything of else of importance that we might need if we had to flee for our lives. People who intended to leave by car if 'it' hit the fan went as far as getting the necessary police clearance for their vehicles.

March was an unsettling month. Friday 8ᵗʰ, and Monday and Tuesday, 11ᵗʰ and 12ᵗʰ, saw the schools closed because of voting. This was a worrying time for all in our volatile land. April was a horrific month for our farming friends Rob and Val, as they were finally forced off their farm on 16ᵗʰ April

2002. I don't know how our friends coped with their ordeal; I suppose there was no alternative but to cope. Val had phoned me in the morning - thank goodness for cell phones - and said that the police, War-Vets (land grabbers) and union representatives were at the farm and that she and Rob were unable to do any of their packing before their imminent departure. She asked if we could go and collect their computer for safekeeping. There was only Mark and I at home at the time and I'm not proud to admit that I was very nervous, to put it politely. This wasn't just a simple of case of driving to a friend's house to collect the computer. These people had been to hell and back and the perpetrators were the ones forcing them to leave. The road to the farm went through two compounds where the farm labourers and their families lived and I wasn't sure what kind of reaction two lone whites would have at this volatile time. As it turned out, it was fine. The scene that greeted us at the farmhouse is indelibly etched on my mind.

It was a bleak day with a cold drizzle falling. Rob and Val hadn't been permitted to farm since the beginning of the invasions thus depriving them of a source of income. This day, their final one on their farm, when they should have been packing, they were having to sit outside around a fire with members of the war vets, police and labour representatives and not only work out the termination packages for their staff, but also to pay them out, all this before they would be permitted to pack and leave. They were told that once they had gone through the gates, they would never be coming back. They were amongst the 'lucky' farmers, if you can call them that; they were being allowed to take their furniture and belongings with them.

The removal van had arrived, but Rob and Val couldn't supervise the packing and had to leave it all to their teenage son and daughter, Doug and Tracy, who did an admirable job under almost impossible conditions. Mark helped Doug dismantle the TV and the satellite dish. Tracy and I packed as many of Val's precious plants into the boot of our car as we possibly could. Val has green fingers and loves gardening. When Mark and I finally left after five o'clock, the car laden with plants, the computer and a fish bowl complete with fish, Rob and Val were still sitting in the cold negotiating. Later Mike and Heath went to the farm with flasks of tea and sandwiches as the family had had nothing to eat all day, but the war vets wouldn't allow Mike to give the food to the distressed family.

Mark and Heath writing their Cambridge exams wasn't even straightforward. Cambridge exams are, as the name denotes, British exams. Those of us with the financial means ensure that our children write not only the Zimsec (Zimbabwean local exams) equivalent of 'A' and 'O' level, but also the Cambridge ones as Zimsec is not recognized outside our borders. The schools writing Cambridge exams, the parents and the pupils had had a year fraught with uncertainty. The Zimbabwean Ministry of Education announced that it would no longer consent to Cambridge exams being written here. This just a few months before the exams were due to take place. It was panic stations. Schools and private individuals were frantically writing, emailing, phoning, educational institutions in South Africa and Zambia to see if our students could go there to write the Cambridge exams. We were trying to find exam centres where our children could write their exams – for a fee of course – more forex required.

There was a contingency plan that there was a chance that the students could use the facilities of the Harare International School in which to write, as this establishment didn't fall under the jurisdiction of the Ministry of Education. However this wasn't a certainty. Our wonderful friends in Johannesburg, Adele and Kets, made the incredible offer that Mark and Heath could go and stay with them while writing their exams. This was even more generous on their part when you take into consideration that two of their sons would also be writing exams, these being Matric and first year university. Could you imagine the stress levels in that household if that had come to pass!

Then the government changed its mind. The furore died down, the exams were written where they had always intended to be written. This kind of yo-yoing frustration plays havoc on stress levels. Every time some 'funny' like this happens here, more people emigrate and it's just another nail in the coffin. This was the year my parents left their home of fifty years. This was the year, nine months after submitting our passport applications; we again went out to Bindura on Thursday 29th September to collect our passports. I can't begin to describe the turmoil my mind had been in for the past nine months. We had had all the problems with the invasions, the exams and just the general unrest and Mike and I couldn't have left if we'd wanted to – we didn't have any travel documents. September also saw my parents celebrating their Golden Wedding anniversary, alone. We would have made it a momentous, joyous family celebration had we all been together. Conditions deemed otherwise. Another milestone in our family's lives that we haven't been able to share.

A lot of time was spent during November trying to find mealie meal, the basic food, for our staff and making trips out to the Grain Marketing Board premises in Concession to collect maize when it was available. It was not all bad this year. Wednesday 4th December graced us with an eighty-six percent Eclipse of the sun. Not as spectacular as the full eclipse the previous year, but still breathtaking. Then we had a treat. Friends of ours Stephen and Sheelah had booked in for a few days into Dombowera Game Ranch near Bindura and asked us if we'd liked to join them. We were the only two families there and the seven of us had the camp to ourselves. I'm afraid that I was a bit too over-wrought to fully appreciate the beauty and serenity of the ranch. It had been a lousy year.

That's not to say I didn't enjoy myself. We had long walks through the bush, the meals were lovely and the boys enjoyed themselves, which is what counted. There were stables and horses available for game rides. Everyone had arranged to go for a game ride one morning and I decided that I would stay behind in our lodge and relax. I like horses, but not when I'm on the back of one. Everyone was pressuring me to go along. The game ranger was a super person and very understanding and assured me that my horse couldn't move fast if its life depended on it, he also said that he would be at my side the whole time. I succumbed. Why do I let myself be persuaded to do things that I *know* I won't enjoy? As previously mentioned, the only horse I've ever enjoyed riding was the one in Woolworth's on First Street Harare, where you put 20cents into the slot on its back and my feet can reach the ground!

The horse I was given was definitely old and steady. Even so, I was nervous and any movement is too much movement for me and we obviously had to move! The ranger had given us a talk before we left explaining the rules of the bush while on horseback. He explained that the horses had been trained not to fear wild animals and they wouldn't react if they saw for instance, an antelope or a giraffe, but there was a bit of difficulty in training the horses to cope with ostriches. The horse would see an ostrich and then suddenly the bird would flap its wings and become twice its size scaring the horse. No one could be sure how the horses would react in these conditions.

I was holding everyone up yet the horse was still walking way too fast for my liking. I told the ranger that he didn't have to stay with me as he was needed at the front to show the way and everyone very kindly took turns to come back and walk alongside me. I kept looking at my watch. I was convinced it had stopped.   We were told that the ride would take approximately two hours and I seemed to have been on the back of that horse for an eternity. We were travelling along a path with wide stretches of grass on either side of us when it happened. Nothing against Sheelah, I do like her and she's a good friend, but I'm so grateful it happened to her and not me, because if it had, I'd be six foot under right now. We had stopped to view some animals. There were a couple of giraffe on the left of the path and a couple of ostriches to the right. We stood there for a few minutes; an ostrich stretched out its wings and it just all seemed too much for Sheelah's steed. With an impressive rear and a snort, it did its 'Hey Ho Silver' imitation, turned round and galloped full tilt into the sunset, well, it was only midday, but you know what I mean.

The giraffe we were admiring

To give Sheelah her due, she hung on. She hung on for her life. She must have been scared out of her wits, which was obvious by the crescendo of screeches emanating from her mouth. I don't know what the horse was more afraid of, the flapping ostriches or the screeching Sheelah. That horse could move. I'd have laid a bet on it any day. The ranger whipped his horse round, told us to stay put and galloped after Sheelah, shouting, "Madam, please be quiet."

More galloping.

"Madam, please be quiet."

More galloping.

"MADAM, PLEASE BE QUIET."

Finally,

"Madam, SHUT UP!"

That did the trick. There aren't many people who would dare tell Sheelah to shut up and get away with it. She shut up. The horse calmed down. It slowed down. It all ended well. I was sorry for the stress that this incident had put Sheelah through, but YES, it was worth it to witness it. I was impressed with Sheelah's riding skills. I could never have done what she did. I could have done the screeching bit, perhaps not. Bet my throat would have constricted. I might have been able to produce little squeaks, but there is no way that I would have been able to stay astride the horse at that speed.

The two hours thankfully came to an end and my horse lethargically dragged its hooves back to the stables. I don't think she could have cared one way or the other whether I was on her back or not. That was our excitement for the trip. No other encounters with dangerous life, wild or otherwise. The fishing was a waste of time, but the men enjoyed being at the water's edge and doing fisherman stuff. I would be interested to know if the camp is still open. The tourist industry has taken a serious knock in the past few years and having a camp with only seven occupants couldn't have been a viable option.

TEA, ANYONE?

We had the privilege of having an American couple, Tom and Alice, as neighbours. They lived in the States, but their hearts were in Africa. Alice was an incredible woman who spent many years fund raising for the Smithsonian Institute, with her last project being her absolute passion, that of the building of The National Museum Of The American Indian in Washington, which Mike and I were fortuitous enough to visit in April, 2005. Through Tom and Alice, our family was introduced to Pina Coladas, bacon bits, maple syrup, Hershey's chocolate, freeze dried coffee and all the other essentials. When our boys were young, they used to write their letters to Father Christmas and made sure they were 'posted' to the North Pole in plenty of time. As Tom and Alice tried to spend every Christmas in Africa, this made life easy for Father Christmas. A phone call to Alice in the U.S (our landline worked in those days) and Father Christmas would go into the nearest 'Toys R Us' and get the shopping done and deliver the presents to Mike and I a week or so before Christmas.

Christmas morning would see the boys up at the crack of dawn opening their presents, then they couldn't wait to go visiting Tom and Alice to show them what Father Christmas had brought! One year though, Father Christmas did a bit of a daft thing. He brought each boy a magnificent set of coloured crayons, magic markers and paints. Unbeknown to him Tom and Alice gave the boys a wonderful electric pencil sharpener. It doesn't take a rocket scientist to figure that one out. We were visiting Tom and Alice one evening for dinner, the boys were both very young at this time. After a lovely meal, we were sitting in the lounge chatting when Mark went off to the toilet. He came back. He sat for a while. He fidgeted. He went back to the loo. He came back. He whispered in Heath's ear. Heath went to the loo. He came back. He whispered to Mark. They both went to the loo. Being a mother, I'm not only able to multi-task, but also multi-converse and multi-watch kids and multi-wonder what on earth they were up to!

By this stage, even Mike, Tom and Alice were noticing the frequent trips to the loo. Finally I could take it no longer. I asked, "Mark, what's the problem?" with a sinking feeling that perhaps he'd broken something in the bathroom, after all, little boys will be little boys. He excitedly grabbed my hand and led me through to the bathroom.

"Look mummy! When you flush the toilet, the water's all blue like in a swimming pool!" On my return to the lounge I explained the great discovery and Alice burst out laughing. "Oh that's because we have 'Two Thousand Flushes' in the toilet cistern," she explained, and she went off to get a packet to show Mark and Heath the secret of making blue swimming pool water in the toilet. She took a photograph of these two little Zimbabwean boys, sitting in her lounge in Africa, grinning from ear to ear while holding a packet of 'Two Thousand Flushes'.

Mark wanted to know if anyone had ever counted to make sure you got two thousand flushes and as we were in the middle of one of our periodic droughts, I really didn't need him to go and try to verify this fact. Mike wasn't concerned, "He can't count up to two thousand anyway, so we're safe," was his take on the situation. When Tom and Alice returned to the States, they left us a packet of the 'flushes' for our loo. Several months later Alice phoned from the States to let us know that they would be coming back to Zimbabwe and to ask if there was anything that we needed.

Alice, "Can I bring you another Two Thousand Flushes?"

Me, "No thanks, we're still going fine. The one we're using has got quite a lot left."

Alice, "Oh my goodness Eilidh! It's not meant to last *that* long! You're not flushing the toilet enough!"

I had to assure Alice that indeed the toilet was being flushed adequately. We were experiencing one of the worst droughts ever in 1992 and had to be very frugal with water. It was a quick up and down with the handle on the cistern, so most likely, our Two Thousand Flushes had become Four Thousand Flushes!

Our home is in a rain shadow area and even in a normal rainy season we have to be careful with water. The 1992 rainy season was exceptionally bad. We kept emphasizing to our boys and the staff to be vigilant where water was concerned. It was during this period that we began to wonder if we'd have to change from our favourite brand of tea. It tasted foul. We couldn't understand it. It was the same brand that we'd used for years, the packet smelt ok. It wasn't the milk that had gone off, it was fine. I love the taste of our water, I checked the water out our tap and it was ok. It was a puzzle. I was in the kitchen one morning when Mark came in with the hot-water bottle that he'd used the night before. It didn't take long to solve this mystery. Mark thought he was doing his bit towards saving water by re-cycling the water from the hot-water bottle back into the kettle! No wonder the tea was 'off', it was the rubbery taste of the water that was causing it!

Tom and Alice would often host lunches or dinners for prominent American businessmen and women who were visiting Zimbabwe and we the neighbours would be invited. At the end of October 1996, Alice phoned me from the States and said that there would be a party of businessmen and women and some Smithsonian representatives who would be in Zimbabwe for a very limited period and that she had invited them for afternoon tea. I was delighted. This meant that we were going to be seeing our friends again. Then Alice dropped the bombshell – she had commitments in the U.S and wouldn't be able to fly out here and she asked if I'd organise the event for her! Wow. I had been out of the work place for years. I had been doing 'mummy' things and they did not include entertaining high-powered people. It was quite a responsibility. It's also a weird thing to be entertaining guests in a home that is not yours. Usually when we are entertaining, I'm running around like a mad thing, but this time it was easy. There were caterers, florists, hire people – I didn't have to actually do any work, just organize and supervise.

The day came. Tuesday 19th November 1996. November is in the rainy season and in the morning the heavens decided to show the Americans what an African downpour is all about! Our guests were not expected until mid afternoon, but the ground was saturated, the mud was viscous and, as nearly always happens when we have a storm, we had a power outage! For once it wasn't my problem. The caterers had been to the house many times before and were very aware of the fickle power supply, so they'd come prepared with gas! Clever people! Alice had given me a list of Zimbabweans that she wanted to invite and said that we could invite any of our friends that we wanted so that there would be a good cross section of people. We had a high-ranking politician from Colorado, American businessmen and women, Smithsonian representatives, Zimbabwean businessmen and women, friends, neighbours, and two young boys who had bunked out of cricket that afternoon and had come to the tea party. Altogether there were about fifty of us. I had a quiet smile to myself when I passed Heath earnestly explaining the intricacies of cricket to a distinguished-looking American gentleman. The afternoon was a success. The rain stayed off. Everyone mingled and when our foreign guests returned in their mini bus to Harare, the rest of us had a party!

Sadly Alice lost her valiant struggle with the ravages of cancer in January 2006. It was a privilege to have known her and to have had her as a part of our lives, she is genuinely missed.

ASTRIDE A JUMBO

Wednesday 27th August 1997 was my father-in-law, Yvo's eighty-eighth birthday. We wanted to make it a special occasion and we wracked our brains to know what to do. So few of his friends were still alive or were still in the country, that to give him a lunch or a dinner would be a bit of a damp squib. It was school holidays, Mark and Heath were both home, it meant we could do something as a family. We booked to spend the day at Ballyvaughn, a private game park, about fifty kilometres out of Harare on the Shamva road. On our arrival while we were enjoying our morning tea, we were given a history of the game park and its aims and objectives, a walk to have a look at various animals in enclosures followed this. These animals had either been injured or rescued and were behind the wire until hopefully, they could be returned to the wild.

Ballyvaughn is situated near a small river. A part of the days activities included canoeing down the river to a beautiful natural restaurant built amongst the trees at the waters' edge where lunch was to be served. Yvo decided he'd give the rowing a miss and he made the journey from the drop off point where the canoes were moored, to the lunch spot, by means of the game-viewing vehicle. Clever man. It was a deceptively long journey and I found out the hard way just how out-of-condition my arms were. Mike had to do nearly all the rowing. It's not really that he's all that chivalrous, he had to row if he wanted any lunch – and judging by the greed at tea time by some of the other guests, if we didn't get there at the same time, if not before them, we were going to go hungry. Mark and Heath were in a canoe slightly ahead of us. They were so busy arguing with each other that instead of making any progress, they were going round and round in square circles.

"You idiot! You're rowing the wrong way."

"Spaz. I'm not wrong, you are!"

"I'm not a spaz. You are!"

"I'm not rowing the wrong way!"

"Idiot, then why aren't we going straight?"

"Cos you're a spaz and you're rowing the wrong way!"

It was like this when Mike and I, who are by no stretch of the imagination tennis aces, were on our tennis court with the boys, we could beat them in straight sets even if we'd had our hands tied behind our backs and were in wheelchairs.

"Idiot. That was your ball."

"It wasn't! It was on your side."

"You were at the net, not me."

"You could have got there easier than me."

"Are you crippled?"

"Idiot!"

You get the idea.

Eventually we all arrived at the picnic destination, even the boys. A scrumptious feast followed. After a relaxing hour or so we were driven to what was to be the highlight of the day, the elephant rides. Yvo was game to climb up on the back of one of the pachyderms, but the ranger in charge of the beasts was gently, but firmly, adamant that Yvo's age made it too dangerous to allow him to take a ride. Yvo was disappointed, but we decided that it was better to err on the side of caution. Mike and Mark climbed onto the back of one elephant, Heath and I on another. Poor Heath lost out on this occasion. All he saw from his perch was the back of the elephant driver's shirt. I squashed Heath between the driver and myself, and he resembled a Pekinese dog with a flattened nose by the time we got off.

I was hanging on to the driver's sides for dear life and I didn't realize just how apprehensive I was until the driver said,

"Excuse me madam. Please you are making holes in my body with your nails." I think I rank elephant riding even lower on the totem pole than horse riding. At least you don't have to be able to do the splits when you're on the back of a horse! The Indian mahouts make it look like there's nothing to it. Although Yvo had had the frustration at not being able to ride an elephant, he thoroughly enjoyed his day, as did we, it definitely was a birthday to remember.

Just shortly after Yvo's birthday treat, he had another incident, which should have gone down in the annals of motoring history. He had been driving a Mazda 323 hatchback for several years, a popular car in Zimbabwe. The one thing that is unforgettable about Yvo is his quiet stubbornness concerning his independence. Although it was admirable, many a time, it was to us, a major headache. We popped in to see Yvo one Sunday after he had just returned from church. He was parking the 323 under the lean-to parking shelter near his front door when Mike noticed that the back window was smashed. Mike is a perfectionist, he *would* notice if the slightest thing were amiss! Yvo hadn't noticed. He thought it was a bit breezier than usual going to church, but wasn't unduly concerned. Mike being Mike, made his father check that nothing was missing from the vehicle and that everything seemed to be in order. Yvo was getting annoyed with his son and he was a bit short with Mike and said that he was perfectly capable of checking the car!

Monday came along and was another busy day as usual. We later found out that Yvo had also had a busy day. Before I go any further, I should point out that the round journey from his house to church was six kilometres. Back to Monday, he left home and went to the bank in town, from there went out to the industrial area of Msasa to a place called Chipungu Village. Chipungu started off as a small centre for stone carvers to produce, show and sell their incredible art. It has blossomed to not only the carving village, but next door is Doone Estate, which is a tourist Mecca. There are all the traditional goods for sale. There's artwork, clothing, coffee shop, restaurant.

Chipungu is sometimes hired as an outside venue for various organizations and on this Monday, it was where Yvo had been invited to address a gathering of engineers. By the time he arrived in the parking area of Chipungu, he had covered approximately twenty-two kilometres and then we have to add the six from the journey to church on Sunday, making a grand total of twenty-eight kilometres. Another car, driven by a younger engineer who was also attending the talk, pulled up next to Yvo. The younger man went over to greet Yvo, and as he did, he commented on how hot Yvo's car smelt. By now, even dad had to agree that there was something not right. The two men opened the bonnet and made an astonishing discovery, the thieves who'd smashed the rear window had stolen something after all – they'd stolen the radiator and the fan! It's amazing to think that the car kept going with these vital parts missing! The younger man had to diplomatically veto Yvo's statement that he'd drive the car back home as it was. He reckoned that if he could drive twenty-eight kilometres without the fan and radiator, why couldn't he just drive the car back home like that and then call a garage from the comfort of his own house!

LIGHTNING

Storms in Africa are frightening. The build up to the storm can also be spectacular. The sweltering, debilitating heat, is one of the first signs. The magnificent heavenly hues in the sky range from indigo to black that few artists could do justice to. The foremost heavy drops that come as a warning and which within seconds become an absolute blinding deluge in a solid sheet of rain. Even more terrifying than the torrential sheet of water, is the lethal lightning. Every year lightning is the cause of several deaths.

We live on the top of a hill flanked on both sides by hills and faced from across the valley by another range of hills. These hills all contain iron ore, which make for sensational lightning strikes. As a result we take extra precautions. Our TV lounge has a lightning conductor on the chimney and we always automatically disconnect the batteries to the burglar alarm in a storm. Mike devised one switch that we have to press to disconnect the entire alarm system; we've learned the hard way about leaving the alarms connected. Even with the use of surge protectors, we never leave TVs, sound systems, computers or other electrical appliances plugged in at the wall socket. In the kitchen we automatically switch appliances off at the wall when we've finished using them. The fluctuation in voltage at times is frightening. We can go from below a hundred to about three hundred volts, when we should be averaging two hundred and thirty volts. Admittedly this doesn't happen very often, but when it does, it can have a devastating effect on electrical items. So we tend to err on the side that it's better to be safe than sorry.

During the festive season we often endure some horrendous storms and this was no exception on Thursday 1st January 2004. What made this even more unusual was that this storm occurred ten in the morning. Storms in the afternoon were typical, not in the morning. Everything seemed to happen at once. Blinding flashes of lightning, deafening peals of thunder and the four of us running from room to room to make sure that everything was unplugged! Dramatic silver and blue flashes were emanating from empty plug sockets in the walls. The wall plug for our phone exploded out of the wall socket and went flying across the room. We rushed into the kitchen to make sure that frigs and freezers were unplugged – which they were, as Mike rested his hand on the top of one freezer he was thrown across the kitchen coming to a stop at the kitchen sink. The jacaranda tree by the front door was bent double with the ferocity of the wind and we expected at any moment to hear it crashing through the roof of the entrance hall.

It was then time to ascertain what damage, if any, had taken place. If I ever needed a reason to be wary of lightning, the events of the past few minutes put it all into perspective. Every television set and music centre was damaged, some beyond repair – and not one of them had been connected to wall sockets. The lights in certain rooms were destroyed, but not in others. The television aerial cable comes into our TV lounge through the ceiling. Despite a lightning conductor close by, despite the aerial being disconnected, still the lightning somehow earthed itself via the aerial and smouldered a black patch in the corner of the ceiling. Two of the four plates on the stove were damaged as was the swimming pool pump and motor. We have security lights along our driveway and the cable is buried under the tar- well it was. After the lightning, the cable was blasted out of the tar. A jacaranda tree nearer the security gate had a black burn stripe up and down the length of its trunk. One window was damaged in the kitchen where there was a large pane of glass sporting a perfect oval sandblast – it was an exquisitely precise piece of work.

The dogs were terrified and had dived into their kennels for refuge. I had been anxious about the safety of our staff and their families and it was a great relief to learn that no one had been injured. The war-vets on the neighbouring farm had suffered serious damage to boreholes. Tom our neighbour had the most dramatic destruction with his electric transformer almost split in two. All in all, it was a miracle that no one had been injured. The storm stopped almost abruptly as it had started and we were left to lick our wounds and ascertain the extent of the damage. Our first port of call was to get estimates to repair anything that was repairable and worth resurrecting. Then we went to the insurance company to lodge a claim. That was another learning curve.

We knew we were underinsured so that we could only expect a pro-rata payout on the claim. The reply we got was a complete and utter bombshell! The claim was rejected because according to the Meteorological Office there was no lightning strike in our area on 1st January. The onus was on us to prove that there had been lightning. How exactly do you go about proving something like this? Mike went straight to the top – of the insurance company that is. Mike told the C.E.O that our neighbours had also been affected. The C.E.O said that we should get affidavits from the neighbours stating this fact. Mike was furious. It wasn't up to us to prove the fact, surely it was up to the insurers to prove or disprove it. In the end, the C.E.O did do a bit of research on his own and at our next meeting, wrote out a cheque there and then, albeit for a fraction of the cost of repairing and replacing, but it was better than nothing.

We have had many storms since then, but nothing like the lightning we had that unforgettable day. It must be terrifying for the millions of Zimbabweans who live in grass huts. Let's hope that it's true that lightning doesn't strike in the same place twice!

WE'RE NOT CRAZY

We're not crazy. Zimbabweans are different. Zimbos come in all colours, creeds, shapes, sizes and anything else you can think of, but we're still Zimbos. In these days of rampant inflation when people are talking in billions and trillions, it's not a compliment to tell a Zimbabwean woman that she looks a million dollars! Cheapskate! It's also not advisable to accept an invitation to a candlelight dinner (eat your heart out Hyacinth Bucket), there's nothing elegant or romantic about it, it just means that it's during the nightly power outages. If you really want to impress overnight guests, tell them they can have a hot bath ..... that's the height of luxury, running water AND electricity to heat it! We spend our time having to make a plan. Transport is a luxury for majority of people in Zimbabwe. If patience is a virtue, then there must be an awful lot of virtuous Zimbos hopefully waiting for the supposedly imminent arrival of the bus or E.T.

We used to have a man working for us, Raphael. You really couldn't help being partial to him he was a likeable rogue. He worked for us for years and in a roundabout way we were related to him – his Heinz 57 dog, Mary, was the mother of our very first pups, Prince and Caesar. Mary spent as much time in our house as she did her master's, but in the end, she always knew where her loyalty lay and, after eating us out of house and home, would happily trot back to Raphael. He started off as a general labourer, then Mike taught him how to build during the construction of our house. Eventually he left us for greener pastures. One day, Mike and I were going into Harare and it seemed as if all our staff wanted a lift into town that day! We couldn't squeeze another body into the car. We were just about to drive out of the driveway when Raphael suddenly appeared, all spruced up and ready for an outing to town. He was crestfallen when Mike said that we couldn't help him, that the car was full to bursting point. We'd both forgotten about

Zimbo optimism. Raphael had a simple solution. He made a plan. He'd travel in the boot of the car!

Mike and I were horrified. We tried to explain to Raphael that it wasn't humane to transport someone in the boot of a car. He remonstrated with us saying that he'd be perfectly happy going that way – he could even have a bit of a snooze en route, he also pointed out that any mode of transport was better than no transport at all. Finally we relented, albeit, reluctantly. Raphael was a happy soul at the best of times, but he sported an extra wide grin now. He climbed into the boot. Mike closed the lid. We set off. The indignant car groaned with its heavy load. There is an almost permanent police roadblock on the main Mazowe road into Harare. Sometimes they just wave you through, other times they stop you. We didn't think the police would take too kindly to finding a body, especially a live body, in the boot of the car, so we stopped a good distance away from the roadblock, released Raphael and told him to walk and we'd meet him on the other side. Isn't it typical, this time we sailed right through without the police giving us a second look! It would just be our luck, that had we not emptied our boot of its human cargo, the police would have decided to give our car a thorough going over!

What I like about the crazy situation here is that we're not alone and it makes me feel relatively normal. Note I didn't say perfectly normal. One of things I can't stand about staying at our house in Borrowdale is the water supply or the lack, thereof. The Harare water supply is erratic to say the least. When either one of us is in the shower, all lathered up, then some twit next door decides to flush the loo we're left standing in our birthday suits twiddling our thumbs until there's enough of a trickle to rinse us. The city's water system is antiquated at best. It needs to be completely revamped and upgraded, but that requires money, so the rejuvenation isn't likely to happen any time soon. The daily power outages exacerbate the situation. The area in which our house is situated seems to be especially vulnerable to the vagaries of the water supply. We have a tap in the very far corner at the front of the garden, which is fractionally lower than the tap at the back. Often when there is literally not a drop of water in any of the taps in the house, we might just get a trickle of the front tap. That's Mike's duty. He's an early riser. He'll meander down to the tap with a container, switch it on, come back to the house, get dressed; go back down to the tap, and by then, the container should be full. It takes about three of these trips to get enough water to fill the cisterns in the two toilets. This followed by a few more trips to get water to fill the ancient geyser in the kitchen, which sits just above the sink.

I don't like the taste of Harare water. I'm not always so sure just how safe it is. I realize that hundreds of thousands of people in the city have no choice but to drink it. We made a plan. Every time we make the journey from Mazowe to Harare, we have containers of drinking water with us, we also take a couple of twenty-five litre containers with water that we can put in the cistern to flush the loo and wash dishes. In June and July 2007, 29 people died from cholera, hence my distrust of the city's water.

In July 2007 the element in the kitchen geyser in our Harare house, died. Mike went around the local hardware stores sourcing a new element, which wasn't an easy task as the geyser was decidedly old-fashioned. His luck was in and he had the choice of four elements ranging in price from one point two million dollars to twenty-eight million dollars for the same thing, so it won't take a rocket scientist to guess which one he purchased. That was the easy part of the repair. The old element had been in place for a long, long time and was firmly wedged in place. Not having the necessary equipment, Mike made a plan and had to make-up a tool of sorts to insert into the narrow opening of the geyser in order to remove the defunct element. We were up early just after dawn and were still in our pyjamas both standing near the kitchen sink when Mike finally managed to dislodge the burnt out geyser.

As the bottom of the geyser and the element came away, so did a deluge of thick, black, liquid sludge. We were showered with the disgusting gunk, as were the walls, the curtains, the floor and the kitchen cupboards. We both resembled wannabe black and white minstrels and on seeing each other, simultaneously burst out laughing. Don't know what I was laughing at as not only was I the mug who was going to have to clean it all up, but we had no water with which to do it! I know it's years and years of build up, but the sight of the liquid black mud that came out of that geyser made me concerned for the residents of Harare who have no choice but to use this water.

Water is the major problem when staying in Borrowdale. I can count on one hand the number of times that there's enough water pressure to have a shower. If we lived here full time, Mike would have sorted out a water storage tank and we most possibly would have a borehole. I've become quite adept at keeping myself clean. Hair is always washed in the kitchen sink. There is, for the most part, water in the geyser – even if it means that we have to fill the tank from water collected from the tap at the bottom of the garden at dawn, or from containers that we've brought into town with us from home. I have often stood in the buff (NOT a pretty sight) in the middle of winter (NOT a whole bundle of fun) in the kitchen, sponging myself down in the kitchen sink.

It's amazing just how little water I actually need! There is also the added bonus that I get to do a yoga session at the same time when I put my feet (one at a time, of course) in the basin to give them a scrub. Getting them back out and onto terra firma is not always easy, it would help if I were a couple of inches taller. Mike's not a yoga adept like me. He also has an added complication of larger, much larger, feet than mine in a basin that's too small for him. We appreciate getting back home to Mazowe. The sheer, absolute bliss of standing under running water (gravity fed) and enjoying its heat (solar heaters) makes all the difference.

Zimbabweans don't always appreciate how inured we've become to the deteriorating conditions until now and again, something will crop up to remind us. We tend to accept the lack of water, the lack of power, the lack of commodities in the shops, the lack of services from local authorities. A neighbour said that it hit her just how much she was suffering from 'Zimbo-itis' when she was watching the popular television show, "The Weakest Link". Anne Robinson asked, "What do you call the thing that travels through the sky and carries information?" Our neighbour shouted out the answer before the contestant on the show had a chance to open his mouth, "Pigeon!" Then realization sunk in. We've learnt to be able to laugh at ourselves.

I seldom watch the local television news. The ruling party controls the media, thus the news tends to be a bit one-sided. Mike periodically watches it as he feels he has to keep abreast of local affairs. On occasions the newsreader doesn't arrive in time to read the six o'clock news, so we're subjected to the same three or four adverts being looped round continuously until a presenter is available. Thursday 24th May 2007 was one of the most entertaining news broadcasts that I've ever watched. It took me on a trip down memory lane. It took me back to my childhood. No news, no explanation, instead an ancient, really ancient, re-run of "Lassie". This was one of the best news I've ever watched, although probably not the most informed and enlightened way to start the day.

Diamonds, blood, or otherwise, have taken Zimbabweans by storm. There are legal and illegal dealers. There are authentic and there are fake, 'finds'. Quite often the finds are nothing more than quartz. Times are hard. People are struggling. People are desperate. The economy is in tatters. The local news on 31st May 2007 carried the report about a school in a township on the outskirts of Harare, Dzivarasekwa, where diamonds had supposedly been found. A young boy, a student at the school, had been put on manual labour by the headmaster for some misdeed. In the course of his digging he discovered some interesting little stones. These interesting little stones turned out to be diamonds! Instead of the school benefiting from this find, the impoverished public descended on the school in hordes and began to dig and dig and dig. They had actually started undermining the very structure of the school in more ways than one.

Or there is the case of the man who lives near us and has been in the area forever. He (legally) owns a fair quantity of land on which there is borehole water and he has a business providing residents in the area with water. One day he noticed a pile of bricks on his land, as well as some members of the public who had no right to be there. He was curious. In these times of land invasions, we're all a bit twitchy about 'undesirables' being on our land. In the course of chatting to this group, the landowner discovered that these people belonged to two church groups who had supposedly recently bought the land from the local council. The landowner took himself off to the local council offices post haste to clarify the situation. The council employee conceded that perhaps a mistake had been made – especially as the landowner pointed out that he still had the title deeds to the property. The council employee then went on to say that it would be a very nice gesture to the two church groups if the landowner could 'donate' the land to them, thus solving all the problems! Whereby the extremely patient landowner proceeded to explain to the council employee that the bulk of the water for his business comes from this particular piece of land. The council employee was nonplussed, he had a simple solution ..... the church groups could collect the water and sell it back to the landowner!

Visits to the hairdresser are a luxury for many now. On average I go to the hairdresser twice a year and for the rest of the year I go to 'Chez Michael' – the cheapest, weirdest hair establishment out. Mike and our sons also frequent this 'salon'. Weather permitting, the 'salon' is usually to be found in the outside courtyard off our bedroom where the 'customer' perches on the stonewall while facing the stunning view of the Mazowe valley while Mike weaves his magic. There has been the odd disaster when Mike has had an off day, but on the whole, he's ok. Our sons have carried on the tradition of 'Chez Michael' in the UK after learning the tricks of the trade from their father. As they said it saves money and when you're a student with limited funds, every penny counts.

Zimbabweans returning from trips outside the country bring back an inordinate quantity of goods that in a normal situation, we'd be able to purchase in our own shops. It's staggering to see the contents of the luggage or vehicles of returning Zimbos. The list is endless: electrical appliances, olive oil, cooking oil, other grocery items, cosmetics, sanitary items, medicinal supplies, tools, motor spares, CDs, books and stationery. Mark and Heath complain that if their suitcases are ever searched on their return to Zim on holiday, the customs officials are going to be giving them funny looks – they bring little in the way of clothing, but their cases are bursting with my hair colours, nail varnishes, cosmetics, perfume, deodorant, accessories, women's clothing, rechargeable batteries, gadgets for Mike, cheese, tuna fish – the list is endless. When the boys come home, we go straight into the lounge with their suitcases and it's like Christmas. We have friends who've even brought pig's ears back as a treat for their dogs!

Good friends of ours had to leave our country to try and earn a liveable wage. Their journey took them over the border to Botswana. With our wild inflation it's often cheaper to buy goods outside the country depending on the rate you've had to pay for black market forex. Years ago, these friends bought a little generator in Botswana to bring back home to Zimbabwe. Not wanting to have all the documentation on them at the customs that would show that it was a new generator, they had a brainwave. They made a plan. They placed the papers in a sturdy plastic bag, dug a hole next to a distinctive tree along the road, and buried everything in the hole. A year later on a return trip to Botswana, they decided to dig up the papers so that they could get the instruction manual as they were having a few problems with the generator and wanted to see how to go about repairing it. This is Africa and the one thing we do have, is an abundant supply of insects. When the tree was eventually located, the package dug up, it was discovered that the white ants had had a feast! There was nothing left. The secrets of the quirky generator were lost forever.

Before leaving Zimbabwe for university in the UK, Heath spent many hours typing out step-by-step pages for Mike and I of how to use the computer and all its idiosyncrasies. He made it in basic, easy-to-follow form. Step one; plug the computer in at the wall. Step two, switch on power to computer. Step three; ...... At the very end of the file of notes that he'd compiled for us, he said 'do not have a drink until you have been successful'. Mike and I have been stone cold sober for a LONG time! It would help if Mike could tell his left from his right. To combat this when driving when I'm navigating I started saying, 'your side' and 'my side'. This works. Mike and I had been trying to follow Heath's instructions for taking the photos off the digital camera and put them onto disk and it was a disaster. Mike was sitting at the computer and I was standing on his left, reading out the instructions. O.K. I'm not blameless, I did leave out a step or two, but Mike would right click when I told him left, he didn't double click when told, then would double click when he didn't have to. This was divorce material.

I emailed my frustrations to Heath. The solution was simple, why hadn't I thought of it? Why did I have to wait for my youngest child to email me from six thousand miles away with the answer? It was so obvious. Heath said that when we were using the computer and I was reading out instructions, I should always stand on Mike's left and that instead of my saying 'right click' or 'left click' I should say 'your side' or 'my side' and if a double click was required, all I had to say was 'your side your side' rapidly, or 'my side my side'! It worked.

Zimbabweans are friendly people. Yet, some of us are loath to wave to each other. The reason is simple. The open hand resembling someone waving is the sign of the opposition party, the Movement for Democratic Change, the MDC. When travelling in areas that are politically tense, the local population often greet you with a 'thumbs up' sign rather than an open hand. I know I do. It's safer. This way you can't offend anyone no matter what their political affiliations.

I AM NOT THE ONE

Zimbabweans have our own language. No, I don't only mean Shona (the literal English translation of the word means 'Where the sun sets'), or Ndbele or English. I mean the many words that we've borrowed from our South African neighbours. I mean the words that we've taken from the British, Americans or Australians. I mean our very own brand. Our own compound of words. It's what makes any nation unique. When you take the Zimbo brand of slang it's actually quite cosmopolitan. It's what leads us to take 'padkos' (food for the road) on a journey with us. It's what leads us to enjoy 'sadza' (mealie meal porridge) and relish at a 'braai' (barbecue), along with our 'boerewors' (South Arican sausage). It's what leads brothers to refer to each other as 'boet'.

In his workshop, Mike has a 'bobbejaan' spanner. I've never worked that one out. I don't get the connection with a baboon and a spanner. It's what makes us wary when buying goods 'voets toets', as this means that the goods are sold as they are, with no guarantee, what you see is what you get. It's what leads us to describe the ZANU (PF) headquarters building in Harare as the 'shake shake' building, which is a reference to the shape that it resembles, that of the pointed cardboard carton of a local beer that needs to be shaken before it's opened. The name of the traditional beer 'Chibuku' is derived from 'by the book' and originates from earlier times when an enterprising entrepreneur decided that this beer could be marketed and asked the local people for the recipe. They didn't use a recipe. It was a handful of this and a bucket of that. So our entrepreneur asked them the next time they made it, to keep a list of the various handful and bucketfuls, so that he could manufacture it for himself 'by the book'. The beer is made from sorghum, maize and other cereal grains. It's what makes us use bits of 'simbe' or metal when carrying out repairs. We eat 'huku' (chicken), 'hove' (fish) and 'nyama' (meat), which, if we're having a braai, are cooked with 'moto' (fire). If any of the family is sick, we take 'muti' (medicine). We have signs on our gates with the words 'Chenjera imbwa', or beware of the dog, accompanied by the picture of a ferocious dog baring its fangs, and in case the you are being attacked by the dog you can shout at it to 'voetsek!' (Go away!).

Once a week Zimbabwean supermarkets give a small discount on purchases to senior citizens, that is, people who are sixty-five and over. Every bit helps. My pride is hurt when vendors refer to me as 'ambuya' (grandmother)! I'm far too young! I'm nowhere near that age! I feel vindicated when they refer to Mike as 'sekuru' (grandfather) – but it's not nearly as often as my 'ambuya'! However, pride goes out the window when we're in the queue at the supermarket and on reaching the cashier, we're asked, "Are you senior citizens?" I have to weigh up between my vanity and the benefits of a ten percent discount on my groceries. I'm sure you know which way I decide all the while knowing that on the inside I'm a recycled teenager!

However, the Zimbo saying that is possibly used most is "I'm not the one". You're on the phone complaining about shoddy service and the person at the other end of the receiver will tell you that he's 'not the one'. You stand for hours in a queue to pay a bill, only to find that you've been standing in the wrong (and of course, unmarked) queue, and that the cashier in front of you is 'not the one'. It's a great phrase. It shirks all responsibility. It covers all situations. We all use it. Like the time that Mike and I went running through to the TV lounge after we'd heard any almighty crash and a scream, dreading the worst, we arrived to see Mark purple in the face trying to stop the TV from crashing to the floor! We, to this day, still don't know what he was up to, but he was the only one in the room at the time. When questioned his reply was, "I'm not the one!"

Our neighbour Tom had (and I must point out here, still has, although it's been parked in our garage for many years) a three-wheeler, all terrain motorbike. It was a great way of entertaining children. One year he very kindly offered it to us for the use of our children. The boys thought they'd died and gone to heaven. Mark being the eldest, laid claim to 'ownership' and he monitored Heath's use of the bike. It was fine while driving the bike on flat ground, but we don't have a whole lot of that on our property. Going uphill I always had the sensation that the bike was going to tip backwards, it just didn't feel very steady. Mark and Heath had great fun giving their grandparents rides on the bike and when the boys had their friends visiting, it was a great source of entertainment. As a real treat, we'd not only let them drive around the garden, but would allow them outside the security fence to ride down to the dam and the campsite. Before their departure, they'd get an earful of exhortations about driving too fast, being careful – and all the other warnings that parents give to their children.

It was a Sunday afternoon I was busy in the kitchen. Mike and the boys were somewhere in the grounds and I was enjoying being able to work in the kitchen without having the grubby fingers of all of my boys (the one that I'm married to, included) being dipped into the raw mixture for tasting, or having everyone hanging around to lick the bowl and pleading with me to leave more raw mix in the bowl, or doing 'quality control' on the finished goods ...... Heath's quality control tends to finish the whole batch. An hour or so later, Mark arrived at the back door, completely dishevelled. He was covered in grass and leaves, his tee shirt was torn and he had a few grazes. He wasn't looking too happy. I asked, "What happened to you?"

"We were on the bike and it overturned on the road up from the dam."

"That's it! I KNEW this would happen! That bike's unsafe. I'm grounding you from using it, except in the garden. You're not going to go down to the dam on it ever again. I told you ...."

"But mum!"

"No buts! How's Heath? Where is he?"

"He's with dad."

"O.k. I want that bike back and put in the garage. No more driving to the dam, and ...."

"But Mum! I'm not the one! I wasn't driving! It was Dad!"

Do boys ever grow up? There were THREE of them on the bike. Mike was driving, Heath behind him and Mark at the back. They were driving up from the dam and on a particularly steep section of the road the bike flipped backwards and "I'm not the one" Mark, was flattened under his brother, father and the bike! The boys have never let their father forget that 'He was the one'!

We have quite a few outbuildings on our property for all our junk. I mean junk. Junk to anyone else is treasure to Mike. His theory being that it may come in handy one day. To give him his due, he has utilized many bits and pieces in his various projects, and he has cannibalised one appliance to make another one work. Our laundry is just outside the kitchen. It's a great room, the walls are out of natural stone and as a result it's like an oven in summer and nice and warm in winter - perfect for drying clothes and even better for proving dough for bread and pizzas! It was school holidays and I had sent the boys to go and play outside, we were expecting quite a crowd for dinner in the evening and I was up to my elbows in the kitchen. I don't know what game the boys were playing, but it did entail them being in the laundry and locking the door from the inside. The lock had been a bit dodgy for a while and was temperamental.

The kitchen window faced that of the laundry and I was keeping an eye on the boys. I went out and told them not to lock the door. I needn't have wasted my time. Boys will be boys. Heath's piping little voice rang out, "Mummy! Mark won't let me out."

"Mark, let him out."

Mark, "I can't."

Me, "Why not?"

Mark, "Cos the door's stuck."

What I'd warned about had come to pass. The door was stuck. Or, in Zimbabwean, the lock was 'buggered'. That descriptive expletive is used to describe anything that is broken. I spent ages fiddling with the key. Taundi spent ages fiddling with the key. Mike was at work and I didn't think he'd be overly impressed with me if I tried to break the door down. The boys were well and truly stuck. There are three windows in the laundry, all with extra heavy-duty burglar bars, there was not way out. I phoned Mike and he said there was nothing for it but to leave the boys where they were until he came home. I went outside to give the boys the news.

"I've phoned Dad and he says you'll just have to stay in there all day until he comes home."

"That's not fair!"

"I DID tell you not to lock the door. Maybe you'll listen to me next time."

"But mummy, it's a long time till Dad comes home."

"That can't be helped. I'll bring you sandwiches and juice for lunch, and if you need a wee, you'll just have to hang out the window! At least you won't get cold."

Mike came home a few minutes earlier than usual and he had to take the door off its hinges, I suppose I could have done that – well, I could have if I'd known how to go about it. Mark and Heath looked quite relieved when they were finally released. Funny thing, the laundry seemed to lose its appeal after that.

HIPPO POOLS

Beautiful Hippo Pools

Mark came back to Zimbabwe from Britain on holiday and although our finances were a bit tight and fuel was the usual headache, we managed to get a few days away to a fishing camp along the Mazowe River called Hippo Pools. We set out to our destination on Friday 3ʳᵈ September 2004. When we made our booking we were advised that we had to take everything that we would need as there were no shops for miles around, so quite a bit of planning went into the catering and the packing. I usually pride myself on being highly organized, but this time I made an awful boo-

boo – I left the wine behind at home! Of course I found out too late! Four days on holiday along the banks of a river in a beautiful African setting with no wine! Horror of horrors! I survived somehow. Our truck was laden and we made good time going out towards Shamva. That was short lived. When we turned off the main road we were travelling at a snail's pace. The booking agent had said that the camp, which is within a national park, was accessible by car! I don't know what kind of car they were talking about! Our truck battled.

Mark was driving and we had to crawl along the road, it was in terrible condition. Our arrival at our lodge was somewhat of an anti-climax. Even a bit of a disappointment. This was not laying blame on the management. The country was still reeling from the effects of the land invasions and this fishing camp had not been spared. The lodges had been all but stripped of their fittings. The squatters were no longer on the premises, but they had been there and their presence had been destructive. The owner had done his best to get the lodges back on track and habitable, but they still had quite a ways to go. There were about three or four of the larger lodges such as ours, all well spaced out, several smaller chalets and a campsite.

Our lodge was basic. There were two bedrooms on either side of a lounge, the front wall of which consisted of chicken wire above a low wall. The kitchen had a gas stove and running water. The basic ablution facilities were adequate and hot water for showering was supplied by means of a Rhodesian boiler. The setting was truly African. It was superb. The camp was quite high up with steep slopes leading down to the water and with a commanding view up and down the river for quite some distance. There was a patch of grass in front of the lodge dotted with indigenous bushes and trees, which led to the braai (barbecue) area situated on the riverbank overlooking the Mazowe River. We were near a bend in the river, which widened quite extensively for a short distance and immediately opposite us was a tiny island that was home to a family of hippos and a resident croc. We couldn't have asked for better surroundings. We unpacked, sat on the riverbank and communed with nature. It was almost possible to believe that our country was at peace with itself and that we hadn't had any problems.

Our first night we had the camp to ourselves. There were so few people staying there that I wonder how the place paid for itself. Most of our meals were braais cooked outside in the coolness of the setting sun, accompanied by the enchanting grunts of the hippo family. The booking agent had omitted to tell us that we needed to take candles and matches with us. We knew there wouldn't be electricity in this remote area, but we thought there might be hurricane lamps. Whenever we go away in Zim, I never go without a couple of candles, power outages have been with us for years. However, a couple of candles weren't going to last for four nights and wouldn't be enough for the various rooms. The camp provided an attendant, a young inexperienced woman. I think we were the first guests she had ever worked for, as I had to show her the rudiments of washing dishes. We negotiated with the young manager for a packet of candles and he did very well out of us, so we were all happy.

At Hippo Pools we were really out in the bush. It took quite a bit of getting used to at night with the sounds in the bush. I wasn't feeling totally relaxed, the invasions had left me with a touch of paranoia. Once we blew the candles out the night was dark, pitch black. I'm not sure how the young manager communicated with the main camp, as there were no telephones. The road to the club was awful. And it suddenly hit me that if we had an emergency of sorts we were on our own, completely on our own. A few years back this wouldn't have fazed me. The recent traumatic happenings in Zimbabwe had left me tense. Thus it did nothing to restore my equilibrium when, on hearing a noise, I tiptoed to the bedroom window and glanced outside. With the aid of a weak moon, I made out the silhouette of a man cradling a rifle! That was it, we were all going to be murdered in our sleep, - except that I wasn't asleep. Mike went to investigate and the outcome was that the camp management was concerned about the safety of the guests in these volatile times, so provided a guard for our protection. We sometimes caught a glimpse of the guard during the daylight hours as well. I would have preferred for his presence to have not been necessary.

My three men would take themselves off fishing fairly early in the mornings. Although they weren't successful, they enjoyed themselves and I had a bit of 'time out' doing one of the things I love, reading. There were several canoes for hire at a nominal rate and Mike informed me one morning that he had booked two of the larger ones for the use of our family that afternoon. I took pleasure in observing the hippo family and the croc from my elevated vantage point on our riverbank and I had no intention, nor any wish, to get any closer to them. Mike should know by now that anything short of the 'Q.E.2' would be too small as far as I was concerned. I pointed this out to him, and his rejoinder was "Oh come on! You'll love it!" Why do I allow myself to be manipulated like this? What on earth made me think I was going to enjoy the water now? Mark and Heath looked at each other; at least they've got a better handle on their mother than Mike does. They knew what the outcome would be.

Mike, Mark and Heath go fishing

I should have chickened out the moment we got to where the canoes were tied up. They looked like toys. I pointed out that there was water in the bottom of each canoe and this just earned me withering stares from three pairs of eyes. Mark knew better than to even offer to let me go with him, so he took his father. Poor Heath always gets the raw end of the deal where I'm concerned. We'd gone about two feet when I started getting nervous. The canoes seemed awfully low in the water and I kept anxiously looking around for the hippos. The croc slid into the water as we neared the island, so I kept my hands well and truly inside the vessel. From the confines of the canoe, the river looked massive, never-ending. I wanted out. I wanted dry land under my feet. Talking about feet, I admit it happened gradually, but my tackies (trainers) were beginning to get damp. The dampness grew to form wet patches. We were going to sink. We were all going to die! I steeled myself. I lowered my gaze from its fixed point on the horizon where I'd earnestly been beseeching God to keep us safe and looked at the floor of the canoe. At a spot near my feet was a hole. Someone had attempted a Heath Robinson (no relation to my Heath) repair with some sticky stuff (blue tak), as a matter of interest, once wet, sticky stuff loses its stickiness and is useless for repairing holes in boats.

I mentioned our dilemma to Heath in my most dulcet, panic-stricken shriek and his solution was that I change my name to Peter, my nationality to Dutch, and use my finger! I nearly gave Heath the proverbial finger. His proposal did nothing to allay my fears, neither did his discovery of a plastic milk bottle with its cap firmly screwed on and the bottom cut off, thus making it an effective scoop with which to bail. I bailed. Heath rowed. I panicked. Enough was enough. Mike and Mark were rowing alongside us with differing views on my plight.

Mike, "Just keep bailing. You'll be ok. You'll see, you'll love it."

Mark, "Chuck her out. Dump her on dry land, she's not enjoying herself."

Me, "She is not enjoying herself, and she wants to get off NOW!"

Poor Heath was rowing in square circles. He would row in the direction we were meant to be heading. Then I'd say I wanted to go back, so he'd start turning round. Then Mike would say that I was being silly and that we should continue and Heath would start going forward again. Yes, I wanted out. I didn't fancy being chucked out anywhere along the riverbank. I know I'm a wimp, but I kept remembering the manager warning us to be careful as just a few days prior to our arrival a local fisherman had been snatched from the banks by a croc.

By now, even my patient, long-suffering youngest son had had enough. He headed for the nearest bank and said, "Out!" I climbed out gingerly, constantly on guard for any flat dogs in the nearby environs. I was safe. I made it back to our lodge and treated myself to a strong cup of coffee to quell my beating heart. Eventually even Heath had to call it quits. The hole in his dyke seemed to be growing and with no Peter to help him, he decided that caution was the better part of valour. He returned the canoe to its mooring and waited for his father and brother to come back for him. The three of them rowed off together and were away for hours and thoroughly enjoyed themselves. Later in the day I bumped into the manager, a nice young man called Simba. When he enquired why I wasn't with the men, I told him about my harrowing experience. He said that I'd had nothing to be worried about and that the canoe never filled up with more than a couple of pints of water at any one time and that it was perfectly safe. I wasn't prepared to find out. Water is water. A couple of inches or a couple of pints is still too much as far as I was concerned.

The land on the opposite of the river was communal lands, or what in Rhodesian days were called Tribal Trust Lands, (TTLs) and as such, were set-aside for the local people. The chief of this particular area was young, barely in his twenties. He and the owner of the fishing camp had decided that it would be a win-win situation if they worked together on the tourism aspect. Initially the opposite bank was full of crops of maize and pumpkins, not exactly the bush experience that tourists would expect. It was explained to the young chief that if he left the dense virgin bush to grow along the edge of the water, he could hide his crops behind it and the tourists would be none the wiser. The chief had also made an investment of ten thousand dollars, which was quite a sum in those days, and his investment had paid for itself time and again. We paid the young chief the princely sum of one thousand dollars for our family, in order for him to row us across the river to his lands and to visit his investment. Notice I said 'row', that means that I had bravely got back on the horse, or in this case, back in the canoe. It was a bigger canoe than the one I'd been in earlier in the day, and I felt that if the chief was prepared to risk his life for us and if we were going to drown during the five minute journey across the water, it would be better to drown as a family. Mark later pointed out to me in some places the water was so shallow we could almost have walked across.

We made it safely to the other side without being savaged by marauding hippos or malevolent crocs. We landed on a beautiful little sandy beach and were met by a couple of the chief's younger siblings and our entourage made our way to go and find the 'investment'. "Lola", the investment, was worth every cent of the ten thousand dollars used to purchase her. She was exquisite. She was a young, probably half grown eland. The chief and his family guarded her jealously. Their main concerns were crocs and other dangerous predators. Lola had been hand-reared; she didn't know that she was an antelope. She was like an over-grown puppy with six-inch long eyelashes to die for. As a precaution, the chief had cut short lengths of rubber hosepipe to cover the tips of her horns so that she couldn't unintentionally inflict damage. She loved to be petted and couldn't get enough attention. Heath's legs had got quite sunburnt earlier and he'd smothered them in aqueous cream to try and combat the pain. We couldn't figure out whether it was agony or ecstasy, Lola would sniff his legs, put her head in the air, curl her lips back and shake her head. Then out would come the long, *very* long, black tongue; she'd lick his legs and start the whole process over again to the great amusement of all. We were loath to take our leave, but the sun was getting lower, so farewells were said. Ever gracious, Lola and her human family accompanied us back to the beach and stood and watched as the chief rowed us safely back to our side of the river.

Lola and Mark getting acquainted

I've often wondered whether Lola survived as the odds were stacked against her. Our sojourn at Hippo Pools is especially poignant as not only was it the last time the four of us holidayed as a family, but while we were relaxing, we missed the ravages of the worst bushfire at our home in Mazowe that our area has ever experienced. Bush fires are an annual event. No matter how meticulous Mike is about cutting the grass on our border and burning firebreaks, every year we are faced with the horrifying aspects of these fires. August and September are the windiest times of the year and they are dry as the last rains to fall would most likely have been in March. All the right ingredients for the perfect fire. I don't know what made Friday 3rd September 2004 any worse than any other year, but it was.

At the bottom of our road lives an enterprising man Isaac, who amongst other agricultural ventures, has a grinding mill and there is always a string of people leading to his property carrying bundles of maize kernels. On this fateful day, one young customer had just left the miller's property and was wheeling his bicycle when he inadvertently threw his cigarette stub into the bush with devastating consequences. As we neared home after our fishing trip we noticed how black everything was, but not the normal burnt black, we're used to bush fires and blackened bush, this was an intense black to the very tops of the trees. Weighton, our gardener, said there had been a ferocious wind and there was little anyone could do to control the fire, he said that the smoke was so thick and the sky so black that you couldn't see your hand in front of your face.

Our neighbours, who live closer to the miller, had been out fighting the fire to protect their property. They were exhausted. Hilary had just got under the shower, clothes and all, to cool down when she heard a sound emanating from the garage. She rushed out in time to see one of their cars on fire. There was no way of saving it, so she got the other car out as quickly as she could and then she and her husband Alan, set about dousing the fire on the vehicle and in the garage. The car didn't blow up in spectacular fashion, but it was finished. A house on our eastern border was razed to the ground, completely gutted. Eleven huts belonging to war-vets or squatters, were destroyed, along with the contents and livestock. Fortunately no lives were lost. We suffered no damage ourselves. We are vigilant about doing our firebreaks, but it doesn't help when the 'new' owners of the neighbouring farm neglect to do theirs.

TELEPHONES

The communication system in Zimbabwe leaves much to be desired. Cell phones do work – intermittently. Often when you send a text message, it can take hours, even days, to be delivered. Sometimes it never reaches the intended recipient at all. The stratosphere or atmosphere or whatever sphere it is that the messages are floating around in limbo, must be packed to capacity. I'm amused when the little icon on my phone informs me that my message is 'pending' but I've already received a reply from the person I sent the message to. It can all be a bit confusing. Then there are the days when you're expecting the worst and hey presto, the message bursts out of your phone and is delivered immediately.

A major worry is if we ever need to use the cell phone in an emergency. I'm not exaggerating when I say that the networks in Zimbabwe are so congested that it's nothing to try for literally hours on especially bad days to get through to a number. Then just when you think you've been successful and you're having a conversation, you get cut off. I've explained about our party-line telephone in a previous chapter. I felt like Hyacinth Bucket in the television comedy "Keeping Up Appearances" when one day the phone company, P.T.C now renamed, Tel-One, delivered my 'green, slim-lined, push-button telephone' .... and we do also have room for a pony! It was such a glam-looking phone after the ghastly big square black affair that used to adorn the table. Well, that is, if you didn't look too carefully, along with the modern phone came a big metal box containing six 1.5volt batteries, which sat most inelegantly on the floor under the telephone table.

After installation the set never actually worked long enough for us to discover the life-time of the batteries, so presumably, if everything was normal, we'd have to call the phone technicians to come and replace the batteries when our speech started getting s – l – o – w – e – r and slurred.

The battery box has been sitting on the floor gathering dust for over three years and the phone hasn't worked since September 2005. The batteries are probably corroded out of existence by now.

Our neighbours were tired of the erratic phone service (this was back in the days when we had a service) and they also wanted an extension put into their art studio, which was separate from the main house. They phoned Tel-One to see what the chances were of repairing the fault and also to install another handset. One of the major causes of interrupted phone service is that of the theft of copper wire from the phone cables. Tel-One apologized to our neighbours and said that they were unable to attend to the fault, as they didn't have transport or fuel. The usual bugbear of Zimbabwean life. Not a case of a pub with no beer (not yet anyway), but of the service station with no fuel. Neighbour Alan magnanimously offered his own 'bakke' (pickup truck) and fuel and time, to go down to the Tel-One facility in Mazowe village, collect the technicians and bring them back to his house. A date and time were arranged.

The day duly arrived. Alan was at the premises at the pre-arranged time, that's right, you guessed, he was the only one there. A wait of an hour or more produced the technicians, then another wait was required to find an unobtainable battery box and batteries – there wasn't one so like true Zimbos, they 'made a plan'. Alan and the technicians patiently waited while amiably chatting until an arbitrary member of the public drove in with a battery box in his car ostensibly being brought in for repair. Not a problem. Just a short wait until the gullible gentleman left the premises, and voila, an additional box for Alan's second handset. Back to the house. First problem, the technicians didn't have a ladder. Not a problem, Alan whipped out his own ladder. Next problem, the technicians had forgotten some of their tools. Not a problem. Alan produced tools that although not perfect, would suffice. Next problem, they didn't have any phone cable. Not a problem, Alan had bought some on one of his shopping trips to South Africa. So it was all systems go. The extra handset was installed; things were looking good until the line was tested. It was, in true Zimbo, 'buggered'.

Alan and the technicians were not daunted. They jumped into the bakke together with the ladder, the tools, the cable and accordingly set off along the road testing the line. Every now and then they would stop, the technicians would alight from the vehicle, un-strap the ladder and one of them would nimbly climb up and inspect the line and equipment. This was done for the length of our little road, in the region of five kilometres long. The fault was not located there. So back onto the main road and heading back towards the Tel-One offices in Mazowe, this must have been somewhat of a relief to Alan since it was his precious supply of fuel that was being utilized. It was drive a bit, stop, ladder up, climb up, back down, back into the bakke, along the road a short distance and repeat the episode. A good distance down the road the whole rigmarole was repeated, but this time it was *the* pole, this was definitely where the problem lay. Success was but a moment away. The ladder was taken off the roof, placed against the pole and the technician began his ascent. The pole had other ideas. It went from being vertical to horizontal in the space of a few seconds, the ladder took its lead and was soon lying parallel to the pole and the technician took his lead from the pole and the ladder!

Alan saw success escaping from his grasp. The pole was left on terra firma. The ladder was secured to the roof and the technician was carefully placed in the back of the bakke. The journey this time actually took Alan past Mazowe and further out, to the Concession hospital to deliver the unhappy technician. Herein endeth the landline. Alan did ask for a repeat performance, minus the act with the flying pole and technician, but the Tel-One staff decided that they'd give it a miss. Alan was out of pocket. We were still phoneless. The handsets do make useful paperweights, so all is not lost.

We've had an almost never-ending feud with Tel-One, for over a year the phone company kept sending us invoices for the rental of the phone. Since the phone hadn't worked during that period we didn't feel that we were entitled to pay rent. We sent back letters telling them to come and reclaim their inoperable sets. The letters went unanswered. The next invoice not only had the accumulation of rental charges, but also interest on the overdue amount. We sent more letters to the phone company. This went on for months and months and months. At our own expense we made the trip into Harare to Tel-One head office to get forms to investigate the usage of the phone, we could only get these forms from town as our phones were part of a party-line and weren't digitalized, then at our own expense, we posted (and postage is expensive) the forms to Tel-One in Mazowe.

Finally, we could hardly believe it; we received an invoice with a nil balance. I'd far rather have a phone that worked. As things stand, the chances of us getting a useable landline within the foreseeable future are not good. Before the farm invasions, the phone company had started installing in rural houses phones with radio link in the hopes of thwarting the theft of the copper cable. All these projects have had to be shelved for the time being. The phone company has run out of money to continue the installations, the vast majority of the houses either stand empty or the 'new owners' either can't meet their financial commitments – or don't see why they should pay for them. After all, they got a farm for nothing, so why shouldn't they have a phone and line for nothing. I feel defenceless when we have the daily power outages, I know that there is no landline and no cell signal, but so does any prospective thief. The silly thing about all this is that even if the phones worked, I wouldn't even know who to call for help. The police most likely would not have transport and so many of our friends have left the country that we basically are on our own.

More often than not, we have no means of communicating with the outside world. I was watching the news in 2007, when there was the awful massacre of students at an American university by one of the students who'd gone on the rampage with a gun. One of the mothers interviewed said that although she was many miles away from her daughter at that university she and her child managed to stay in close contact by using a web-cam and chatting to each other daily. I was envious! *So* envious! I would give anything to sit and chat and hear my sons' voices, also those of my parents. The horrendous power outages that we experience often mean that we are without a signal for our cell phones.

I was spitting mad, our cell phone provider had run short of forex and therefore we couldn't send text messages to Britain – my only link with my children. To add insult to injury, in June 2007, we were not able to message anywhere for over three weeks, also Net-One, our cell-phone provider put up their fees by one thousand percent! Friday 29th June 2007 caused Mike a few headaches. He had several business calls to make, the landline hadn't worked for two years and we were in the middle of a sixteen-hour power outage and none of our three cell phones had a signal. Forever the pragmatist, Mike found himself a new office. He had discovered that if he went out of our property to the small road where it is slightly more elevated than our house, he could sometimes get a signal. That's what he did on this Friday. He took himself off armed with two phones, a telephone directory, a notepad and a pen. He climbed up on top of one of the stone pillars that acts as a gatepost and had the perfect office. All the feng shui in the world couldn't have provided that view, the fresh air, the inquisitive neighbour's goats, the warm winter sunshine and a phone signal! I went with the camera. He resembled an over-grown leprechaun sitting crossed-legged on top of the pillar.

Mike making phone calls in his office

VISA HEADACHES

Travelling on a Zimbabwean passport isn't a whole bundle of fun. In fact, it's no fun at all. The production of that little green book reduces one to pariah status. I know from experience. Going through the process of getting a visa isn't something I'd wish on my worst enemy. It never ceases to amaze me how desperate Zimbabweans are and what lengths they'll go to, to get out of here. Our supposedly friendly neighbouring countries don't make it exactly easy either to obtain a visa. In June 2007 Mike needed to apply for a holiday visa for Britain. What could be simpler? We have family there who'd vouch for us. We've been before so the Brits knew weren't dodgy. We forgot about being pariahs.

Mike already had the necessary visa application forms. He had the photographs. He had the documentation. That sounds simple. It isn't. The documentation included originals and photostats of his birth certificate, my birth certificate, Mark's birth certificate, Heath's birth certificate, his father's birth certificate, my father's birth certificate, my mother's birth certificate, our marriage certificate, my parent's marriage certificate, our utility bills to prove we live here, our company returns to prove that we have assets here that we will be returning to, letters from the university proving that Mark and Heath are students there, a letter of invitation from my parents, certified copies of my parents' passports showing their British status, copies of all our bank statements showing that we can support ourselves, - I think that about does it. We couldn't pay in either Zimbabwean cash or forex, it had to be by bank certified cheque and the rate rose daily with our crazy rate of inflation. For several years, the Brits have insisted that applicants use the services of the Visa Company, which of course charges for its services.

Mike wanted to submit his application about the 13th June 2007, the earlier he got it in the better as the rate was climbing. He had phoned at the beginning of June and was told that the rate was Z$3 million plus. When he phoned on the 13th, it had risen to Z$8 million. Just as a matter of interest, friends paid Z$22 million for a visa two weeks later. He was unable to put in his visa application as the Visa Company was closed for a few days as they were relocating and also for training as the British had introduced finger printing and photographs for visas to try and cut down on the fraudulent use of visas by many desperate Zimbabweans. Mike had been told that the Visa Company would be open for business on Thursday 21st June, at the same time he'd enquired about the cost of the visa. He thought that we'd be able to save fuel and time in queues if we first went to our bank in Borrowdale got the certified cheque made out to the British Embassy and then went to the Visa Company. Funny how things work out for the best. The person on the phone advised Mike not to get the cheque in advance in case the rate had changed and to phone on the morning of the 21st. We did this. It was impossible to get through by phone, there was nothing for it but to go to the Visa Company in Belgravia and then backtrack to our bank for the cheque.

Our hearts sank when we arrived at the new location of the Visa Company. The queue was unbelievable. The gates opened at eight in the morning, we arrived at eight twenty. Those at the front of the queue had been there since six in the morning. Just as well we hadn't got the cheque from our bank; a new ruling was in effect, all payments could only be made through one branch of a certain bank – and it was a branch right in the middle of the C.B.D! Most people avoid going into the C.B.D if they possibly can for reasons of security and parking. Luck was on our side. The bank was the same one that we bank with so we only had to transfer money from our account, for us it was a simple procedure. Of course everyone has to take their cut and the bank took one per cent of the value of the visa as a charge. That's one thing banks know how to do well in Zim and that's charge their customers!

We rushed from the Visa Company in Belgravia, headed into town, parked in the Farmer's Co-op car park and hastily made our way. On reaching the bank my heart sank at the sight of the queue ahead of us. The British Embassy obviously had their reasons for using this particular bank. Personally I felt that was unfair. It necessitates a trip into the centre of town, whereas previously, it was possible to pay at the nearest branch of your bank. The elderly couple who had been first in the queue at the Visa Company at six in the morning didn't own a car. They'd been dropped off and left there. They had waited two hours for the gates to open so that like us, they could find out how much was needed for the fee. Then they had to wait at the side of the main road for an E.T to come and take them into town, hopefully near enough to the bank so that they didn't have too far to walk. They would have to reverse the process to get back to the Visa Company. Had we known where they were going we would have offered a lift

We were pleasantly surprised the queue at the bank was handled efficiently and a security guard was present to make sure there were no queue-jumpers. Once inside there were comfortable chairs to sit on, life was looking up. There were quite a few disgruntled prospective visa seekers milling around. One woman in particular in a senior nurses' uniform was so distressed she couldn't sit down. Like Mike, she'd tried the previous week to submit her application and had been told to come back this week. It was 21st June, Thursday, she was booked to fly on Sunday 24th to Britain to start 'caring' work with an agency on Tuesday 26th. It wasn't going to happen. Those who had previously been granted visas by the British Embassy were told that they could get another visa within twenty-four hours. Mike tried that in September 2006, and his twenty-four hour visa took five days as the Embassy's computers were down.

The hour spent at the bank was not wasted, I did what I do best, I chatted. There was a young family next to me with a toddler and the mum was telling me that they had waited for two years to get their Zimbabwean passports to enable them to travel. Mike was chatting to another man, see I'm not the only one in the family who's a chatterbox. This man was fuming. He didn't bank with this bank so had to pay by cheque from his bank. Easy enough. There were three members of his family travelling so he'd come armed with a cheque for twenty-four plus million Zimbabwean dollars to cover the amount. He waited the hour to get to the teller only to be told that he couldn't pay with a single cheque, he had to pay by three separate cheques! He could not, and neither could we, see the reason for this. There was nothing for it, he had to go back to his bank and ask for three cheques. That sounds like a peace of cake doesn't it? Remember that our country was suffering from hyper-inflation, bank charges were out of all proportion, monetary issues aside, it meant time off work, it meant using precious fuel to get from A to B.

An hour later we were back at the Visa Company and I sat in the car and waited for Mike. The company's new location was in what had been a gracious home on the corner of a busy main road. Even though it was in a residential area with grass verges, trying to find parking was nigh impossible. We were in my small Nissan Sunny and managed to squeeze in to a parking fairly close to the corner of the main road. My family tends to scoff at my 'feelings' that I sometimes get. I wasn't happy with where we'd parked, when Mike came back out about half an hour later, I told him that I had a feeling that an accident was in the offing. The main road is always busy and the volume of traffic around the Visa Company together with the pedestrians is a recipe for disaster. We happened to pass by the Visa Company a couple of hours later on our journey, and my 'feeling' had come to pass, two cars had had an accident, from the looks of things, not a serious one, but an accident all the same. Mike submitted his visa application on the Thursday and collected it the following Tuesday, that suited us fine, but I wonder what the nurse going to the caring job did?

THE LADY

We had to go into the Central Business District of Harare and Mike managed to get a parking place right outside where he wanted to be and under the shade of a big, leafy tree, which was just as well as I was being left in the car. On the pavement right next to where we'd parked the car was a black woman and her baby. She fascinated me. She was a vagrant, but had such dignity that it was impossible not to admire her. She was dressed in filthy clothes consisting of a black acrylic blouse and a muddy coloured skirt full of holes with the hem undone and a pair of very well worn rubber slipslops. The baby was dressed in a blue baby bonnet adorned with a lovely white lacey design, a dirty white tee shirt, black cotton trousers and a filthy pair of baby shoes that were in tatters.

The lady was no beauty, but she had a pleasant, friendly face. The lady and her baby were intent on having their lunch on the pavement. She had a small, tatty, navy blue holdall that seemed to be bottomless. She was drinking tea out of an attractive, extra large, dappled emerald green pottery mug. The mug was incongruous with her attire and the rest of her belongings. She poured tea out of her mug into the baby's blue plastic baby-cup with a lid. The little tot didn't have much of the tea, but did manage to pour most of it out over the pavement. The lady and her child shared their lunch. It wouldn't feature in a Michelin guide, but they both appeared to enjoy it. From the depths of the holdall emerged some greyish looking bread, which they shared. I was engrossed watching her breaking a large ripe avocado in half with her bare hands. I doubted if I could have done as well with a chopping board and a knife. She used her forefinger to extract the avocado flesh from its shell and transfer it to her hunk of bread, which she then folded in half and it had all the appearance of a bona fide sandwich.

While she was carrying out this procedure the baby kept crawling all over the pavement getting absolutely filthy in the process. It was an education to see how tolerant the passing pedestrians were of the mother and more so, of the baby who was getting in their way. No one appeared to be annoyed with the child; several brought the fact of the errant baby to the mother's attention. Several greeted the baby, others had passing conversations with the mother. The lady was quite intent on her meal, she didn't even seem to be aware of me sitting in the car within touching distance of her. Although she appeared articulate with the passers-by, she only communicated with her child in a series of grunts, they seemed to have a system that worked for them.

It was entertaining watching the reactions of the pedestrians as they passed by the two completely self-absorbed celebrities. Their faces showed emotions ranging from a passing interest, to amusement, to concern. None of them showed annoyance or anger. Once the repast was complete, the lady once again delved into her bottomless bag and emerged holding a navy blue face cloth, which she used to wipe her own hands and then she attempted to clean the baby. I say attempted, she appeared to make more of a mess than was already there by smearing white snot and green avocado over the baby's brown face. The woman then bent forwards at the waist and in age-old African tradition, hoisted the baby on to her back and secured it there by the means of a bright orange patterned towel. I am fascinated by this means of transporting a child. I tried it many times. I enlisted the help of black women who could do it in their sleep. The towel never stayed in place and my baby would slide out.

My sons never encountered any injury from my feeble endeavours to carry them in this fashion. I eventually had to acknowledge defeat and had to cheat by means of a canvass harness that I wore in the tradition of a backpack. I have enormous admiration for women who can carry their children on their backs using only a towel or a length of cloth it is a form of art. It is a sensible means of transportation in a country where many of the women have to walk for miles and miles to get to their destination. It is not unusual to see a woman walking with a child on her back and she's knitting at the same time, complete with a heavy bundle on her head, they really are incredible.

The baby safely stowed on her back, the lady collected her voluminous, but small, holdall and set off. She was a tidy soul. First stop was to deposit the skin and the pip of the avocado in a huge gaping hole in a broken concrete slab that formed part of the pavement. Her refuse was biodegradable and in years to come, there may even be an avo tree growing there to provide nourishment. She then proceeded down the near-by sanitary lane with her green pottery mug in one hand and the blue baby cup in the other. I surmised that she was going to rinse them out by means of a tap somewhere down the lane. She was only away for about five minutes, on her return from the sanitary-lane, she turned into the architecturally attractive courtyard of one of the restored old buildings of Harare that housed the financial institution where my husband at that moment, was talking to one of the financial gurus about his portfolio. The security guard resplendent in his blue uniform with gold trim didn't challenge her as she made her way through the gate and into the charming reception area of the premises. I doubted if she was in there discussing her portfolio and was proved right when she emerged a few minutes later, minus her green mug.

The kind folk in that establishment obviously provide her morning tea for her. I know it was only a cup of tea. Who knows, that might be the only warm drink that woman ever receives. Life is tough in Zimbabwe. Tough doesn't even begin to describe the hardships that so many of our people are enduring. This is not a welfare state and with the highest inflation in the world and rampant unemployment, it doesn't bode well for the underprivileged in our society. The lady had a quiet dignity that I admired. She didn't try and beg. I watched her for a while after she'd left the financial institution; she stayed in the vicinity chatting to other vendors. I wondered if her holdall contained all her worldly possessions. I wondered where she slept at night. I wondered what life would have in store for her child.

NOW AND THEN

Perhaps if Mike and I had had a crystal ball to see into the future, we wouldn't have built our home in Mazowe. We have loved living on our smallholding, but it has not been the most convenient of locations for a residence. Between the ever-increasing price and availability (or non-availability!) of fuel over the years, it has made living out of 'town' a challenge. With school-going-age children, it has meant that we have had to be very well organised, if anything was left behind it was just too bad. We left home at six thirty in the morning and most days we didn't get back until six in the evening. If one boy finished school earlier than his brother, he would just have to occupy himself while he waited. Of course we were blessed to have wonderful friends who helped out, and grandparents.

Probably one of the most difficult aspects of the Zimbabwean situation is that of families being split up. This is one of the tragedies of our nation, families have been torn apart and have been scattered to the four corners of the earth. The reasons for leaving are many and varied. The main ones being political persecution, financial and deteriorating standards. The politics is not in my realm. I'll leave that for others. The financial side is mind-blowing. For somebody who has not experienced inflation such as we have had to endure, it is impossible to know where to begin to describe what it's like.

For those pensioners who saved hard, bought their own homes and thought that they would be secure in their old age, it must be terrifying for them to realize that they could be homeless, as they can no longer pay their property rates. My parents, if they were still living in this country would fit into that category. I get panicky when shopping. When bread reached Z$12 000 a loaf, I said that I wouldn't pay that. Two months down the line, I paid Z$30 000 for a loaf. In 2008 we are paying millions for a loaf. Mark's girlfriend Vicki was fascinated with prices on her visit to Zimbabwe in 2005. The day that she arrived in Harare we went grocery shopping and I bought a dozen eggs at a cost of Z$16 000 a dozen, by the time she left five weeks later, they were Z$26 000. A dozen eggs is now "only" Z$48 000; *but,* and it's a VERY big but, this is the price in the 'new' money, that's to say, after the government had dropped three zeroes from the currency, so in actual fact, the eggs are Z$480 000 a dozen. In April 2008, one egg cost Z$8 million!

For those whose incomes are linked to the American dollar, this increase is not a problem. For the vast majority it's a nightmare. In my diary the entry for Wednesday 16 April 2003 reads in bold capitals and several exclamation marks: 'PRICE OF FUEL GOES TO $500 lt'. On Wednesday 13 June 2007 we paid Z$85 000 per litre ...... and add the three missing zeroes, then we actually paid eighty-five million dollars a litre, Thursday 21st June 2007 saw us paying one hundred and seventy five thousand dollars (remember to add another three zeroes) a litre. That's when reality hits you. In 2008 you can't buy fuel in Zimbabwe currency, it's all paid for in forex.

The other point that I mentioned was that of falling standards. The month of June 2007 had been one of the worst in memory in Zimbabwe for power outages. 2008 managed to top it, unfortunately. I'm not talking about the odd hour here and there. I'm talking for up to sixteen hours at a time. I don't care if the outage is the result of a fault or load shedding, no power is no power. Again, for those who can afford inverters or generators the power outages aren't really too much of a problem. They can still cook, pump and heat water to their homes, continue to live a normal life. The cost of phone calls has become prohibitive for a multitude of Zimbabweans.

Hardly anyone makes use of the postal service any more. It's expensive and unreliable. In 2007 I only posted one item being a birthday card for my sister-in-law Yvonne. It was a beautiful card that I'd bought for her in England. It was posted at the Borrowdale post office in plenty of time for her birthday in May. She lives in the suburb of Greendale approximately twelve kilometres from the post office. She's still waiting for it to arrive. The lack of affordable medical care is of great concern to many Zimbabweans. It is essential that we subscribe to one of the private medical aid schemes. These schemes are also affected by inflation and the scheme that our family is on increases their subscriptions every three months. I'm not talking by just a dollar or two, their fees often double or even treble.

Mike and I have already downgraded the category of medical aid that we can afford, thus reducing the calibre of coverage that we get. We really can't afford, in medical terms, to go much lower. It's not just the monthly medical aid dues that have to be paid; it's also having to pay cash up front for doctor's visits, treatment and drugs. It is worrying to think what would happen to us in an emergency.

The spiralling crime rate is also distressing. Our family has been fortunate so far. Though we have been victims of attempted robberies, no one has been harmed and nothing of value has been taken. Yet. This is because we live in a five star prison with bolts, alarms, barbed wire, locks and all the other security trappings. I don't want to end up a statistic. At the beginning of June 2007 I went to a ladies' meeting where we were shown various methods of self-defence. There was an elderly lady present she was eighty-three years old. She seemed to be showing more interest than some of the younger women and the thought flitted through my mind that she's such a vulnerable target, and I hoped she'd never have the misfortune to have to use anything that we were being shown. Never a truer word was spoken.

Only two weeks after the self-defence meeting she was brutally attacked in her home. The power outages are infuriating to us, but they're a bonus to would-be thieves. The old woman had gone to her bed early as it was dark and the power was out. Later, when electricity was restored, she decided to get up, on entering her lounge came face-to-face with a man in her lounge. He brutally beat her, tied her up and then went through to the kitchen to get a knife and savagely slashed her. It's not known exactly how long it was before she was found and taken to hospital. She'd lost a lot of blood and shock had set in. I know that other countries have crime. We don't live in other countries, we live here. I can't see a solution to the crime rate as long as Zimbabwe is facing the present difficulties as well as an eighty per cent unemployment rate.

There are die-hard Zimbabweans who say that if we went to another country we'd never have a standard of living like we have here. I feel that some of them have the 'laager mentality', that is, they live mainly in the affluent northern suburbs behind their walls, barbed wire, electric fences, electric gates and security guards, they're not in the real Zimbabwe where it all happens such as the rural areas or the townships. A whole new industry has sprung up where by some enterprising Zimbabweans with access to forex will do shopping, acquire fuel, whatever for those who are unable to do so. It is filling a necessary niche in the market, but it doesn't come cheap. It does save the hassle of having to drive to South Africa or Botswana to do grocery shopping. The ingenious Zimbo Diaspora in the UK is also trying to make life easier for those of us still living here. If we have family or friends in the UK and they are prepared to pay, all they have to do is send money to the Zimbo entrepreneurs and they will organize fuel, cooking oil, sugar, flour and other necessities to be delivered to the door of the recipient in Zimbabwe. There has been criticism of these cell-phone businessmen that they are supporting the Mugabe regime, as without this form of 'aid', the regime would crumble. It is reckoned that it is the Zimbabwean Diaspora that is keeping our economy (what there is of it) afloat. Economists say that if the three million Zimbabweans outside our borders spend on average of fifty British pounds a month, it keeps the economy ticking over.

Rhodesians and Zimbabweans who have gone to live elsewhere have sometimes been referred to as "wenwe's"(when we). 'When we were in Rhodesia, ...'. We know people who fall into this category. For all those 'wenwe's out there who still have a hankering for home, you'll just have to realise that the country that you knew and loved is no more. We still have one of the best climates in the world. We still have wonderful people of all races, if it wasn't for these things, this place could be a living hell. This nation was once the breadbasket of Africa and now we're known as the basket case of Africa.

JULY MADNESS

You're most likely fed-up with me writing about our inflation, so I'll drop the subject, but at least you've got the economic background to follow this next chapter. The government reckoned that unscrupulous businessmen who were making massive profits were in part fuelling the rationale behind our rampant inflation. I'm no economist, but I know when I'm being ripped off. In a normal business environment, there would be competition so we could utilize a bit of consumer resistance, but in many circumstances, Zimbos don't have that option, it's a case of take it or leave it. In other instances the exorbitant prices are legitimate in that the supplier has to pay with black-market obtained forex and as the inflation goes spiralling ever higher and higher, so does the cost of the forex and therefore so does the replacement value of the goods. It's a vicious circle.

A fifty trillion dollar note and other denominations

Whatever the reason, in its wisdom, at the beginning of July 2007, the government ordered that all prices had to be slashed, in some instances by as much as half. Can you imagine if you've paid a supplier a certain price for an item, then put on the government stipulated increase of 45%, then told to that you can only sell the item for half the price, it doesn't take a rocket scientist to work out the repercussions. The euphoria brought on with these reduced prices caused riots and looting in some shops. Zimbos of all colours were going on a stampede shopping as if their lives depended on it. The police and army went round the shops to enforce the price freeze and they usually had an entourage of enthusiastic shoppers who were shopping like there was no tomorrow. Finally many of the shops were rationing 'two' items per person, it didn't matter if it was coffee, bread or televisions. Of course, those 'in the know' were nodded the wink when a certain shop was going to be visited by the enforcers, so the 'shoppers' were there with their massive bundles of Zim dollars.

Thousands of C.E.O.s of companies were arrested for not reducing prices. Many chain stores had to close certain branches and some of the smaller establishments were completely cleaned out and had nothing left to sell. This crazy economic decision has resulted in empty shelves and I really DO mean empty. Mike and I went shopping at the beginning of July and were horrified at the totally empty frigs and freezers. In all our years in this country, we'd never seen anything like it. Mike went shopping again on 18th July, and he said it was actually spooky; the shelves that did have anything on them just had a single line of cool drinks, with nothing behind them. There is no sugar, salt, flour, margarine, meat, milk, bread, coffee, tea – the list can go on and on. So now that the euphoria amongst those who benefited from the price freeze, has dissipated and reality has set in. Empty shelves mean empty stomachs. The black-market is rife. Many of those 'bargain hunters' were hunting for 'bargains' to resell and to make a big profit. You can't get sugar or cooking oil in any shop, but when you're parked at a shopping centre or at the post office, a vendor will approach surreptitiously whilst keeping an eye out for any police in the area, to offer you the commodities at the most outrageous prices. If you haven't got the goods and you need the goods, then you have to pay for the goods.

I met a friend who was in tears and told me that she can't take any more of trying to find food to feed her family, trying to get the school uniforms washed and ironed when she goes for days without running water and electricity. Millions of Zimbabweans have no means of escaping this madness. The schools in this country don't provide meals, the scholars take their own food and drink for the mid-morning break and lunch. When our sons were at school, I used to battle trying to provide enough food for them to keep them going through the day. In summer I was really limited with what I could put into sandwiches as fillings; meat would go off, cheese would melt, vegetables would go soggy, even the bottles of water would become lukewarm. Winter was slightly easier. However, I was able to get food, I was able to buy bread and rolls, I was able to buy the contents to make sandwich fillings. I feel for the mothers in Zimbabwe now.

Mark left school at the end of 2002 and Heath at the end of 2004. We did have power outages then, but not like the twelve to sixteen hours a day outages like we're having now and we didn't go for days and days without running water. Zimbabwean scholars wear school uniforms, how on earth do mother's manage to wash and iron them when there isn't any power during the day? A hairdresser I know told me that she was closing her business at the end of the month. The hairdresser had been in business for thirty years, but she said that with the price freeze she couldn't import the chemicals and colours that she used in her business, she also said that she was tired of trying to cope with no water and no power. She said that customers had to phone before appointments, to check if she had water and electricity. What a way to try and run a business. Wasn't it Chairman Mao who said take everything from the people and they'll be grateful for whatever little they do receive, or words to that effect. I know exactly what he means. We hadn't been able to get bread for several days, when one day, we managed to buy two French loaves from Spar. Between the two of us, Mike and I ate a whole loaf – with me claiming the crusty ends before he could get near the loaf! You have no idea how it felt, just to be able to eat fresh, crusty bread and a whole loaf to boot!

The shop where we normally buy the meat for our cats and dogs has closed its doors. Whether this is a permanent closure or not, will depend on future politics. The manager had been battling with the power outages and trying to keep his meat at the correct temperatures, now he can't even source the meat and chicken that he needs for resale. The government has issued dire warnings against firms who close their doors and don't carry on with 'business as usual'. Prices have to be cut by half, so presumably profits will be cut by half, but no salaries are to be cut.

It is glaringly noticeable that para-statals such as the power company, the water company and the municipality have not reduced their prices, in fact they've just increased them considerably, in some cases, by as much as one thousand per cent. Why is there one rule for one section of the population and another for the other? Makes you wonder, doesn't it. The South African television news on Friday 20th July announced that the Zim government and captains of industry had had discussions about the price freeze and it had been agreed that these new prices were not sustainable and that they would have to be increased! I could have told them that. It's not all madness though, people who were 'in the know' of the authorities going around businesses and forcibly making them reduce their prices, were able to get wonderful bargains such as televisions and cell phones and other luxury items. It makes you wonder doesn't it?

As of the 1st August, a new law will come into being preventing cross-border traders from plying their trade between Zimbabwe and surrounding countries such as South Africa, Botswana and Zambia. If the goods were available locally, these traders wouldn't be necessary, but, as things stand, they provide a very necessary need in our lives. There is a visible presence of military and police personnel in most shopping centres. What is going to happen when people are starving and there's no food? We've put up with the daily power outages. We've put up with the lack of running water. We've put up with drastically falling standards. We've put up with trying to cope with the highest inflation in the world. We've put up with the government's snooping law whereby they can legally intercept and open our mail, read our emails and eavesdrop on our phone calls. We've put up with unnecessary deaths. We've put up with having to cope with saying goodbye to family and friends, and with families being torn apart..

I was standing in a queue in the bank and it seemed to be taking forever. A black man in front of me was chatty and started moaning about the slow progress. I whole-heartedly agreed with him, *but* I have become wary of voicing my 'views' in public with people I don't know, as even if they agree with me, strategically placed 'spies' in the queue could denounce me. This man was most likely a genuine, fed-up Zimbo like me, he was far too old to be a 'green bomber' one of the youth militia, but I wasn't prepared to take the risk. I've noticed on several occasions when we've been chatting to people in public places, there's quite often a young man with his hands in his pocket who's trying to be unobtrusive, but is showing definite signs of being interested in our conversations.

Mike had an incident in TM supermarket where he bumped into an elderly farming acquaintance, let's call him 'Jim'. Jim had been forcibly evicted from his farm, as had his son off his. Jim was understandably bitter and he was the type of man who called a spade a 'bloody shovel!' He was giving Mike a full litany of his woes in colourful language. Mike, like me, has learnt to be 'aware' of who is around, and he noticed a young black couple that seemed to have an inordinate interest in the chickens in the cold counter next to Jim. It was when the young man went round the corner and pulled out a radio and was pointing towards Jim and Mike, that Mike took Jim by the arm and told him to get into his car and '*go*'! I had been sitting in our car waiting for Mike and was surprised to see him hurrying out of the store without any provisions, he jumped into the car, started immediately, it was only when we were safely out on the road that he told me what had happened.

We've put up with a lot. We make a plan. There must come a time when every Zimbabwean will say 'Sokwanele', or, 'enough is enough'.

Lightning Source UK Ltd.
Milton Keynes UK
12 April 2011
170814UK00002B/41/P